Rumiko Takahashi

The spotlight on Rumiko Takahashi's career began in 1978 when she won an honorable mention in Shogakukan's annual New Comic Artist Contest for *Those Selfish Aliens*. Later that same year, her boy-meets-alien comedy series, *Urusei Yatsura*, was serialized in *Weekly Shonen Sunday*. This phenomenally successful manga series was adapted into anime format and spawned a TV series and half a dozen theatrical-release movies, all incredibly popular in their own right. Takahashi followed up the success of her debut series with one blockbuster hit after another—*Maison Ikkoku* ran from 1980 to 1987, *Ranma ½* from 1987 to 1996, and *Inuyasha* from 1996 to 2008. Other notable works include *Mermaid Saga*, *Rumic Theater*, and *One-Pound Gospel*.

Takahashi won the prestigious Shogakukan Manga Award twice in her career, once for *Urusei Yatsura* in 1981 and the second time for *Inuyasha* in 2002. A majority of the Takahashi canon has been adapted into other media such as anime, live-action TV series, and film. Takahashi's manga, as well as the other formats her work has been adapted into, have continued to delight generations of fans around the world. Distinguished by her wonderfully endearing characters, Takahashi's work adeptly incorporates a wide variety of elements such as comedy, romance, fantasy, and martial arts. While her series are difficult to pin down into one simple genre, the signature style she has created has come to be known as the "Rumic World." Rumiko Takahashi is an artist who truly represents the very best from the world of manga.

RIN-NE

VOLUME 4
Shonen Sunday Edition

STORY AND ART BY
RUMIKO TAKAHASHI

Original Japanese edition "KYOUKAI NO RINNE"
published by SHOGAKUKAN Inc.

Translation/Christine Dashiell
Touch-up Art & Lettering/Evan Waldinger
Design/Yukiko Whitley
Editor/Mike Montesa

The rights of the author(s) of the work(s) in this publication to be so identified have been asserted in accordance with the Copyright, Designs and Patents Act 1988. A CIP catalogue record for this book is available from the British Library.

Printed in the U.S.A.

Published by VIZ Media, LLC
P.O. Box 77010
San Francisco, CA 94107

10 9 8 7 6 5 4 3 2 1
First printing, September 2010

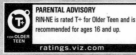

Story and Art by
Rumiko Takahashi

RIN-NE りんね

Characters

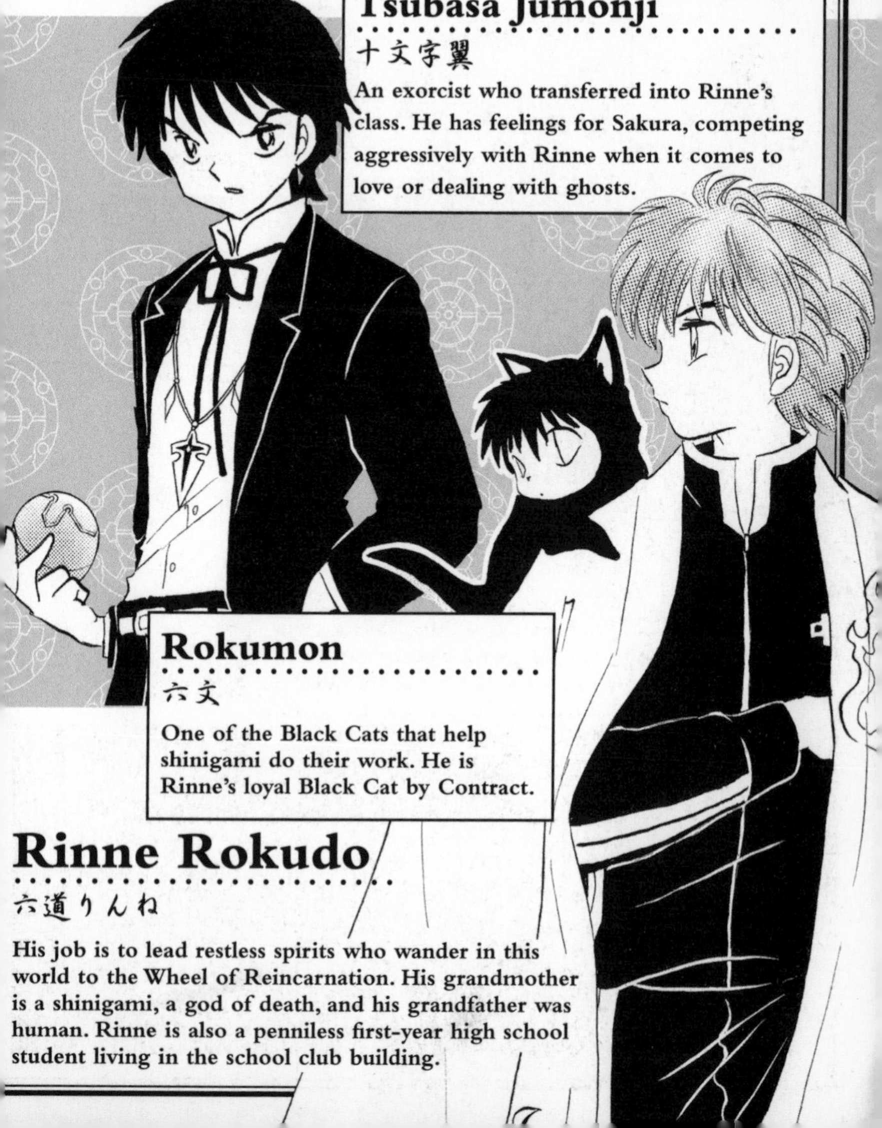

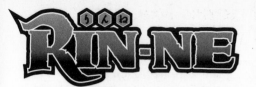

Tsubasa Jumonji

十文字翼

An exorcist who transferred into Rinne's class. He has feelings for Sakura, competing aggressively with Rinne when it comes to love or dealing with ghosts.

Rokumon

六文

One of the Black Cats that help shinigami do their work. He is Rinne's loyal Black Cat by Contract.

Rinne Rokudo

六道りんね

His job is to lead restless spirits who wander in this world to the Wheel of Reincarnation. His grandmother is a shinigami, a god of death, and his grandfather was human. Rinne is also a penniless first-year high school student living in the school club building.

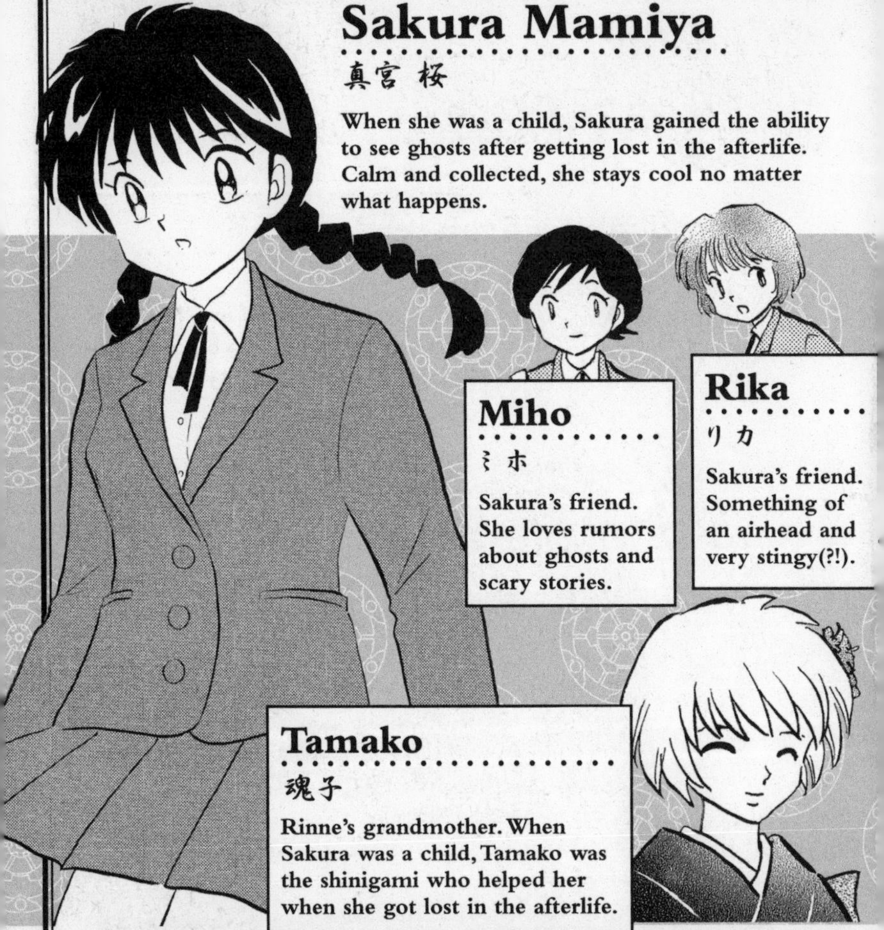

Sakura Mamiya

真宮 桜

When she was a child, Sakura gained the ability to see ghosts after getting lost in the afterlife. Calm and collected, she stays cool no matter what happens.

Miho

ミホ

Sakura's friend. She loves rumors about ghosts and scary stories.

Rika

リカ

Sakura's friend. Something of an airhead and very stingy(?!).

Tamako

魂子

Rinne's grandmother. When Sakura was a child, Tamako was the shinigami who helped her when she got lost in the afterlife.

The Story So Far

Together, Sakura, the girl who can see ghosts, and Rinne the shinigami (sort of) spend their days helping spirits that can't pass on reach the afterlife, and deal with all kinds of strange phenomena at their school.

One day, Tsubasa Jumonji, an exorcist and Sakura's classmate from elementary school, transfers into their class. Tsubasa has long had a crush on Sakura and soon develops a rivalry with Rinne over both ghost-busting and Sakura. Has something changed between Sakura and Rinne?

Contents

Chapter 29: Negative......7

Chapter 30: President......25

Chapter 31: Damshigami Company......43

Chapter 32: Inauguration Ceremony......61

Chapter 33: Kyuketsukasha......79

Chapter 34: Handprint......97

Chapter 35: You Don't Disapprove of That?......115

Chapter 36: Ageha, the Shinigami......133

Chapter 37: Sister's Whereabouts......151

Chapter 38: Bride Screening......169

Translation and Cultural Notes......187

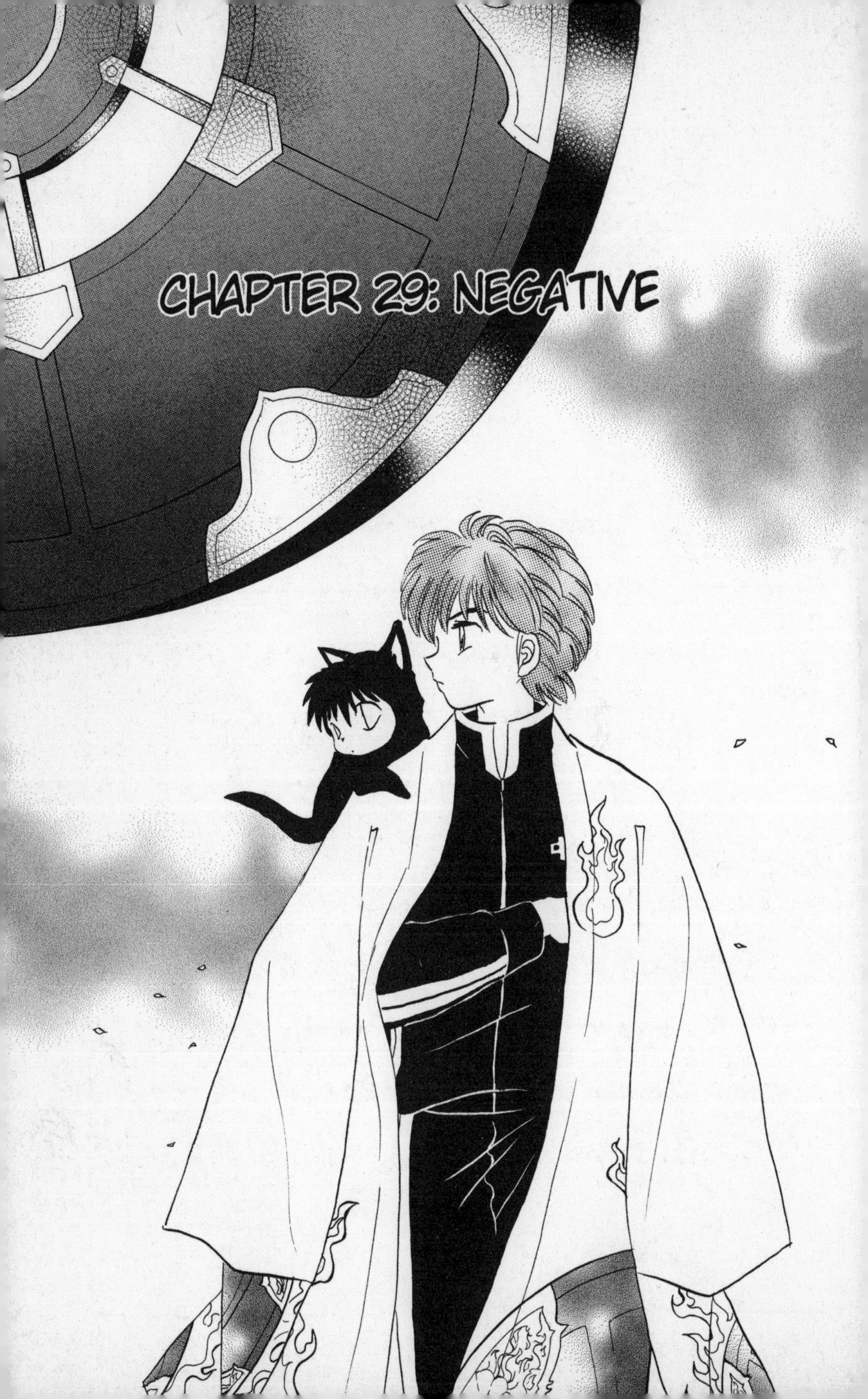
CHAPTER 29: NEGATIVE

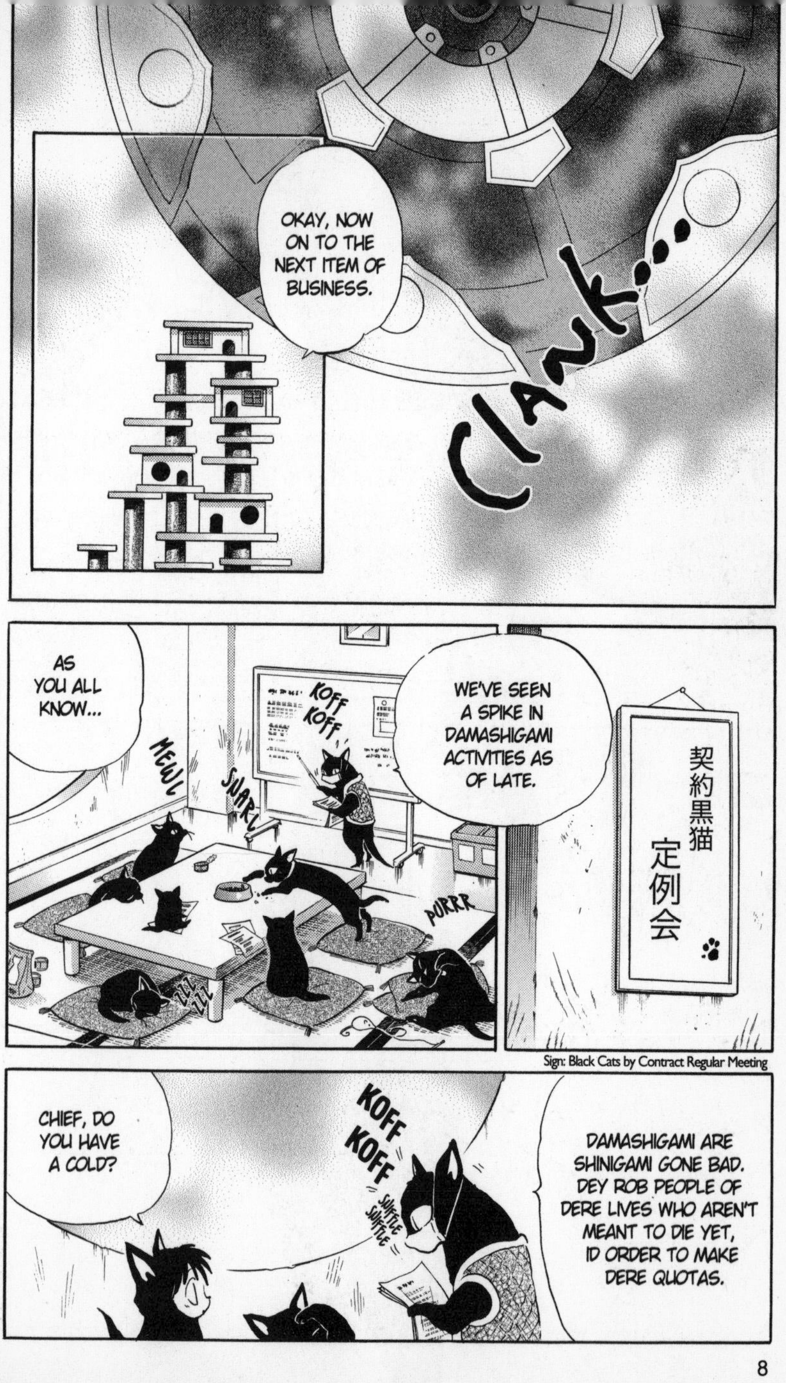
OKAY, NOW ON TO THE NEXT ITEM OF BUSINESS.
CLANK...
契約黒猫
定例会
AS YOU ALL KNOW...
WE'VE SEEN A SPIKE IN DAMASHIGAMI ACTIVITIES AS OF LATE.
KOFF KOFF
MEWL
SNARL
PURRR
ZZZ
DAMASHIGAMI ARE SHINIGAMI GONE BAD. DEY ROB PEOPLE OF DERE LIVES WHO AREN'T MEANT TO DIE YET, ID ORDER TO MAKE DERE QUOTAS.
KOFF KOFF
SHUFFLE SHUFFLE
CHIEF, DO YOU HAVE A COLD?
Sign: Black Cats by Contract Regular Meeting

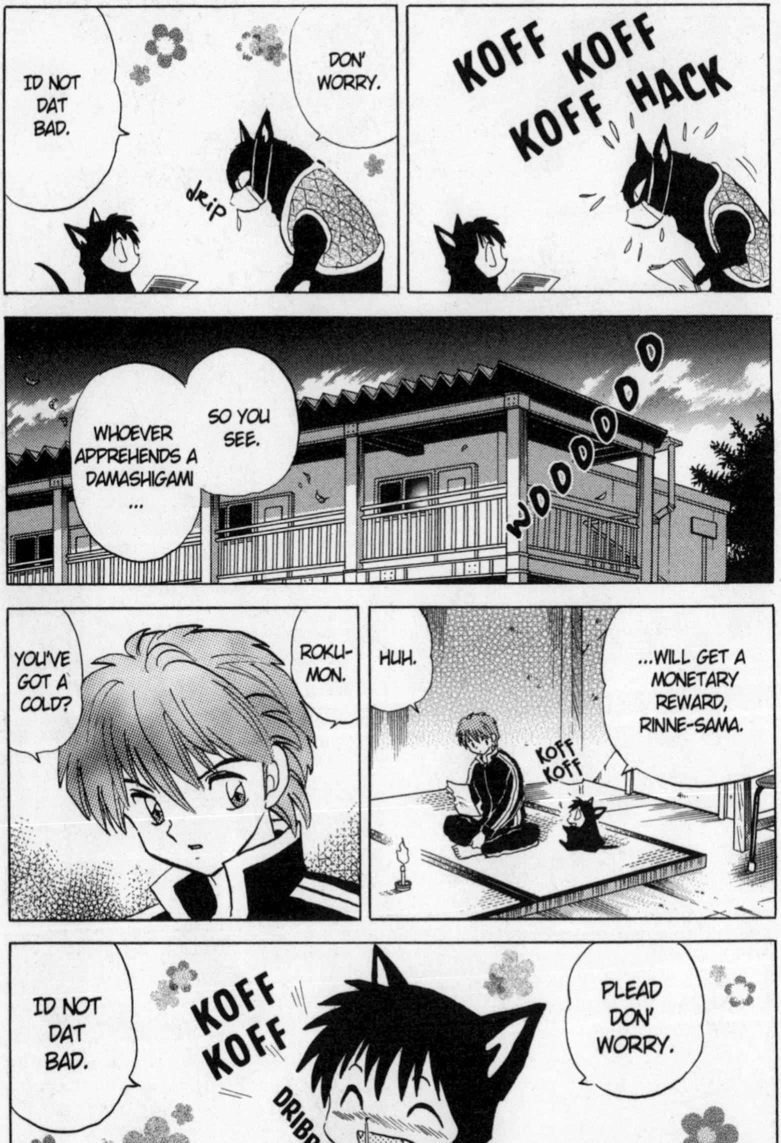
KOFF KOFF KOFF HACK
DON' WORRY.
ID NOT DAT BAD.
drip
SO YOU SEE.
WHOEVER APPREHENDS A DAMASHIGAMI ...
WDDDDDDD
...WILL GET A MONETARY REWARD, RINNE-SAMA.
HUH.
KOFF KOFF
ROKU-MON.
YOU'VE GOT A COLD?
PLEAD DON' WORRY.
KOFF KOFF
DRIBBLE
ID NOT DAT BAD.

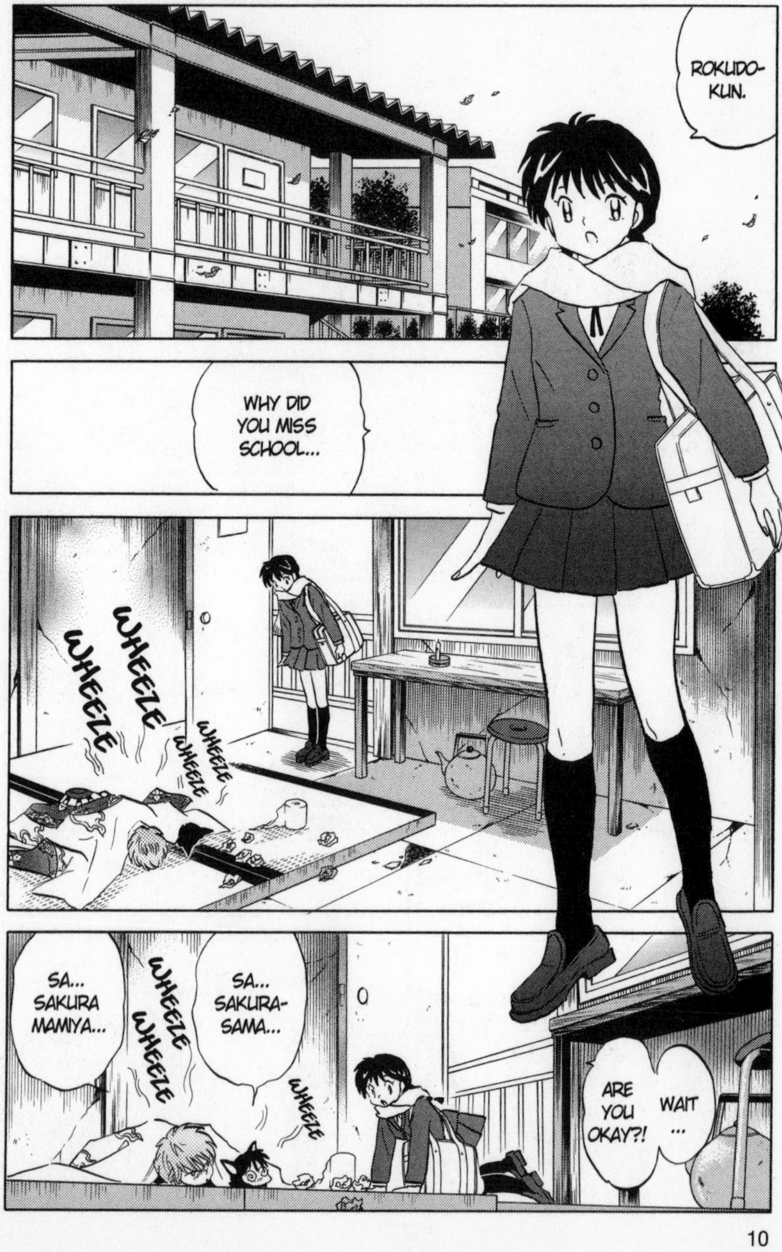
ROKUDO-KUN.
WHY DID YOU MISS SCHOOL...
WHEEZE WHEEZE
WHEEZE WHEEZE
WAIT ...
ARE YOU OKAY?!
WHEEZE
SA... SAKURA-SAMA...
WHEEZE WHEEZE
SA... SAKURA MAMIYA...

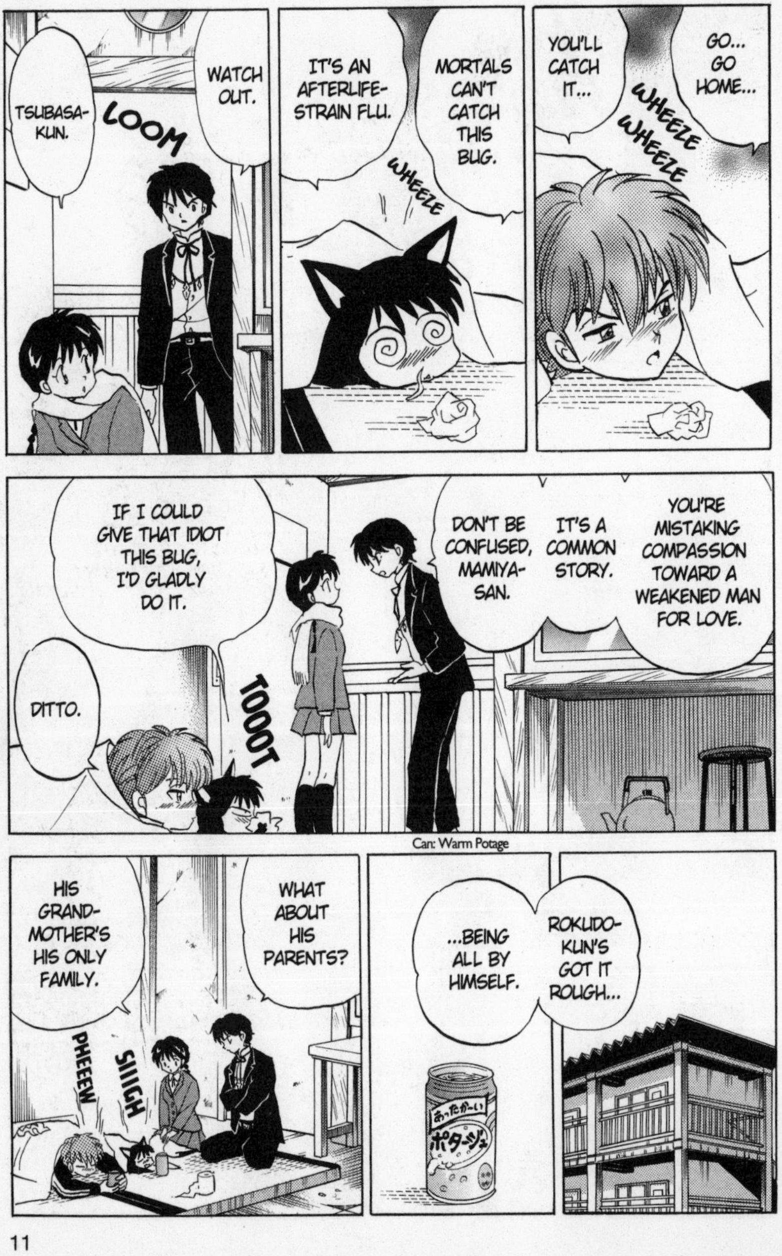
GO... GO HOME...
YOU'LL CATCH IT...
WHEEZE WHEEZE
MORTALS CAN'T CATCH THIS BUG.
IT'S AN AFTERLIFE-STRAIN FLU.
WHEEZE
WATCH OUT.
LOOM
TSUBASA-KUN.
YOU'RE MISTAKING COMPASSION TOWARD A WEAKENED MAN FOR LOVE.
IT'S A COMMON STORY.
DON'T BE CONFUSED, MAMIYA-SAN.
IF I COULD GIVE THAT IDIOT THIS BUG, I'D GLADLY DO IT.
TOOOT
DITTO.
Can: Warm Potage
ROKUDO-KUN'S GOT IT ROUGH...
...BEING ALL BY HIMSELF.
あったかーい
ポタージュ
WHAT ABOUT HIS PARENTS?
HIS GRANDMOTHER'S HIS ONLY FAMILY.
SIIIGH
PHEEEW

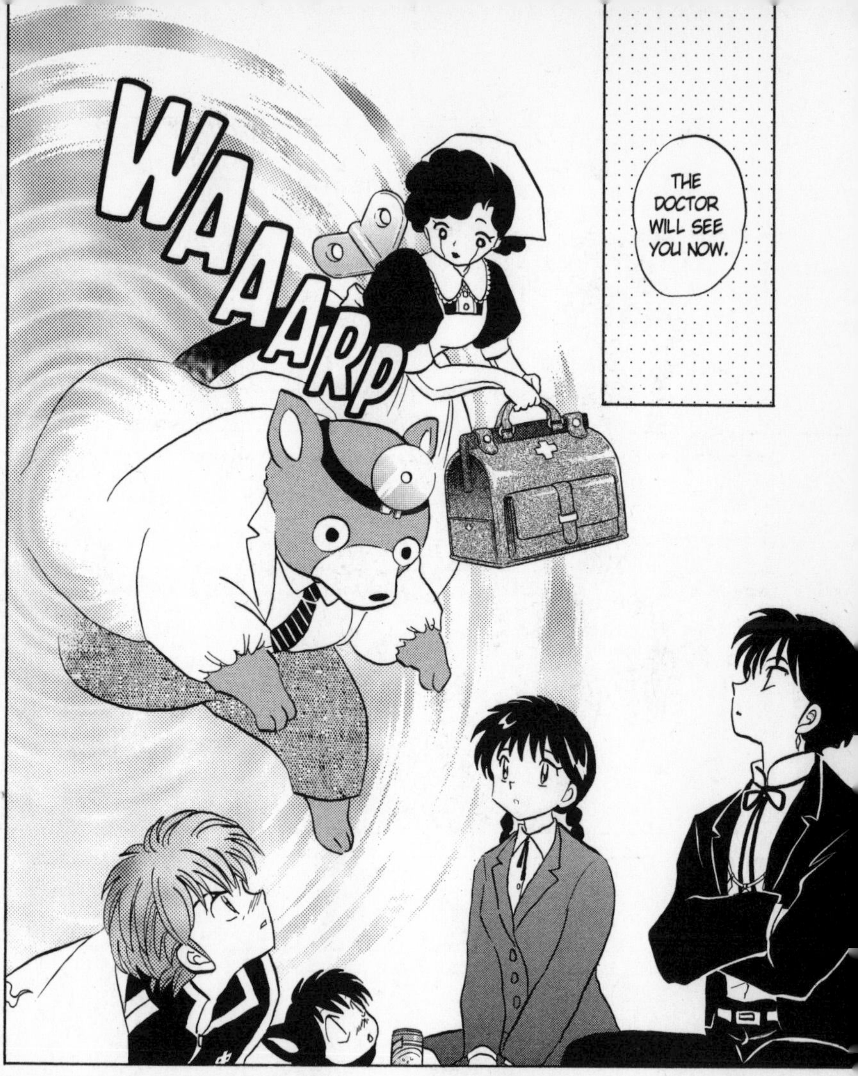
THE DOCTOR WILL SEE YOU NOW.
WAAAARP

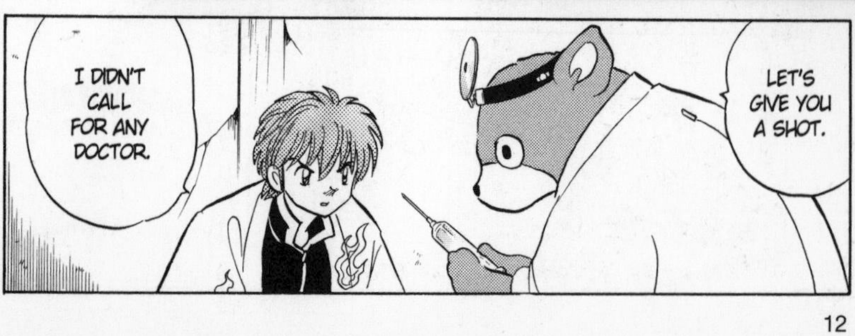
LET'S GIVE YOU A SHOT.
I DIDN'T CALL FOR ANY DOCTOR.

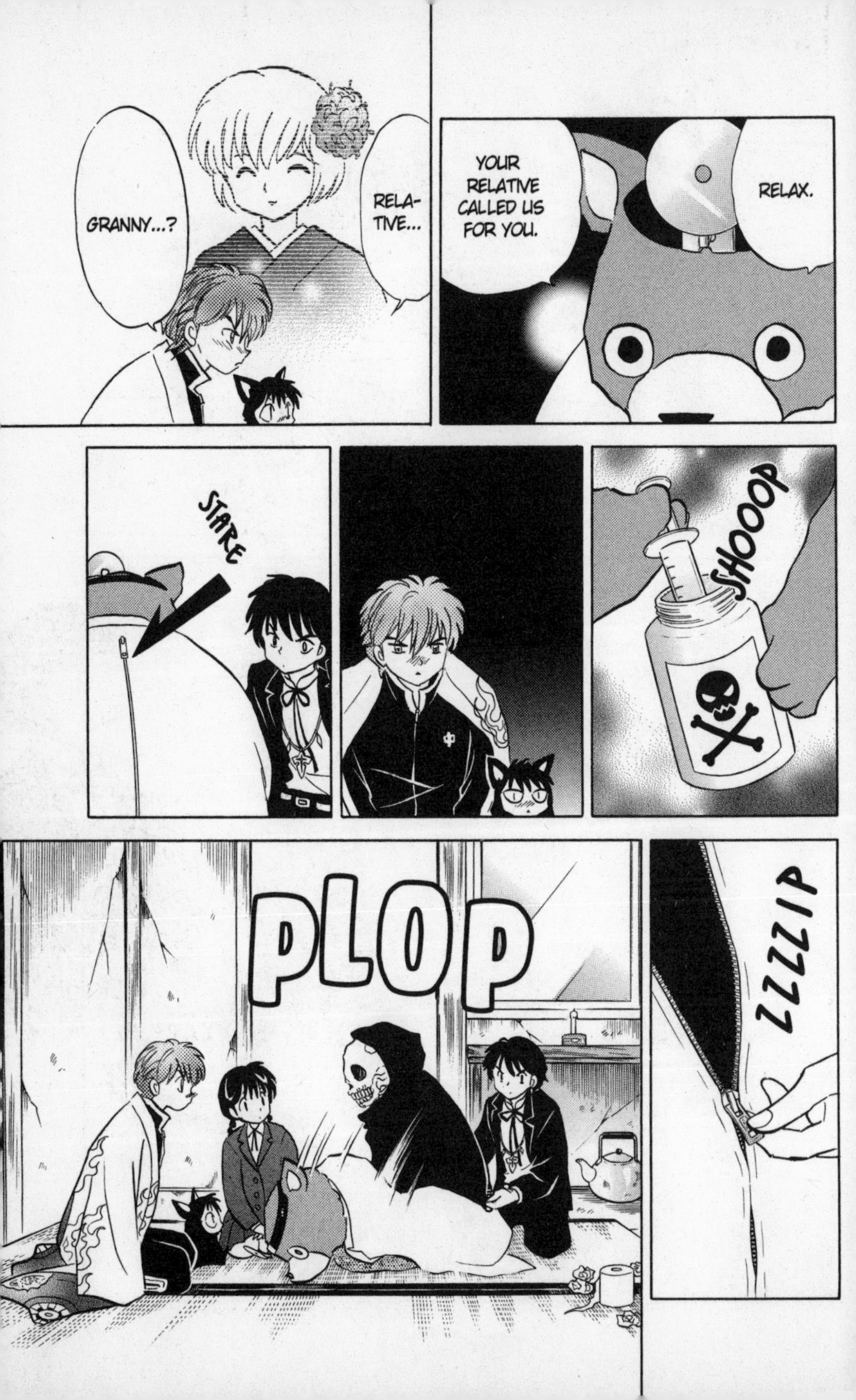
RELAX.
YOUR RELATIVE CALLED US FOR YOU.
RELA-TIVE...
GRANNY...?
SHOOOP
STARE
ZZZZIP
PLOP

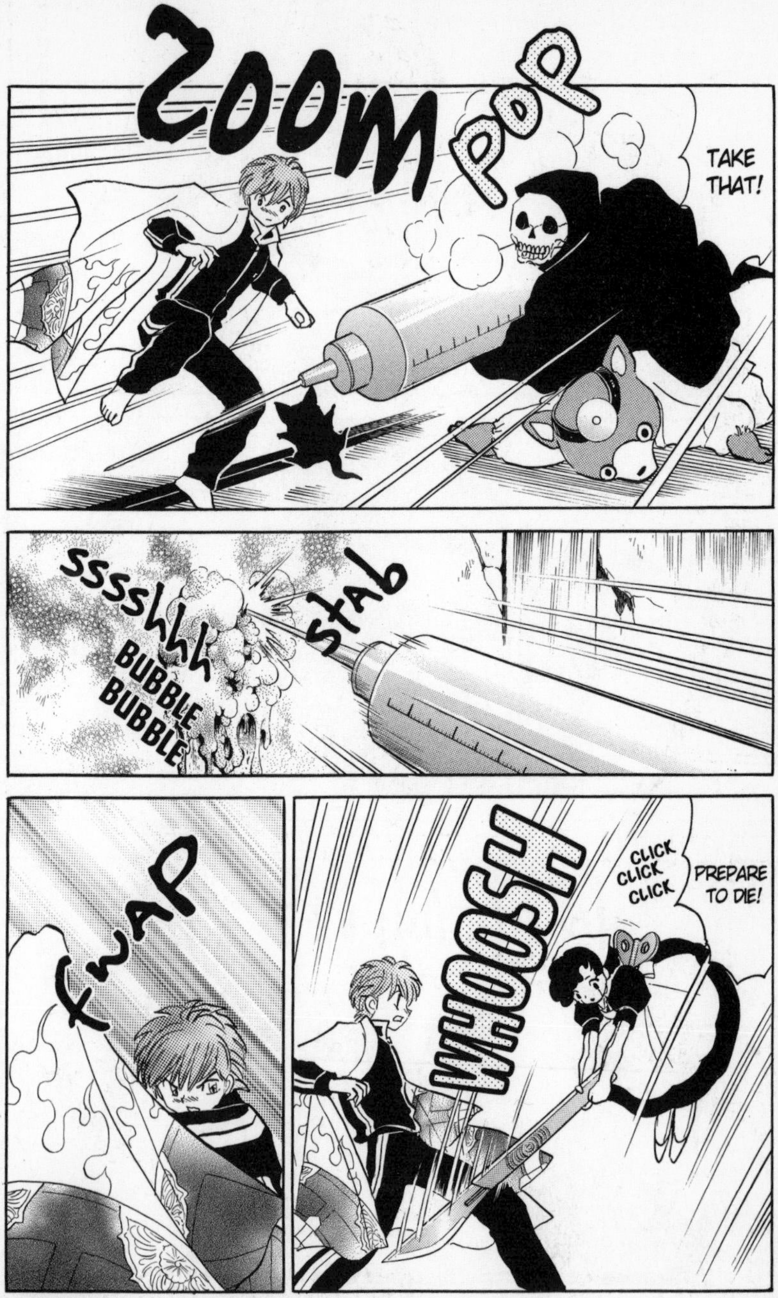
TAKE THAT!
POP
ZOOM
stab
SSSSHHH
BUBBLE BUBBLE
PREPARE TO DIE!
CLICK CLICK CLICK
WHOOSH
FWAP

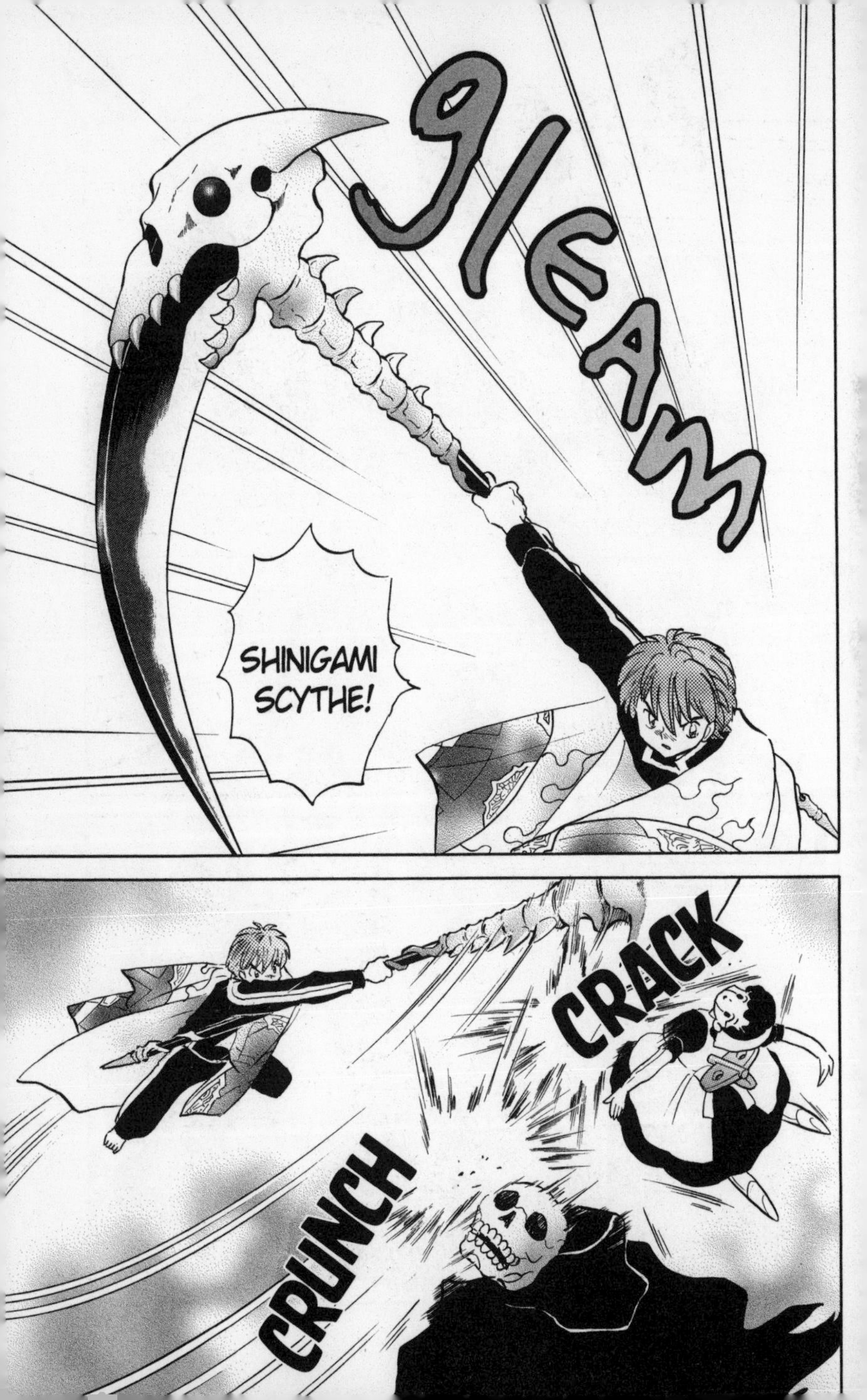
GLEAM
SHINIGAMI SCYTHE!
CRACK
CRUNCH

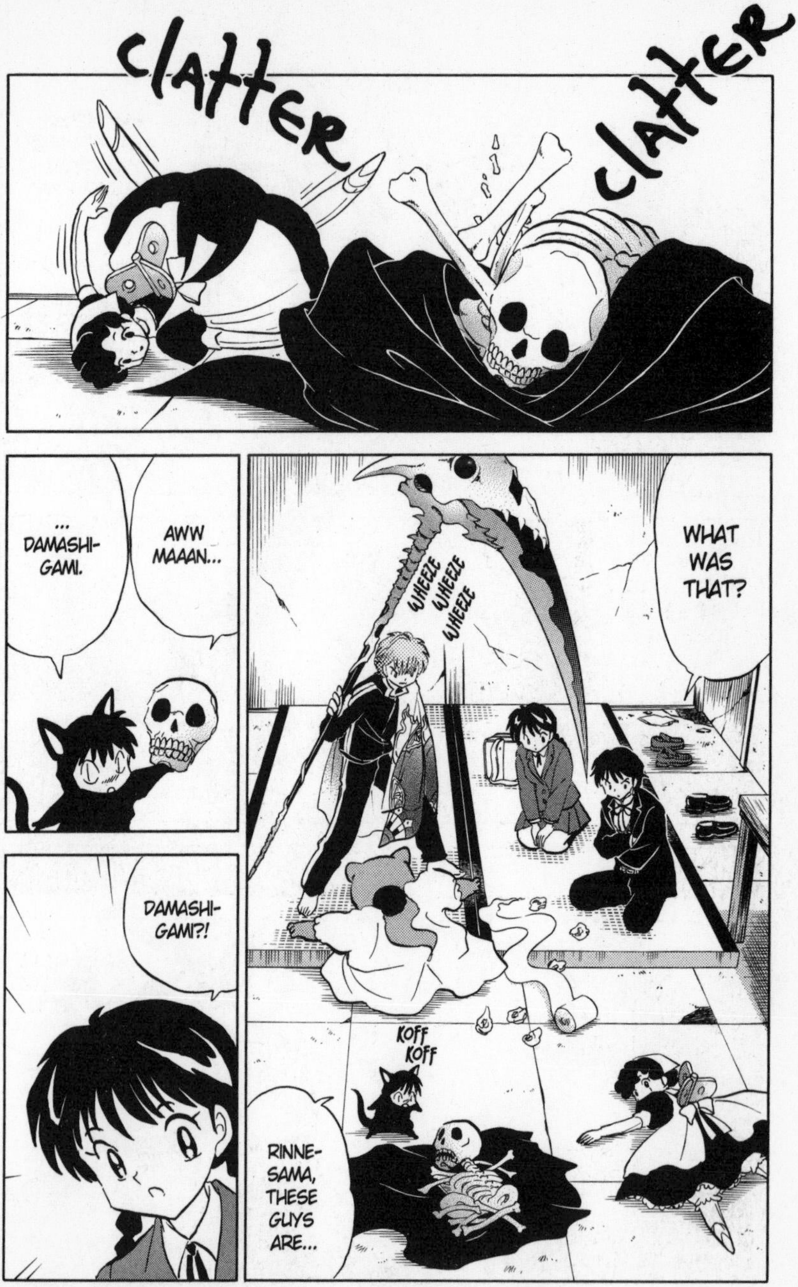
clatter clatter
WHAT WAS THAT?
WHEEZE WHEEZE WHEEZE
KOFF KOFF
RINNE-SAMA, THESE GUYS ARE...
AWW MAAAN...
... DAMASHI-GAMI.
DAMASHI-GAMI?!

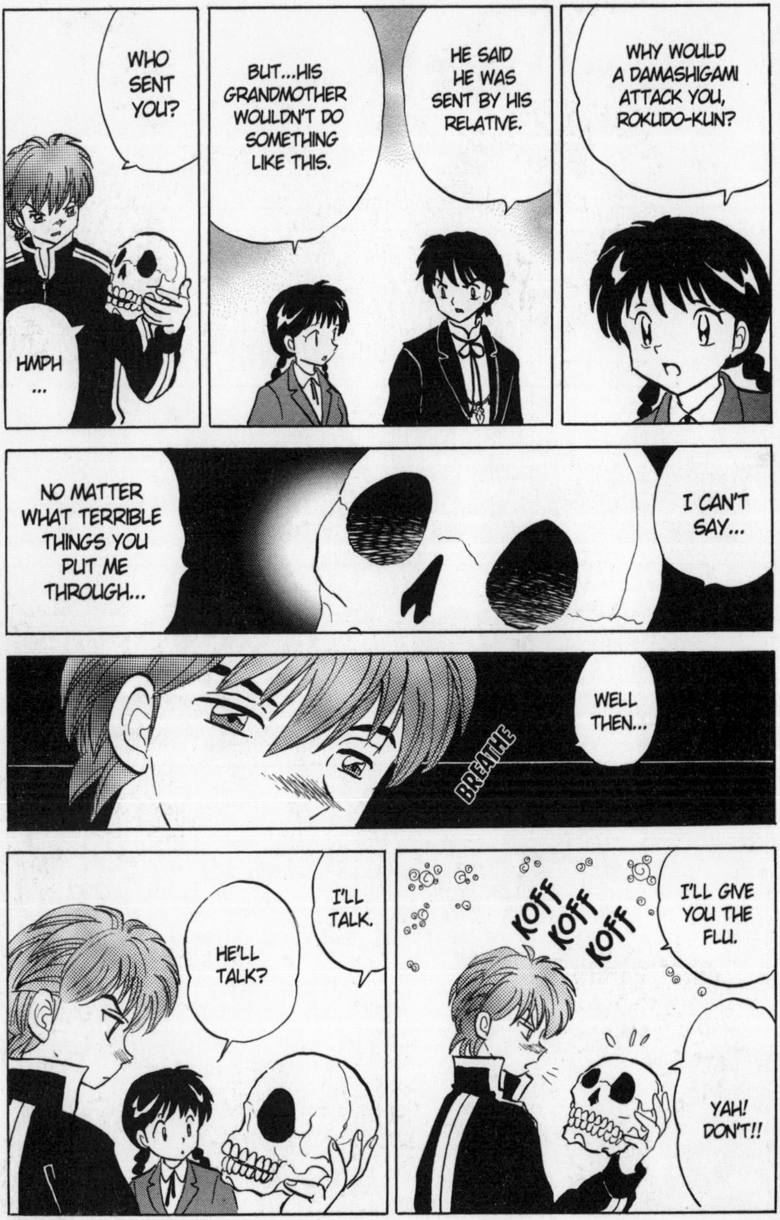
WHY WOULD A DAMASHIGAMI ATTACK YOU, ROKUDO-KUN?
HE SAID HE WAS SENT BY HIS RELATIVE.
BUT...HIS GRANDMOTHER WOULDN'T DO SOMETHING LIKE THIS.
WHO SENT YOU?
HMPH ...
I CAN'T SAY...
NO MATTER WHAT TERRIBLE THINGS YOU PUT ME THROUGH...
WELL THEN...
BREATHE
I'LL GIVE YOU THE FLU.
KOFF KOFF KOFF
YAH! DON'T!!
I'LL TALK.
HE'LL TALK?

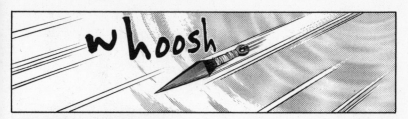

whoosh
STAB
WHAT THE...
limp
SOMEBODY... DIDN'T WANT HIM TO TALK?!
WHO WOULD DO SUCH A THING?
DON'T TELL ME IT'S... HIM?!

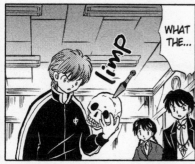

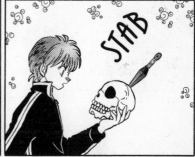

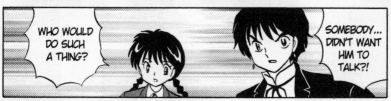

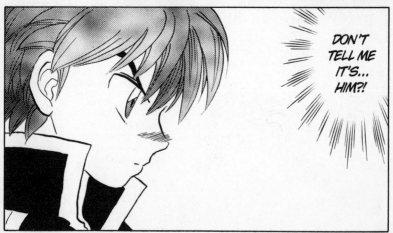

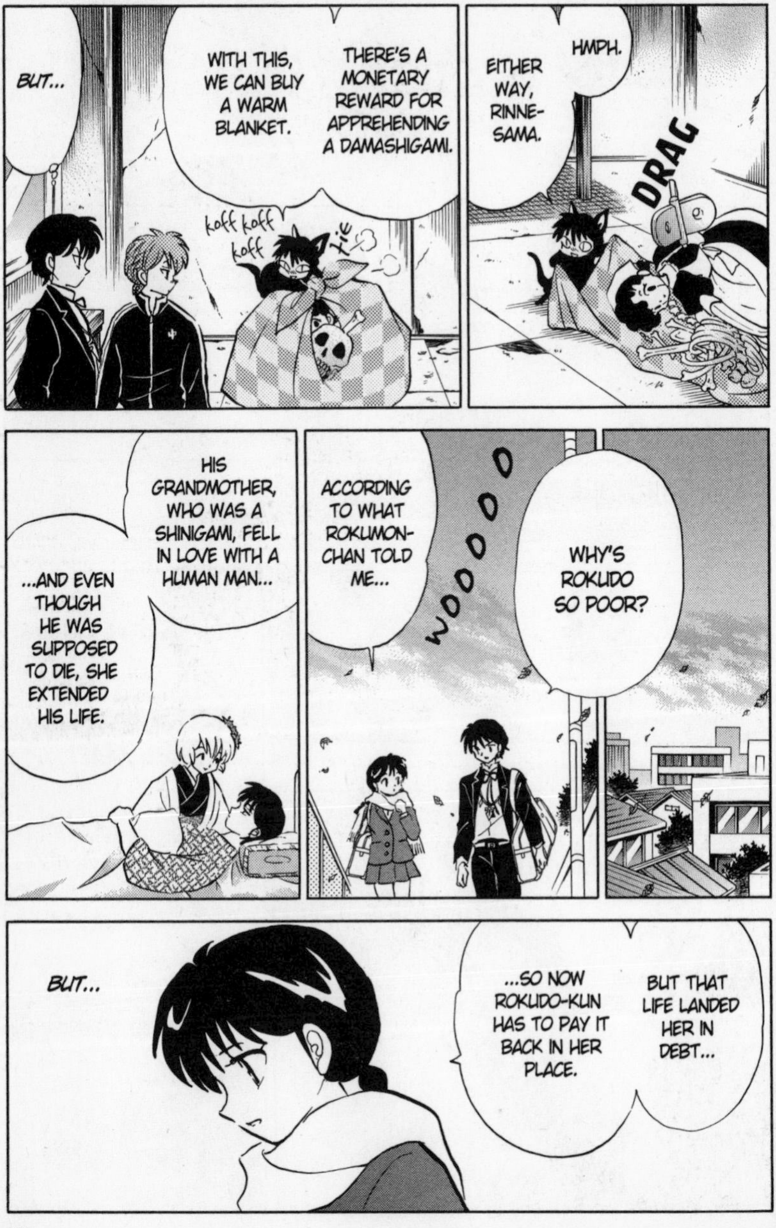
HMPH.
EITHER WAY, RINNE-SAMA.
DRAG
THERE'S A MONETARY REWARD FOR APPREHENDING A DAMASHIGAMI.
WITH THIS, WE CAN BUY A WARM BLANKET.
koff koff koff
tie
BUT...
WHY'S ROKUDO SO POOR?
WOOOOOO
ACCORDING TO WHAT ROKUMON-CHAN TOLD ME...
HIS GRANDMOTHER, WHO WAS A SHINIGAMI, FELL IN LOVE WITH A HUMAN MAN...
...AND EVEN THOUGH HE WAS SUPPOSED TO DIE, SHE EXTENDED HIS LIFE.
BUT THAT LIFE LANDED HER IN DEBT...
...SO NOW ROKUDO-KUN HAS TO PAY IT BACK IN HER PLACE.
BUT...

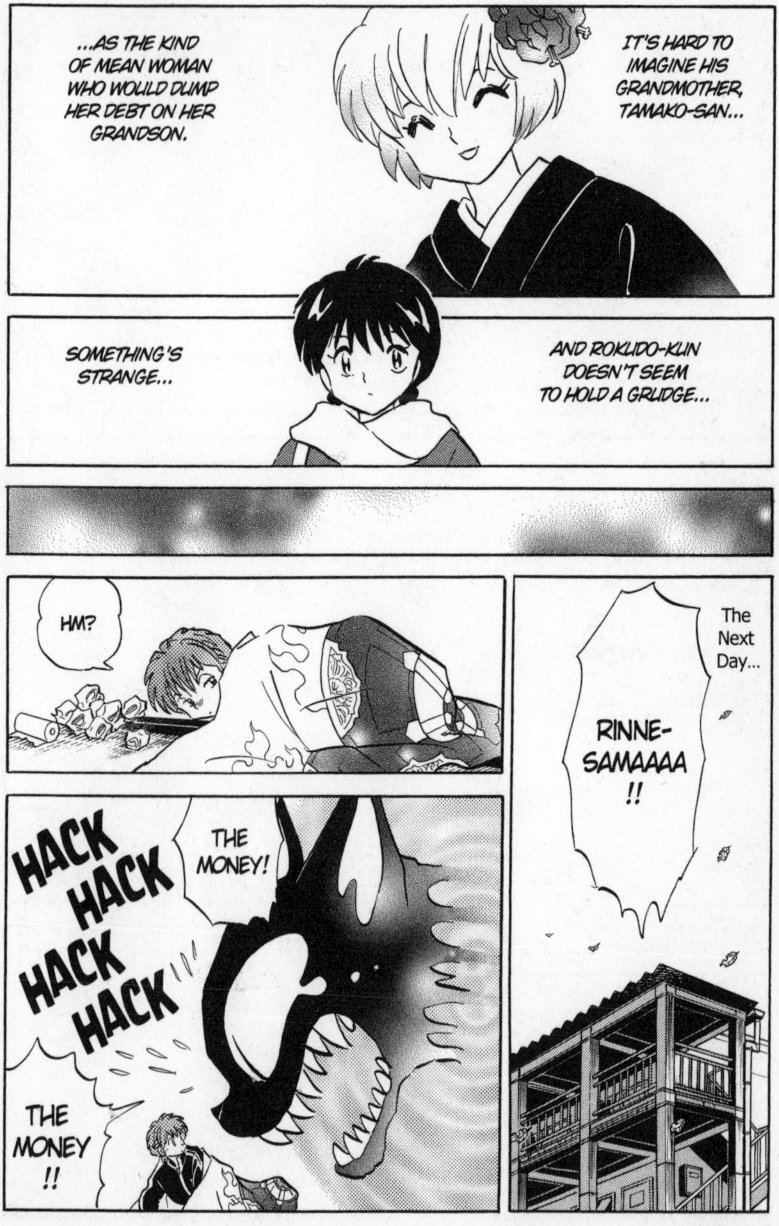
IT'S HARD TO IMAGINE HIS GRANDMOTHER, TAMAKO-SAN...
...AS THE KIND OF MEAN WOMAN WHO WOULD DUMP HER DEBT ON HER GRANDSON.
AND ROKUDO-KUN DOESN'T SEEM TO HOLD A GRUDGE...
SOMETHING'S STRANGE...
The Next Day...
RINNE-SAMAAAA !!
HM?
THE MONEY!
HACK HACK HACK HACK
THE MONEY !!

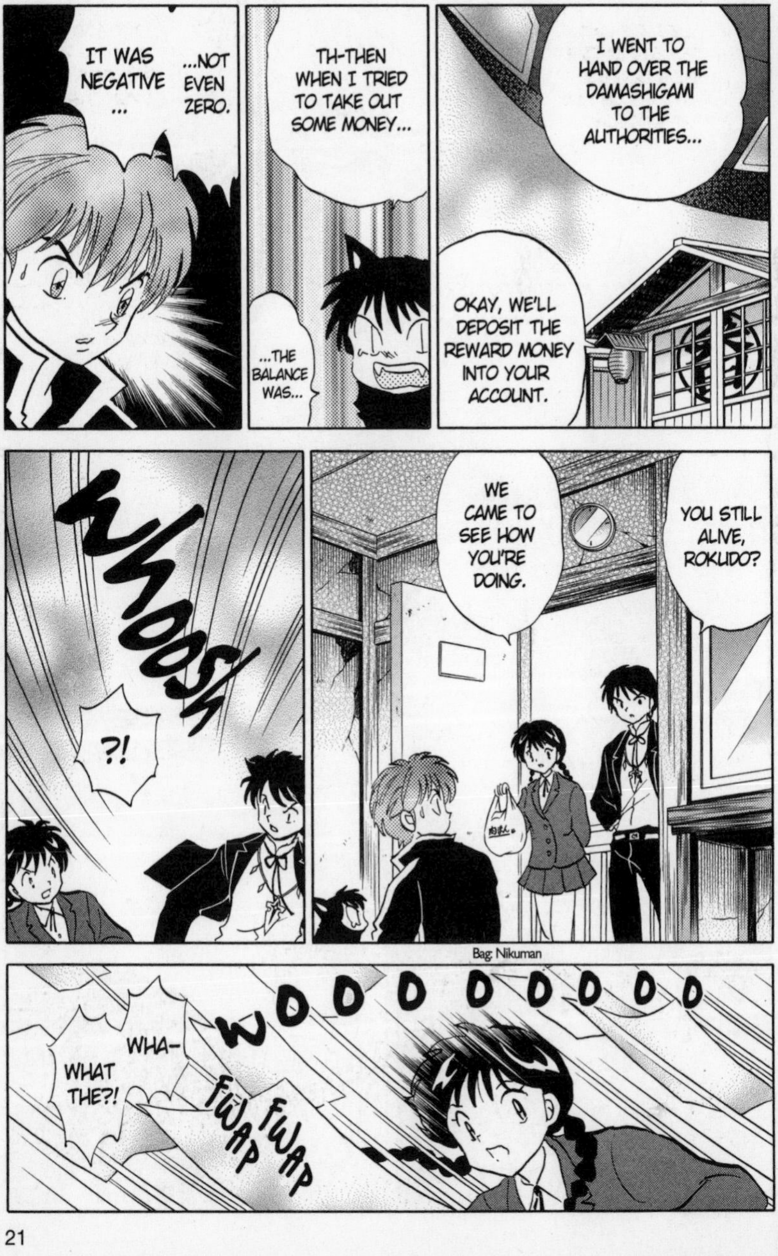
I WENT TO HAND OVER THE DAMASHIGAMI TO THE AUTHORITIES...
OKAY, WE'LL DEPOSIT THE REWARD MONEY INTO YOUR ACCOUNT.
TH-THEN WHEN I TRIED TO TAKE OUT SOME MONEY...
...THE BALANCE WAS...
IT WAS NEGATIVE ...
...NOT EVEN ZERO.
YOU STILL ALIVE, ROKUDO?
WE CAME TO SEE HOW YOU'RE DOING.
WHOOSH
?!
WOOOOOOOOO
WHA- WHAT THE?!
FWAP FWAP
Bag: Nikuman

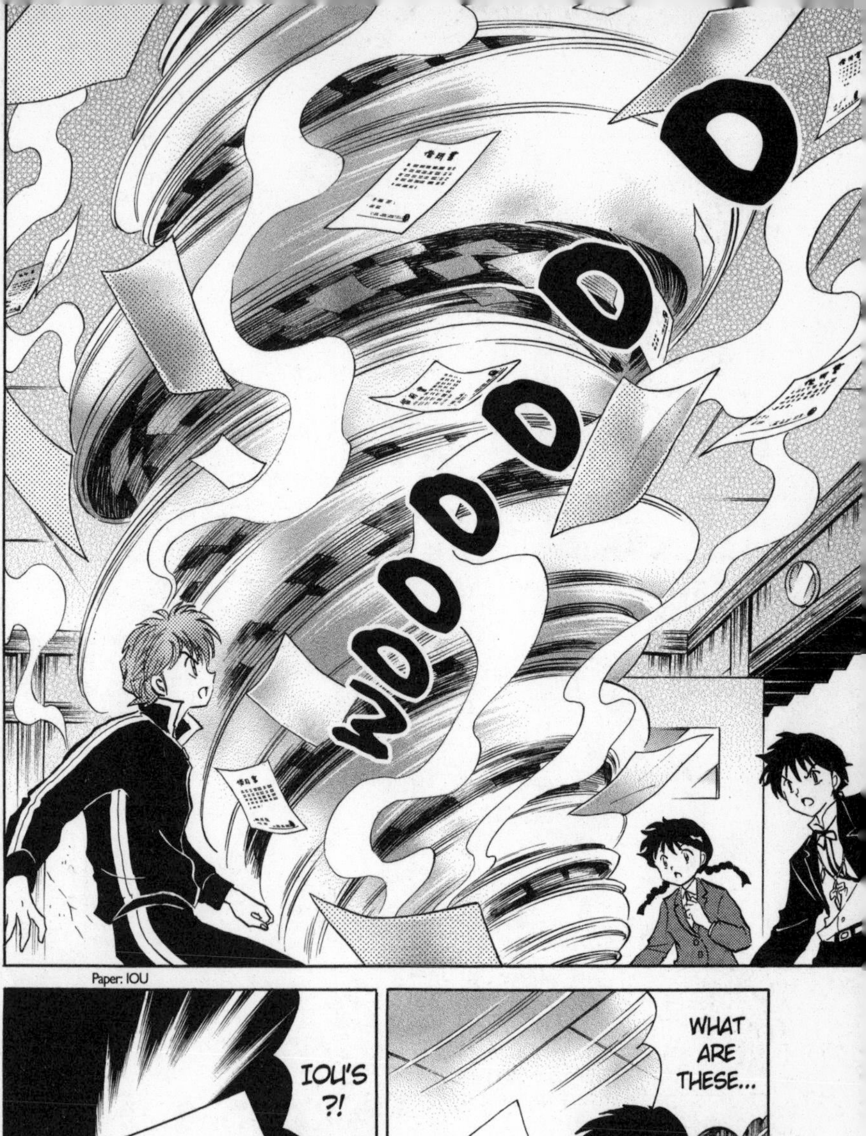
WOOOOD

Paper: IOU

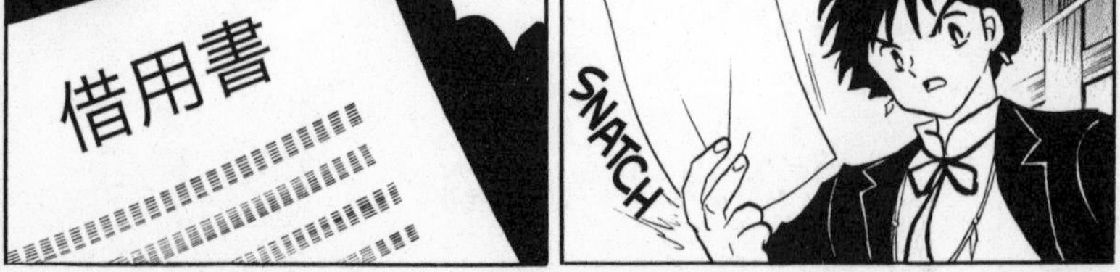
WHAT ARE THESE...
SNATCH
IOU'S ?!
借用書

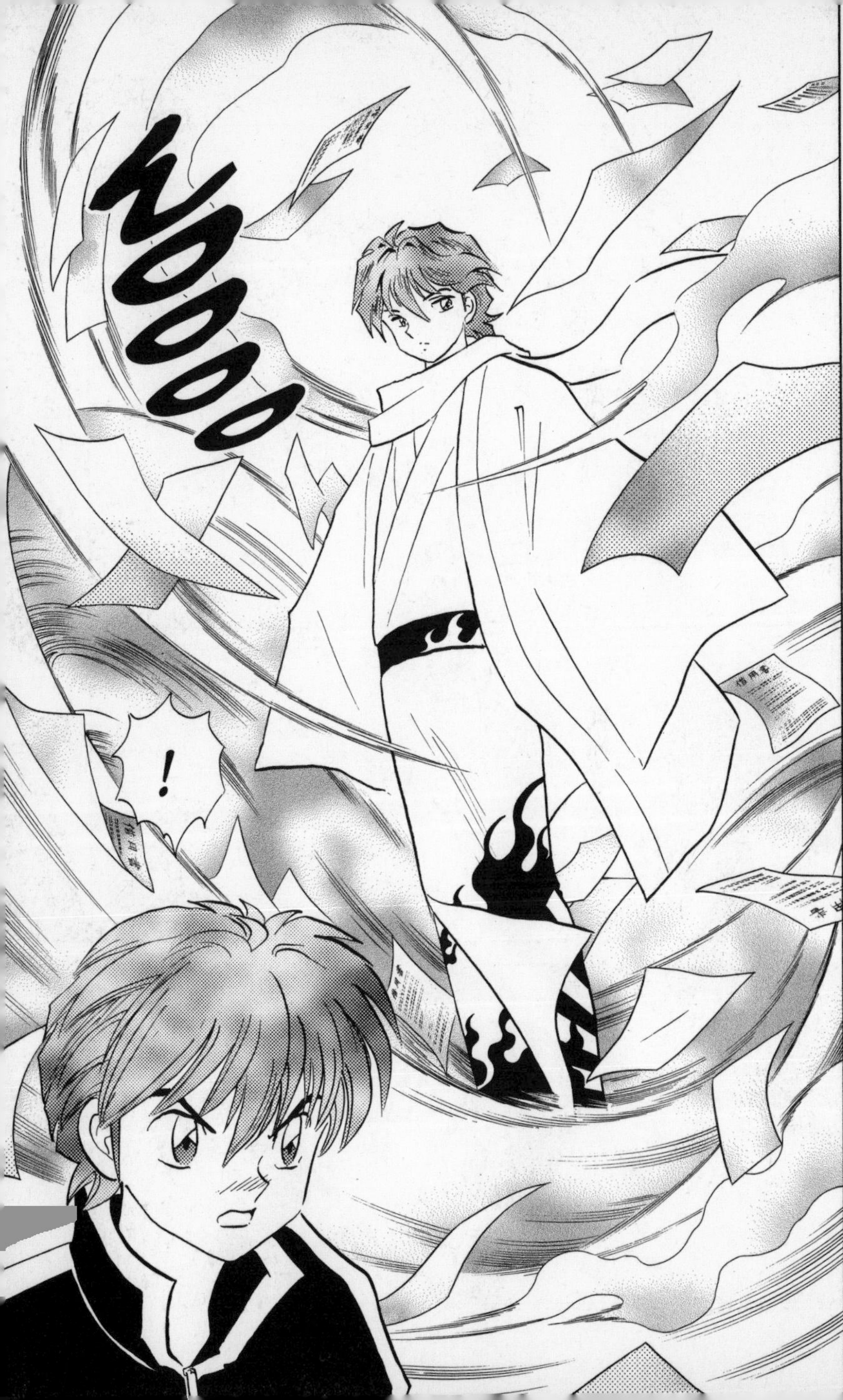
WOOOOO
!

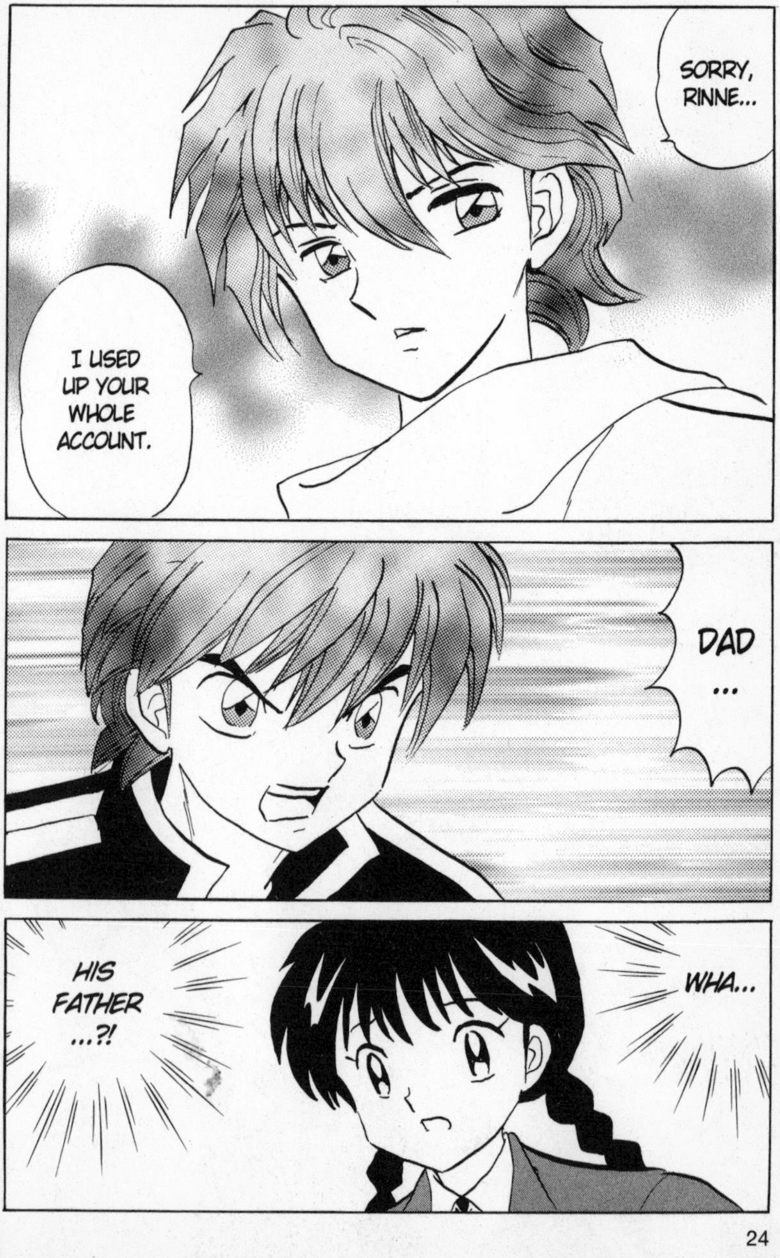
SORRY, RINNE...
I USED UP YOUR WHOLE ACCOUNT.
DAD ...
WHA...
HIS FATHER ...?!

CHAPTER 30: PRESIDENT

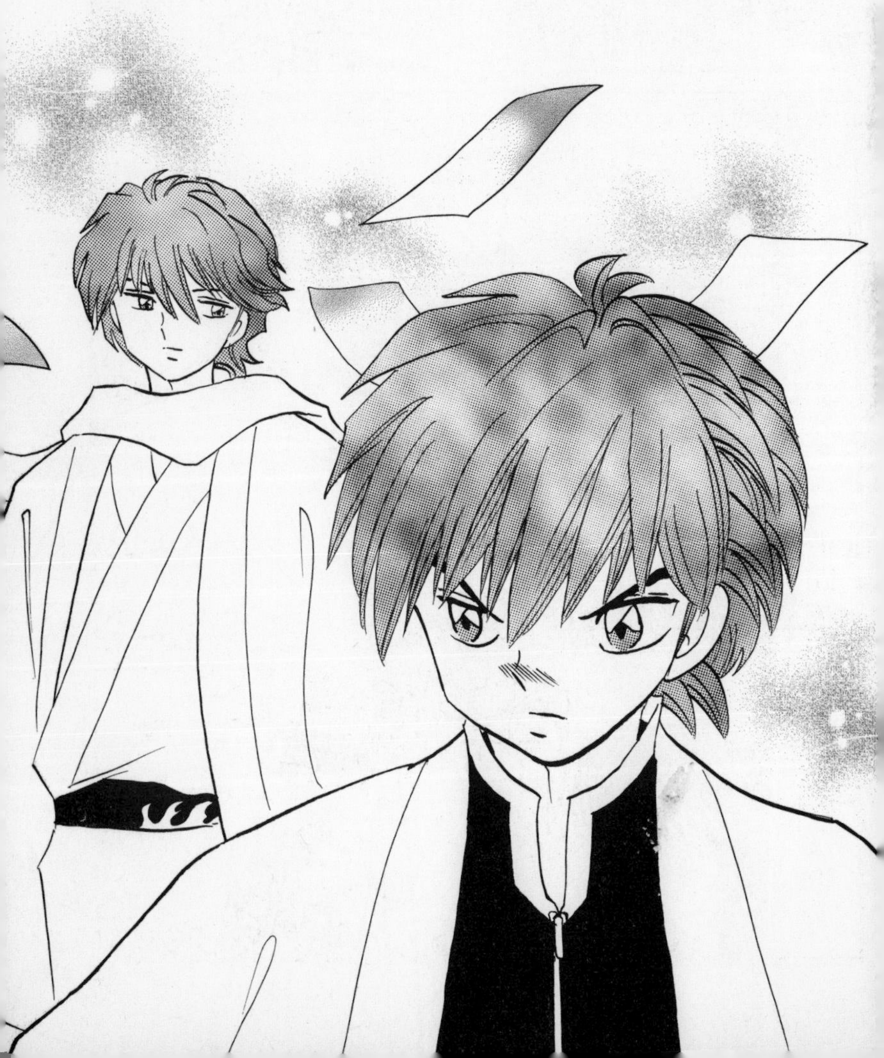

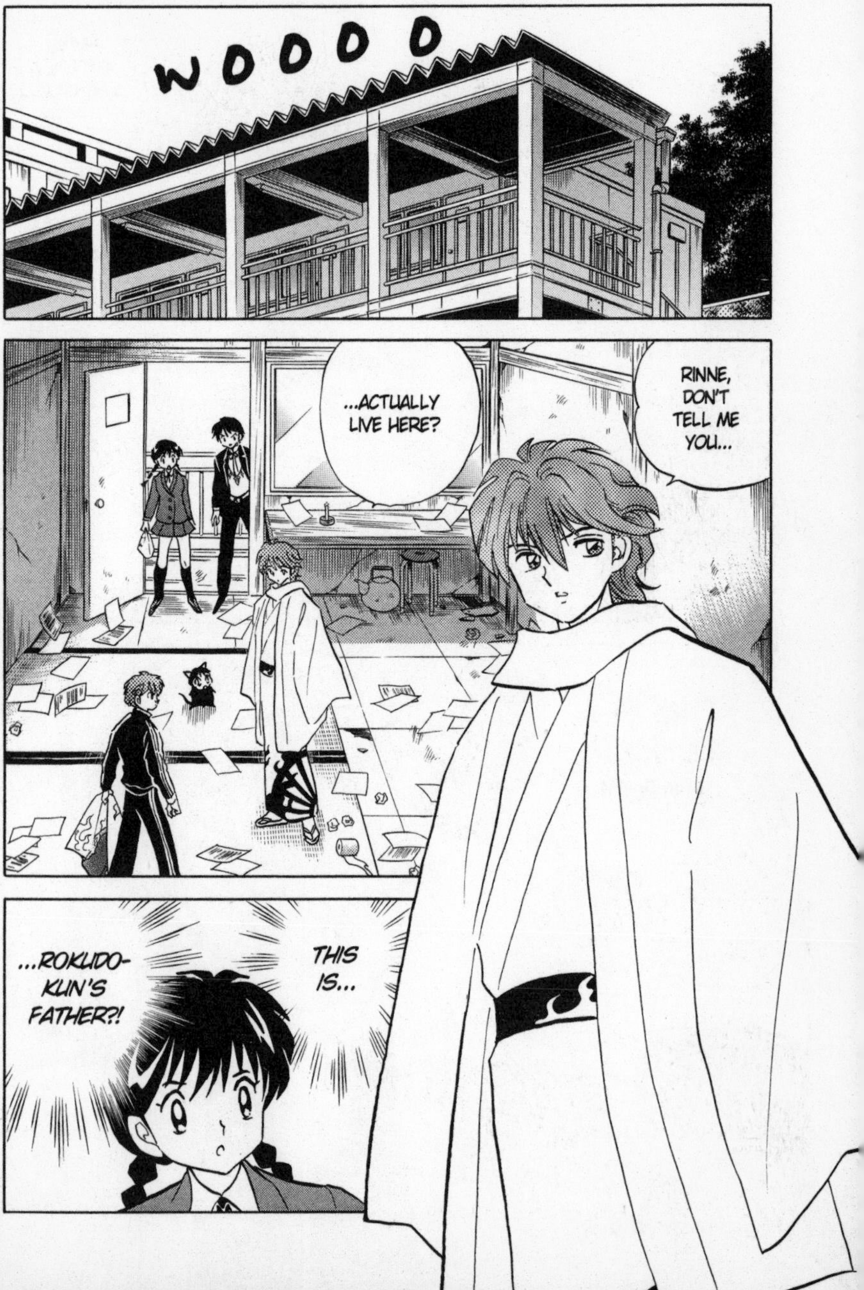
WOOOO
RINNE, DON'T TELL ME YOU...
...ACTUALLY LIVE HERE?
THIS IS...
...ROKUDO-KUN'S FATHER?!

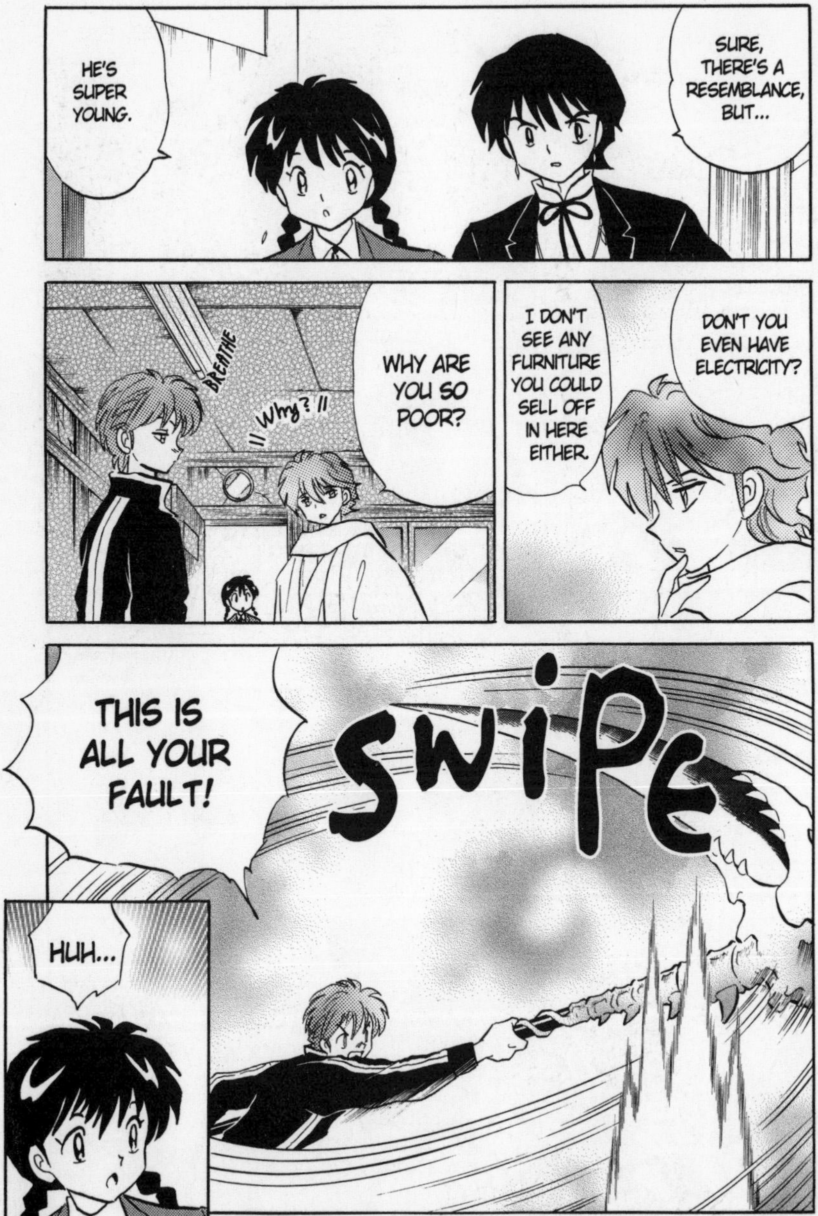
SURE, THERE'S A RESEMBLANCE, BUT...
HE'S SUPER YOUNG.
DON'T YOU EVEN HAVE ELECTRICITY?
I DON'T SEE ANY FURNITURE YOU COULD SELL OFF IN HERE EITHER.
WHY ARE YOU SO POOR?
BREATHE
Why?
THIS IS ALL YOUR FAULT!
SWIPE
HUH...

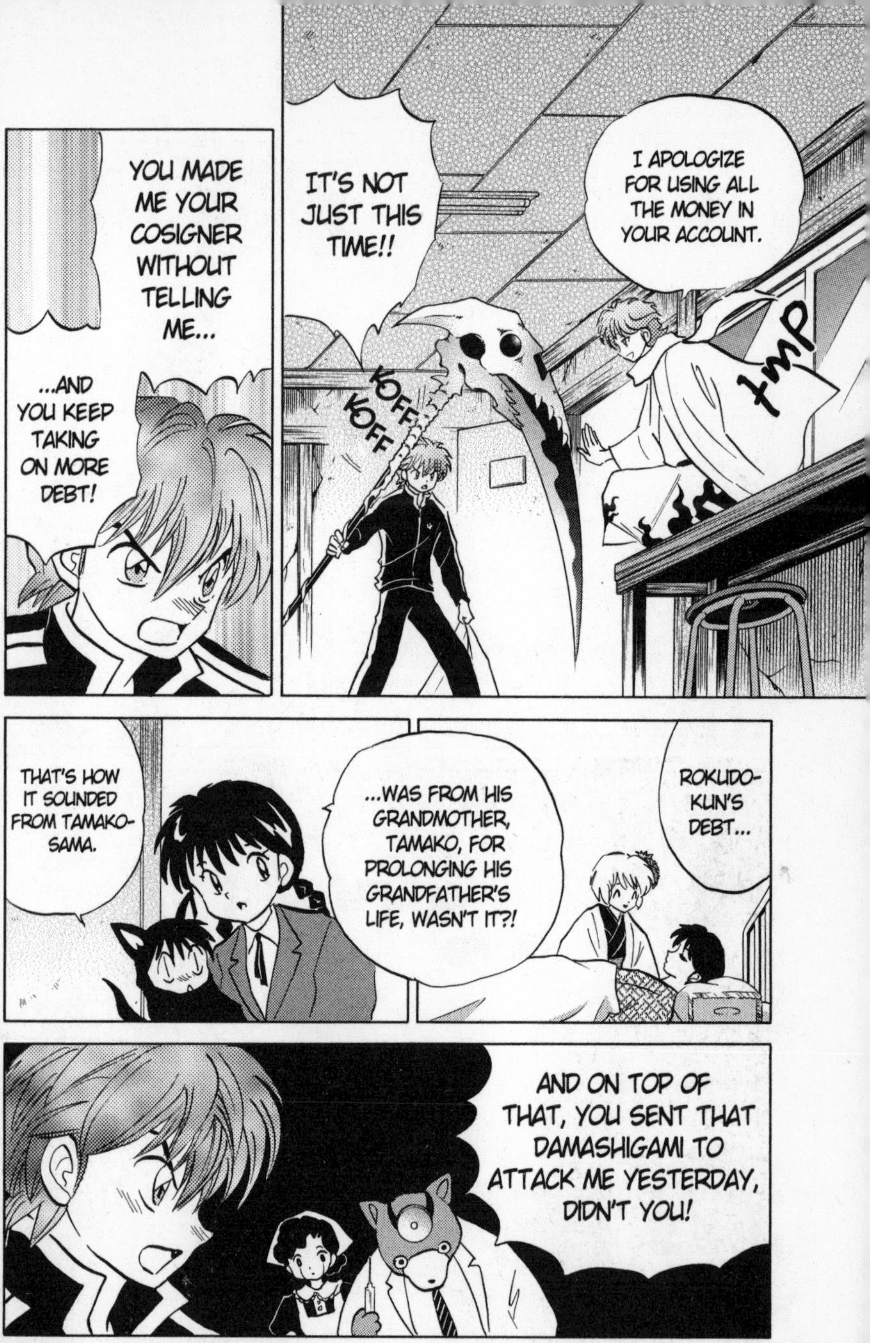
I APOLOGIZE FOR USING ALL THE MONEY IN YOUR ACCOUNT.
TMP
IT'S NOT JUST THIS TIME!!
KOFF KOFF
YOU MADE ME YOUR COSIGNER WITHOUT TELLING ME...
...AND YOU KEEP TAKING ON MORE DEBT!
ROKUDO-KUN'S DEBT...
...WAS FROM HIS GRANDMOTHER, TAMAKO, FOR PROLONGING HIS GRANDFATHER'S LIFE, WASN'T IT?!
THAT'S HOW IT SOUNDED FROM TAMAKO-SAMA.
AND ON TOP OF THAT, YOU SENT THAT DAMASHIGAMI TO ATTACK ME YESTERDAY, DIDN'T YOU!

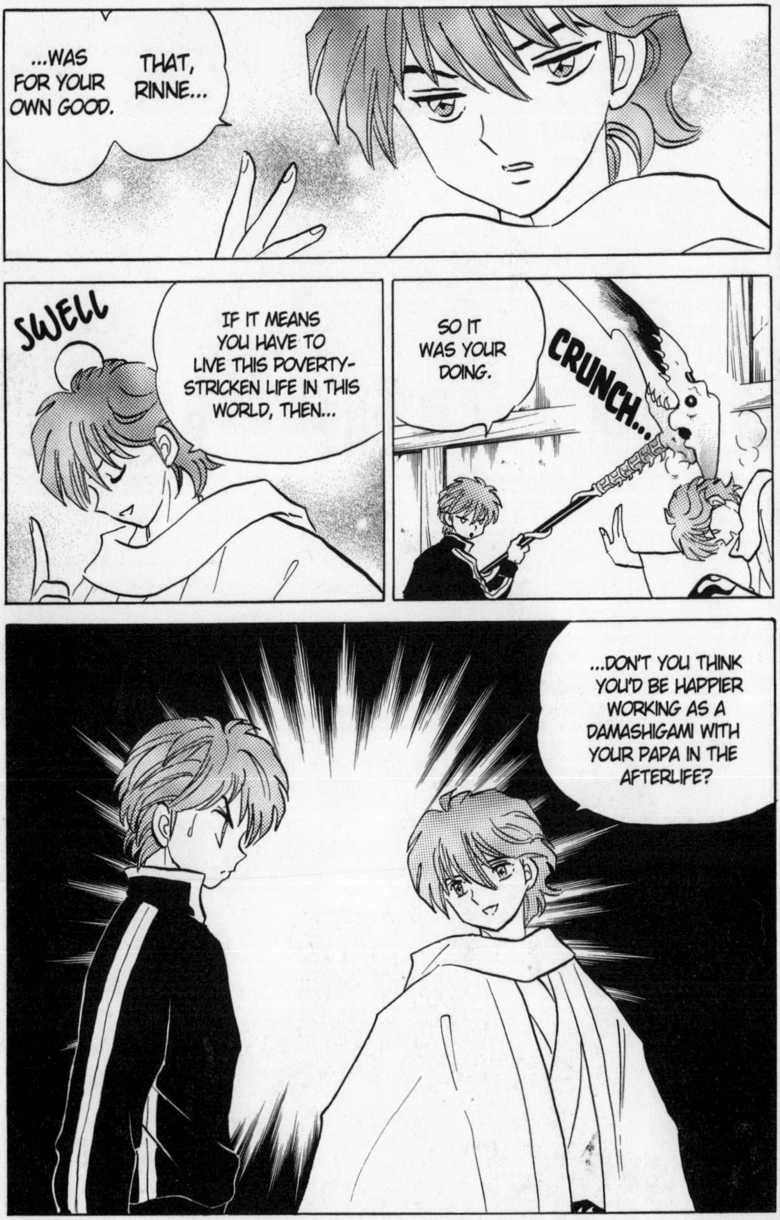
THAT, RINNE...
...WAS FOR YOUR OWN GOOD.
SO IT WAS YOUR DOING.
CRUNCH...
IF IT MEANS YOU HAVE TO LIVE THIS POVERTY-STRICKEN LIFE IN THIS WORLD, THEN...
SWELL
...DON'T YOU THINK YOU'D BE HAPPIER WORKING AS A DAMASHIGAMI WITH YOUR PAPA IN THE AFTERLIFE?

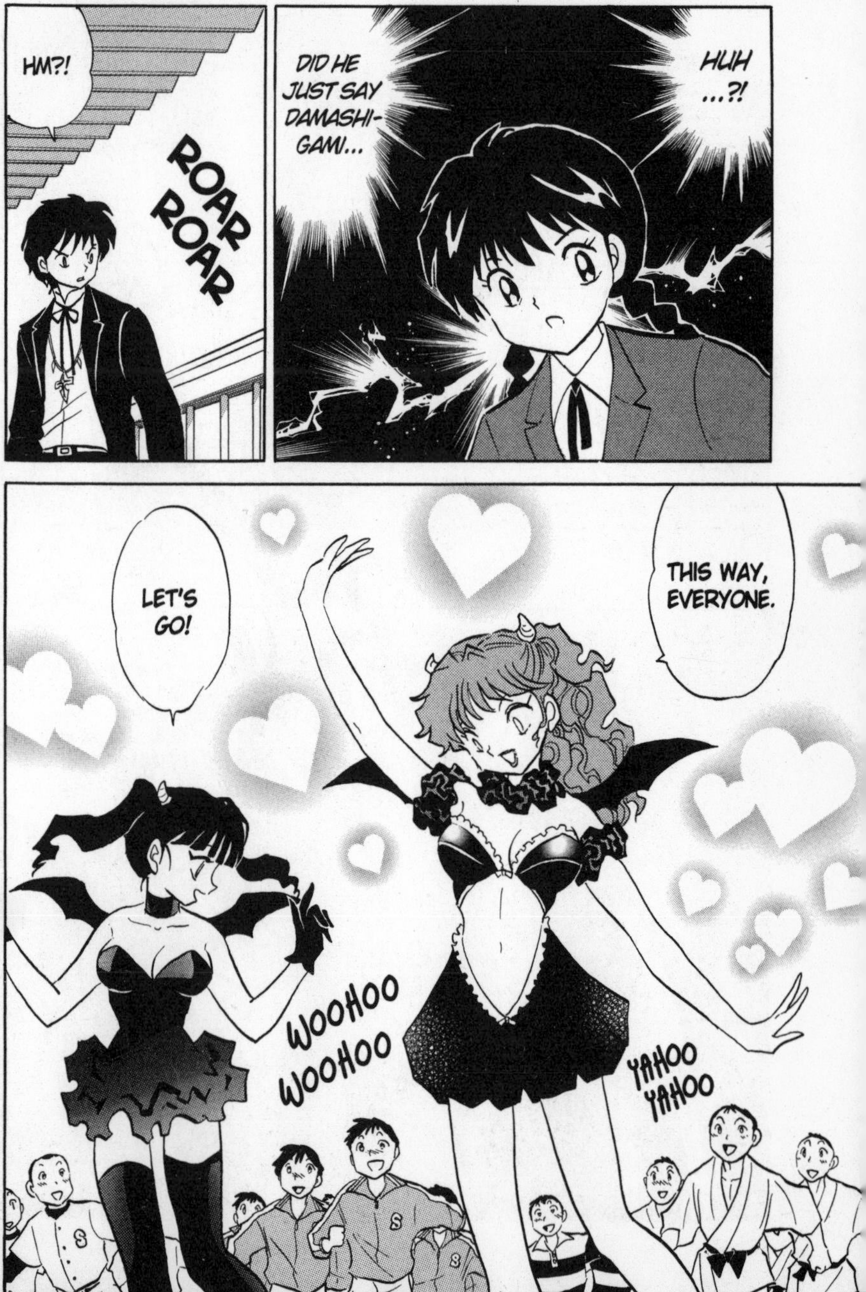
HUH ...?!
DID HE JUST SAY DAMASHI-GAMI...
HM?!
ROAR ROAR
THIS WAY, EVERYONE.
LET'S GO!
YAHOO YAHOO
WOOHOO WOOHOO

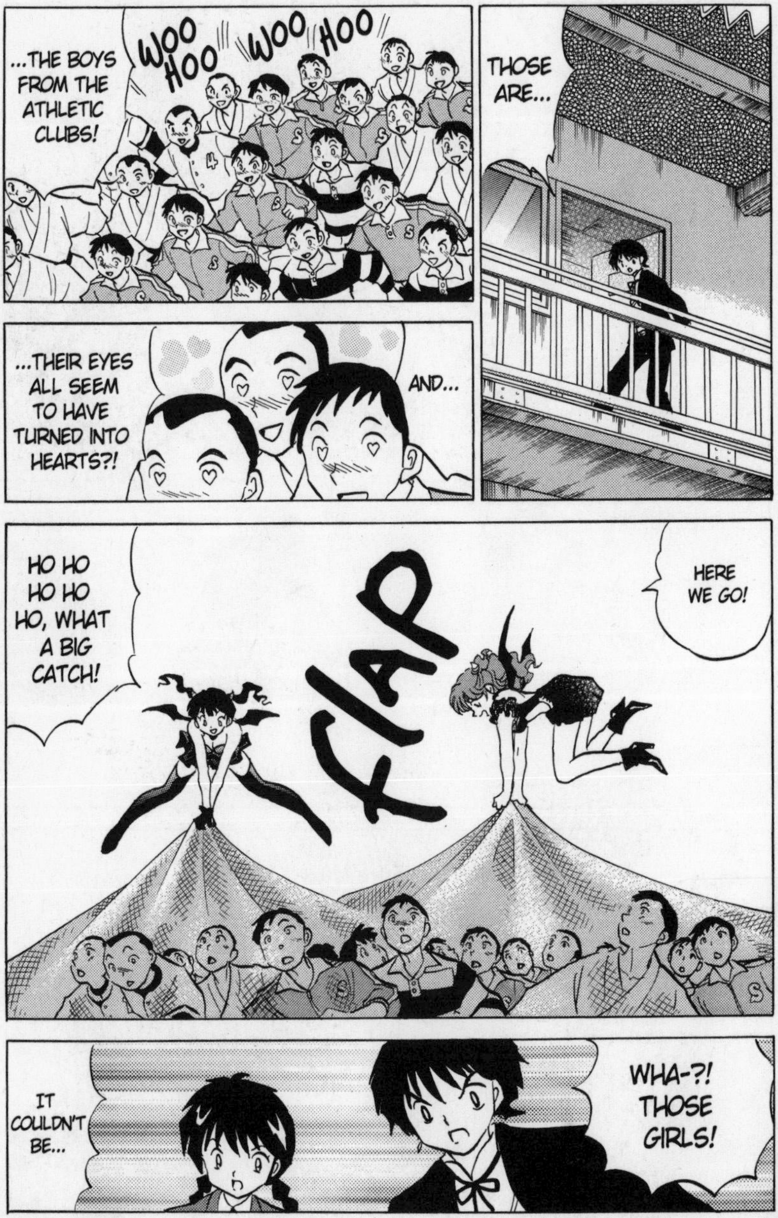
THOSE ARE...
...THE BOYS FROM THE ATHLETIC CLUBS!
WOO HOO
WOO HOO
AND...
...THEIR EYES ALL SEEM TO HAVE TURNED INTO HEARTS?!
HERE WE GO!
FLAP
HO HO HO HO HO, WHAT A BIG CATCH!
WHA-?! THOSE GIRLS!
IT COULDN'T BE...

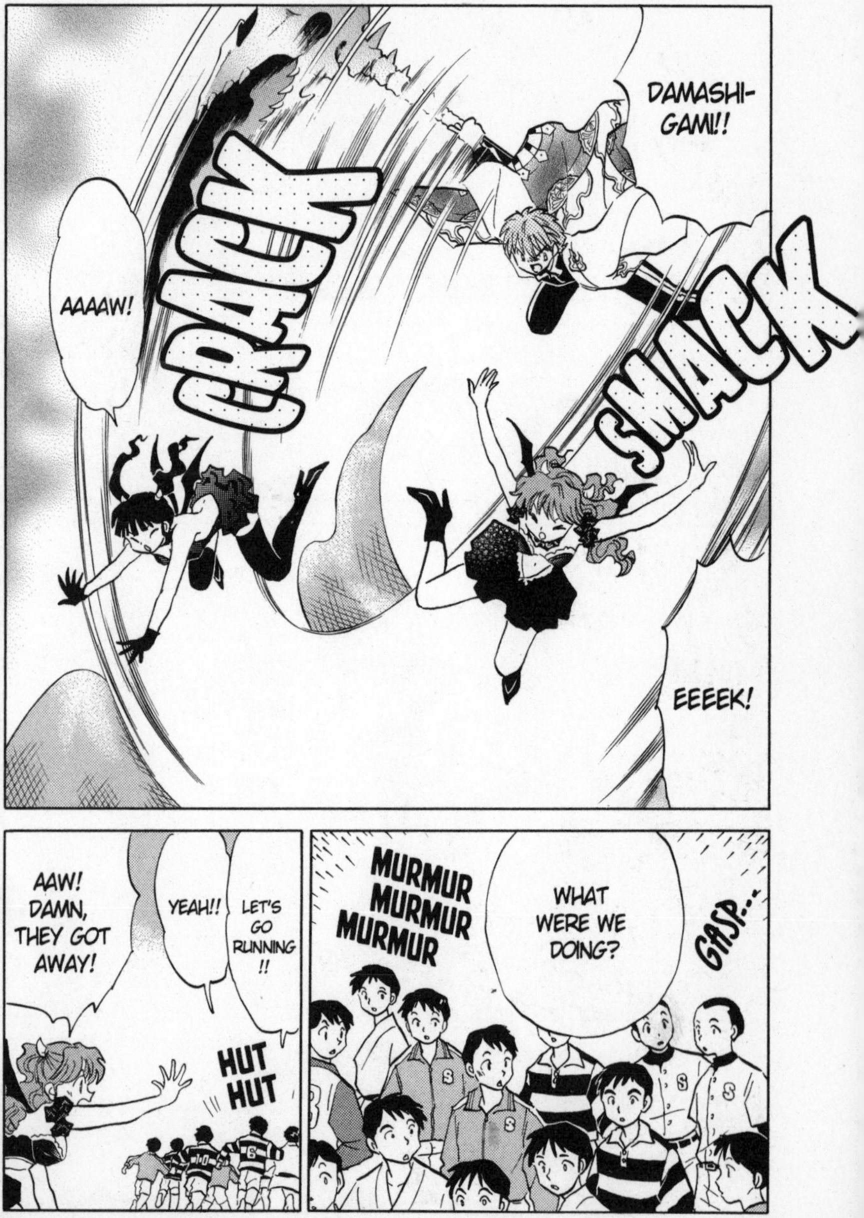
DAMASHI-GAMI!!
SMACK
CRACK
AAAAW!
EEEEK!
GASP...
WHAT WERE WE DOING?
MURMUR MURMUR MURMUR
LET'S GO RUNNING!!
YEAH!!
AAW! DAMN, THEY GOT AWAY!
HUT HUT

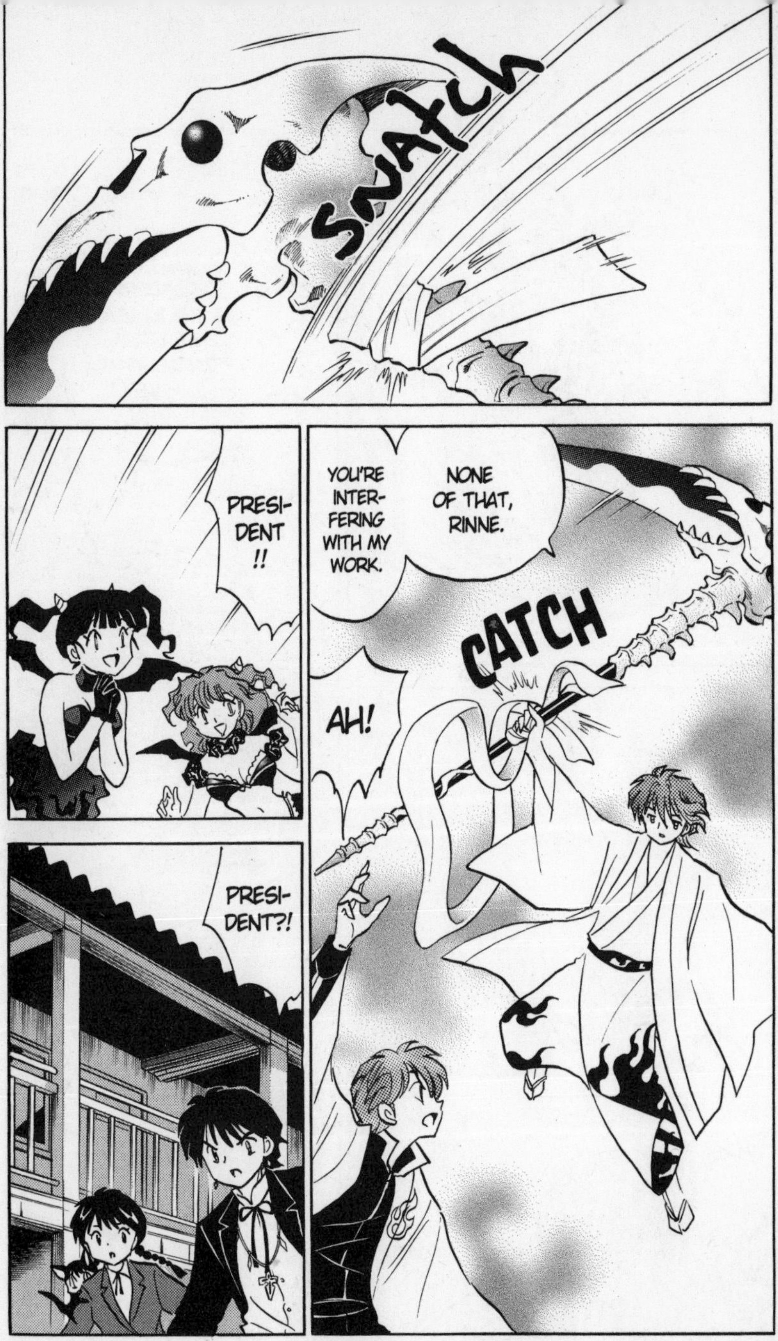
SNATCH
NONE OF THAT, RINNE.
YOU'RE INTERFERING WITH MY WORK.
CATCH
AH!
PRESIDENT!!
PRESIDENT?!

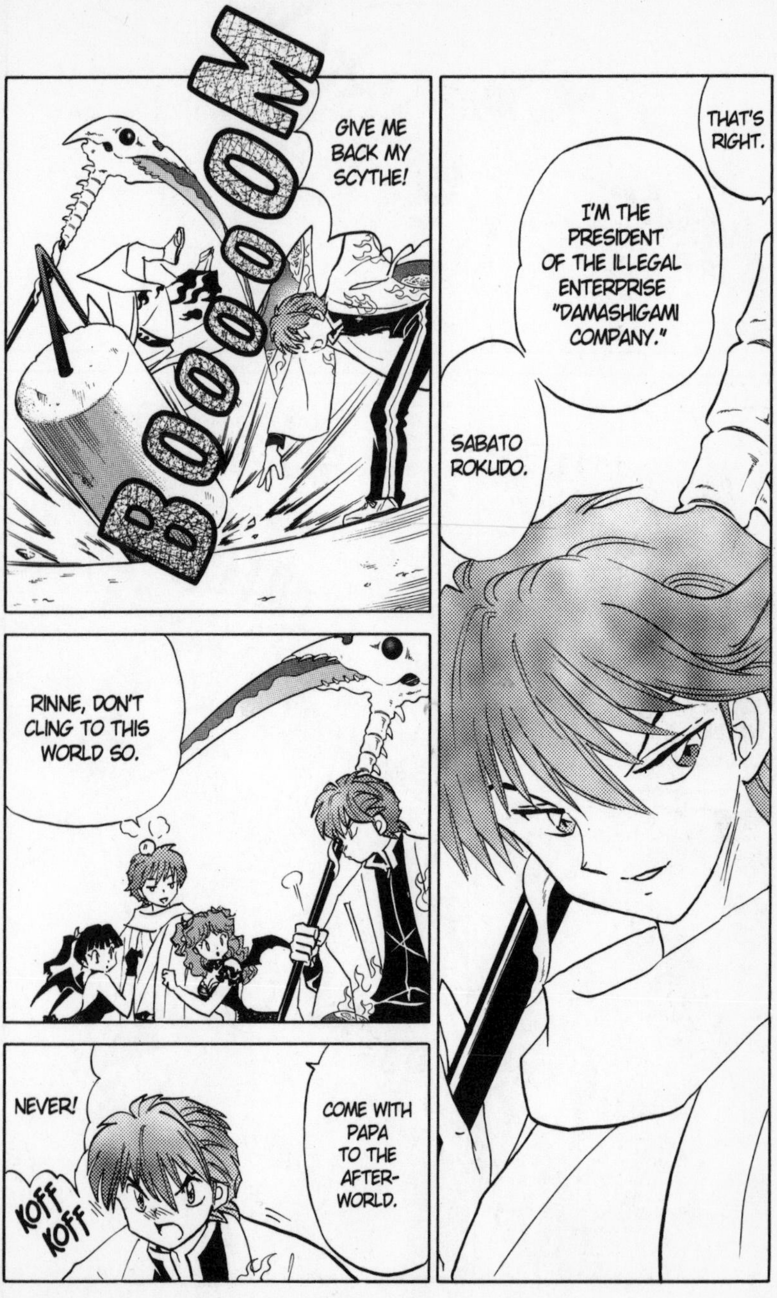
THAT'S RIGHT.
I'M THE PRESIDENT OF THE ILLEGAL ENTERPRISE "DAMASHIGAMI COMPANY."
SABATO ROKUDO.
BOOOOOM
GIVE ME BACK MY SCYTHE!
RINNE, DON'T CLING TO THIS WORLD SO.
COME WITH PAPA TO THE AFTER-WORLD.
NEVER!
KOFF KOFF

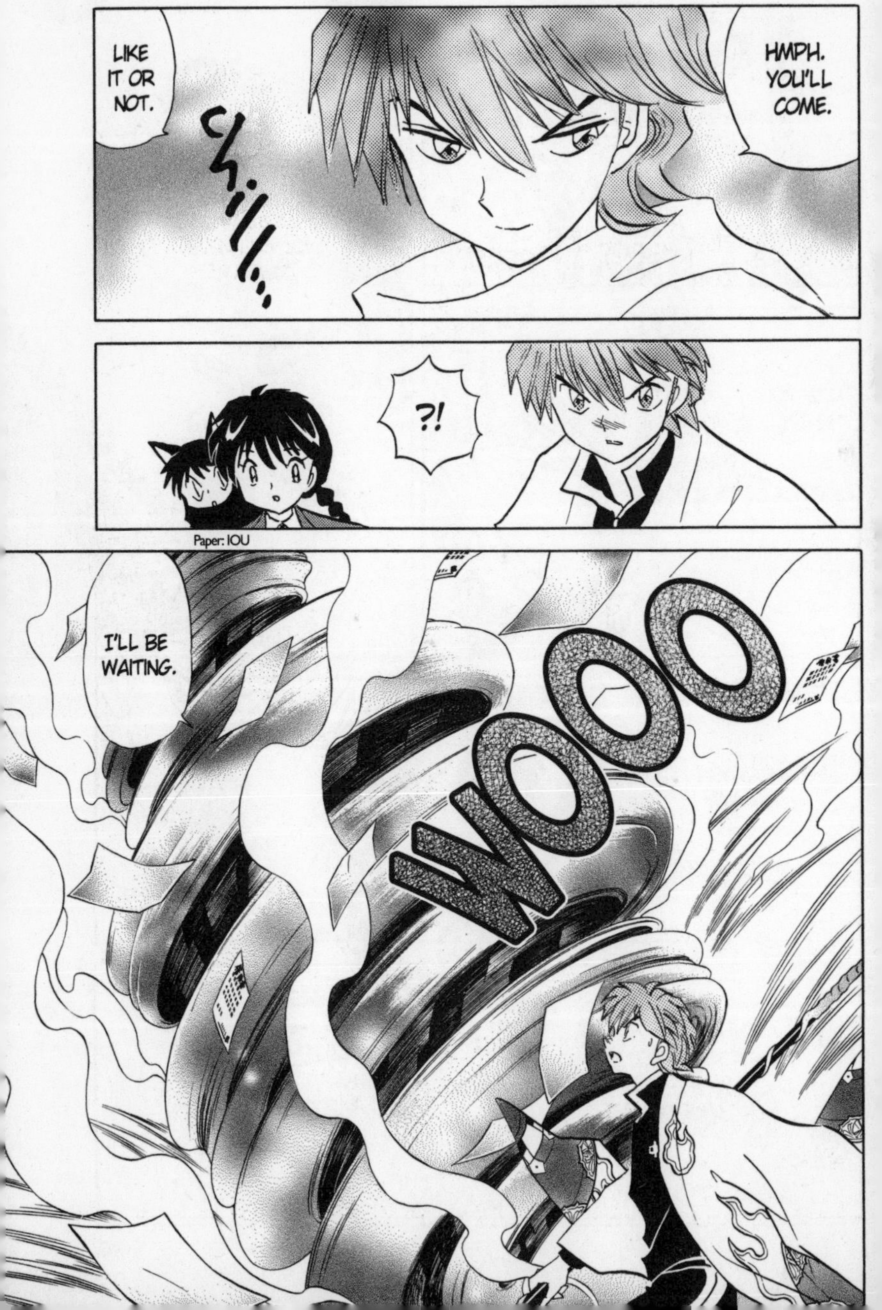
HMPH. YOU'LL COME.
LIKE IT OR NOT.
chill...
?!
Paper: IOU
WOOOO
I'LL BE WAITING.

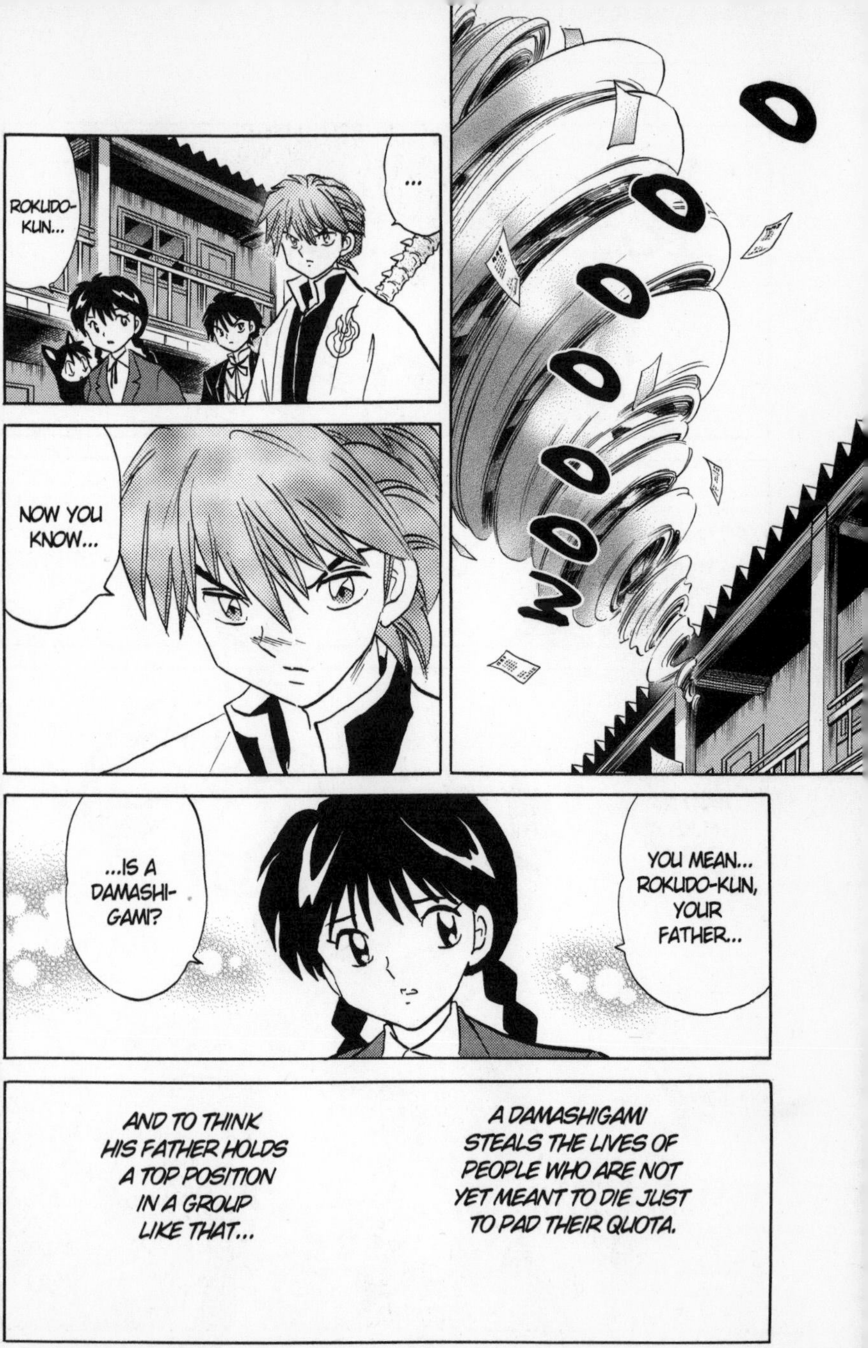
DOOOOOOM
...
ROKUDO-KUN...
NOW YOU KNOW...
YOU MEAN... ROKUDO-KUN, YOUR FATHER...
...IS A DAMASHI-GAMI?
A DAMASHIGAMI STEALS THE LIVES OF PEOPLE WHO ARE NOT YET MEANT TO DIE JUST TO PAD THEIR QUOTA.
AND TO THINK HIS FATHER HOLDS A TOP POSITION IN A GROUP LIKE THAT...

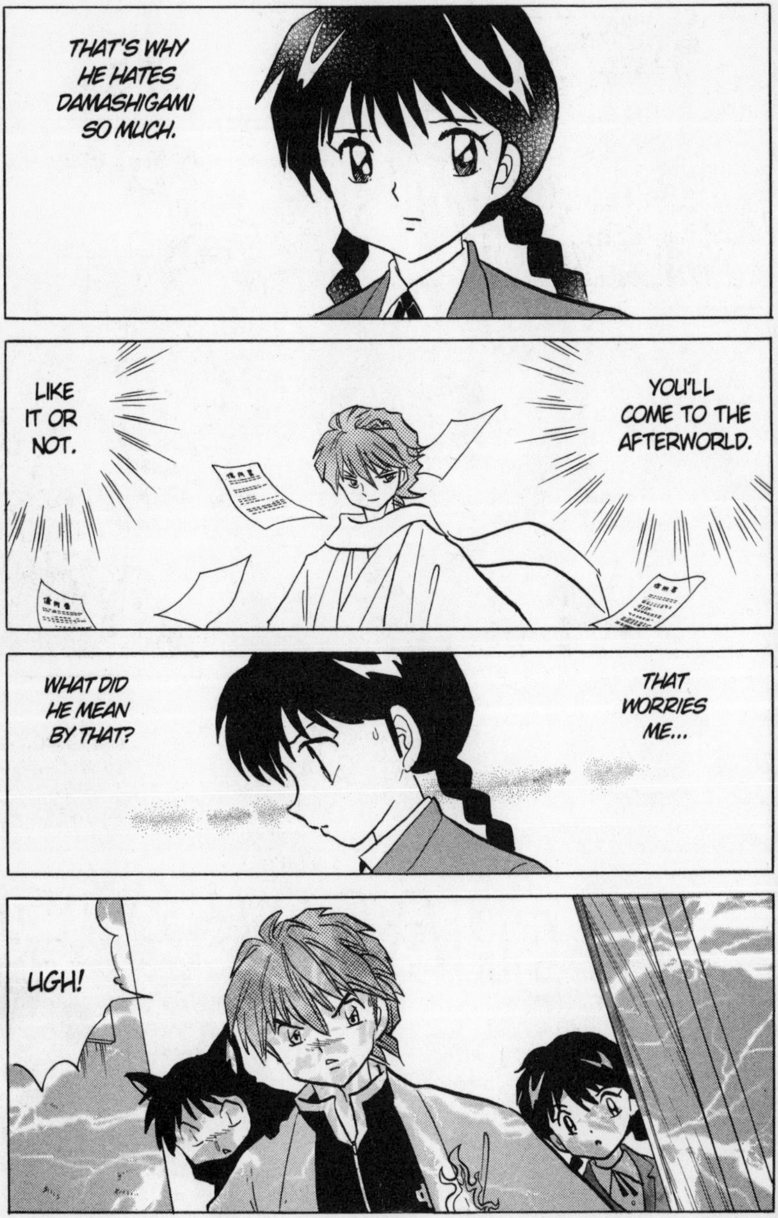
THAT'S WHY HE HATES DAMASHIGAMI SO MUCH.
YOU'LL COME TO THE AFTERWORLD.
LIKE IT OR NOT.
THAT WORRIES ME...
WHAT DID HE MEAN BY THAT?
UGH!

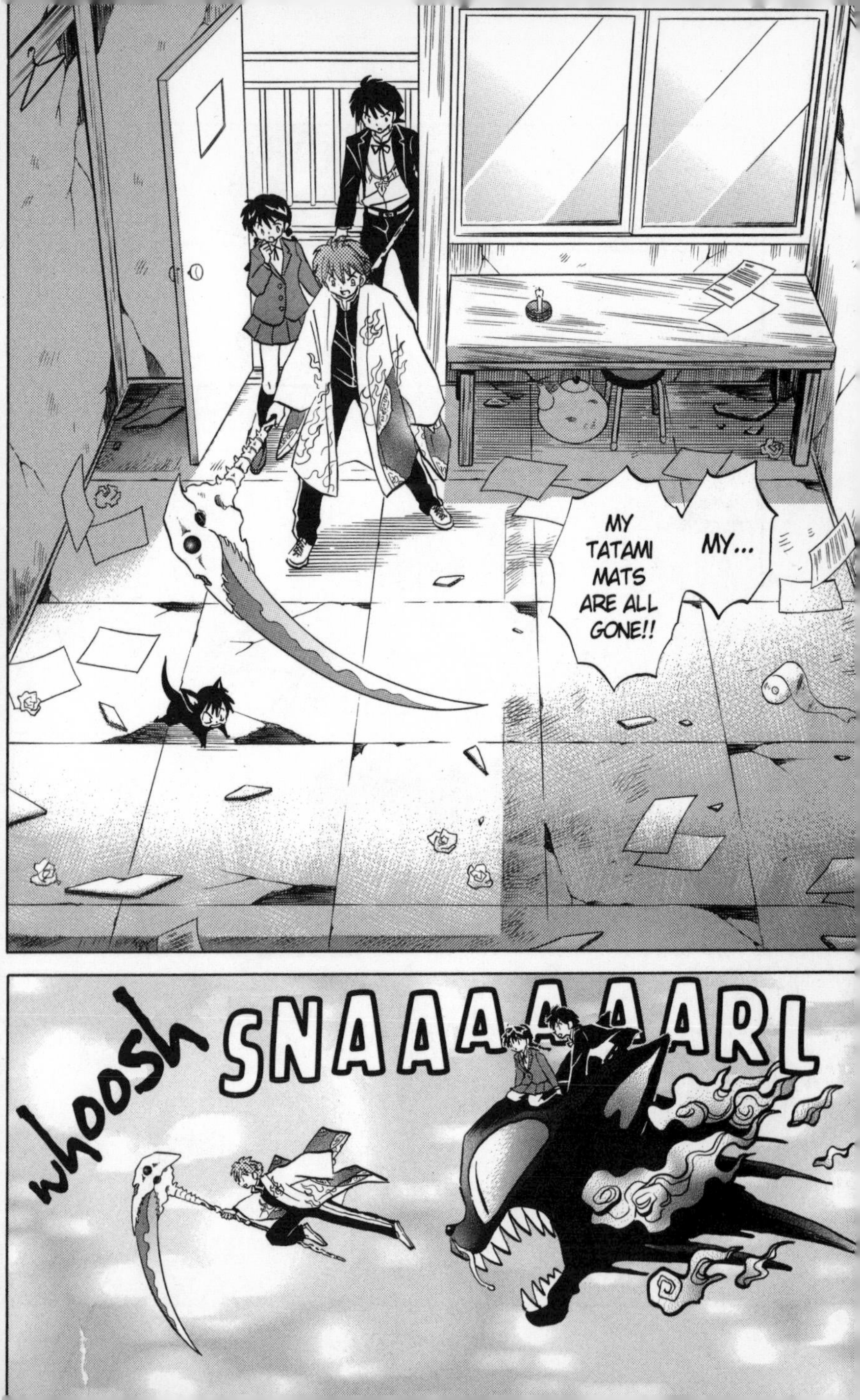
MY...
MY TATAMI MATS ARE ALL GONE!!
SNAAAAAARL
whoosh

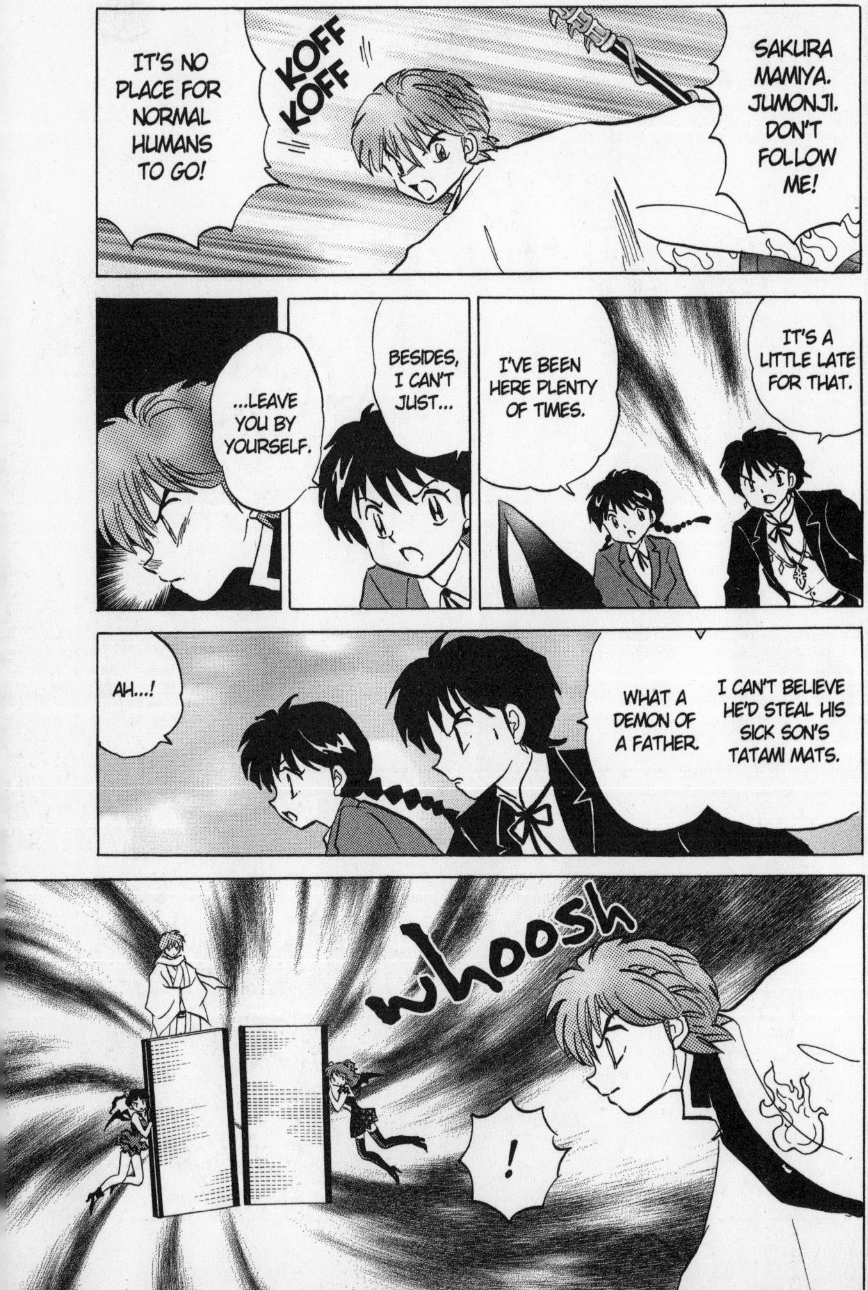
SAKURA MAMIYA. JUMONJI. DON'T FOLLOW ME!
KOFF KOFF
IT'S NO PLACE FOR NORMAL HUMANS TO GO!
IT'S A LITTLE LATE FOR THAT.
I'VE BEEN HERE PLENTY OF TIMES.
BESIDES, I CAN'T JUST...
...LEAVE YOU BY YOURSELF.
I CAN'T BELIEVE HE'D STEAL HIS SICK SON'S TATAMI MATS.
WHAT A DEMON OF A FATHER.
AH...!
whoosh
!

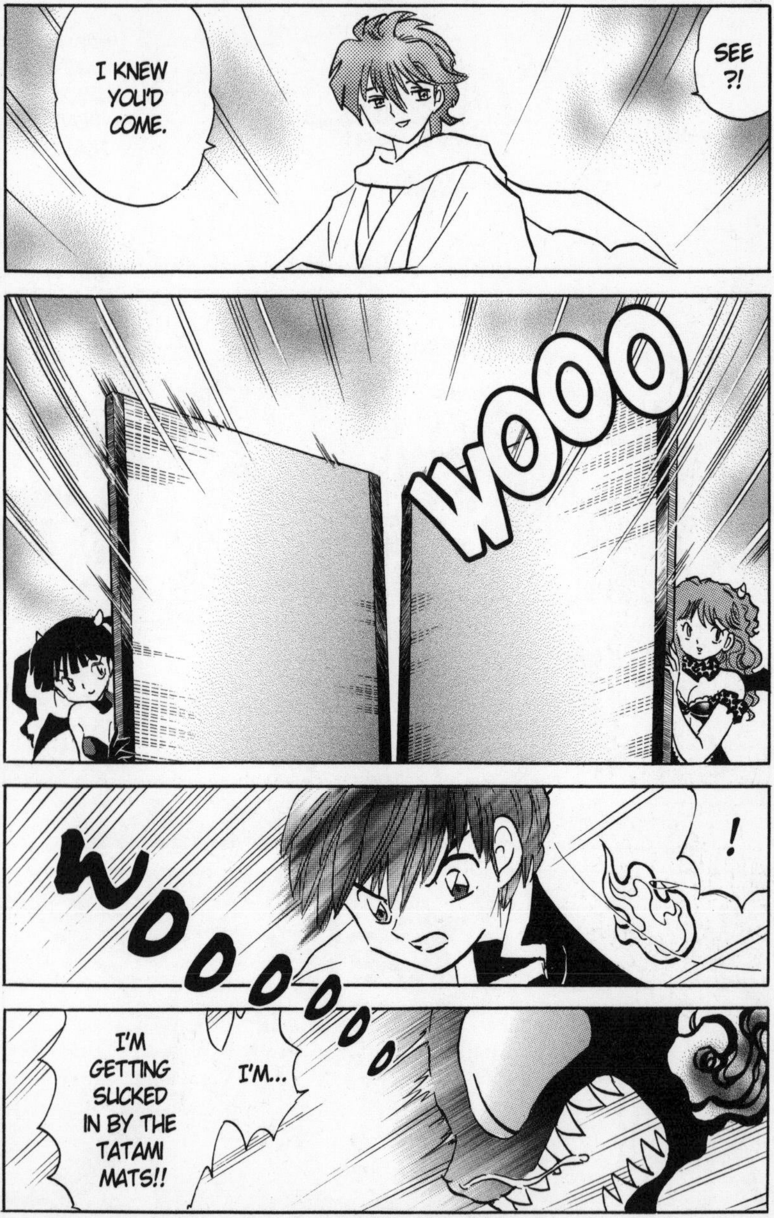
SEE ?!
I KNEW YOU'D COME.
WOOO
!
WOOOOOOOO
I'M...
I'M GETTING SUCKED IN BY THE TATAMI MATS!!

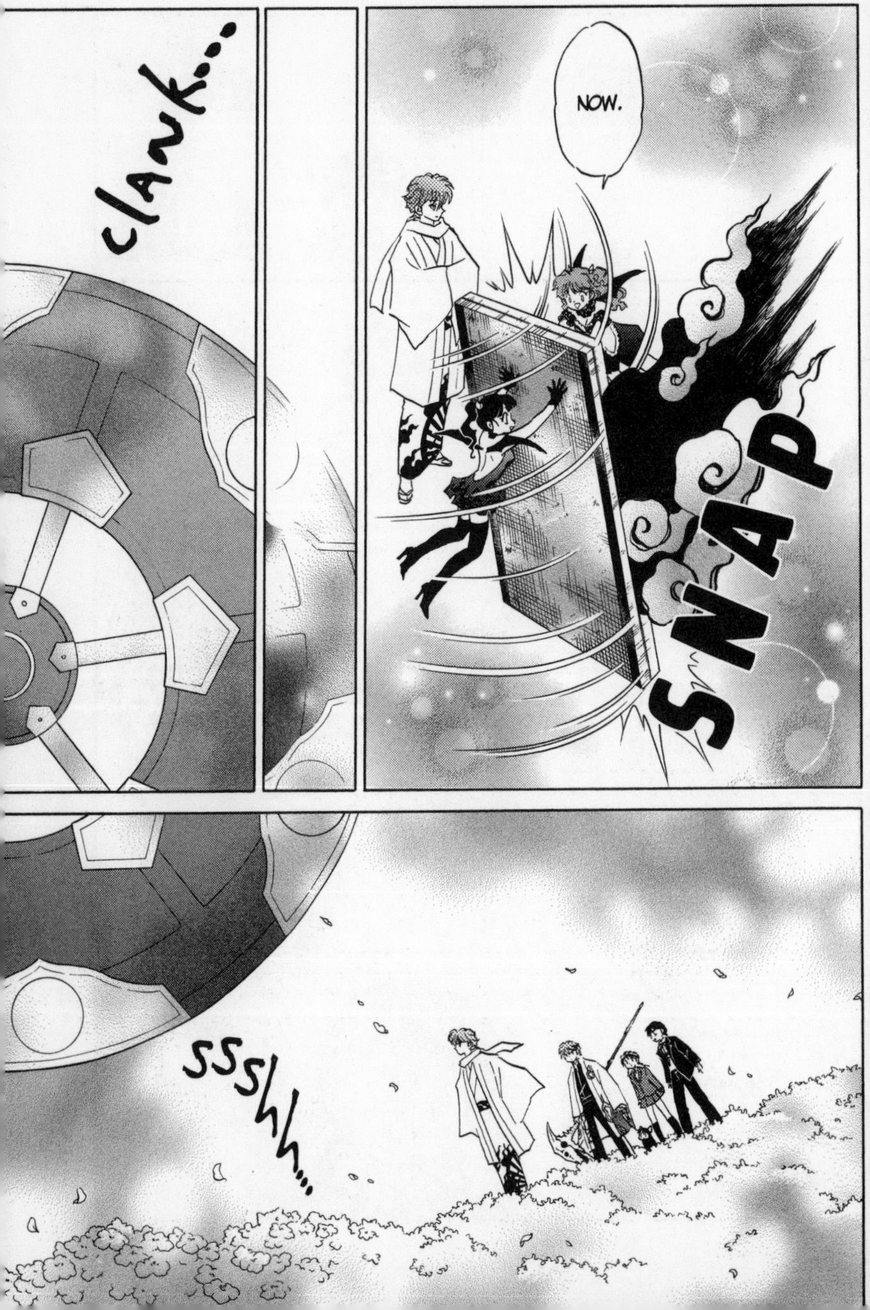
NOW.
SNAP
clank...
ssshh...

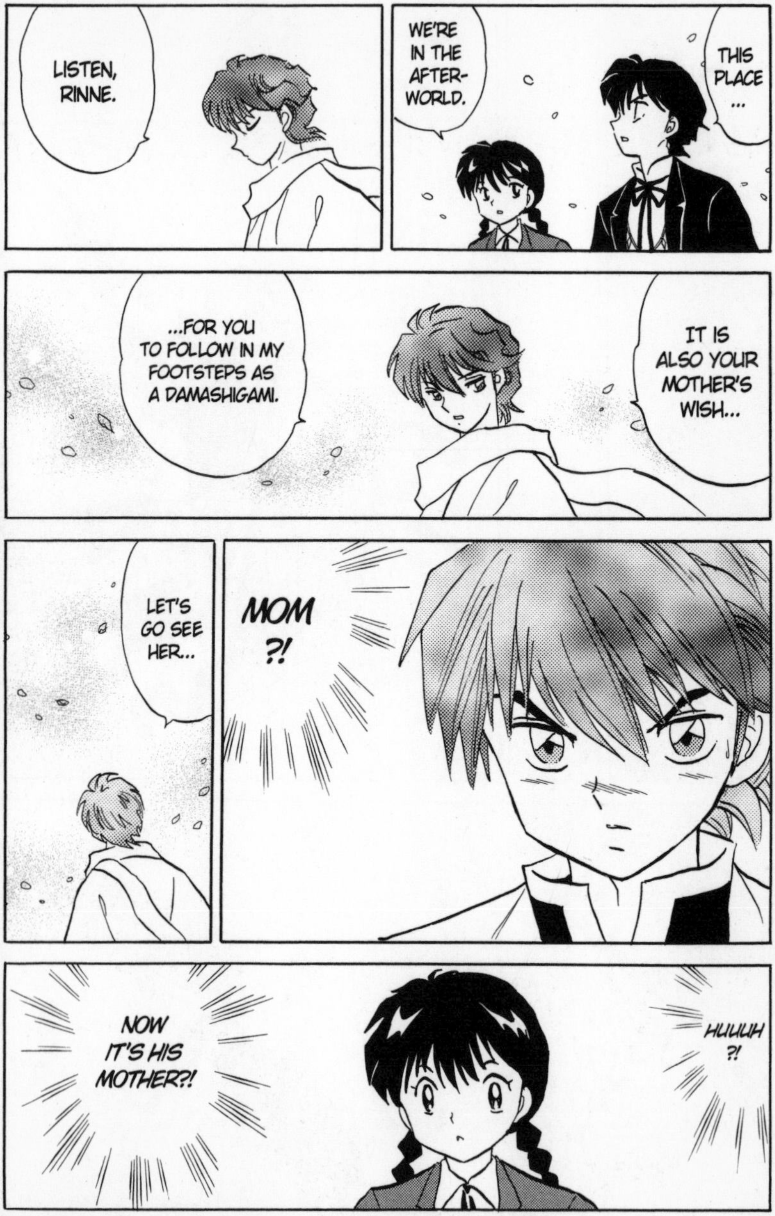
THIS PLACE ...
WE'RE IN THE AFTER-WORLD.
LISTEN, RINNE.
IT IS ALSO YOUR MOTHER'S WISH...
...FOR YOU TO FOLLOW IN MY FOOTSTEPS AS A DAMASHIGAMI.
MOM ?!
LET'S GO SEE HER...
HUUUH ?!
NOW IT'S HIS MOTHER?!

CHAPTER 31: DAMASHIGAMI COMPANY

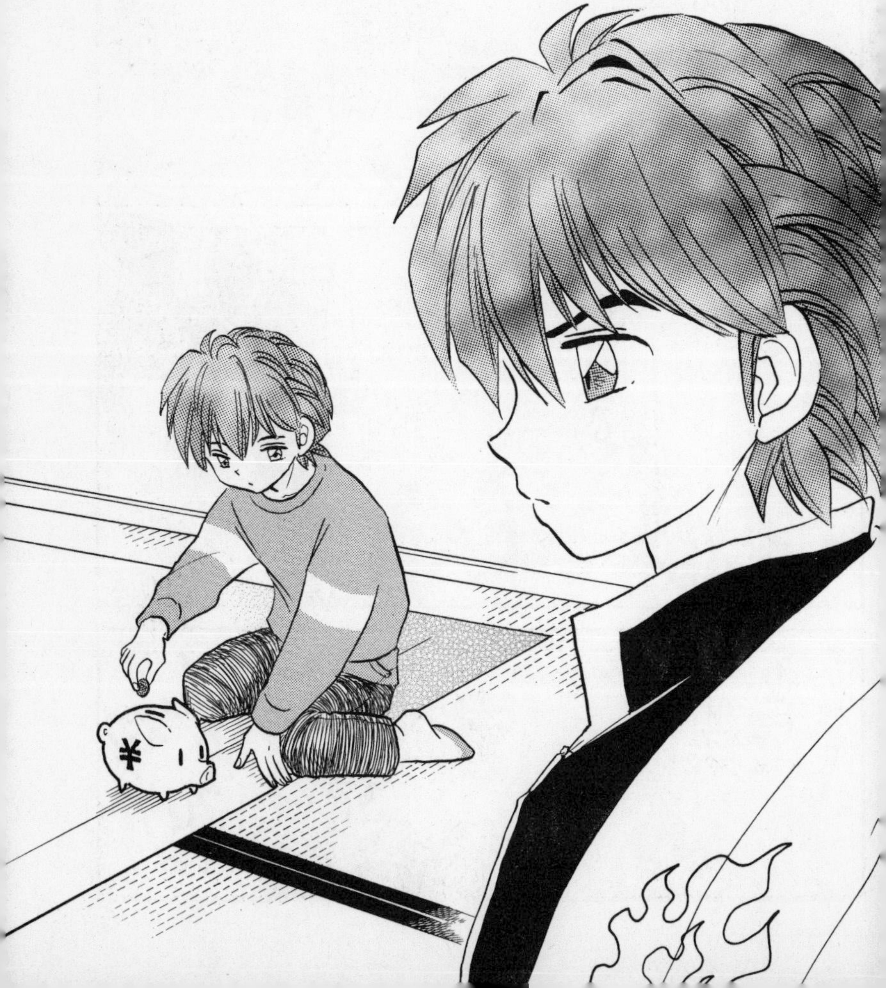
¥

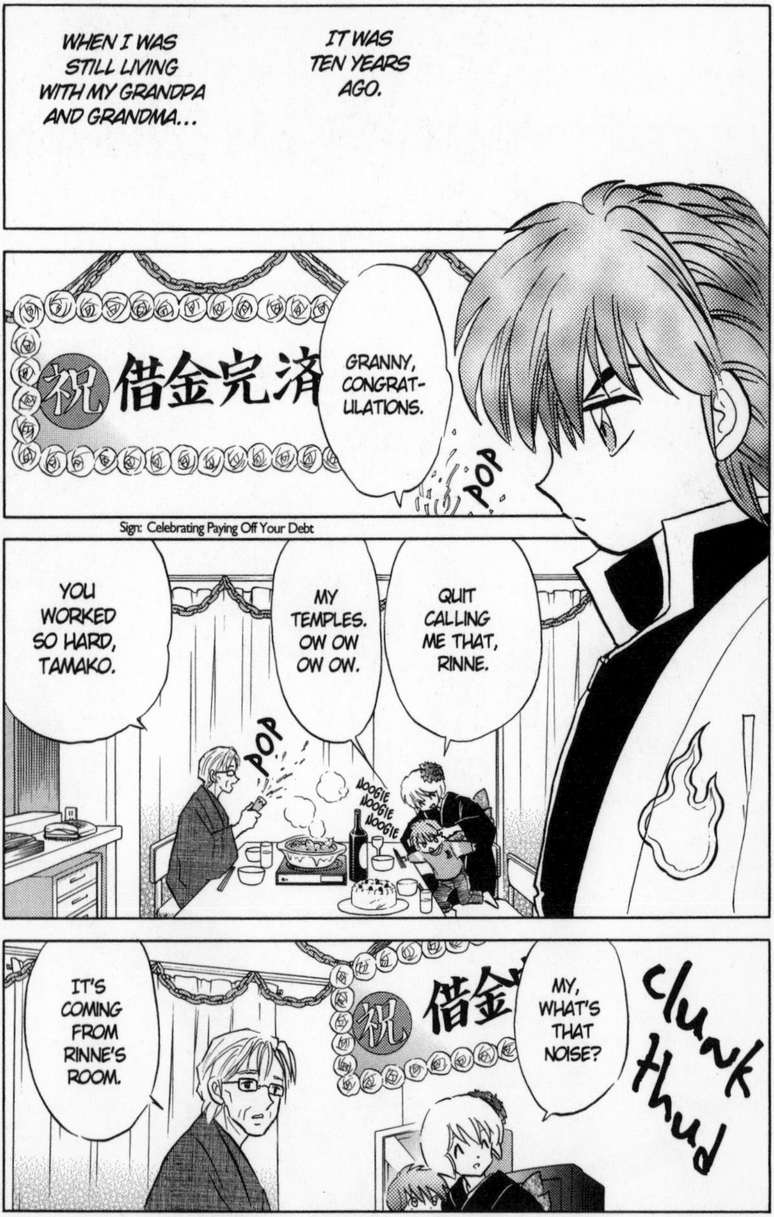
IT WAS TEN YEARS AGO.
WHEN I WAS STILL LIVING WITH MY GRANDPA AND GRANDMA...
GRANNY, CONGRAT-ULATIONS.
POP
祝 借金完済
Sign: Celebrating Paying Off Your Debt
QUIT CALLING ME THAT, RINNE.
MY TEMPLES. OW OW OW OW.
YOU WORKED SO HARD, TAMAKO.
NOOGIE NOOGIE NOOGIE
POP
clunk thud
MY, WHAT'S THAT NOISE?
祝 借金
IT'S COMING FROM RINNE'S ROOM.

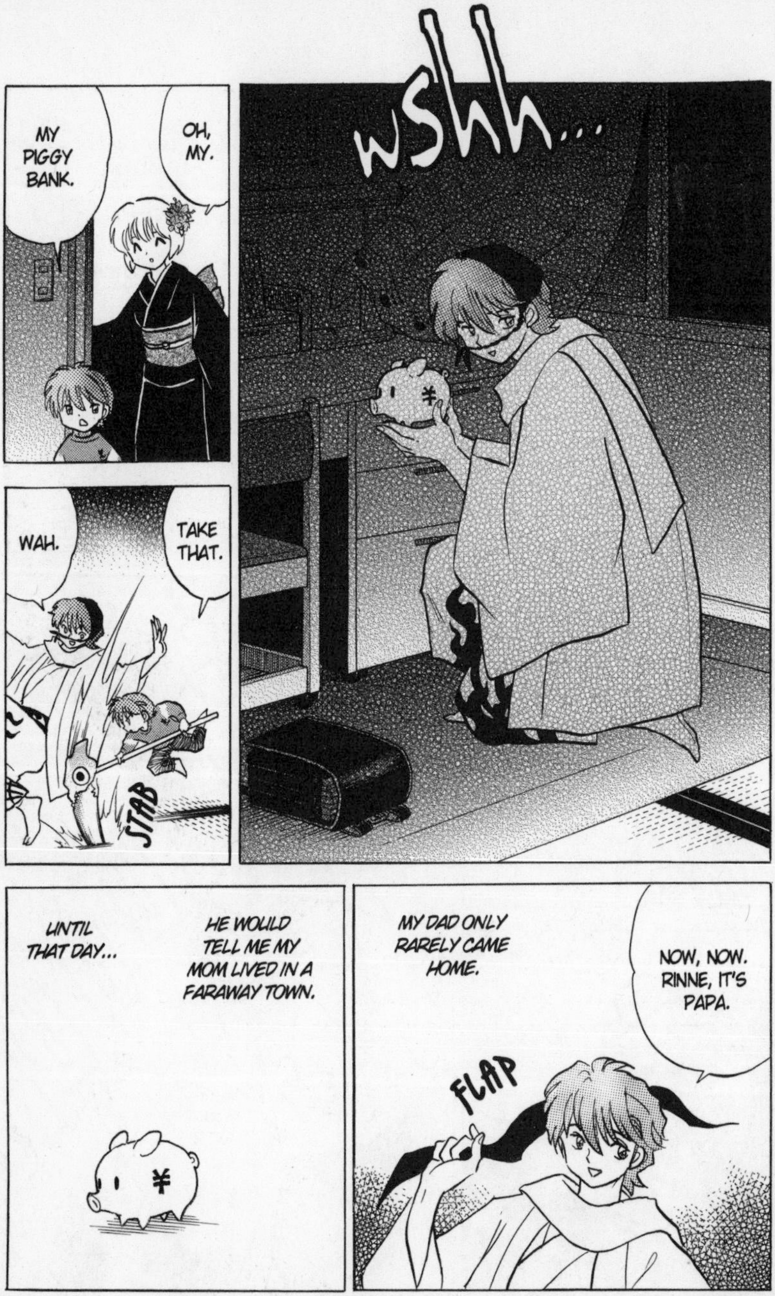
wShh...
OH, MY.
MY PIGGY BANK.
TAKE THAT.
WAH.
STAB
NOW, NOW. RINNE, IT'S PAPA.
MY DAD ONLY RARELY CAME HOME.
FLAP
HE WOULD TELL ME MY MOM LIVED IN A FARAWAY TOWN.
UNTIL THAT DAY...

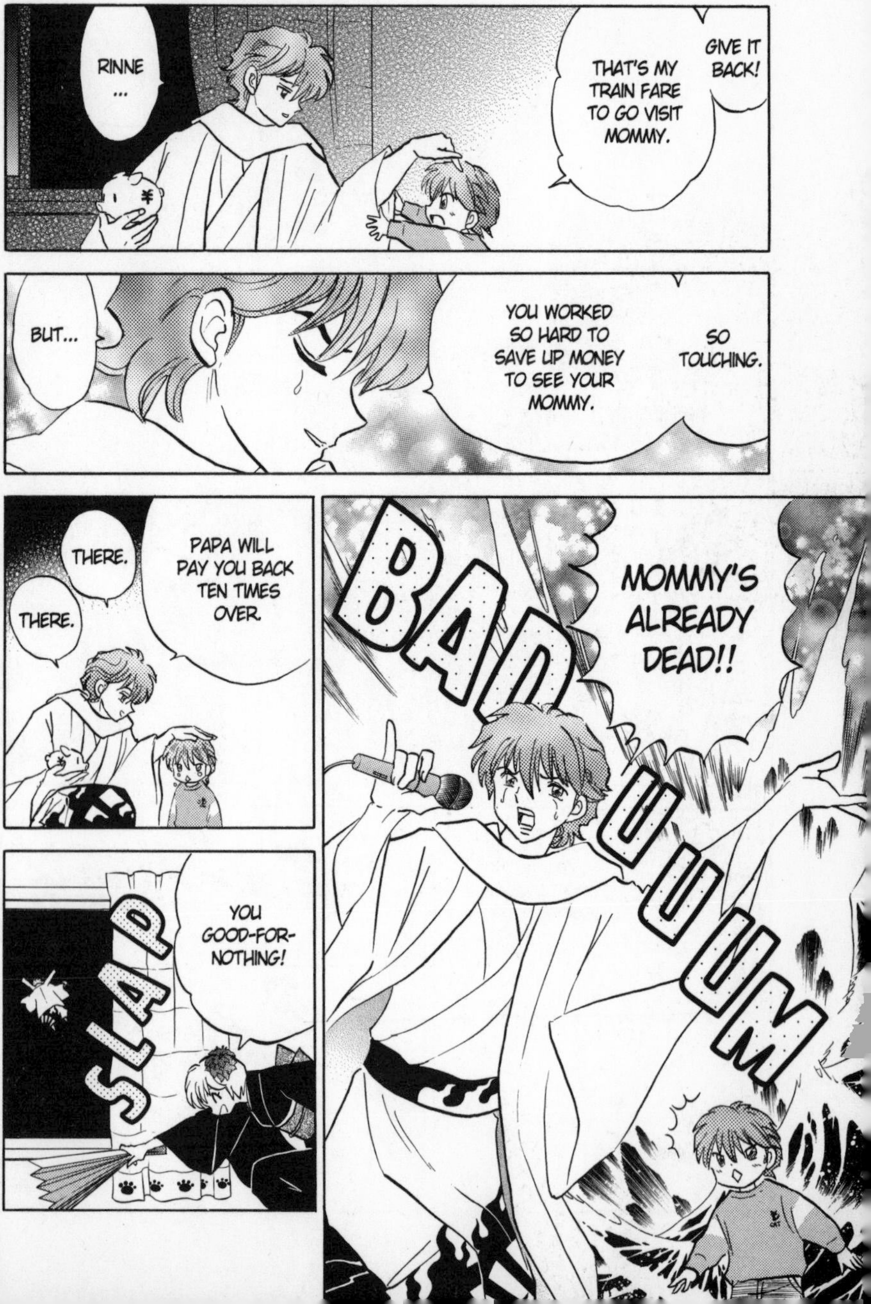
GIVE IT BACK!
THAT'S MY TRAIN FARE TO GO VISIT MOMMY.
RINNE ...
SO TOUCHING.
YOU WORKED SO HARD TO SAVE UP MONEY TO SEE YOUR MOMMY.
BUT...
MOMMY'S ALREADY DEAD!!
BADUUUM
PAPA WILL PAY YOU BACK TEN TIMES OVER.
THERE.
THERE.
YOU GOOD-FOR-NOTHING!
SLAP

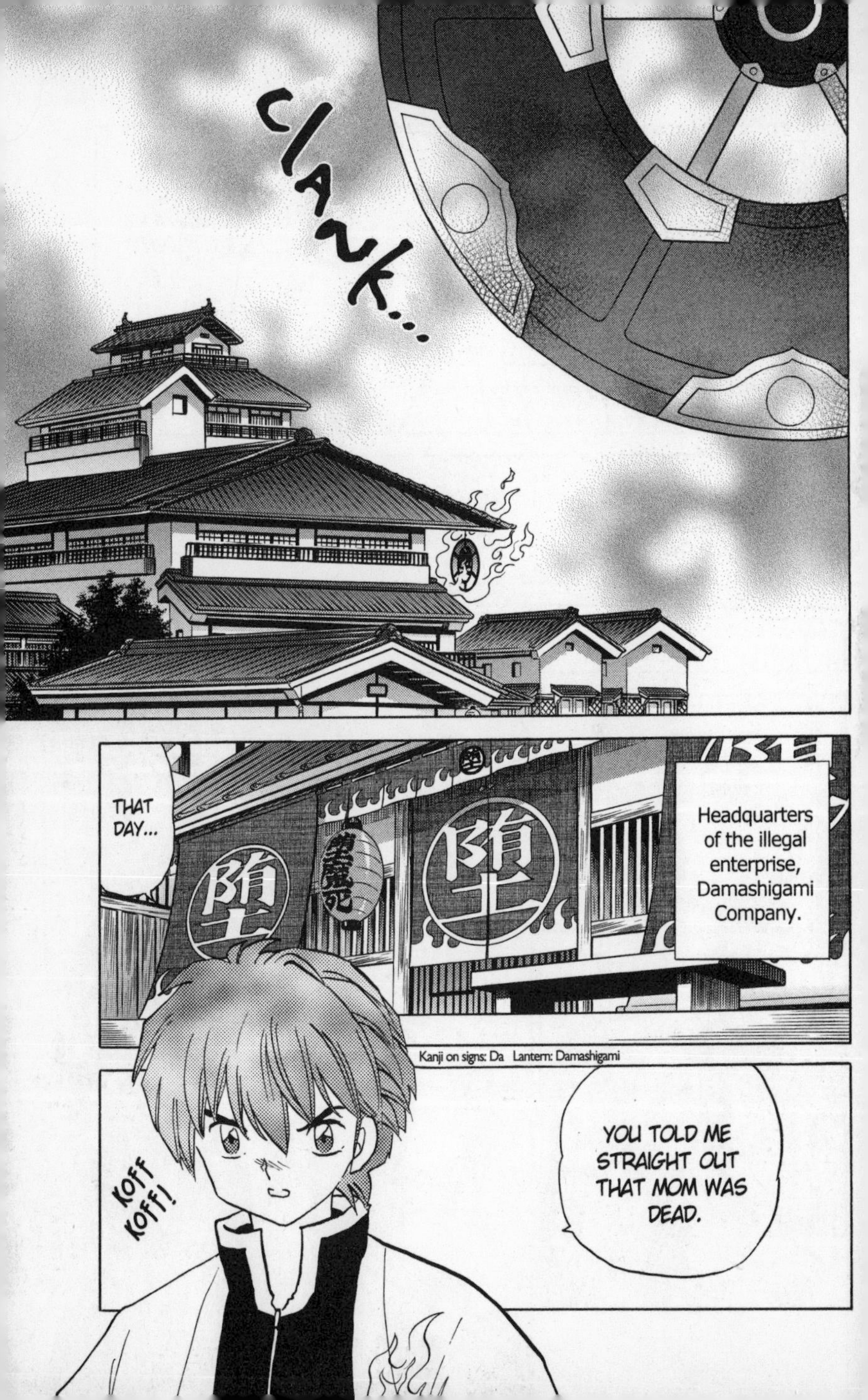
CLANK...
Headquarters of the illegal enterprise, Damashigami Company.
THAT DAY...
Kanji on signs: Da Lantern: Damashigami
YOU TOLD ME STRAIGHT OUT THAT MOM WAS DEAD.
KOFF KOFF!

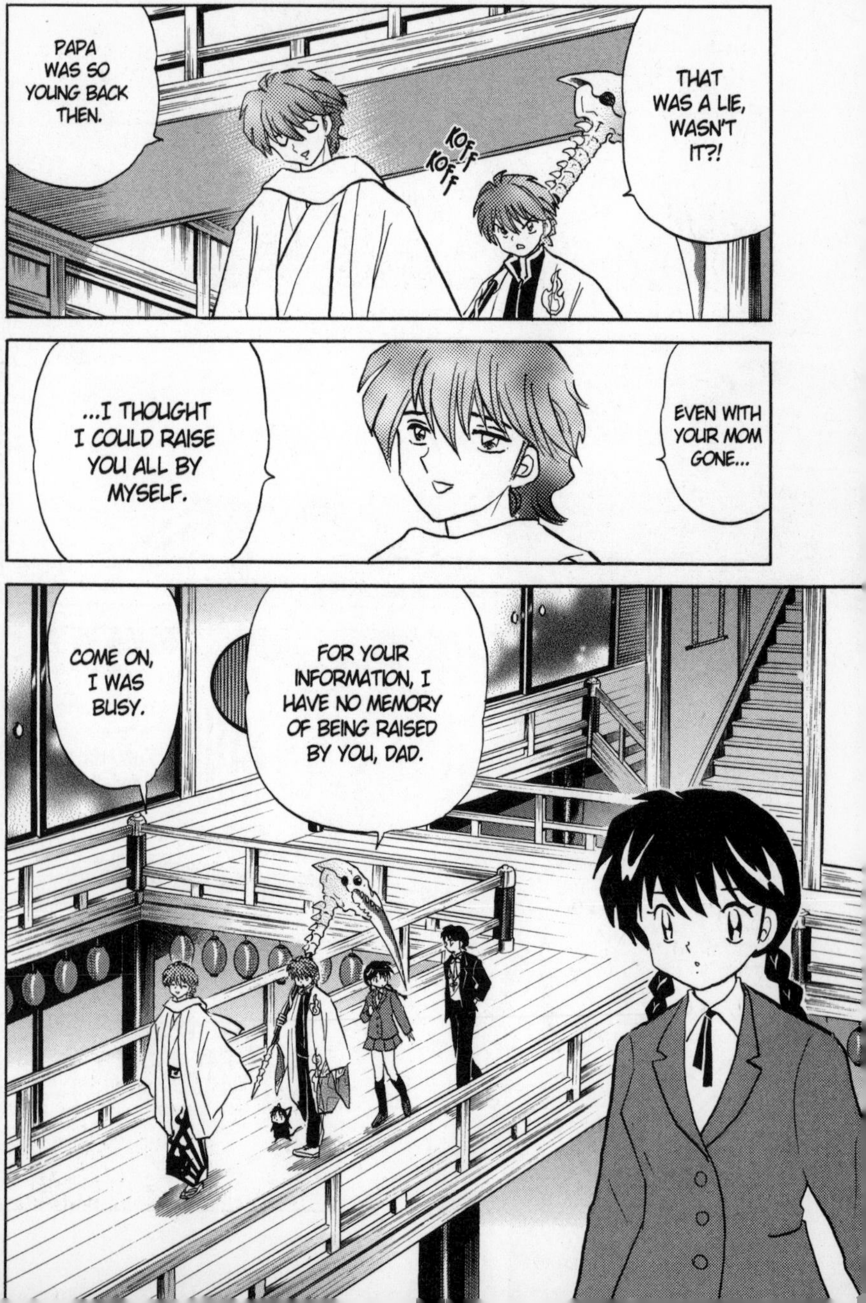
THAT WAS A LIE, WASN'T IT?!
KOFF KOFF
PAPA WAS SO YOUNG BACK THEN.
EVEN WITH YOUR MOM GONE...
...I THOUGHT I COULD RAISE YOU ALL BY MYSELF.
FOR YOUR INFORMATION, I HAVE NO MEMORY OF BEING RAISED BY YOU, DAD.
COME ON, I WAS BUSY.

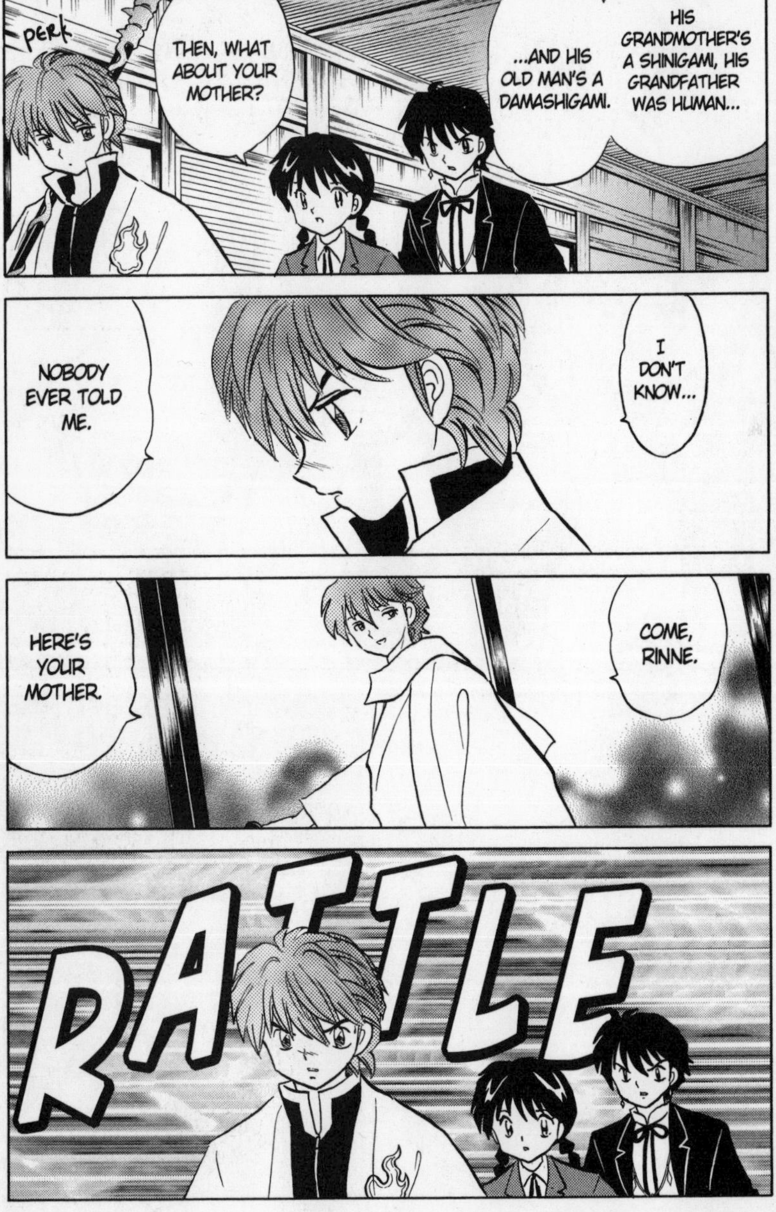

HIS GRANDMOTHER'S A SHINIGAMI, HIS GRANDFATHER WAS HUMAN...
...AND HIS OLD MAN'S A DAMASHIGAMI.
THEN, WHAT ABOUT YOUR MOTHER?
PERK
I DON'T KNOW...
NOBODY EVER TOLD ME.
COME, RINNE.
HERE'S YOUR MOTHER.
RATTLE

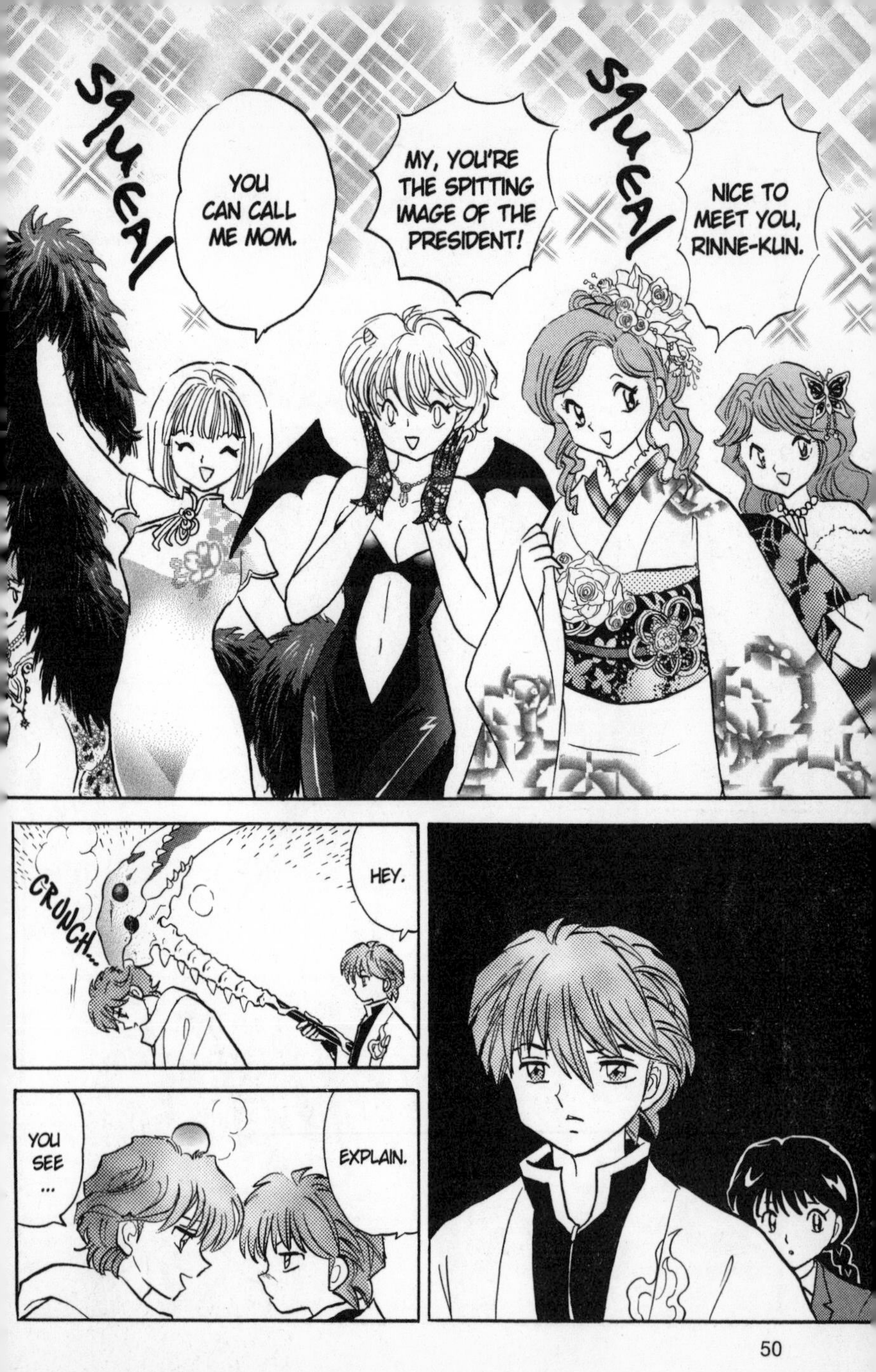
NICE TO MEET YOU, RINNE-KUN.
SQUEAL
MY, YOU'RE THE SPITTING IMAGE OF THE PRESIDENT!
YOU CAN CALL ME MOM.
SQUEAL
HEY.
CRUNCH...
EXPLAIN.
YOU SEE ...

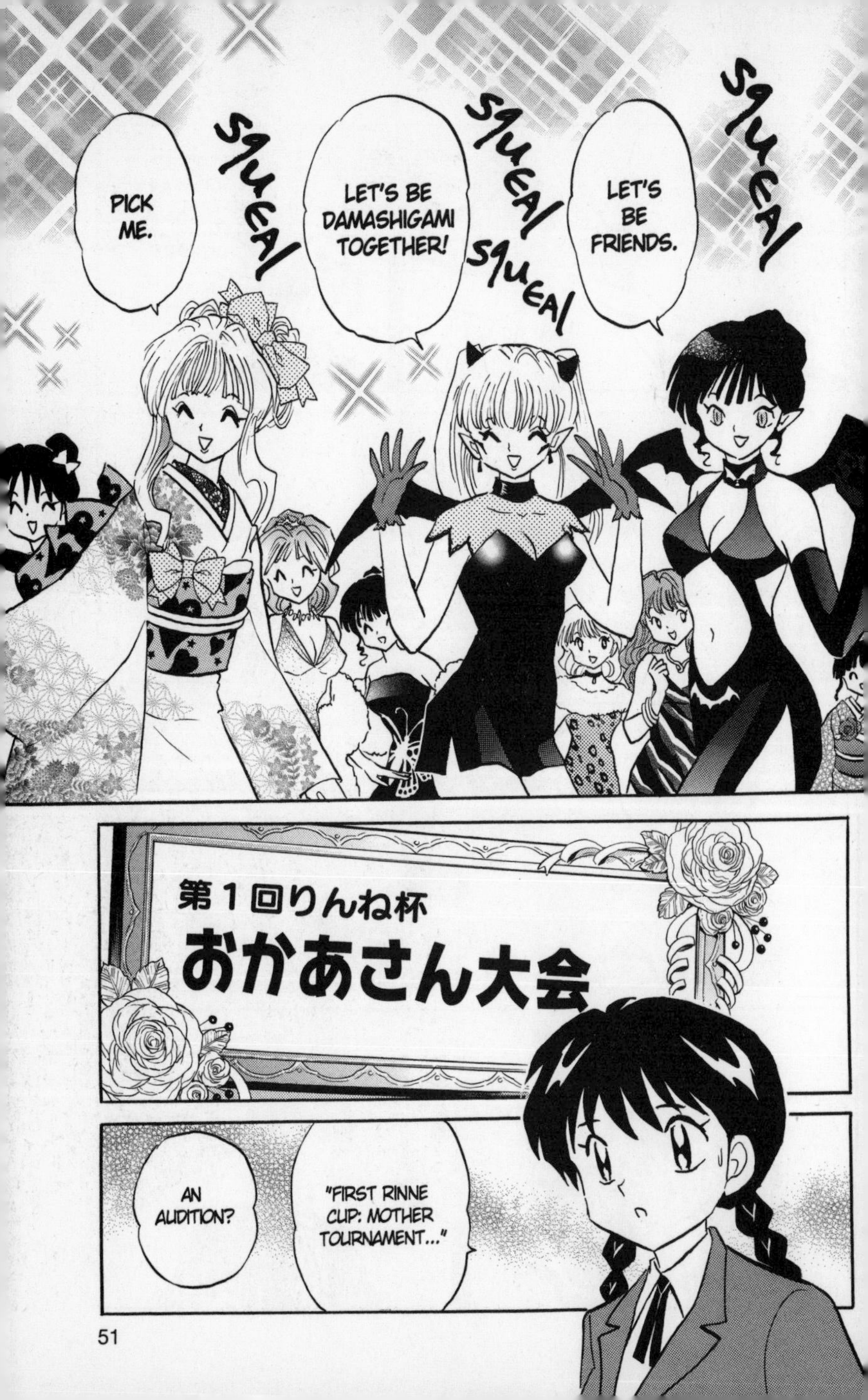
SQUEAL
LET'S BE FRIENDS.
SQUEAL
SQUEAL
LET'S BE DAMASHIGAMI TOGETHER!
SQUEAL
PICK ME.
第1回りんね杯
おかあさん大会
"FIRST RINNE CUP: MOTHER TOURNAMENT..."
AN AUDITION?

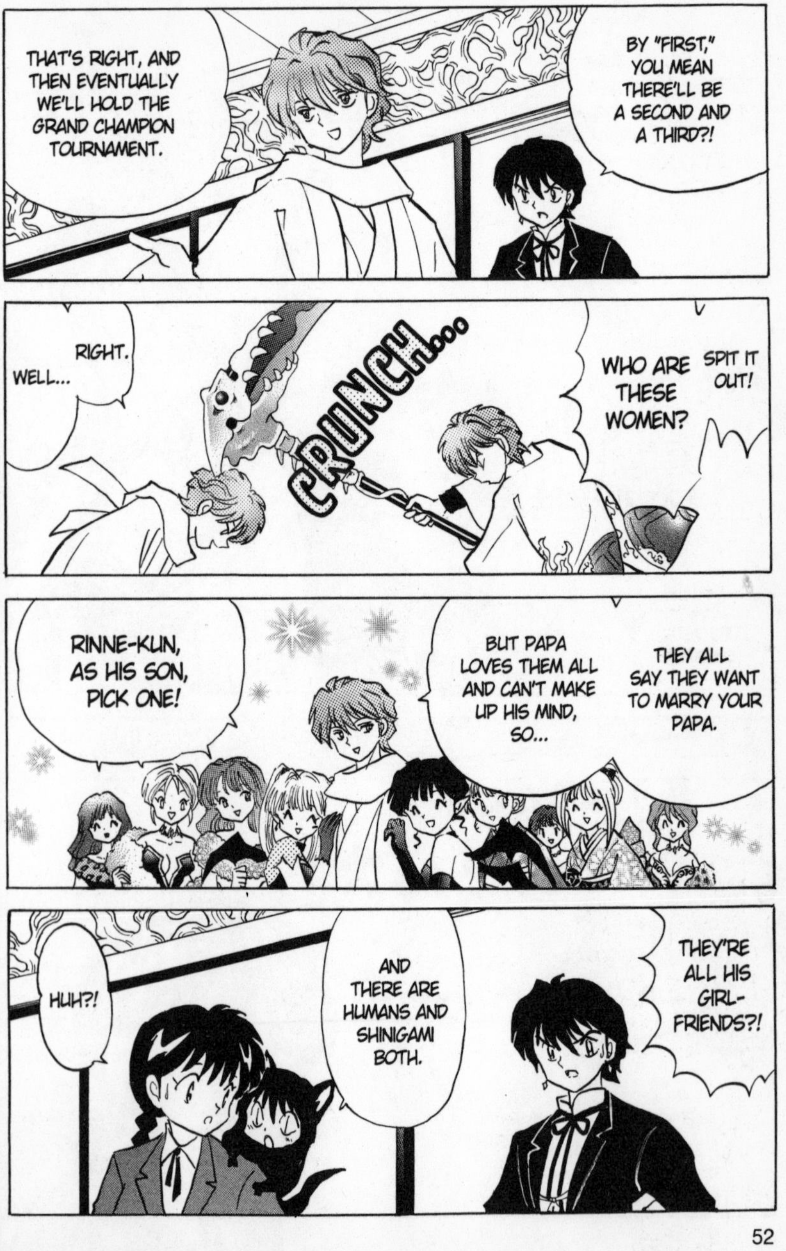
BY "FIRST," YOU MEAN THERE'LL BE A SECOND AND A THIRD?!
THAT'S RIGHT, AND THEN EVENTUALLY WE'LL HOLD THE GRAND CHAMPION TOURNAMENT.
SPIT IT OUT!
WHO ARE THESE WOMEN?
CRUNCH...
RIGHT.
WELL...
THEY ALL SAY THEY WANT TO MARRY YOUR PAPA.
BUT PAPA LOVES THEM ALL AND CAN'T MAKE UP HIS MIND, SO...
RINNE-KUN, AS HIS SON, PICK ONE!
THEY'RE ALL HIS GIRL-FRIENDS?!
AND THERE ARE HUMANS AND SHINIGAMI BOTH.
HUH?!

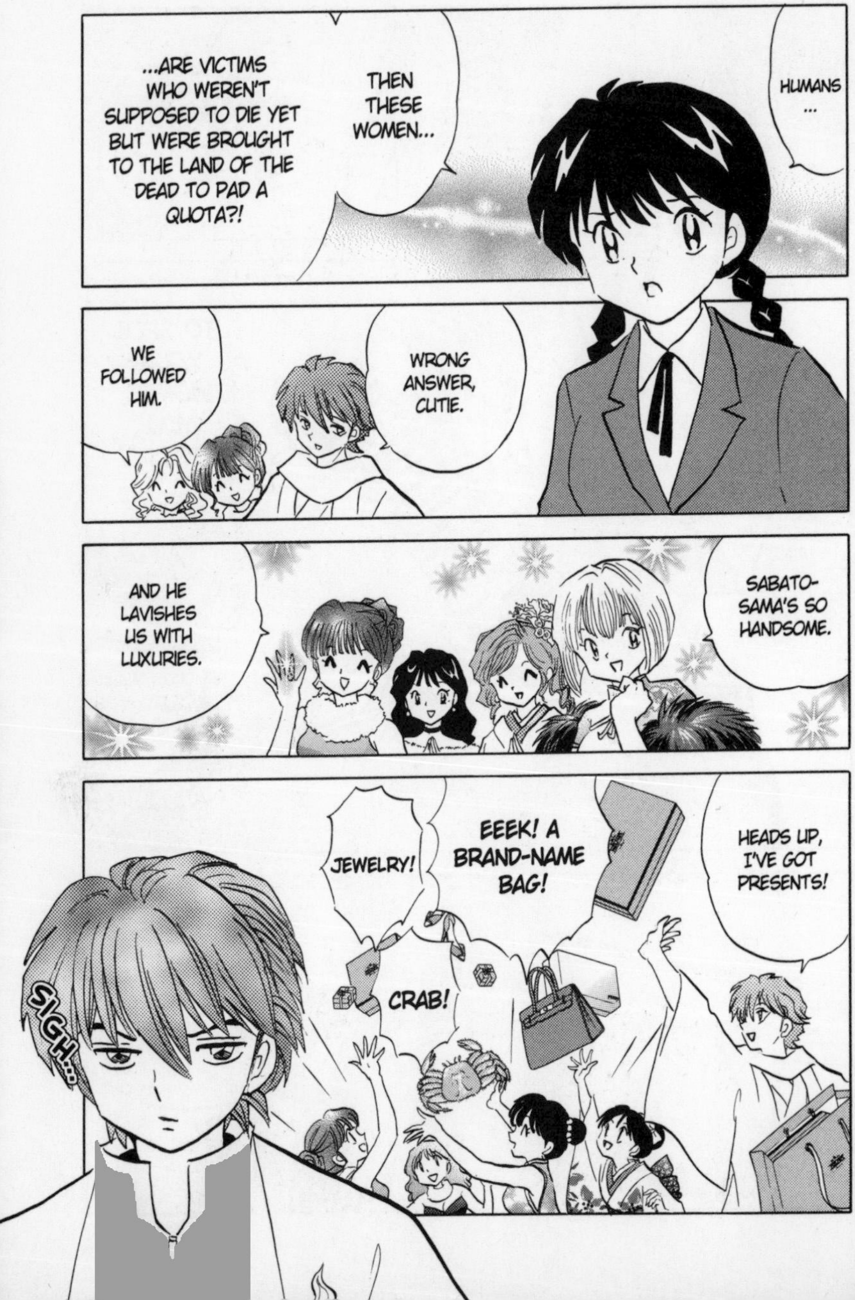
HUMANS...
THEN THESE WOMEN...
...ARE VICTIMS WHO WEREN'T SUPPOSED TO DIE YET BUT WERE BROUGHT TO THE LAND OF THE DEAD TO PAD A QUOTA?!
WRONG ANSWER, CUTIE.
WE FOLLOWED HIM.
SABATO-SAMA'S SO HANDSOME.
AND HE LAVISHES US WITH LUXURIES.
HEADS UP, I'VE GOT PRESENTS!
EEEK! A BRAND-NAME BAG!
JEWELRY!
CRAB!
SIGH...

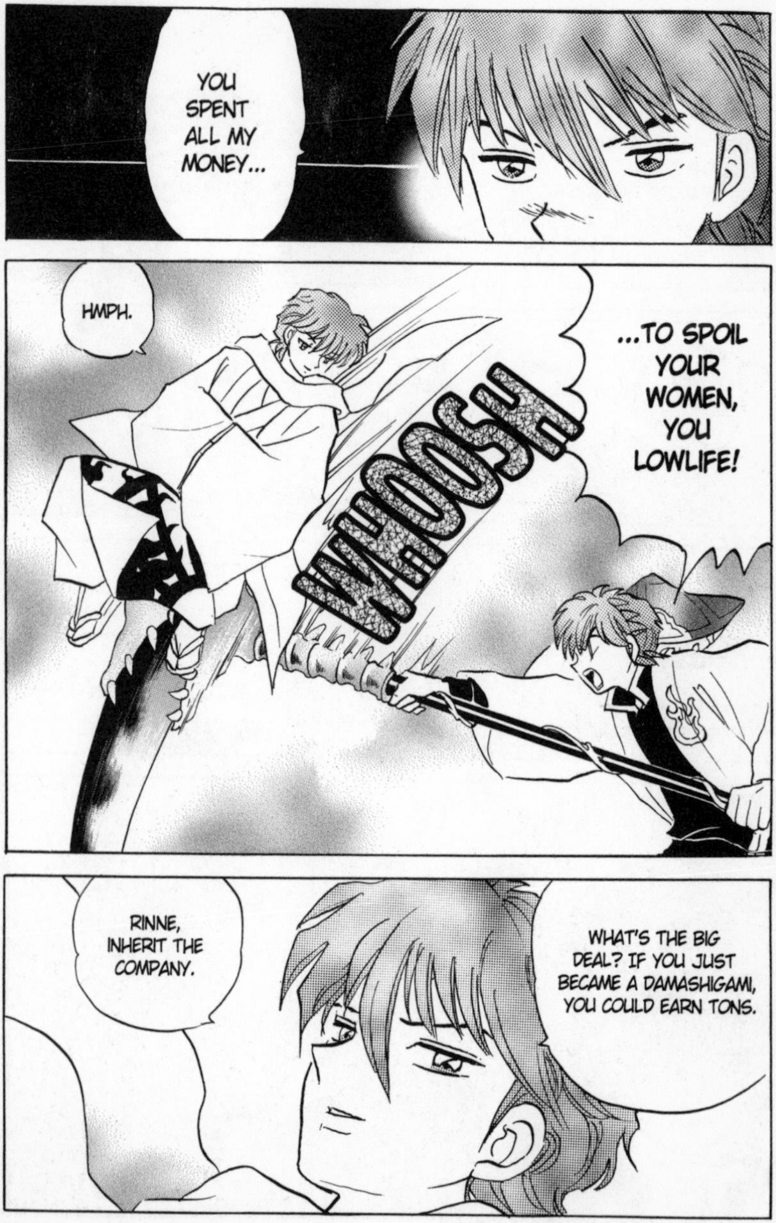
YOU SPENT ALL MY MONEY...
...TO SPOIL YOUR WOMEN, YOU LOWLIFE!
WHOOSH
HMPH.
WHAT'S THE BIG DEAL? IF YOU JUST BECAME A DAMASHIGAMI, YOU COULD EARN TONS.
RINNE, INHERIT THE COMPANY.

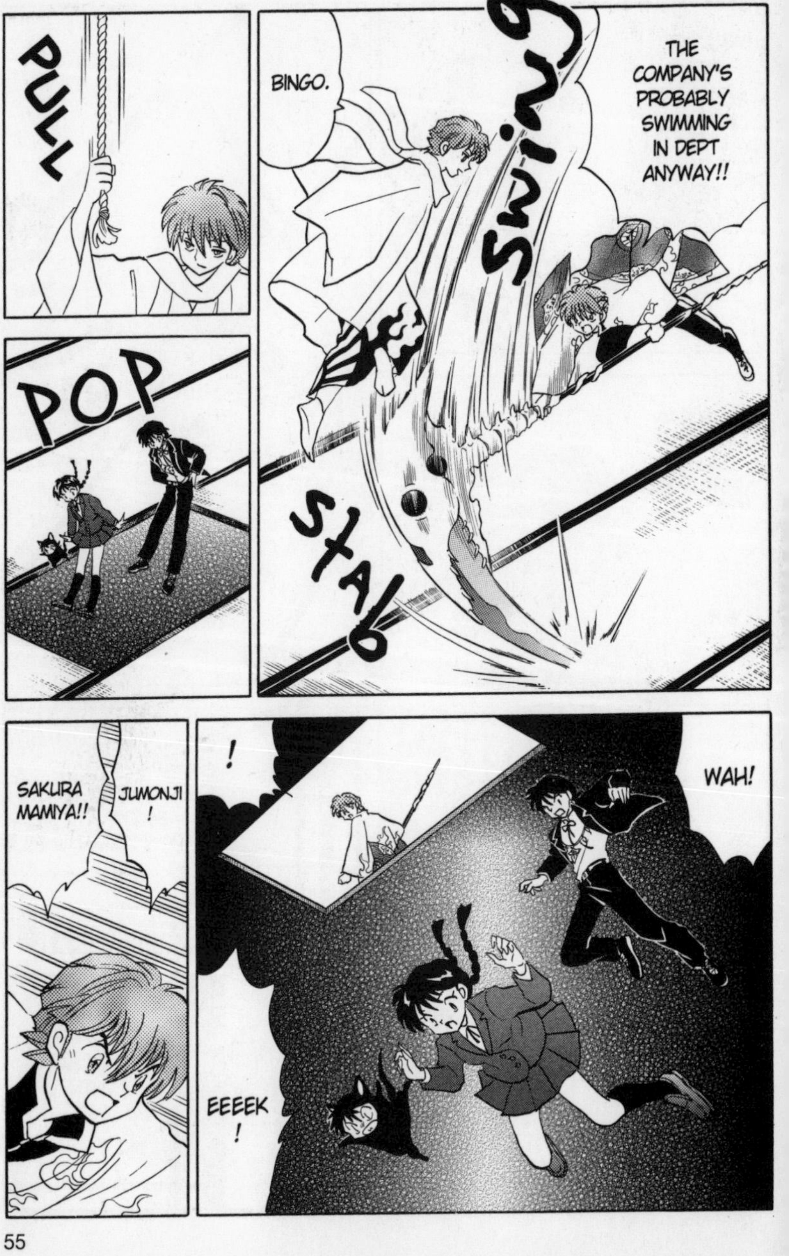
THE COMPANY'S PROBABLY SWIMMING IN DEPT ANYWAY!!
SWING
BINGO.
STAB
PULL
POP
WAH!
!
EEEEK!
JUMONJI!
SAKURA MAMIYA!!

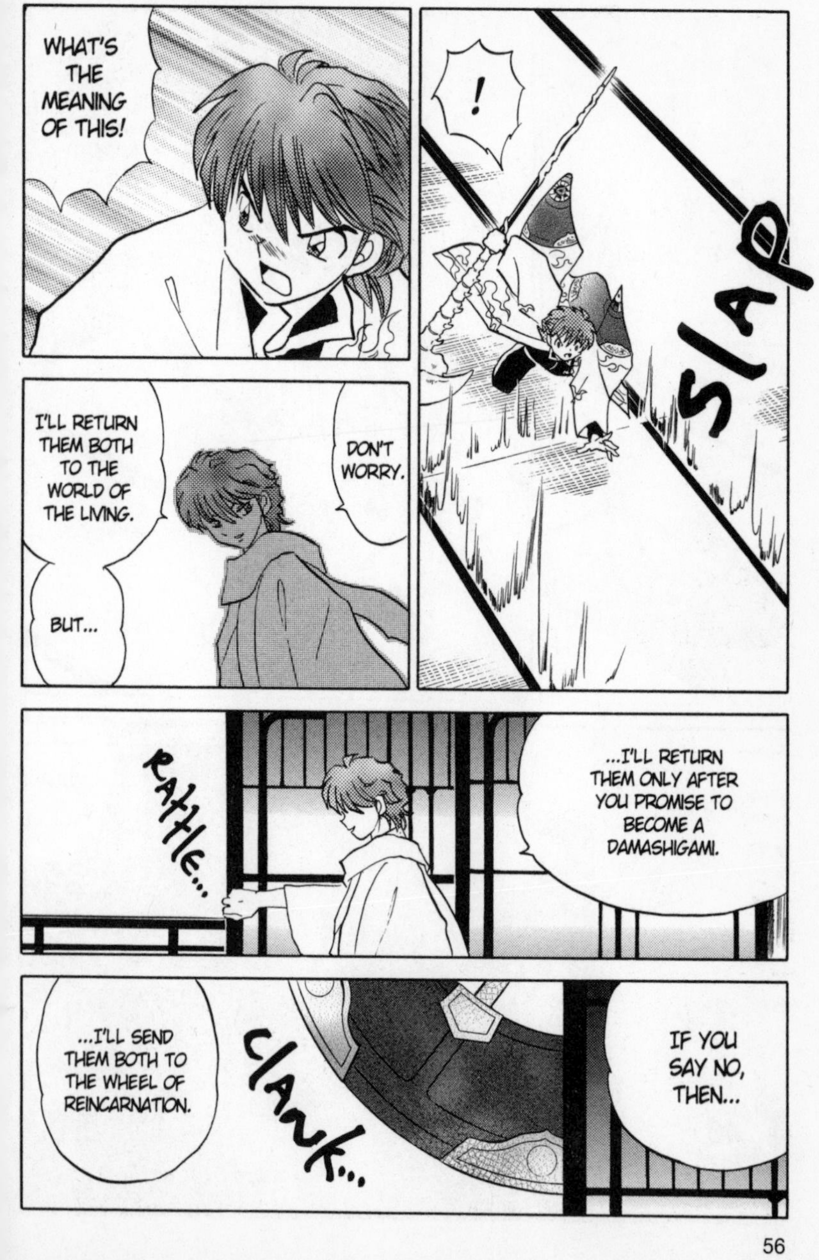
!
SLAP
WHAT'S THE MEANING OF THIS!
DON'T WORRY.
I'LL RETURN THEM BOTH TO THE WORLD OF THE LIVING.
BUT...
...I'LL RETURN THEM ONLY AFTER YOU PROMISE TO BECOME A DAMASHIGAMI.
Rattle...
IF YOU SAY NO, THEN...
Clank...
...I'LL SEND THEM BOTH TO THE WHEEL OF REINCARNATION.

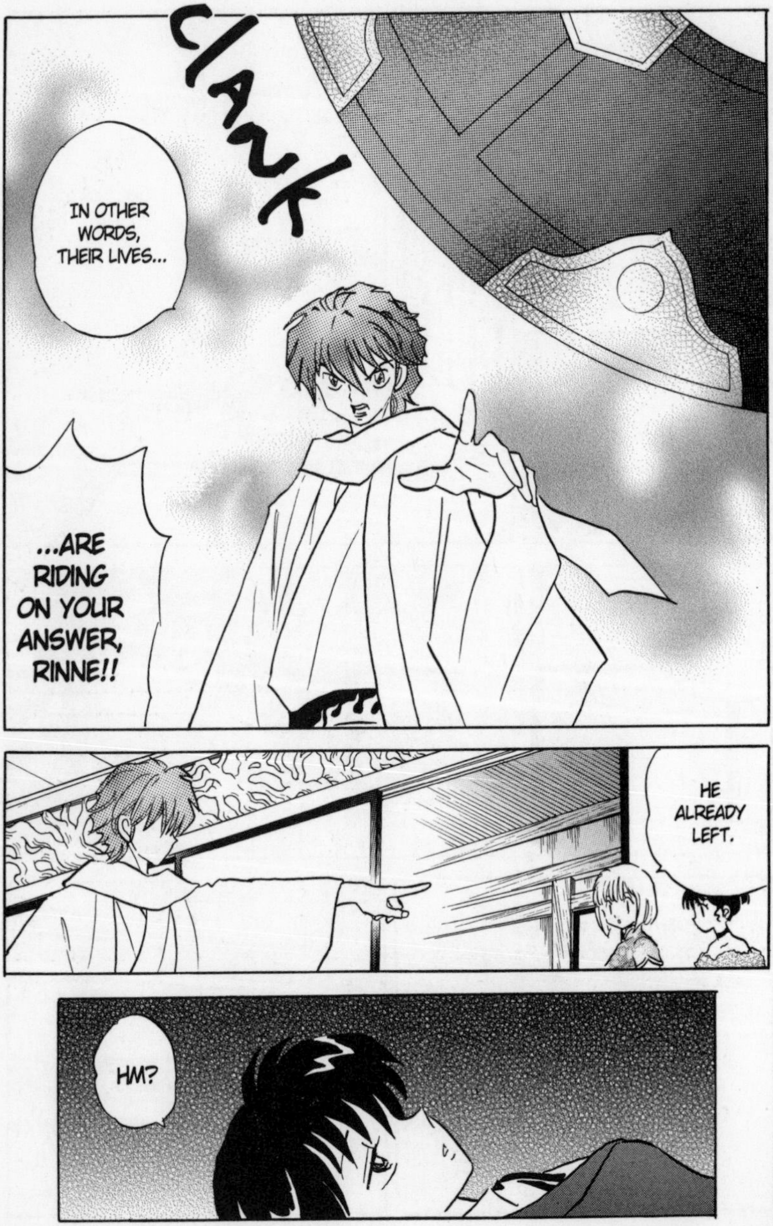
CLANK
IN OTHER WORDS, THEIR LIVES...
...ARE RIDING ON YOUR ANSWER, RINNE!!
HE ALREADY LEFT.
HM?

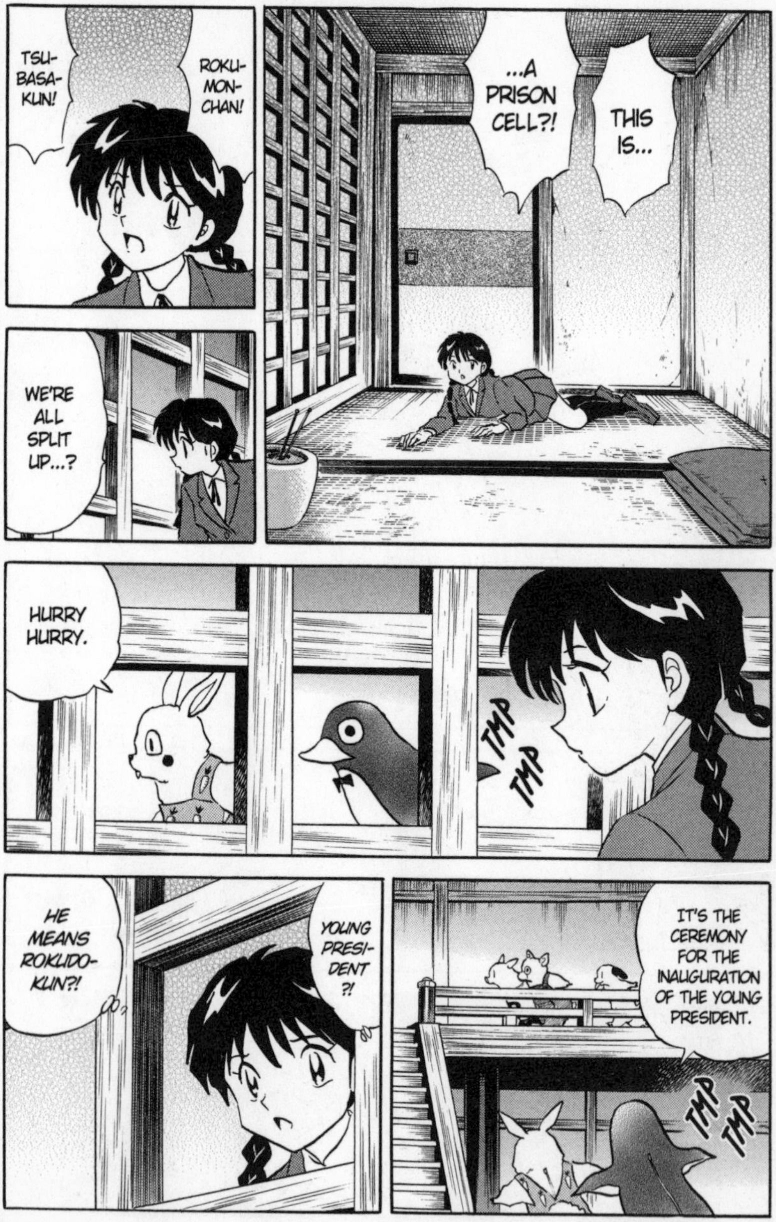
THIS IS...
...A PRISON CELL?!
ROKU-MON-CHAN!
TSU-BASA-KUN!
WE'RE ALL SPLIT UP...?
HURRY HURRY.
TMP TMP
IT'S THE CEREMONY FOR THE INAUGURATION OF THE YOUNG PRESIDENT.
TMP TMP
YOUNG PRESI-DENT ?!
HE MEANS ROKUDO-KUN?!

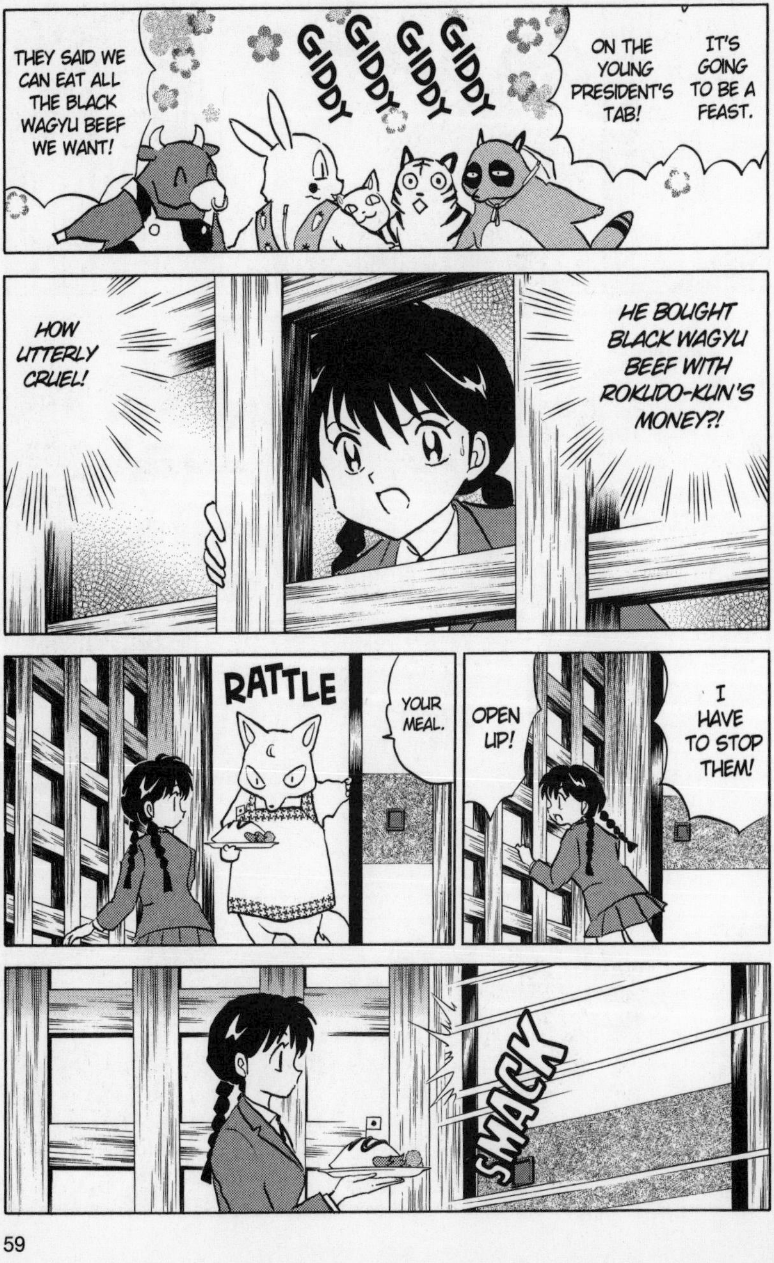
IT'S GOING TO BE A FEAST.
ON THE YOUNG PRESIDENT'S TAB!
GIDDY GIDDY GIDDY GIDDY
THEY SAID WE CAN EAT ALL THE BLACK WAGYU BEEF WE WANT!
HE BOUGHT BLACK WAGYU BEEF WITH ROKUDO-KUN'S MONEY?!
HOW UTTERLY CRUEL!
I HAVE TO STOP THEM!
OPEN UP!
YOUR MEAL.
RATTLE
SMACK

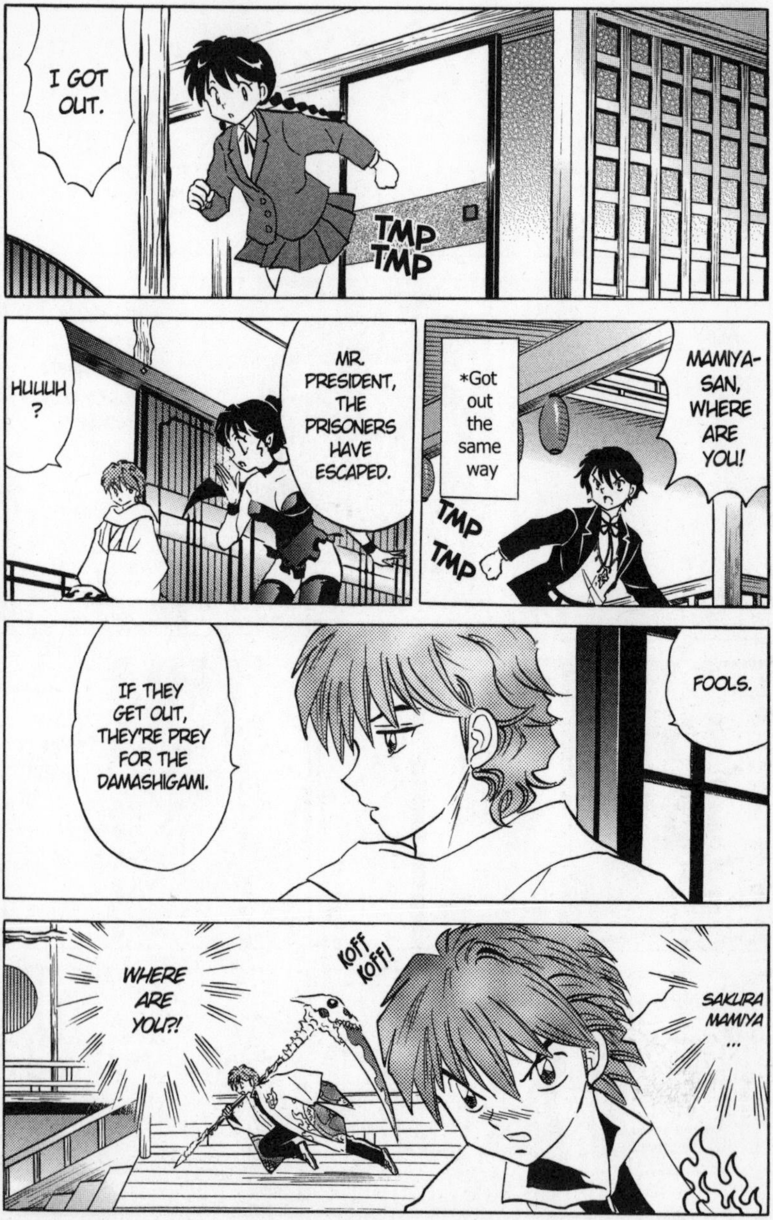
I GOT OUT.
TMP TMP
MAMIYA-SAN, WHERE ARE YOU!
*Got out the same way
TMP TMP
MR. PRESIDENT, THE PRISONERS HAVE ESCAPED.
HUUUH?
FOOLS.
IF THEY GET OUT, THEY'RE PREY FOR THE DAMASHIGAMI.
SAKURA MAMIYA ...
KOFF KOFF!
WHERE ARE YOU?!

CHAPTER 32: INAUGURATION CEREMONY

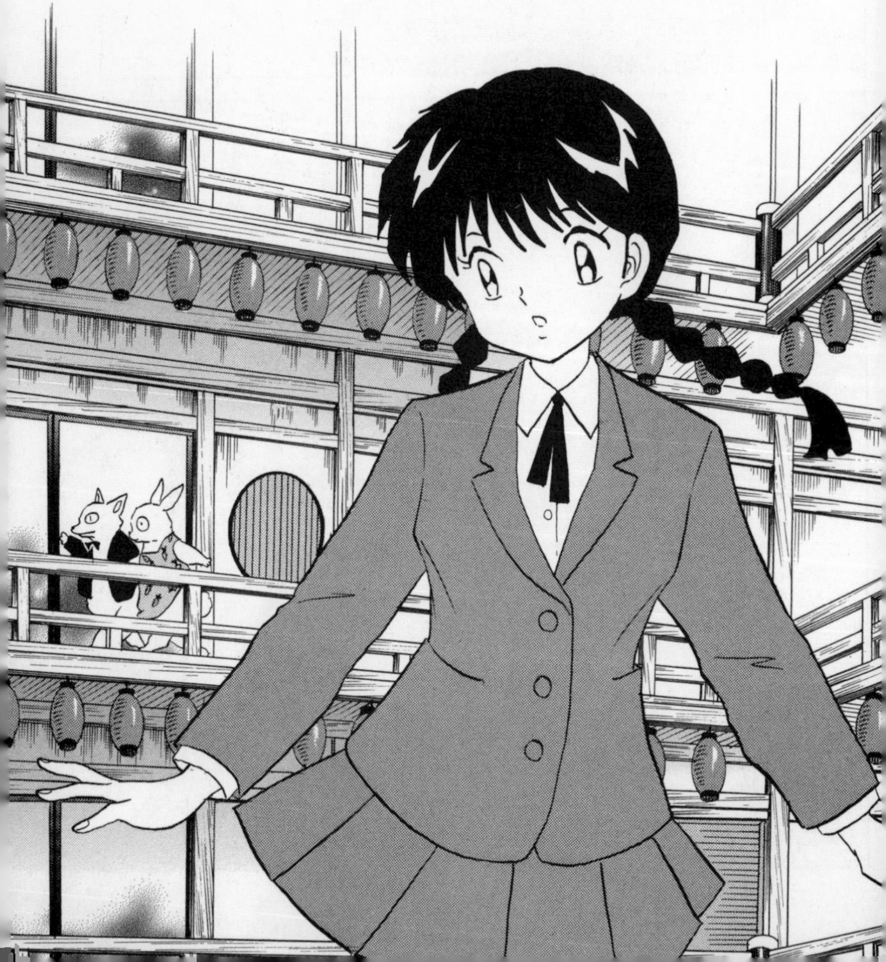

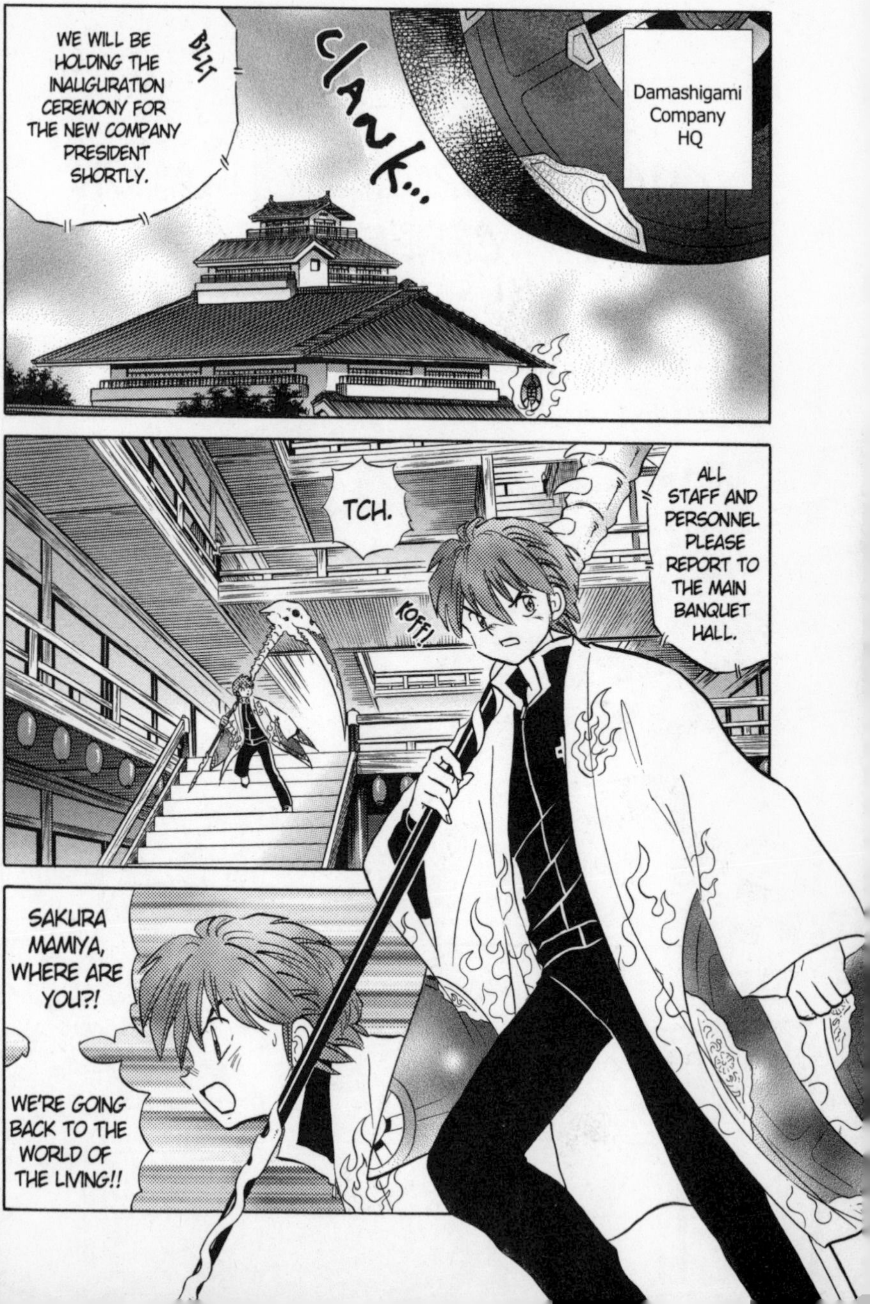
Damashigami Company HQ
CLANK...
BZZT
WE WILL BE HOLDING THE INAUGURATION CEREMONY FOR THE NEW COMPANY PRESIDENT SHORTLY.
ALL STAFF AND PERSONNEL PLEASE REPORT TO THE MAIN BANQUET HALL.
TCH.
KOFF!
SAKURA MAMIYA, WHERE ARE YOU?!
WE'RE GOING BACK TO THE WORLD OF THE LIVING!!

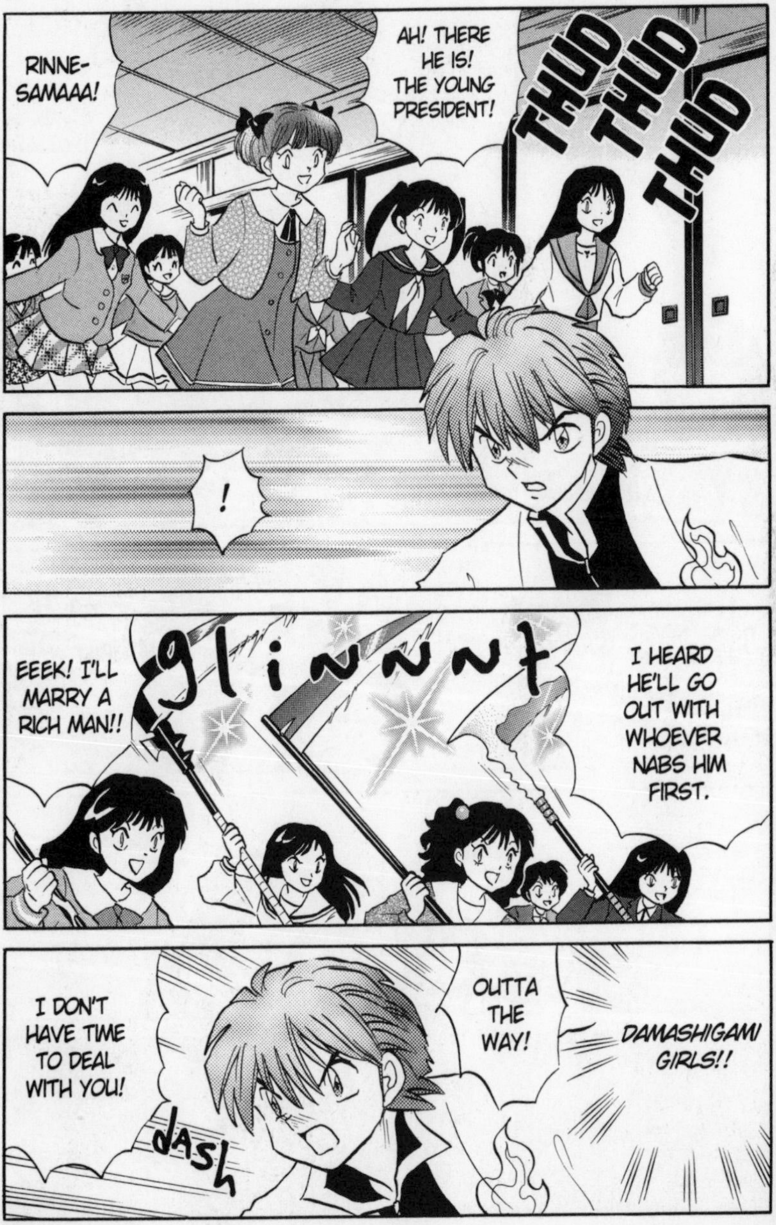
THUD THUD THUD
AH! THERE HE IS! THE YOUNG PRESIDENT!
RINNE-SAMAAA!
!
I HEARD HE'LL GO OUT WITH WHOEVER NABS HIM FIRST.
glinnnt
EEEK! I'LL MARRY A RICH MAN!!
DAMASHIGAMI GIRLS!!
OUTTA THE WAY!
I DON'T HAVE TIME TO DEAL WITH YOU!
dash

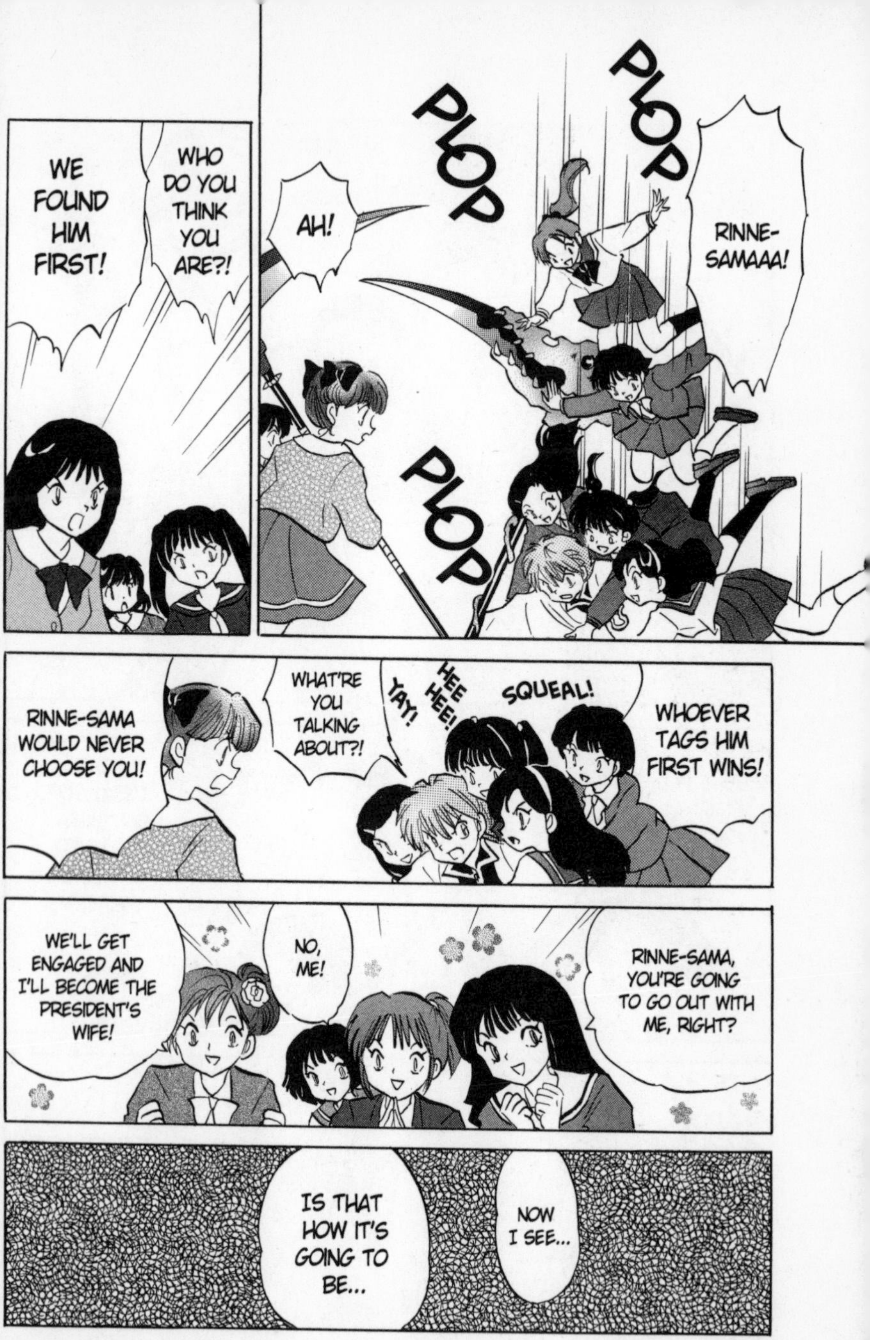

PLOP PLOP
RINNE-SAMAAA!
PLOP PLOP
AH!
PLOP PLOP
WHO DO YOU THINK YOU ARE?!
WE FOUND HIM FIRST!
WHOEVER TAGS HIM FIRST WINS!
SQUEAL!
HEE HEE!
YAY!
WHAT'RE YOU TALKING ABOUT?!
RINNE-SAMA WOULD NEVER CHOOSE YOU!
RINNE-SAMA, YOU'RE GOING TO GO OUT WITH ME, RIGHT?
NO, ME!
WE'LL GET ENGAGED AND I'LL BECOME THE PRESIDENT'S WIFE!
NOW I SEE...
IS THAT HOW IT'S GOING TO BE...

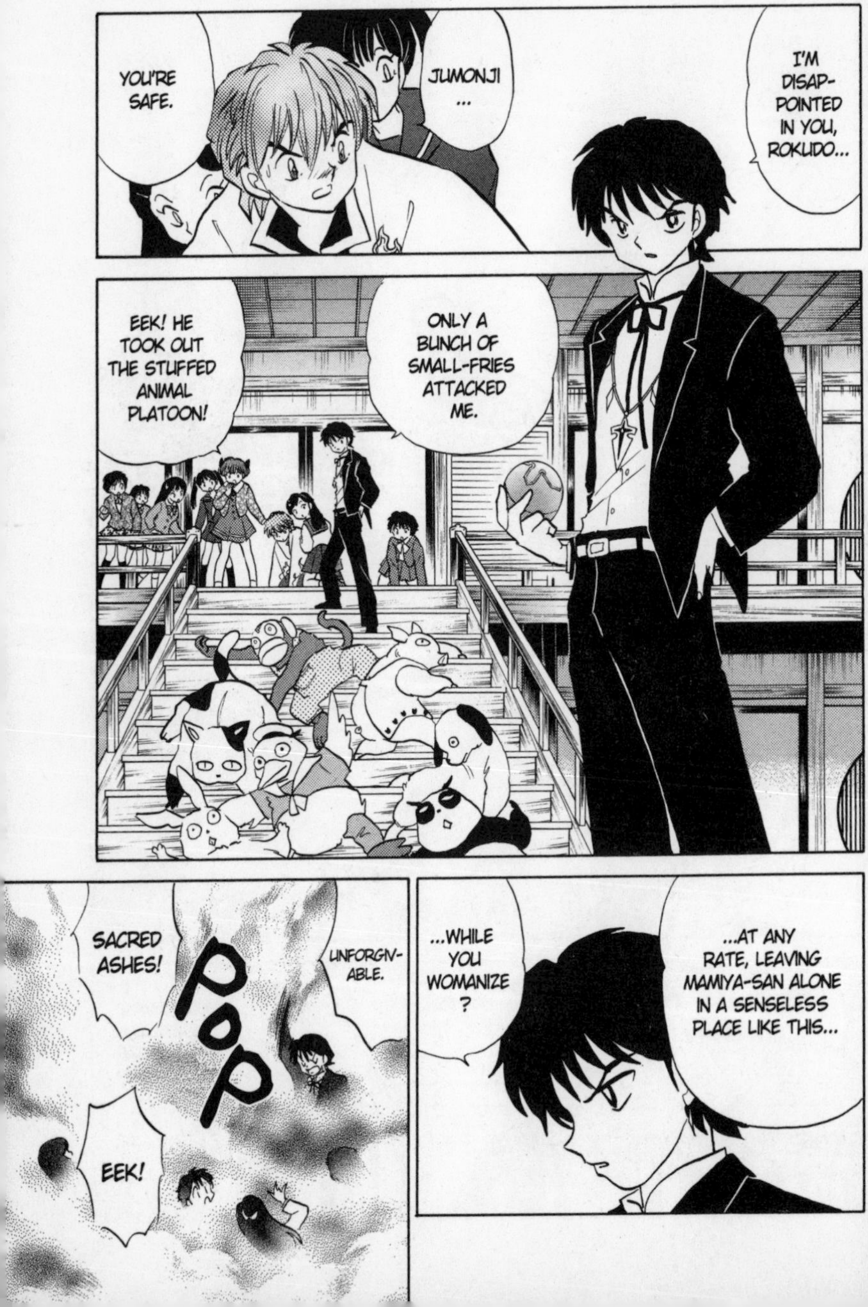
I'M DISAPPOINTED IN YOU, ROKUDO...
JUMONJI ...
YOU'RE SAFE.
ONLY A BUNCH OF SMALL-FRIES ATTACKED ME.
EEK! HE TOOK OUT THE STUFFED ANIMAL PLATOON!
...AT ANY RATE, LEAVING MAMIYA-SAN ALONE IN A SENSELESS PLACE LIKE THIS...
...WHILE YOU WOMANIZE ?
UNFORGIVABLE.
SACRED ASHES!
POP
EEK!

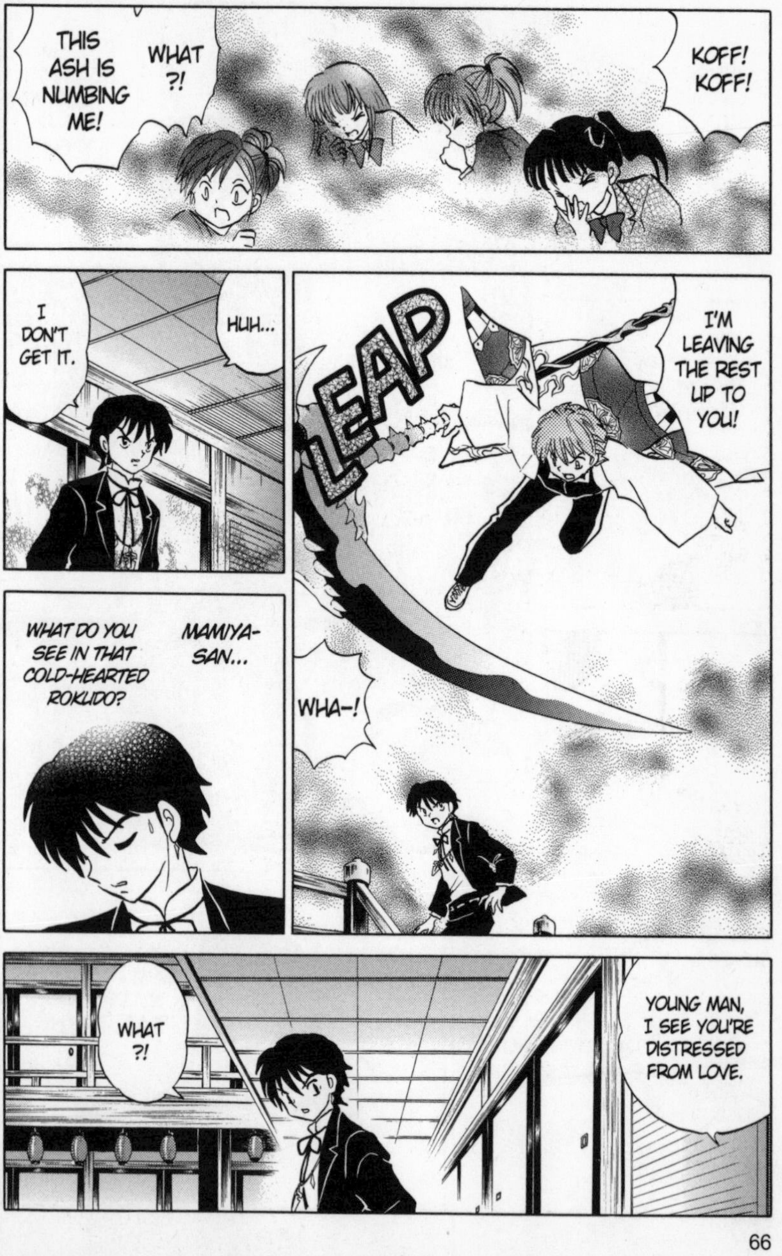
KOFF! KOFF!
WHAT ?!
THIS ASH IS NUMBING ME!
I'M LEAVING THE REST UP TO YOU!
LEAP
WHA-!
HUH...
I DON'T GET IT.
MAMIYA-SAN...
WHAT DO YOU SEE IN THAT COLD-HEARTED ROKUDO?
YOUNG MAN, I SEE YOU'RE DISTRESSED FROM LOVE.
WHAT ?!

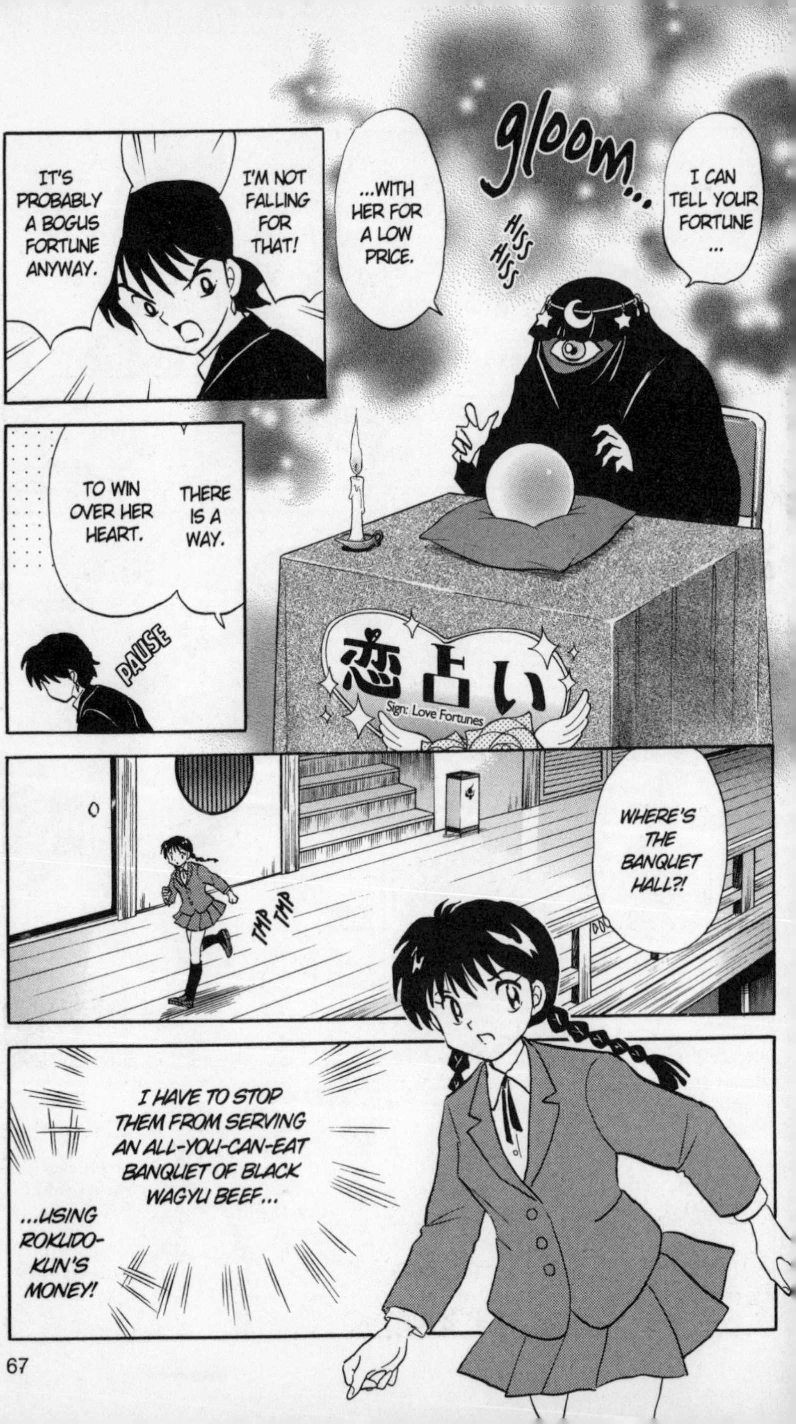
gloom...
I CAN TELL YOUR FORTUNE ...
HISS HISS
...WITH HER FOR A LOW PRICE.
恋占い
Sign: Love Fortunes
I'M NOT FALLING FOR THAT!
IT'S PROBABLY A BOGUS FORTUNE ANYWAY.
THERE IS A WAY.
TO WIN OVER HER HEART.
PAUSE
WHERE'S THE BANQUET HALL?!
TMP TMP
I HAVE TO STOP THEM FROM SERVING AN ALL-YOU-CAN-EAT BANQUET OF BLACK WAGYU BEEF...
...USING ROKUDO-KUN'S MONEY!

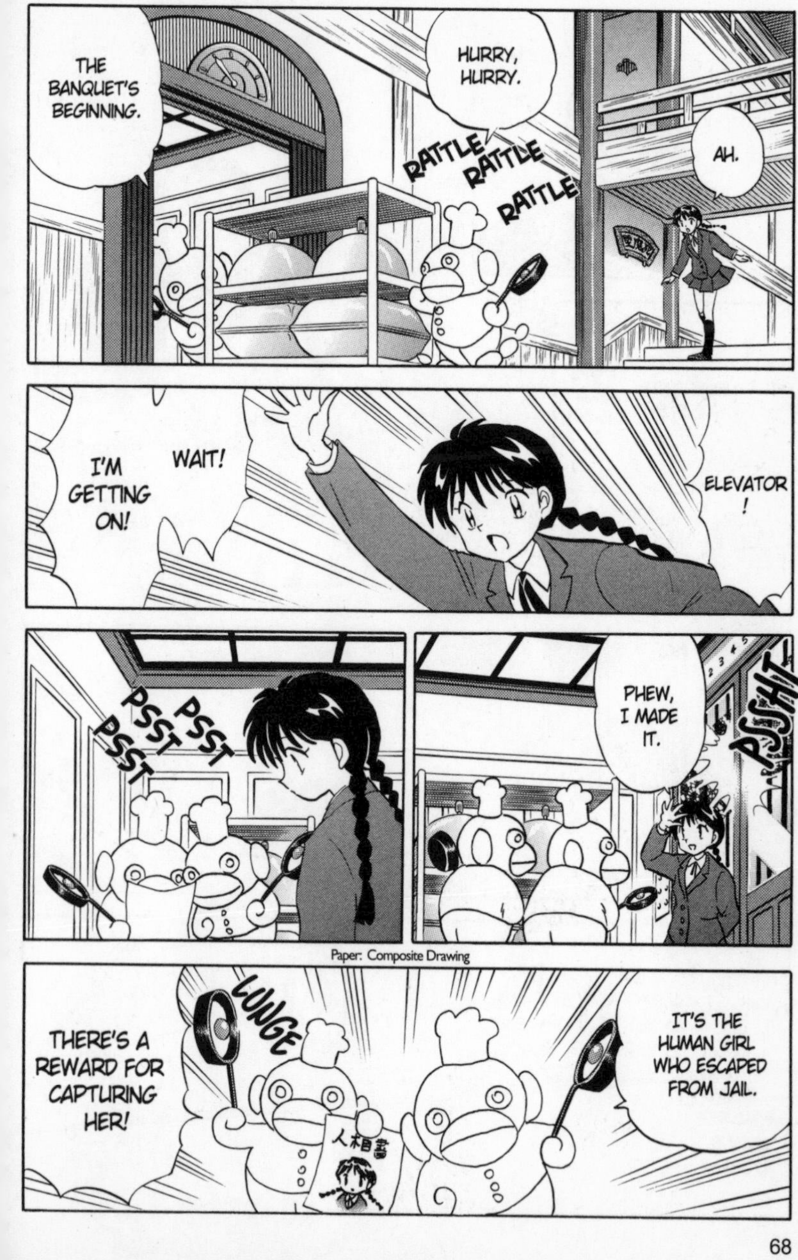
AH.
HURRY, HURRY.
RATTLE RATTLE RATTLE
THE BANQUET'S BEGINNING.
ELEVATOR!
WAIT!
I'M GETTING ON!
PSSHT
PHEW, I MADE IT.
PSST PSST PSST
Paper: Composite Drawing
IT'S THE HUMAN GIRL WHO ESCAPED FROM JAIL.
LUNGE
人相書
THERE'S A REWARD FOR CAPTURING HER!

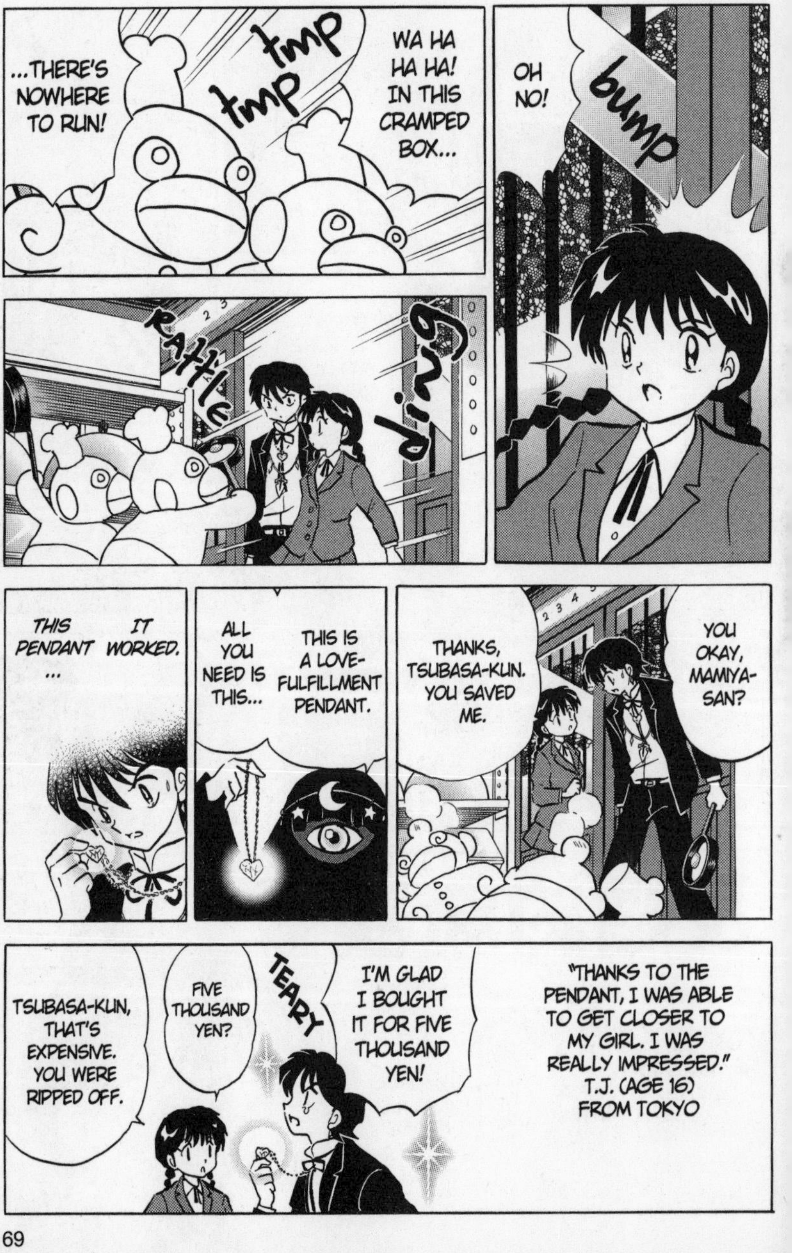
OH NO!
bump
WA HA HA HA! IN THIS CRAMPED BOX...
tmp tmp
...THERE'S NOWHERE TO RUN!
grip
rattle
YOU OKAY, MAMIYA-SAN?
THANKS, TSUBASA-KUN. YOU SAVED ME.
THIS IS A LOVE-FULFILLMENT PENDANT.
ALL YOU NEED IS THIS...
IT WORKED.
THIS PENDANT ...
"THANKS TO THE PENDANT, I WAS ABLE TO GET CLOSER TO MY GIRL. I WAS REALLY IMPRESSED." T.J. (AGE 16) FROM TOKYO
I'M GLAD I BOUGHT IT FOR FIVE THOUSAND YEN!
TEARY
FIVE THOUSAND YEN?
TSUBASA-KUN, THAT'S EXPENSIVE. YOU WERE RIPPED OFF.

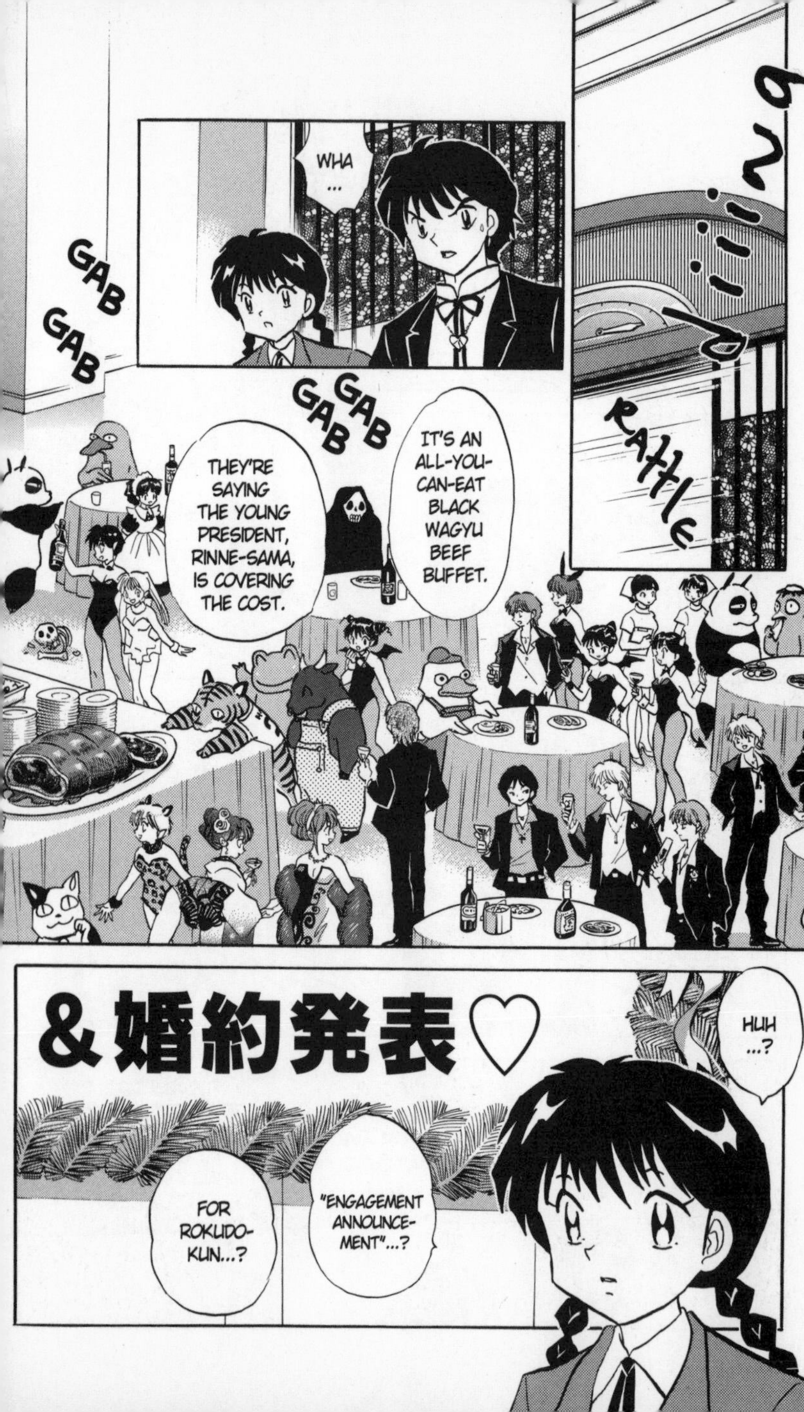
RATTLE
WHA ...
GAB GAB
GAB GAB
GAB GAB
IT'S AN ALL-YOU-CAN-EAT BLACK WAGYU BEEF BUFFET.
THEY'RE SAYING THE YOUNG PRESIDENT, RINNE-SAMA, IS COVERING THE COST.
&婚約発表♡
HUH ...?
"ENGAGEMENT ANNOUNCEMENT"...?
FOR ROKUDO-KUN...?

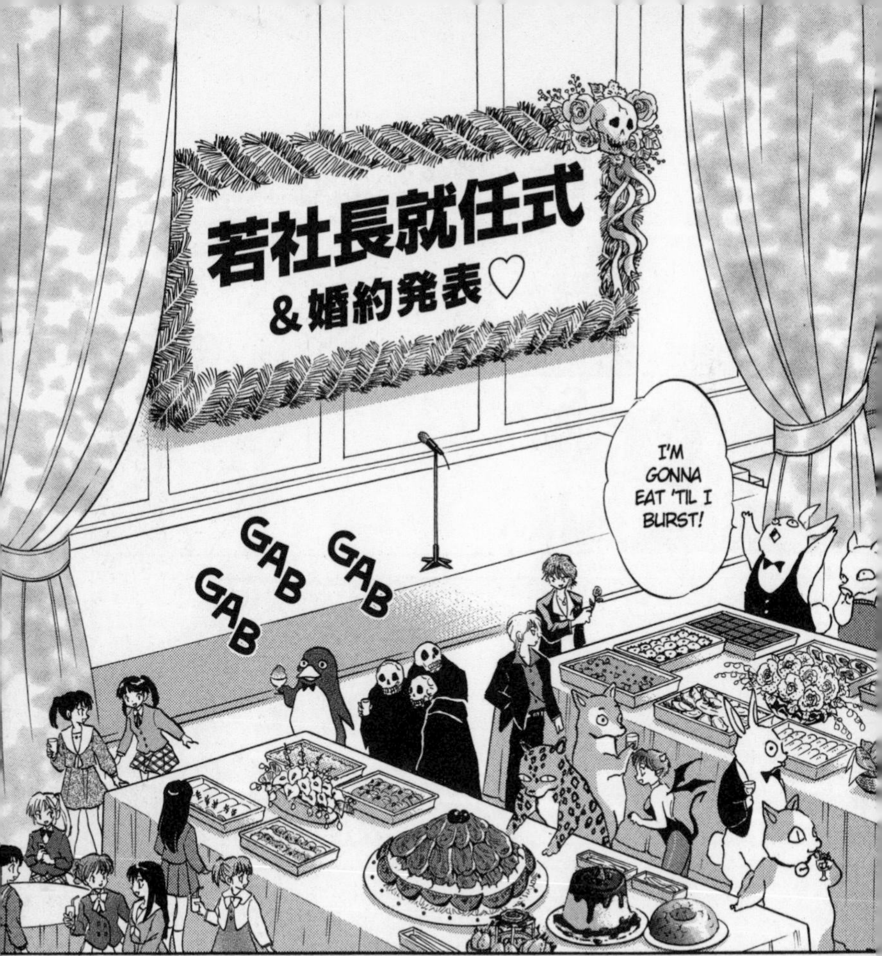
若社長就任式
&婚約発表♡
I'M GONNA EAT 'TIL I BURST!
GAB GAB
GAB
Sign: Young President Inauguration Ceremony & Engagement Announcement

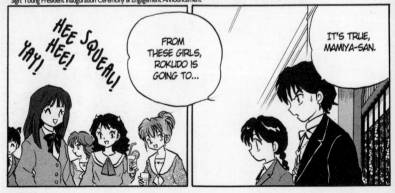

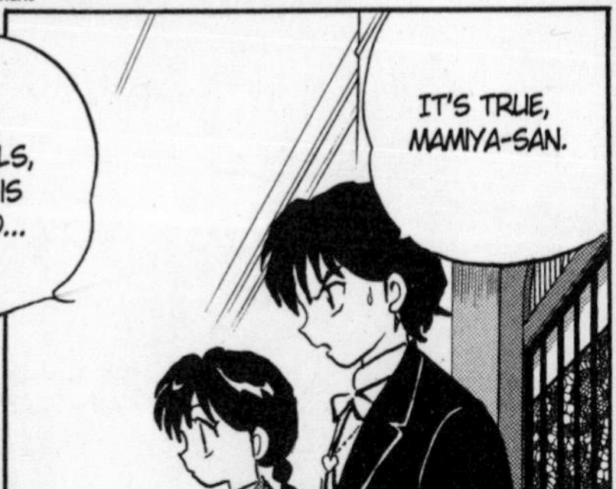
IT'S TRUE, MAMIYA-SAN.

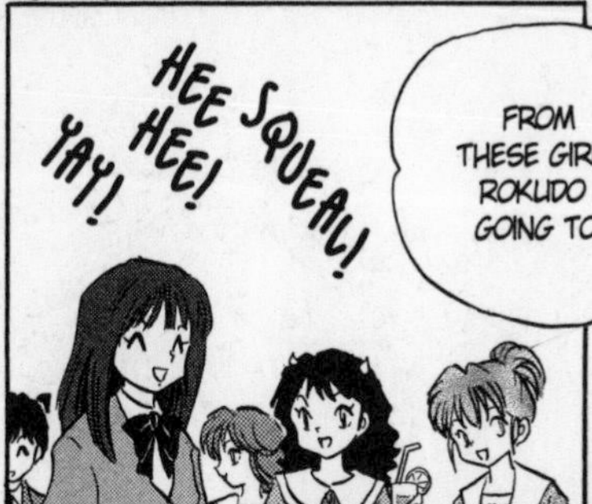
FROM THESE GIRLS, ROKUDO IS GOING TO...
SQUEAL!
HEE HEE!
YAY!

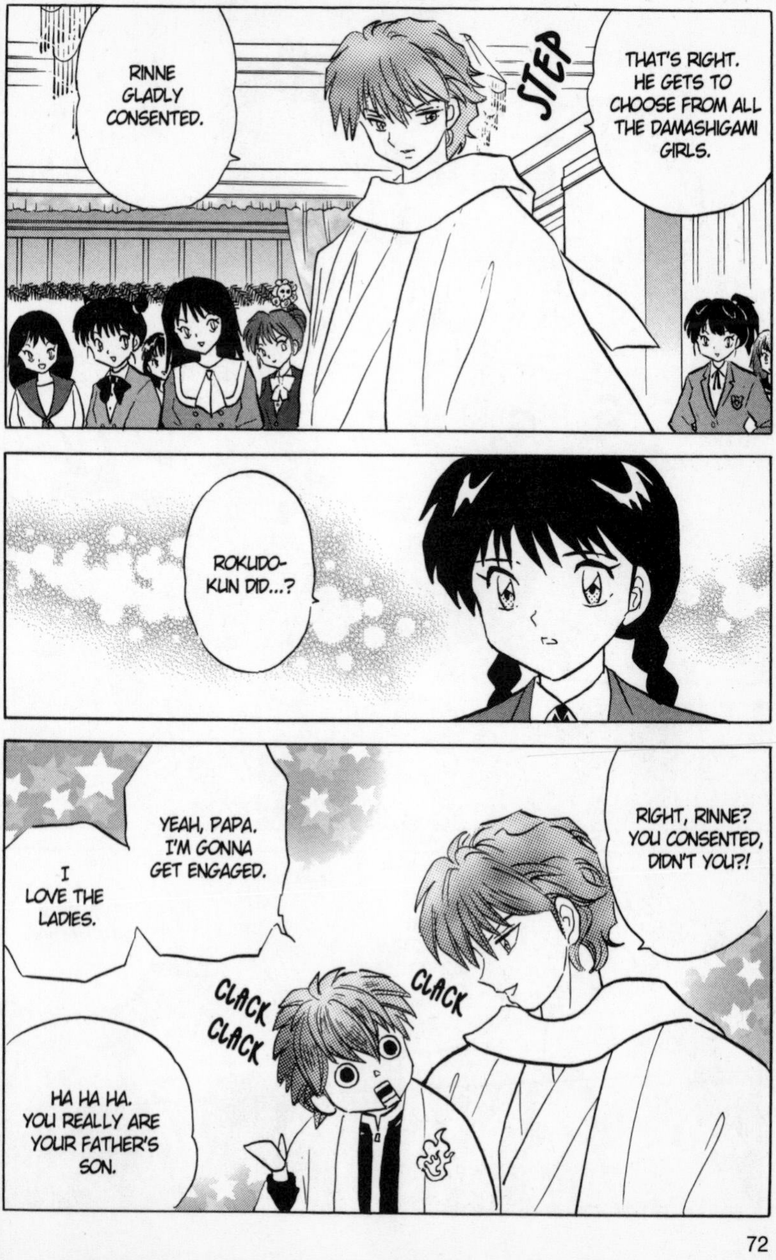
THAT'S RIGHT. HE GETS TO CHOOSE FROM ALL THE DAMASHIGAMI GIRLS.
STEP
RINNE GLADLY CONSENTED.
ROKUDO-KUN DID...?
RIGHT, RINNE? YOU CONSENTED, DIDN'T YOU?!
YEAH, PAPA. I'M GONNA GET ENGAGED.
I LOVE THE LADIES.
CLACK
CLACK CLACK
HA HA HA. YOU REALLY ARE YOUR FATHER'S SON.

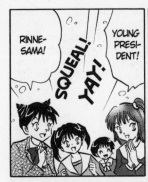

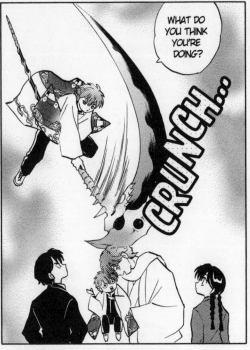

WHAT DO YOU THINK YOU'RE DOING?
CRUNCH...
YOUNG PRESIDENT!
SQUEAL! YAY!
RINNE-SAMA!
STAY BACK!
I'M NOT GETTING ENGAGED TO ANYONE.
WHY NOT, RINNE?
HOW CAN YOU BE DISSATISFIED WITH ALL THESE CUTE GIRLS?
THAT'S RIGHT, RINNE-SAMA.
I SEE... YOU...

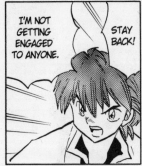

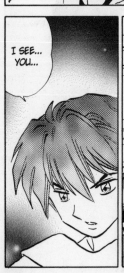

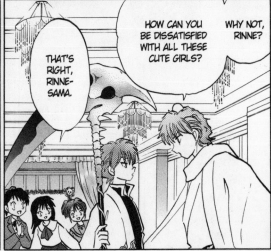

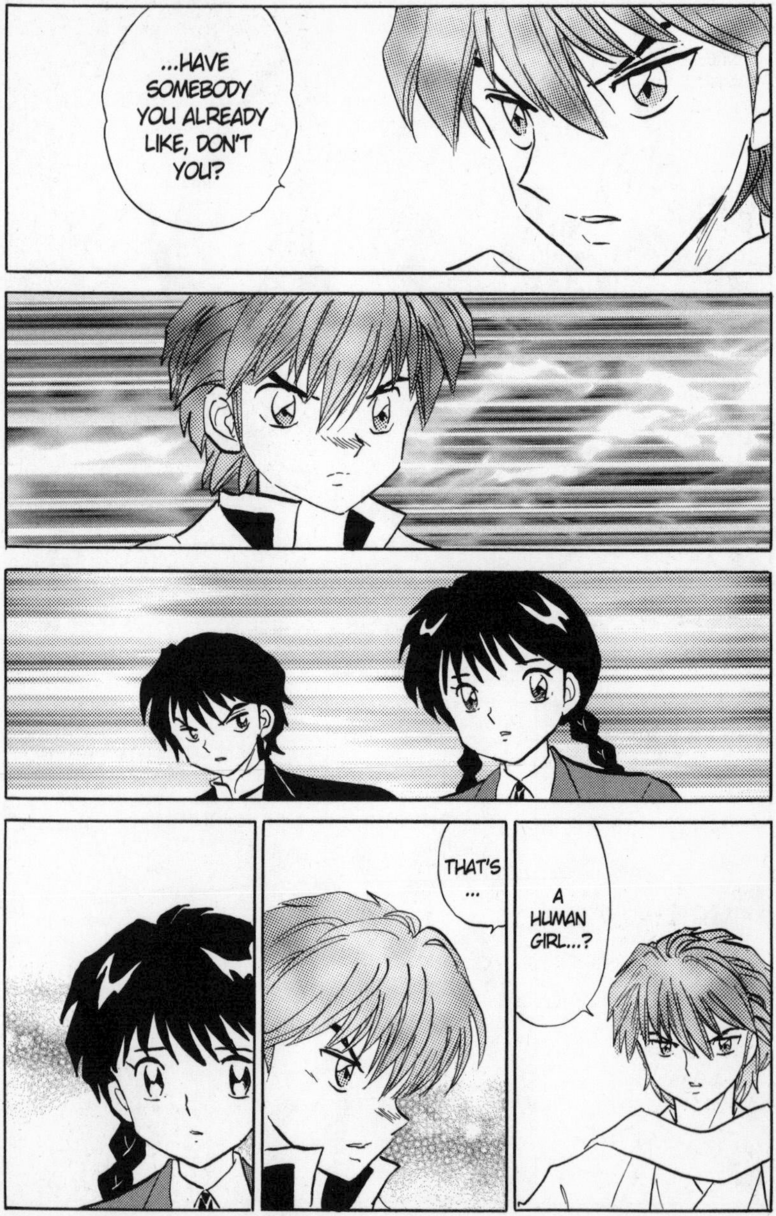
...HAVE SOMEBODY YOU ALREADY LIKE, DON'T YOU?
A HUMAN GIRL...?
THAT'S ...

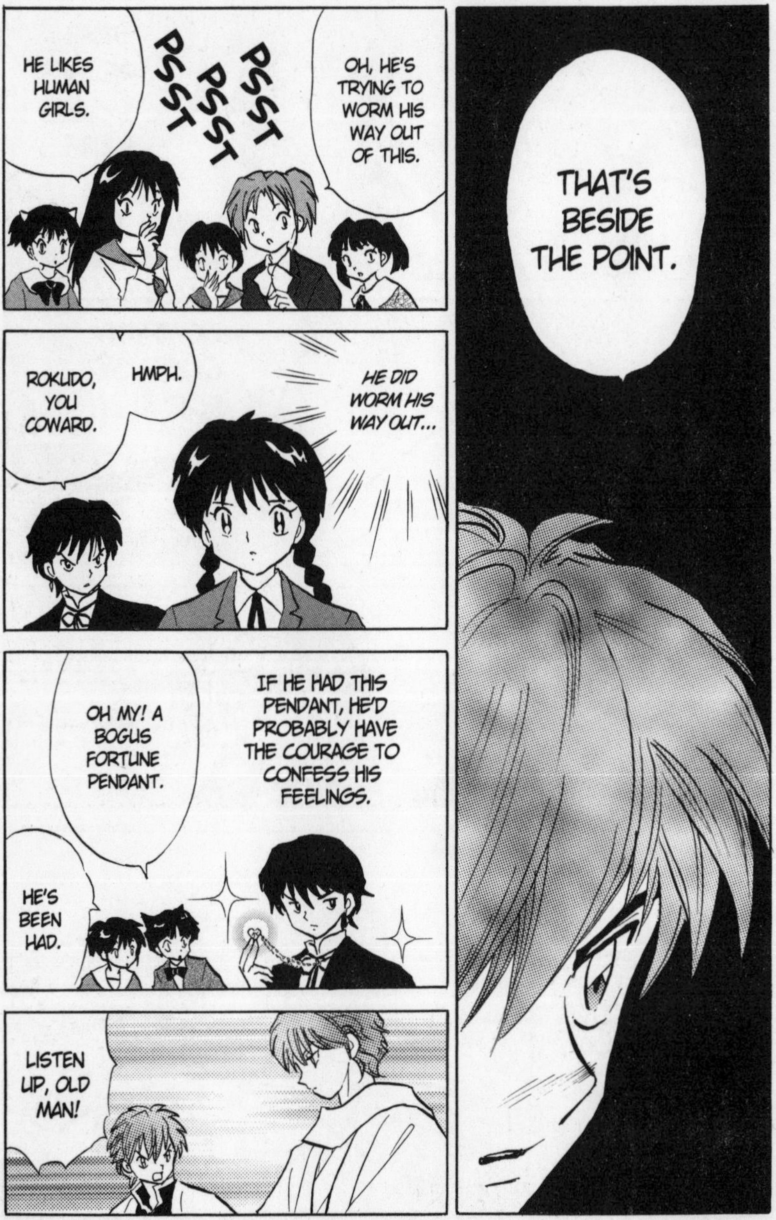
THAT'S BESIDE THE POINT.
OH, HE'S TRYING TO WORM HIS WAY OUT OF THIS.
PSST PSST PSST
HE LIKES HUMAN GIRLS.
HE DID WORM HIS WAY OUT...
HMPH.
ROKUDO, YOU COWARD.
IF HE HAD THIS PENDANT, HE'D PROBABLY HAVE THE COURAGE TO CONFESS HIS FEELINGS.
OH MY! A BOGUS FORTUNE PENDANT.
HE'S BEEN HAD.
LISTEN UP, OLD MAN!

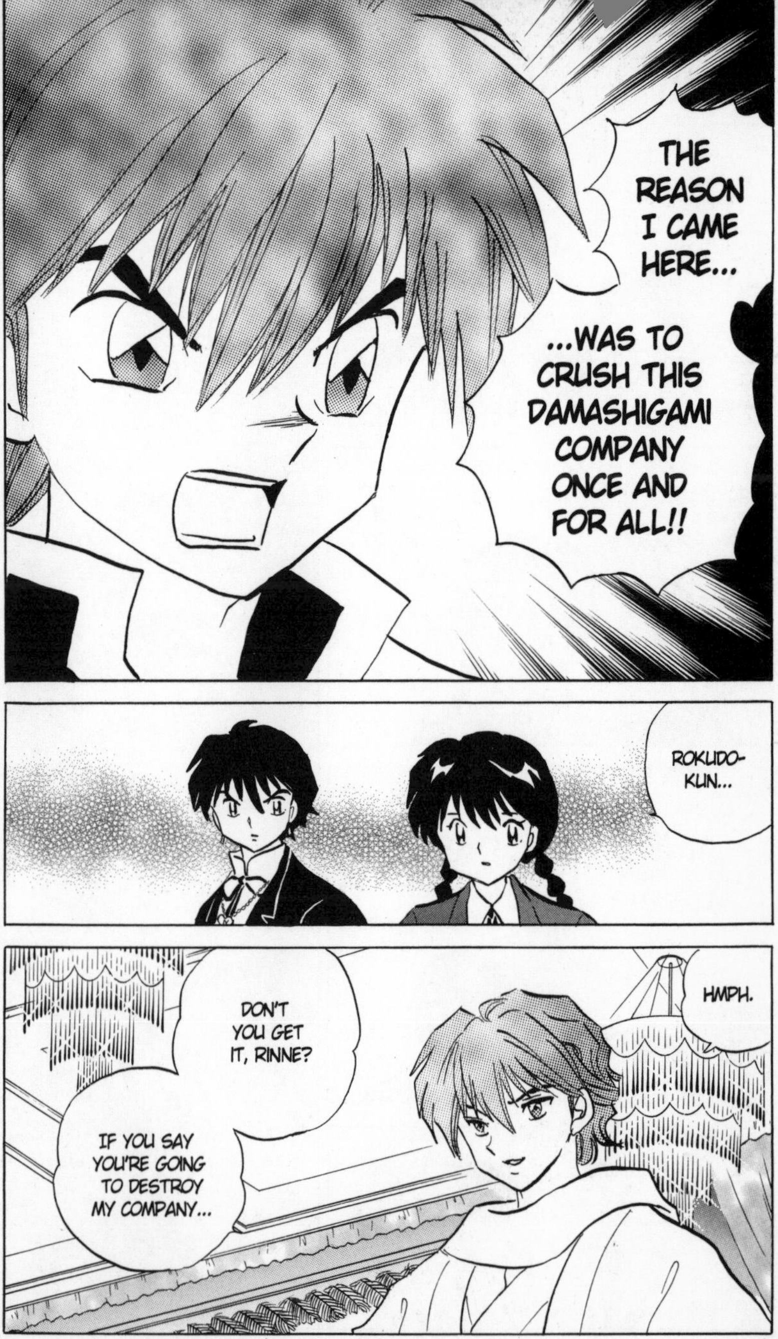
THE REASON I CAME HERE...
...WAS TO CRUSH THIS DAMASHIGAMI COMPANY ONCE AND FOR ALL!!
ROKUDO-KUN...
HMPH.
DON'T YOU GET IT, RINNE?
IF YOU SAY YOU'RE GOING TO DESTROY MY COMPANY...

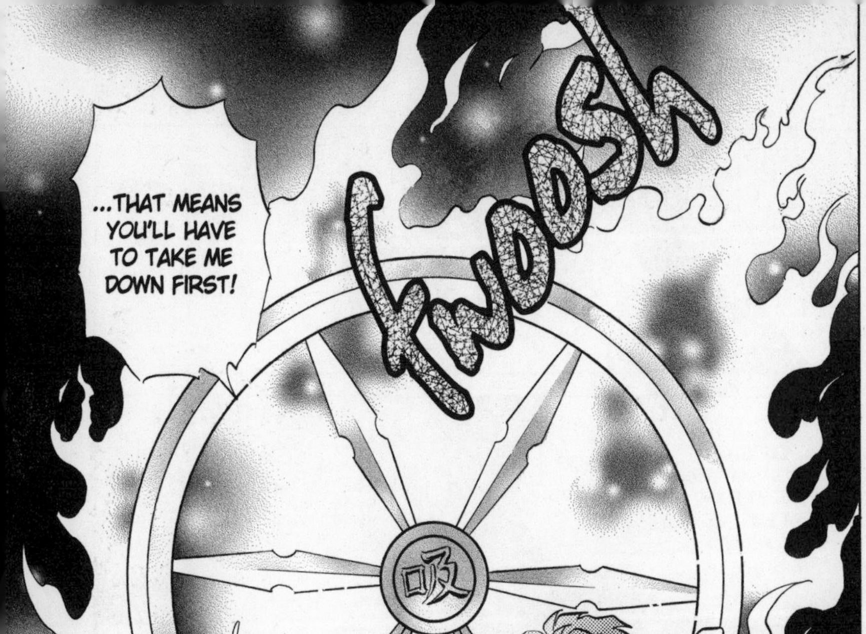
FWOOSH
...THAT MEANS YOU'LL HAVE TO TAKE ME DOWN FIRST!
吸

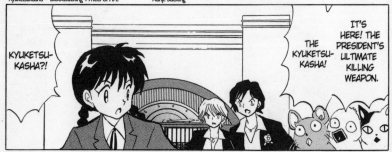

Kyuketsukasha = Bloodsucking Wheel of Fire Kanji: Sucking

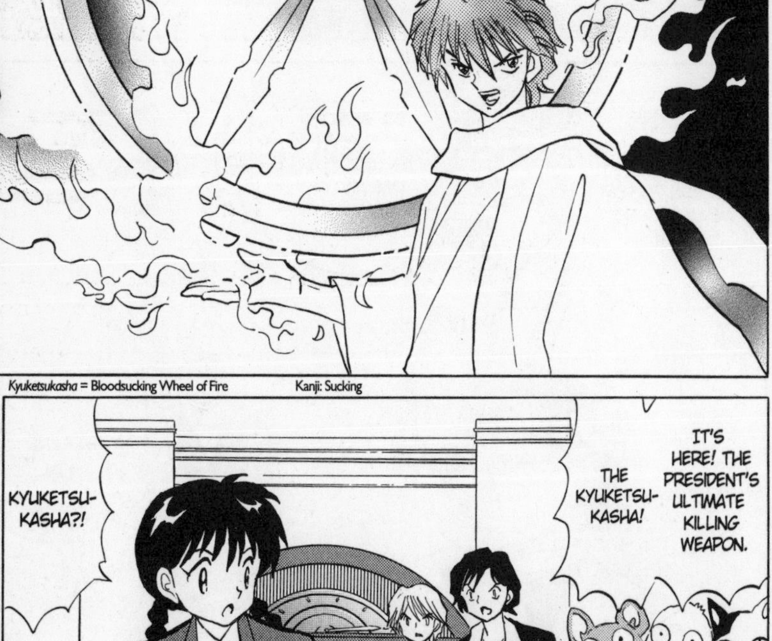
IT'S HERE! THE PRESIDENT'S ULTIMATE KILLING WEAPON.
THE KYUKETSU-KASHA!
KYUKETSU-KASHA?!

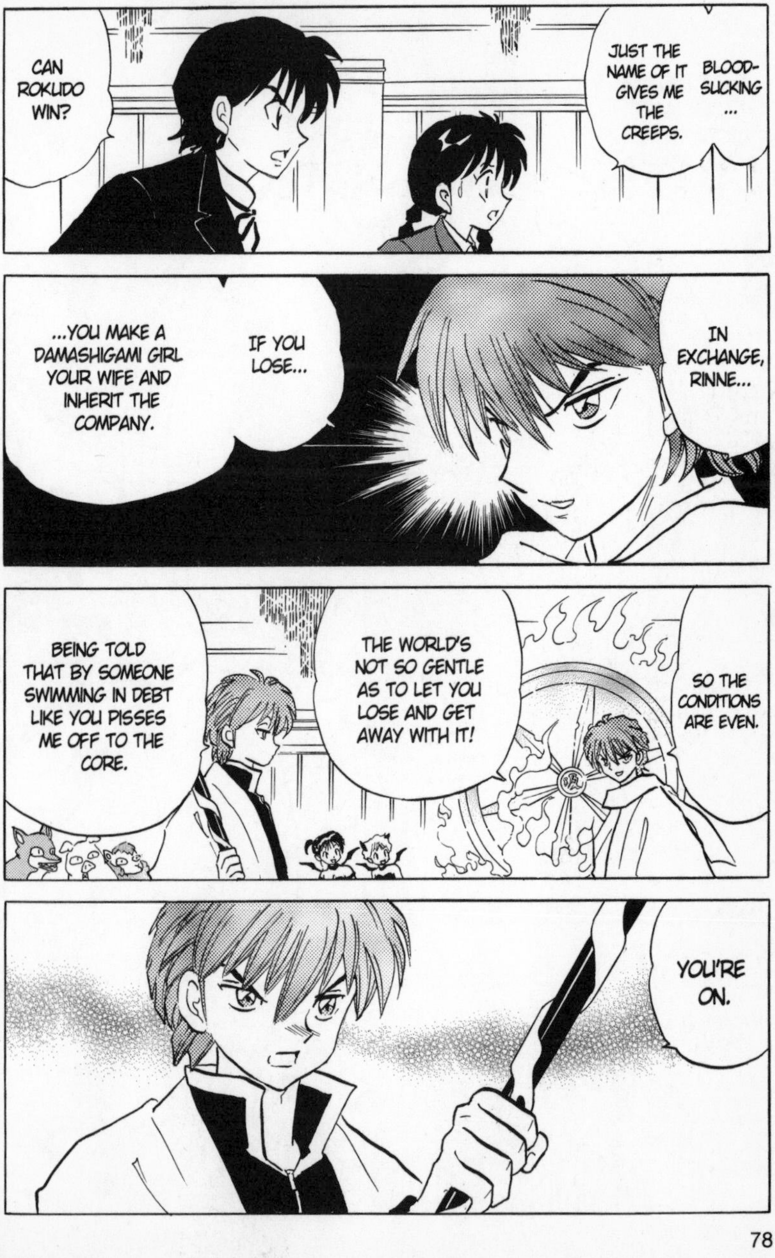
BLOOD-SUCKING...
JUST THE NAME OF IT GIVES ME THE CREEPS.
CAN ROKUDO WIN?
IN EXCHANGE, RINNE...
IF YOU LOSE...
...YOU MAKE A DAMASHIGAMI GIRL YOUR WIFE AND INHERIT THE COMPANY.
SO THE CONDITIONS ARE EVEN.
THE WORLD'S NOT SO GENTLE AS TO LET YOU LOSE AND GET AWAY WITH IT!
BEING TOLD THAT BY SOMEONE SWIMMING IN DEBT LIKE YOU PISSES ME OFF TO THE CORE.
YOU'RE ON.

CHAPTER 33: KYUKETSUKASHA

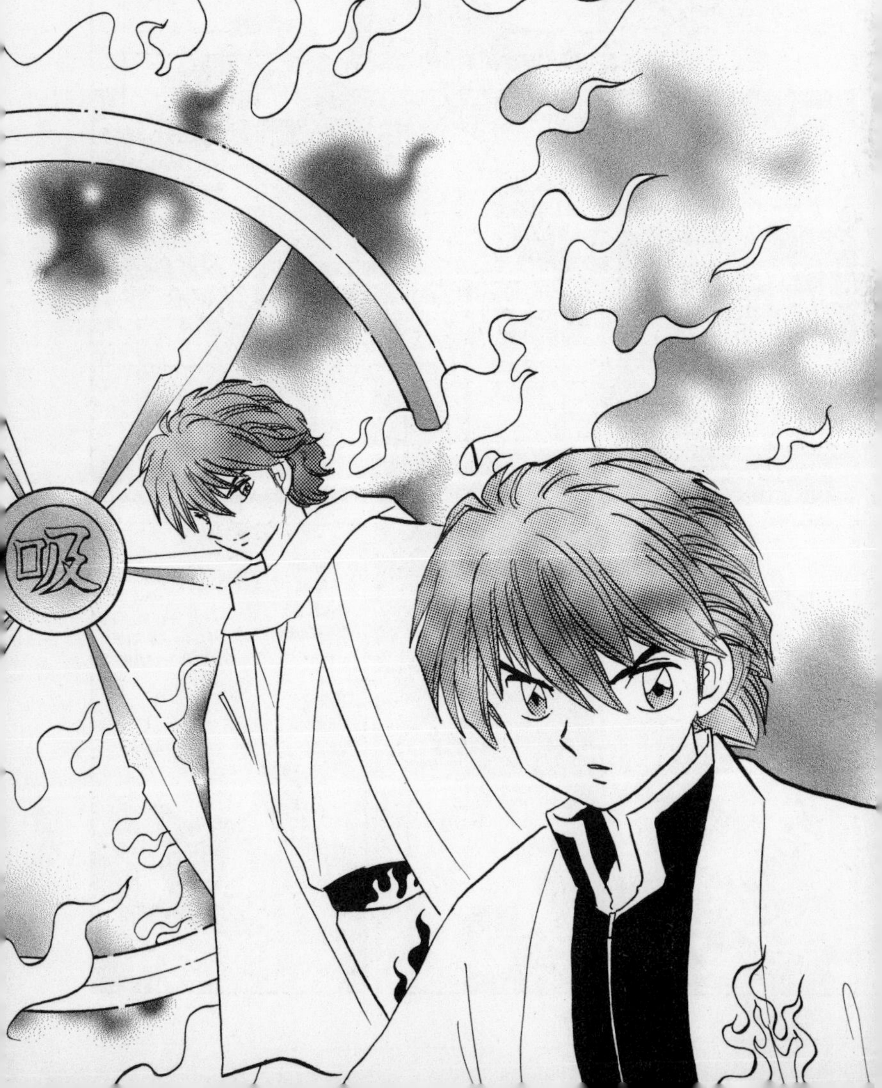
吸

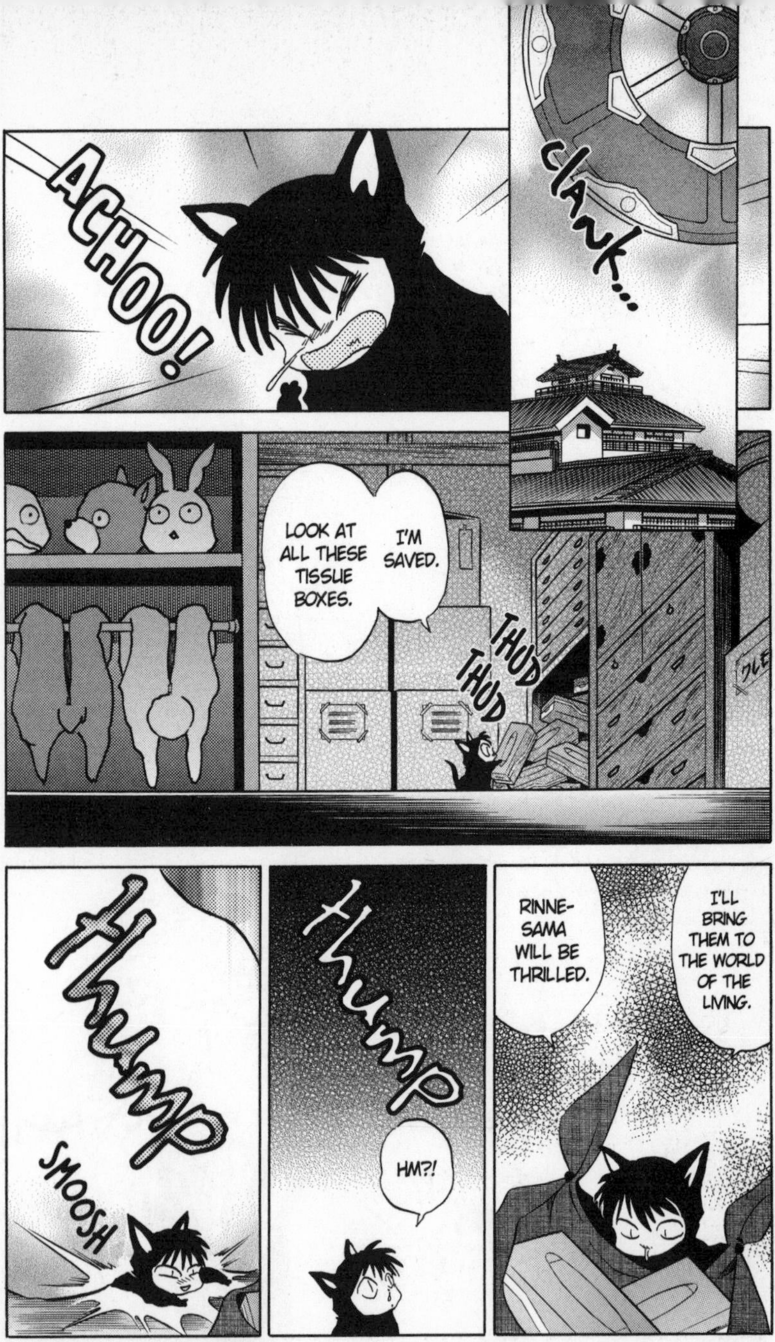
CLANK...
ACHOO!
THUD
THUD
I'M SAVED.
LOOK AT ALL THESE TISSUE BOXES.
I'LL BRING THEM TO THE WORLD OF THE LIVING.
RINNE-SAMA WILL BE THRILLED.
THUMP
HM?!
THUMP
SMOOSH

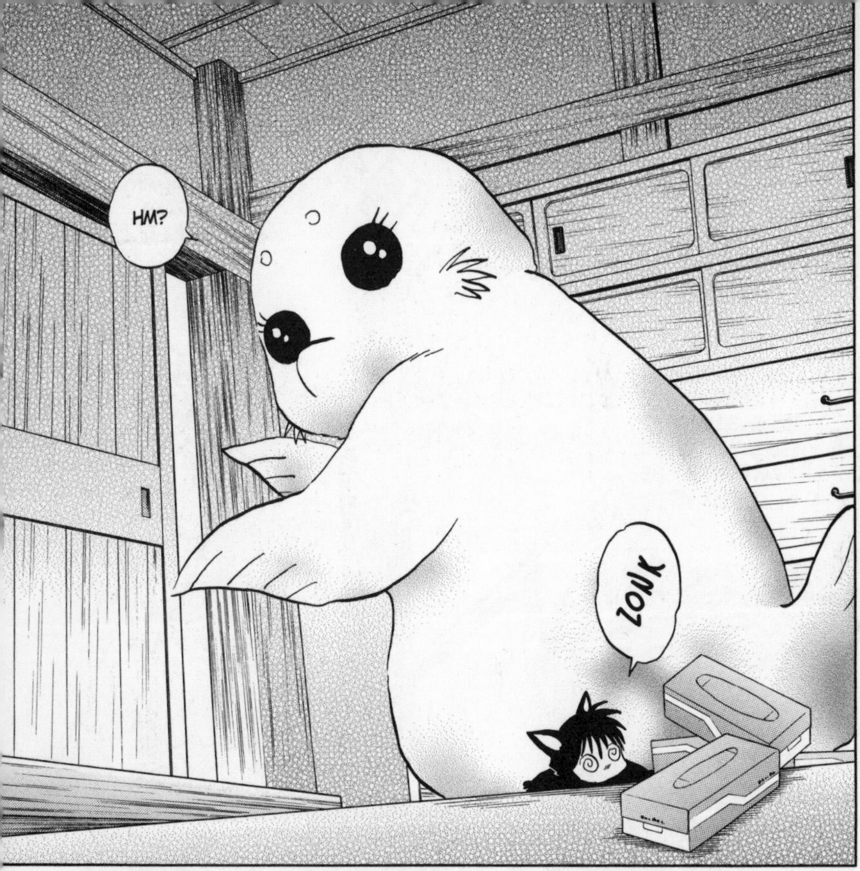
HM?
ZONK

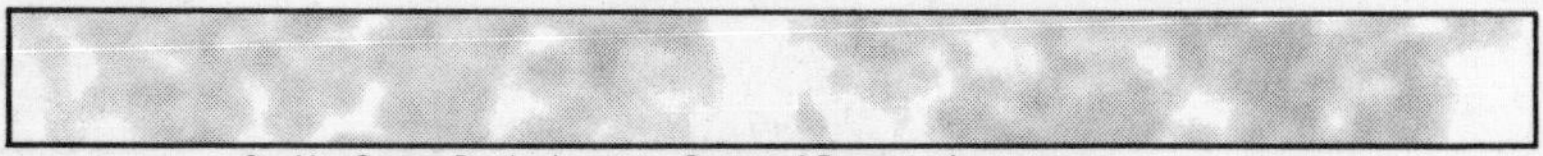

Sign: New Company President Inauguration Ceremony & Engagement Announcement

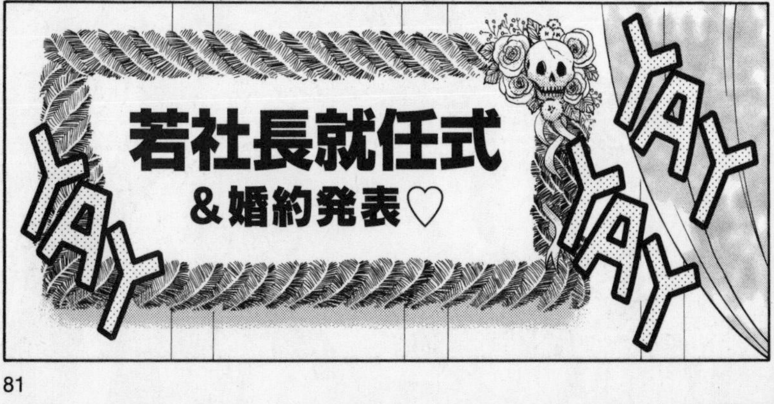
YAY
YAY
若社長就任式
&婚約発表♡
YAY

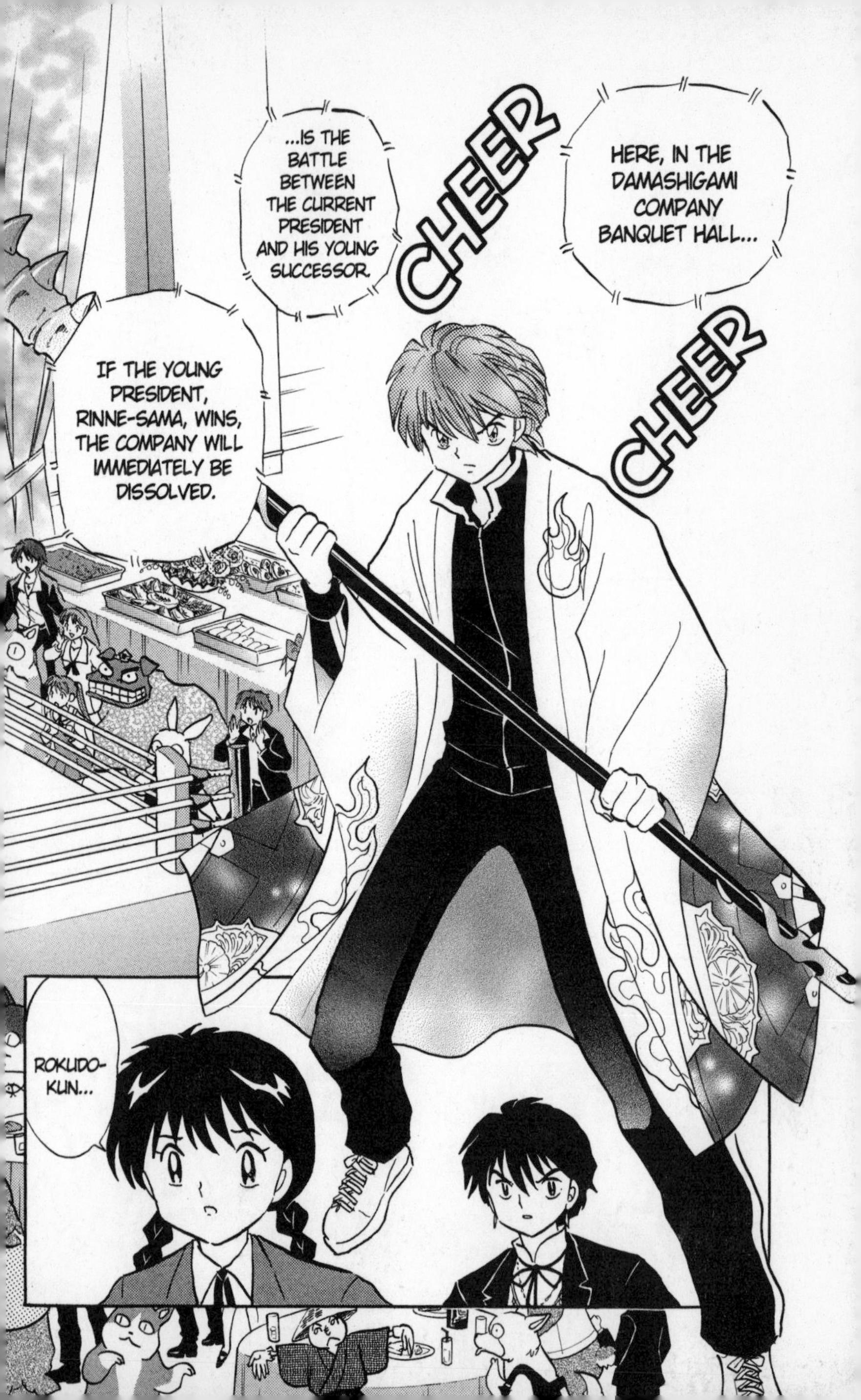
HERE, IN THE DAMASHIGAMI COMPANY BANQUET HALL...
CHEER
...IS THE BATTLE BETWEEN THE CURRENT PRESIDENT AND HIS YOUNG SUCCESSOR.
CHEER
IF THE YOUNG PRESIDENT, RINNE-SAMA, WINS, THE COMPANY WILL IMMEDIATELY BE DISSOLVED.
ROKUDO-KUN...

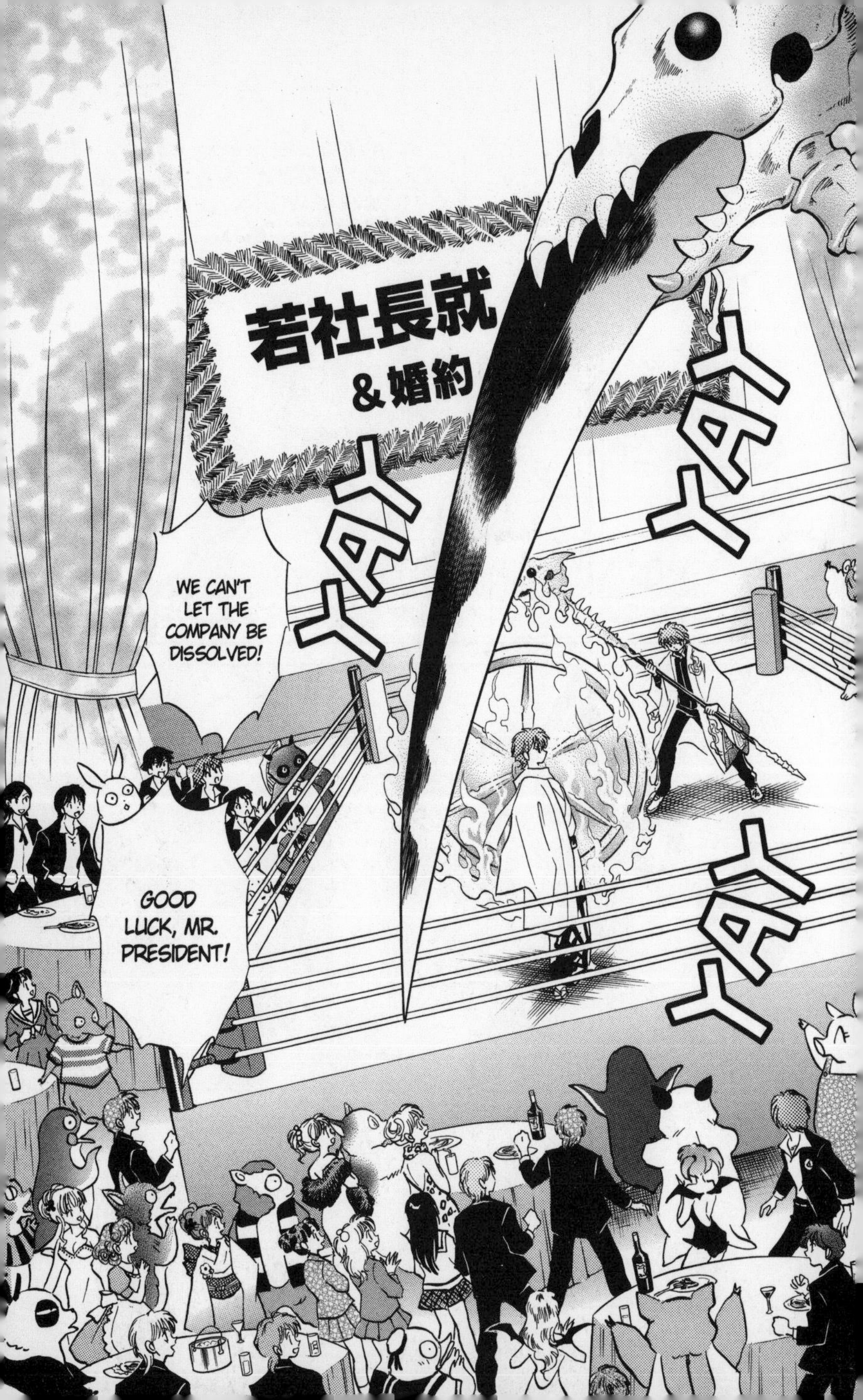
若社長就
&婚約
YAY
YAY
YAY
WE CAN'T LET THE COMPANY BE DISSOLVED!
GOOD LUCK, MR. PRESIDENT!

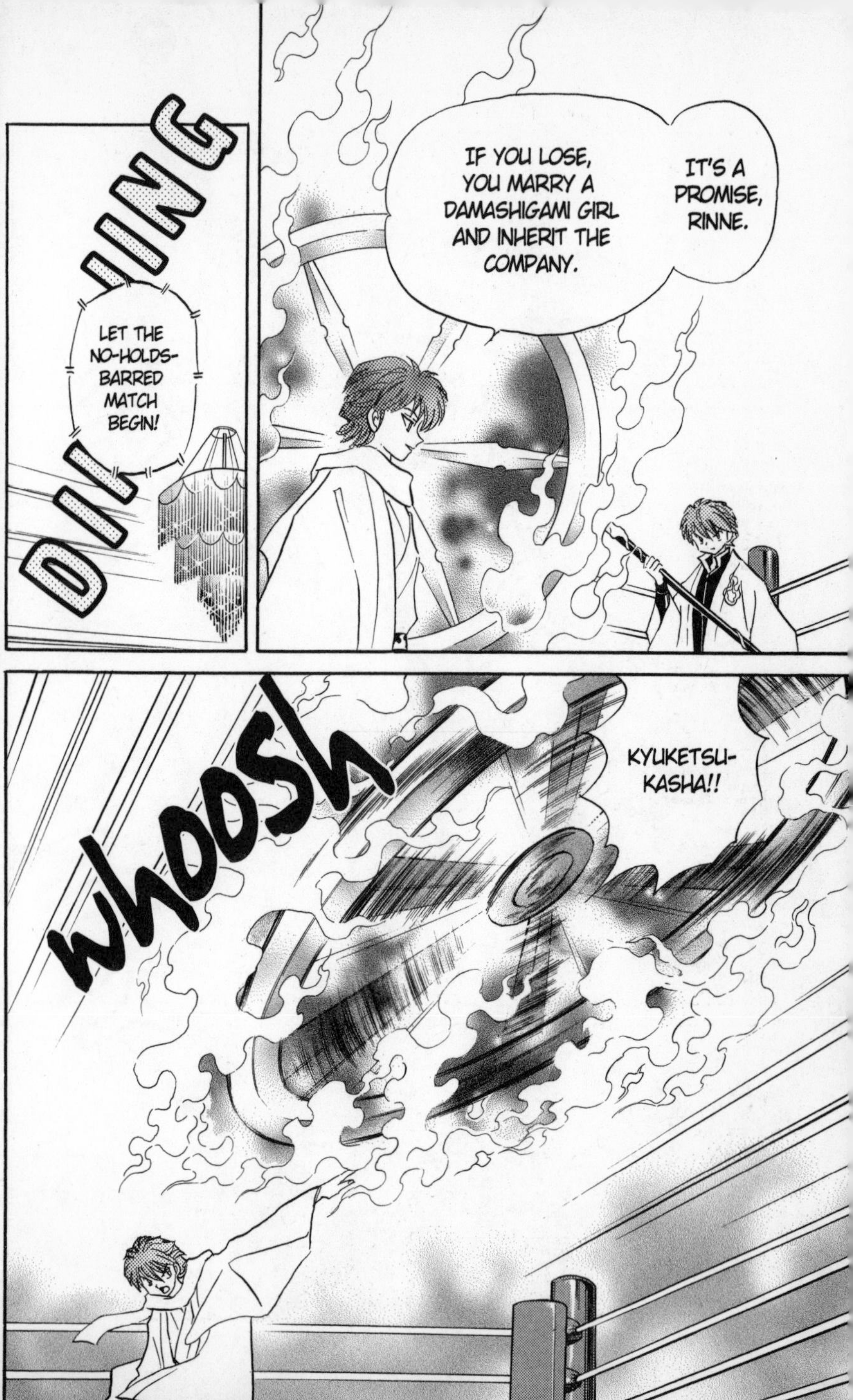
IF YOU LOSE, YOU MARRY A DAMASHIGAMI GIRL AND INHERIT THE COMPANY.
IT'S A PROMISE, RINNE.
DIIING
LET THE NO-HOLDS-BARRED MATCH BEGIN!
KYUKETSU-KASHA!!
WHOOSH

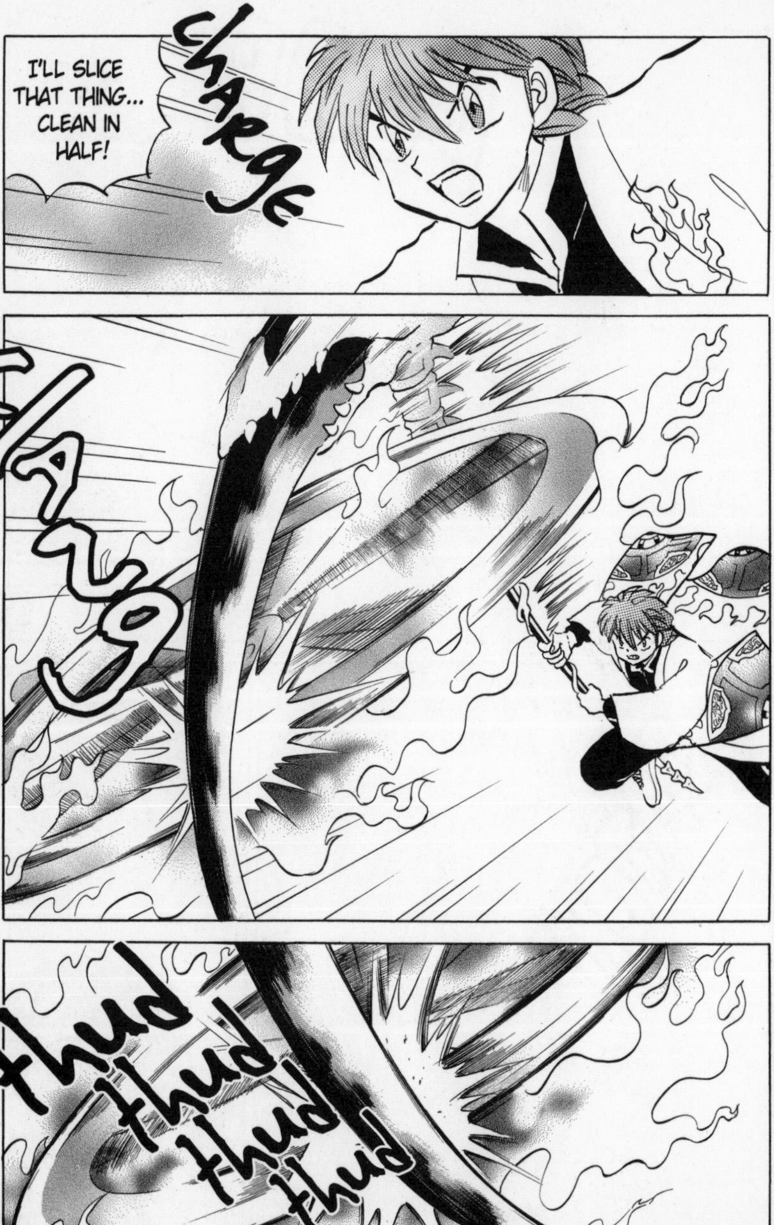
CHARGE
I'LL SLICE THAT THING... CLEAN IN HALF!
CLANG
THUD THUD THUD THUD

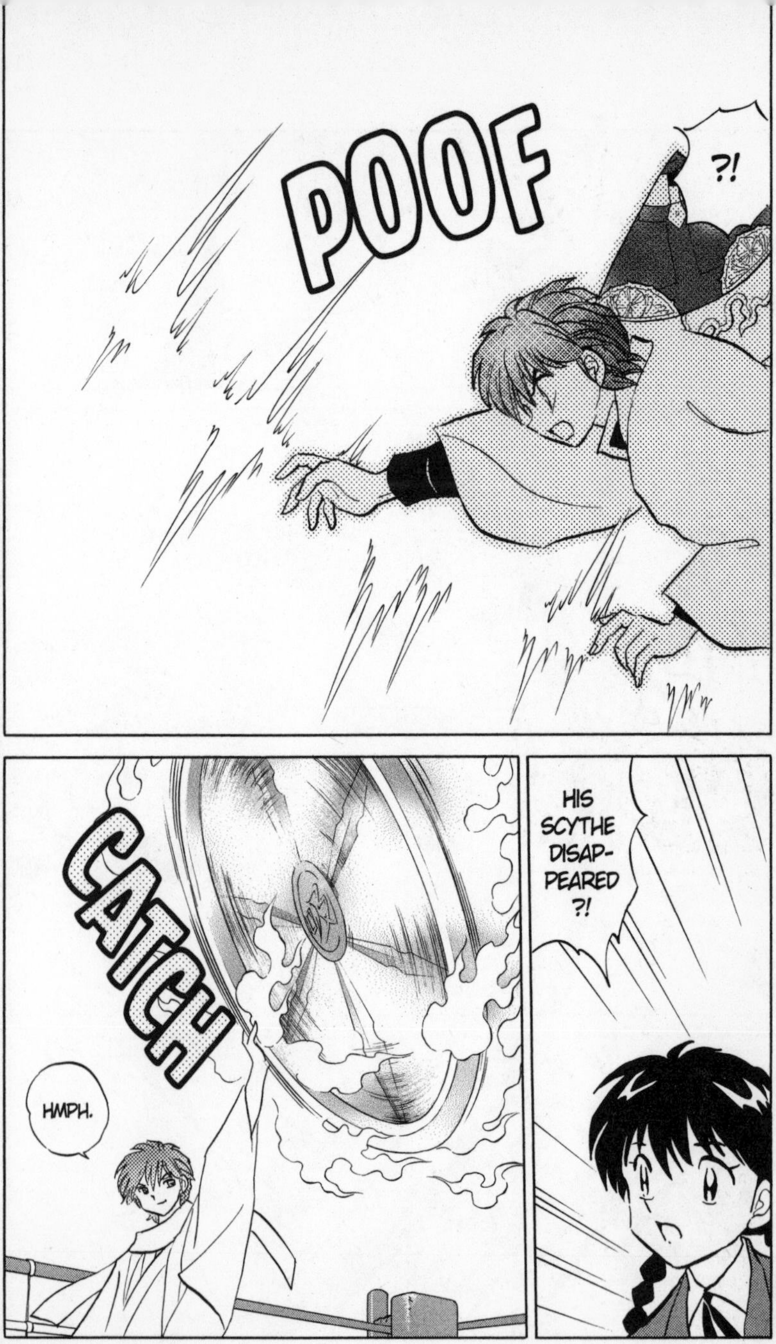
POOF
?!
HIS SCYTHE DISAP-PEARED ?!
CATCH
HMPH.

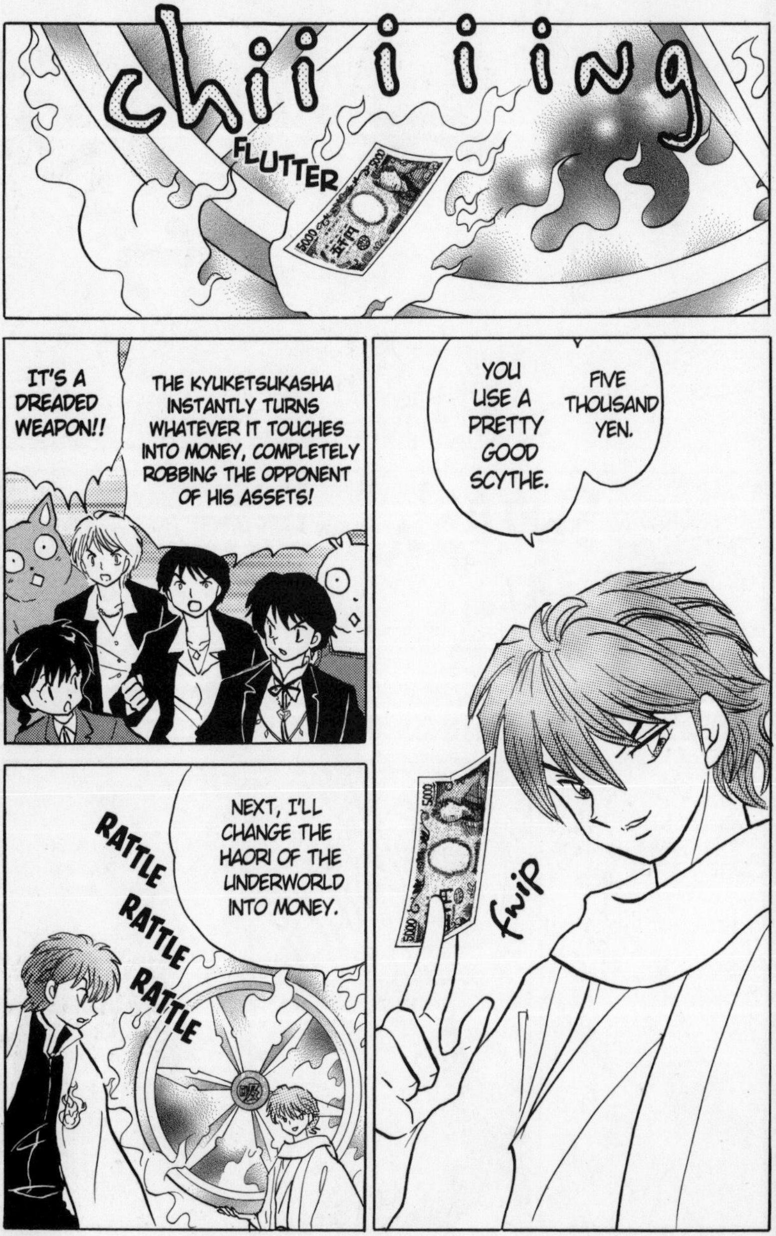
chiiiing
FLUTTER
FIVE THOUSAND YEN.
YOU USE A PRETTY GOOD SCYTHE.
fwip
THE KYUKETSUKASHA INSTANTLY TURNS WHATEVER IT TOUCHES INTO MONEY, COMPLETELY ROBBING THE OPPONENT OF HIS ASSETS!
IT'S A DREADED WEAPON!!
NEXT, I'LL CHANGE THE HAORI OF THE UNDERWORLD INTO MONEY.
RATTLE RATTLE RATTLE RATTLE

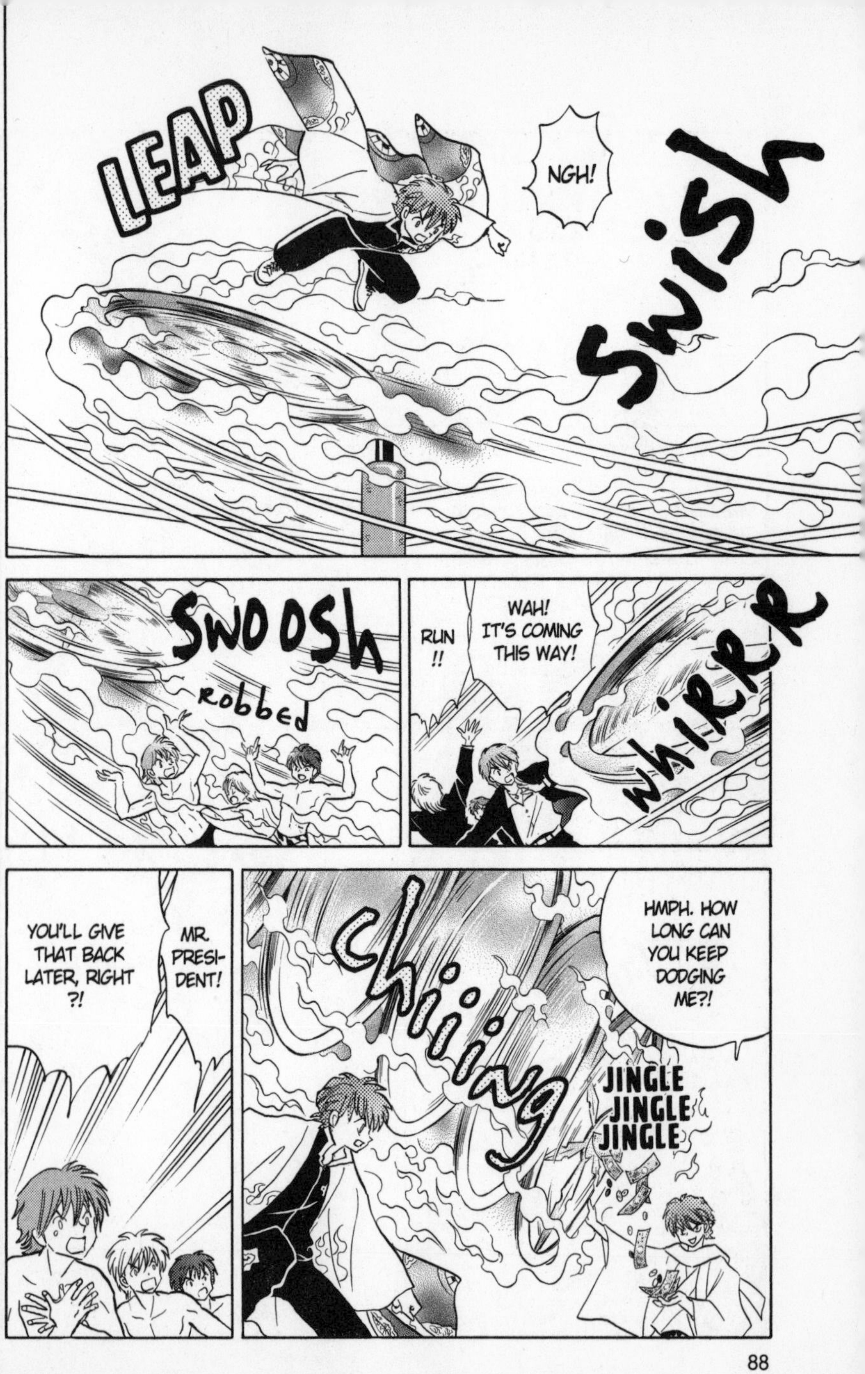
Swish
NGH!
LEAP
whiRRR
WAH! IT'S COMING THIS WAY!
RUN!!
SWOOSh
robbed
HMPH. HOW LONG CAN YOU KEEP DODGING ME?!
JINGLE JINGLE JINGLE
chiiing
MR. PRESI-DENT!
YOU'LL GIVE THAT BACK LATER, RIGHT?!

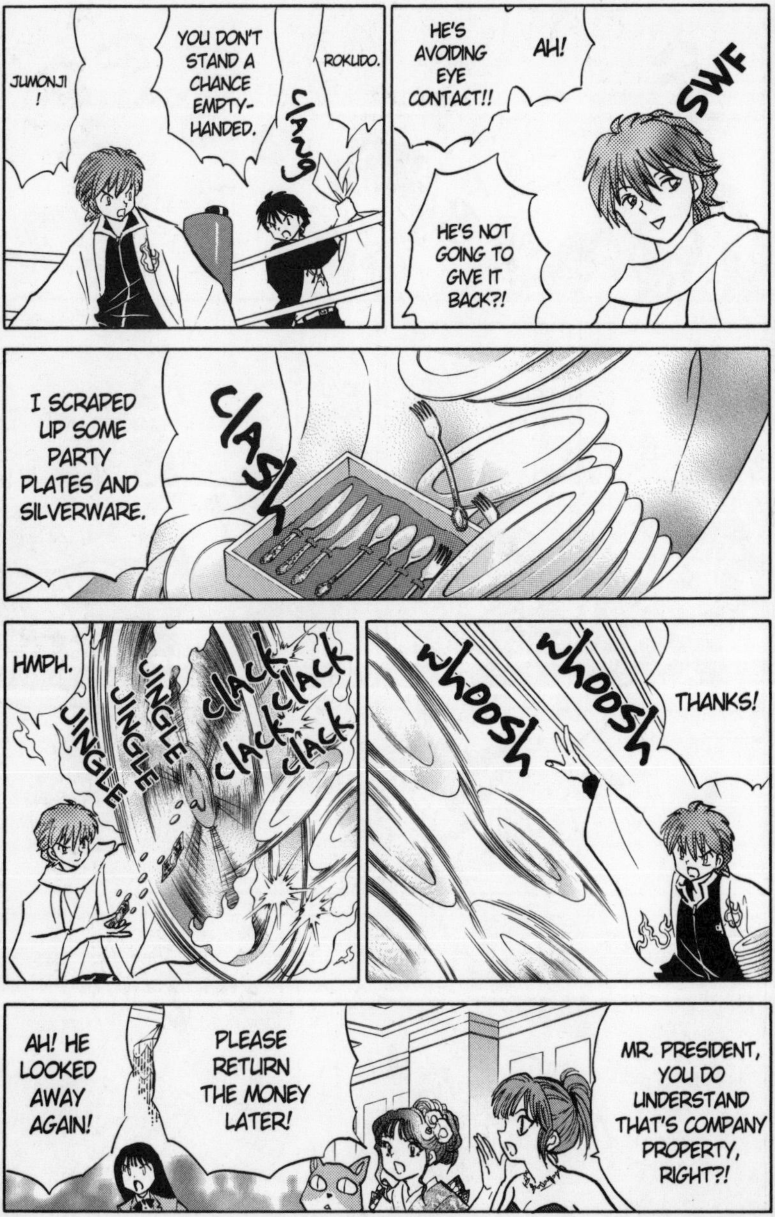
SWF
AH!
HE'S AVOIDING EYE CONTACT!!
HE'S NOT GOING TO GIVE IT BACK?!
ROKUDO.
clang
YOU DON'T STAND A CHANCE EMPTY-HANDED.
JUMONJI!
CLASH
I SCRAPED UP SOME PARTY PLATES AND SILVERWARE.
THANKS!
whoosh
whoosh
clack clack clack clack
JINGLE JINGLE JINGLE
HMPH.
MR. PRESIDENT, YOU DO UNDERSTAND THAT'S COMPANY PROPERTY, RIGHT?!
PLEASE RETURN THE MONEY LATER!
AH! HE LOOKED AWAY AGAIN!

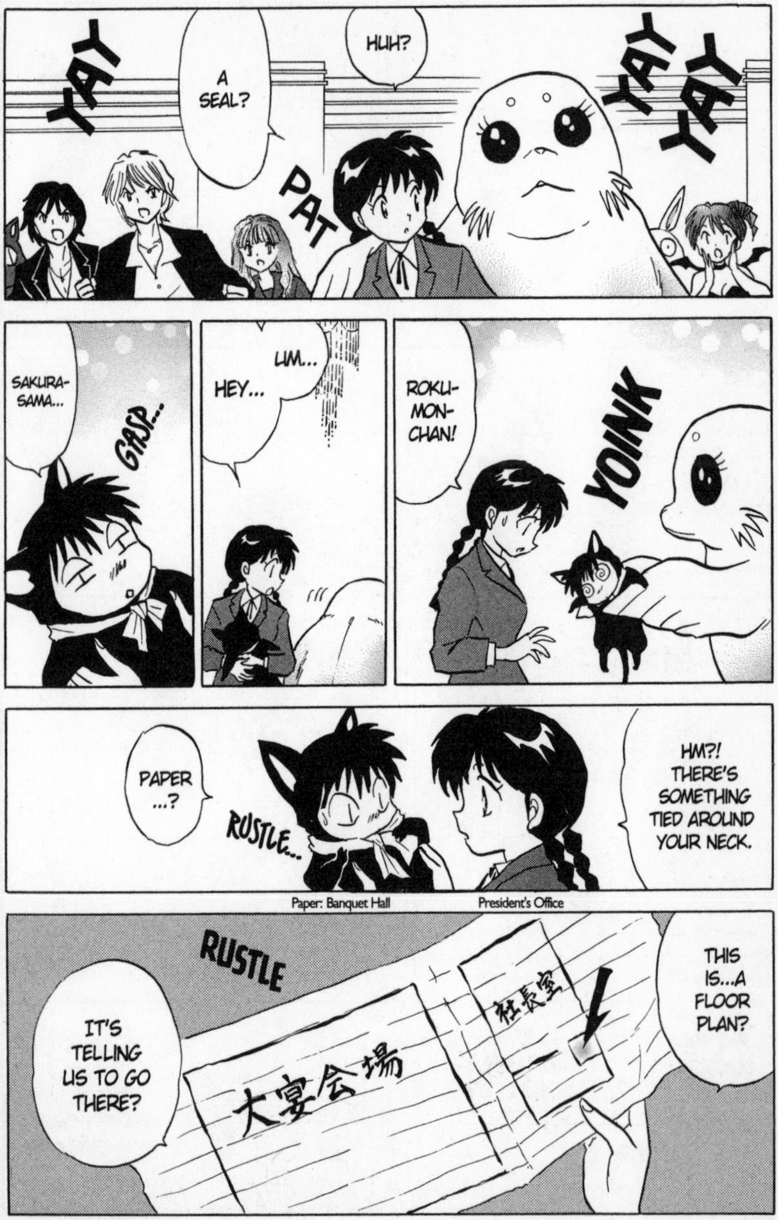
YAY YAY
HUH?
A SEAL?
YAY
PAT
ROKU-MON-CHAN!
YOINK
UM...
HEY...
SAKURA-SAMA...
GASP...
HM?! THERE'S SOMETHING TIED AROUND YOUR NECK.
PAPER ...?
RUSTLE...
Paper: Banquet Hall
President's Office
THIS IS...A FLOOR PLAN?
RUSTLE
社長室
大宴会場
IT'S TELLING US TO GO THERE?

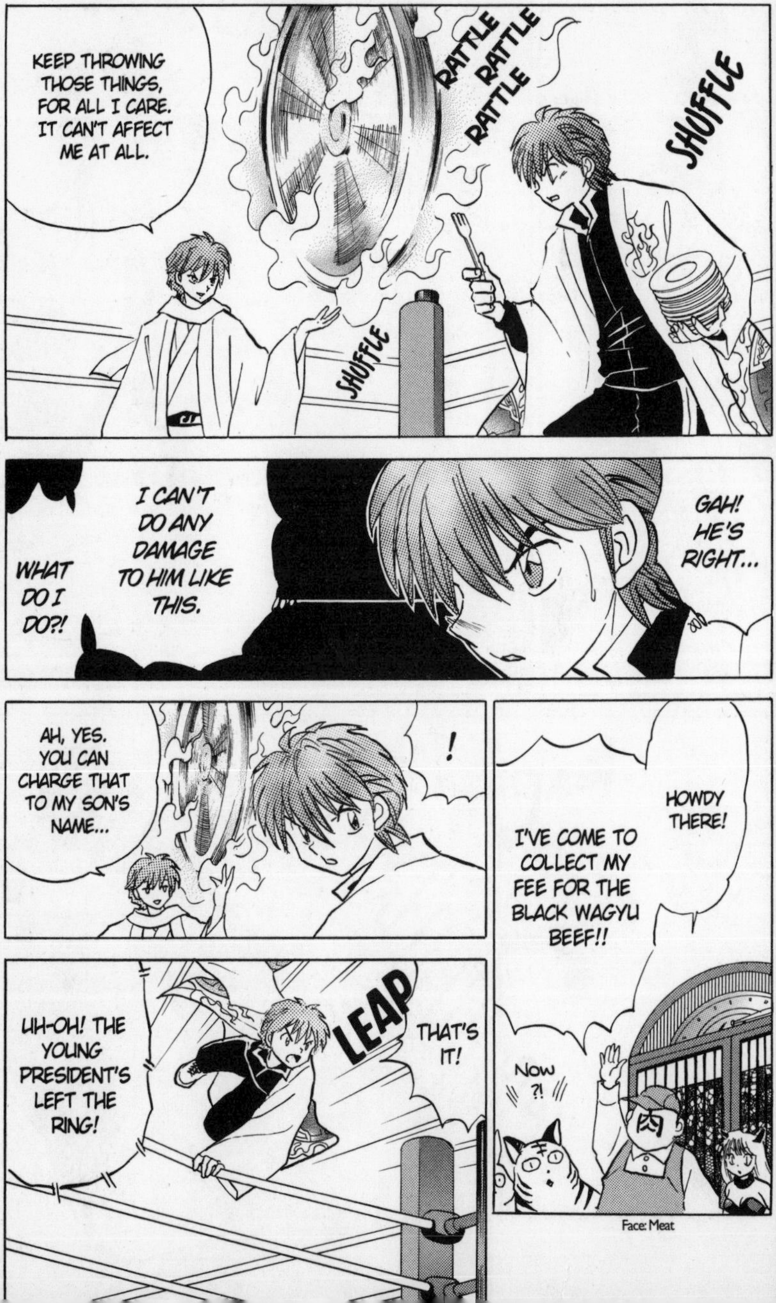
SHUFFLE
RATTLE RATTLE RATTLE
KEEP THROWING THOSE THINGS, FOR ALL I CARE. IT CAN'T AFFECT ME AT ALL.
SHUFFLE
GAH! HE'S RIGHT...
I CAN'T DO ANY DAMAGE TO HIM LIKE THIS.
WHAT DO I DO?!
HOWDY THERE!
I'VE COME TO COLLECT MY FEE FOR THE BLACK WAGYU BEEF!!
Now ?!
Face: Meat
!
AH, YES. YOU CAN CHARGE THAT TO MY SON'S NAME...
THAT'S IT!
LEAP
UH-OH! THE YOUNG PRESIDENT'S LEFT THE RING!

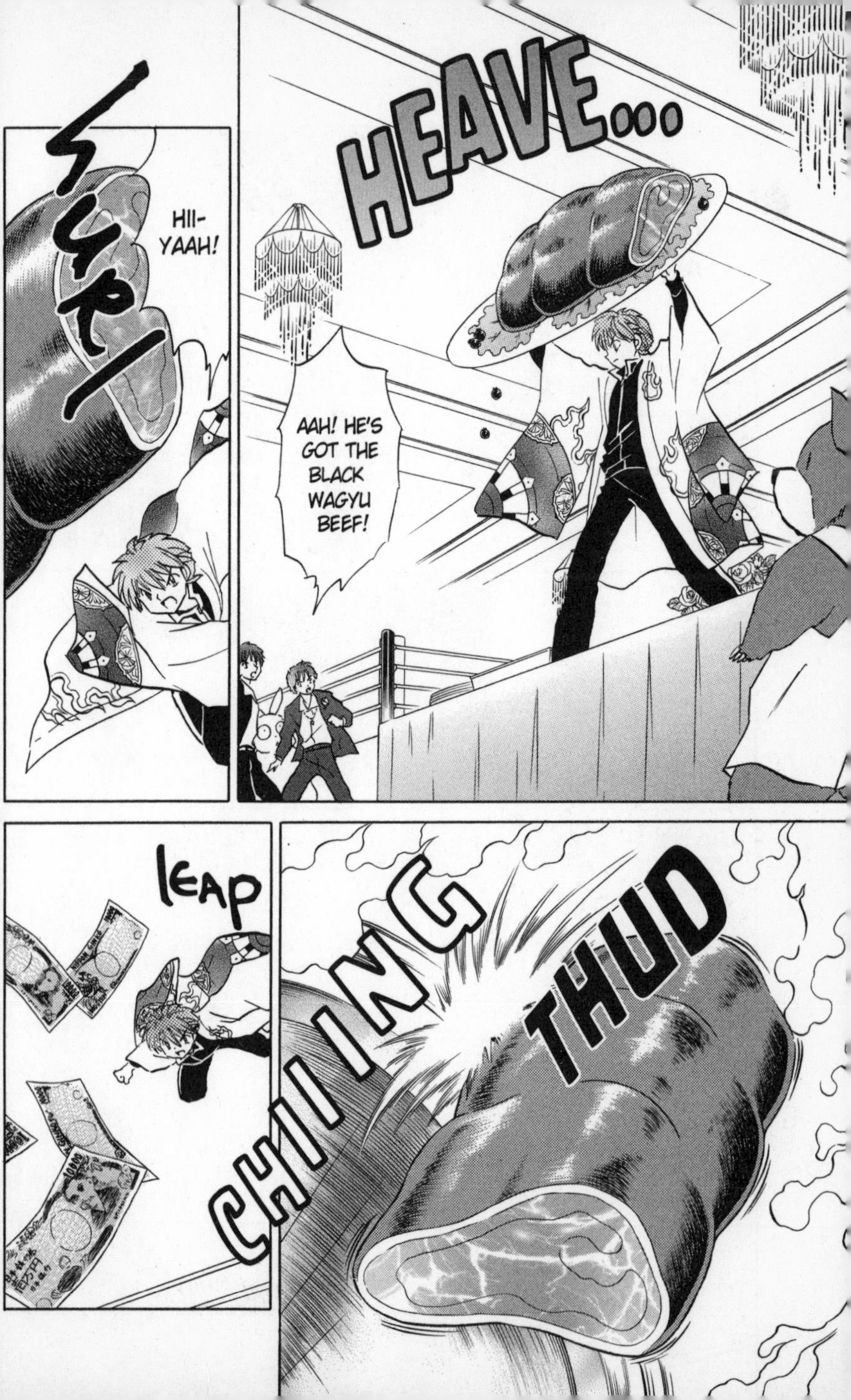
HEAVE...
AAH! HE'S GOT THE BLACK WAGYU BEEF!
HII-YAAH!
CHIIING
THUD
leap

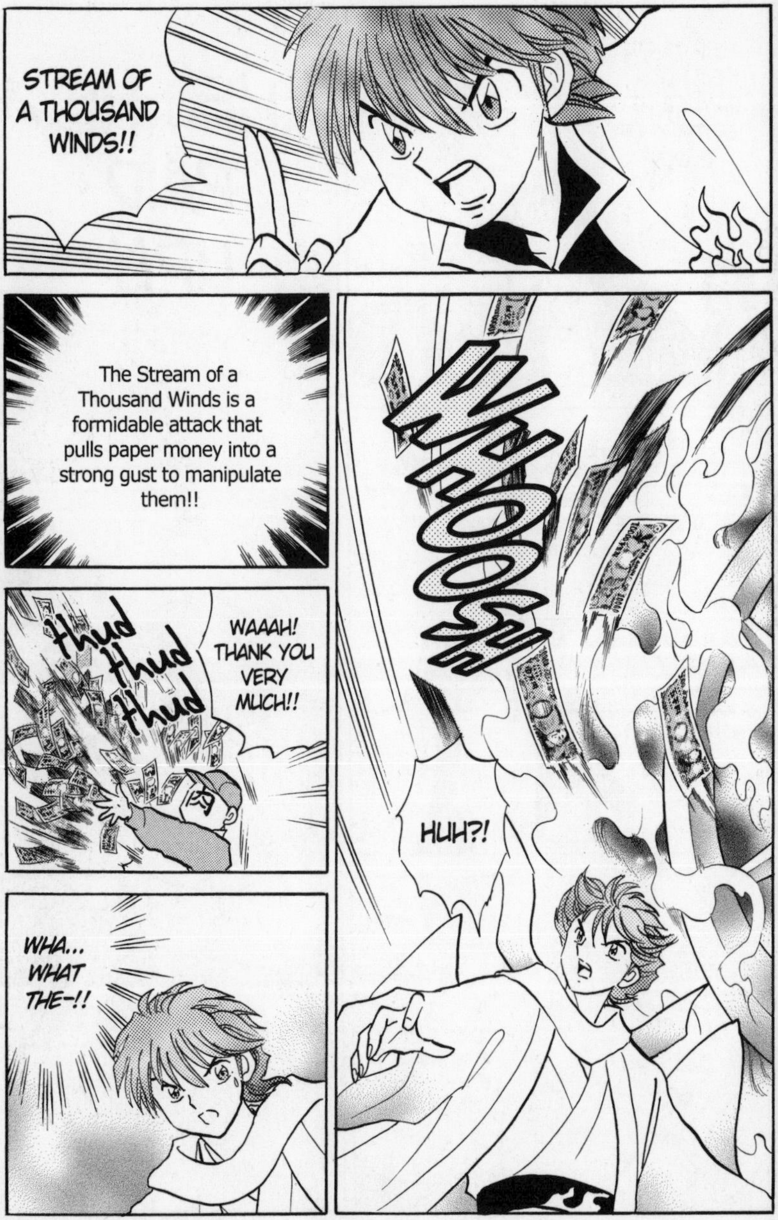
STREAM OF A THOUSAND WINDS!!
WHOOSH
HUH?!
The Stream of a Thousand Winds is a formidable attack that pulls paper money into a strong gust to manipulate them!!
WAAAH! THANK YOU VERY MUCH!!
thud thud thud
WHA... WHAT THE-!!

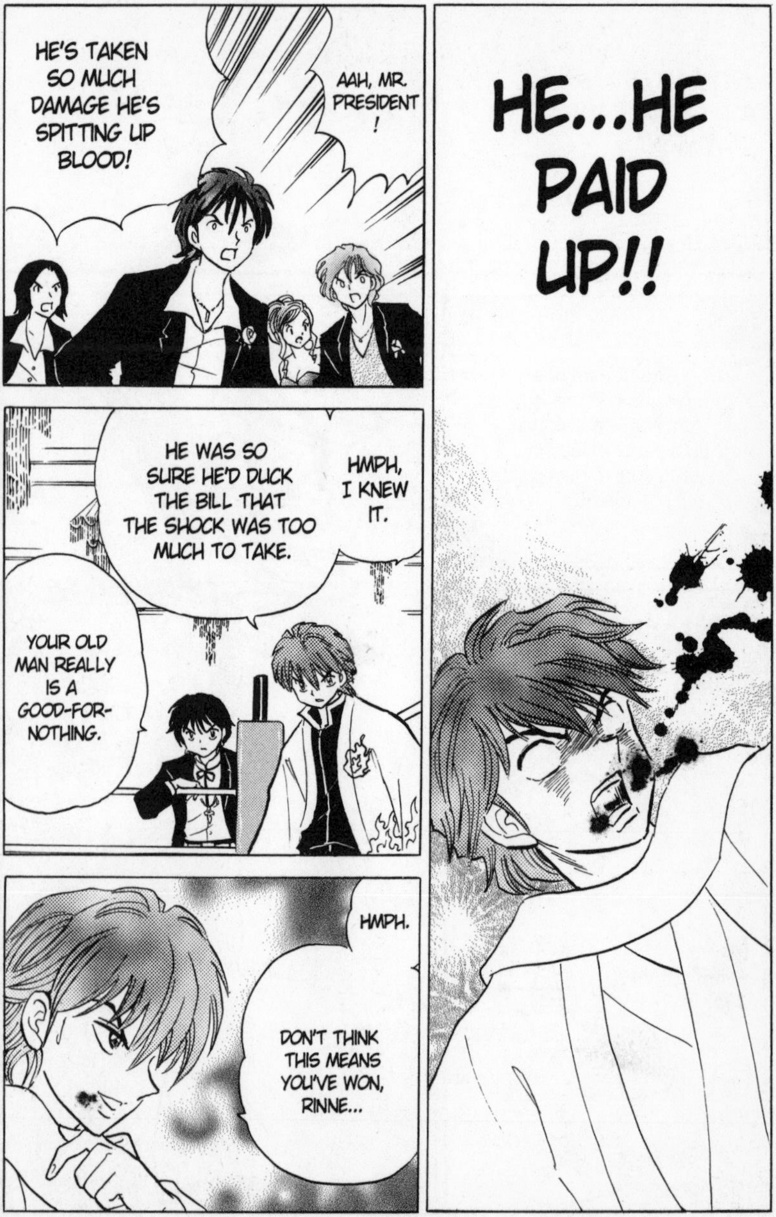
HE...HE PAID UP!!
AAH, MR. PRESIDENT!
HE'S TAKEN SO MUCH DAMAGE HE'S SPITTING UP BLOOD!
HMPH, I KNEW IT.
HE WAS SO SURE HE'D DUCK THE BILL THAT THE SHOCK WAS TOO MUCH TO TAKE.
YOUR OLD MAN REALLY IS A GOOD-FOR-NOTHING.
HMPH.
DON'T THINK THIS MEANS YOU'VE WON, RINNE...

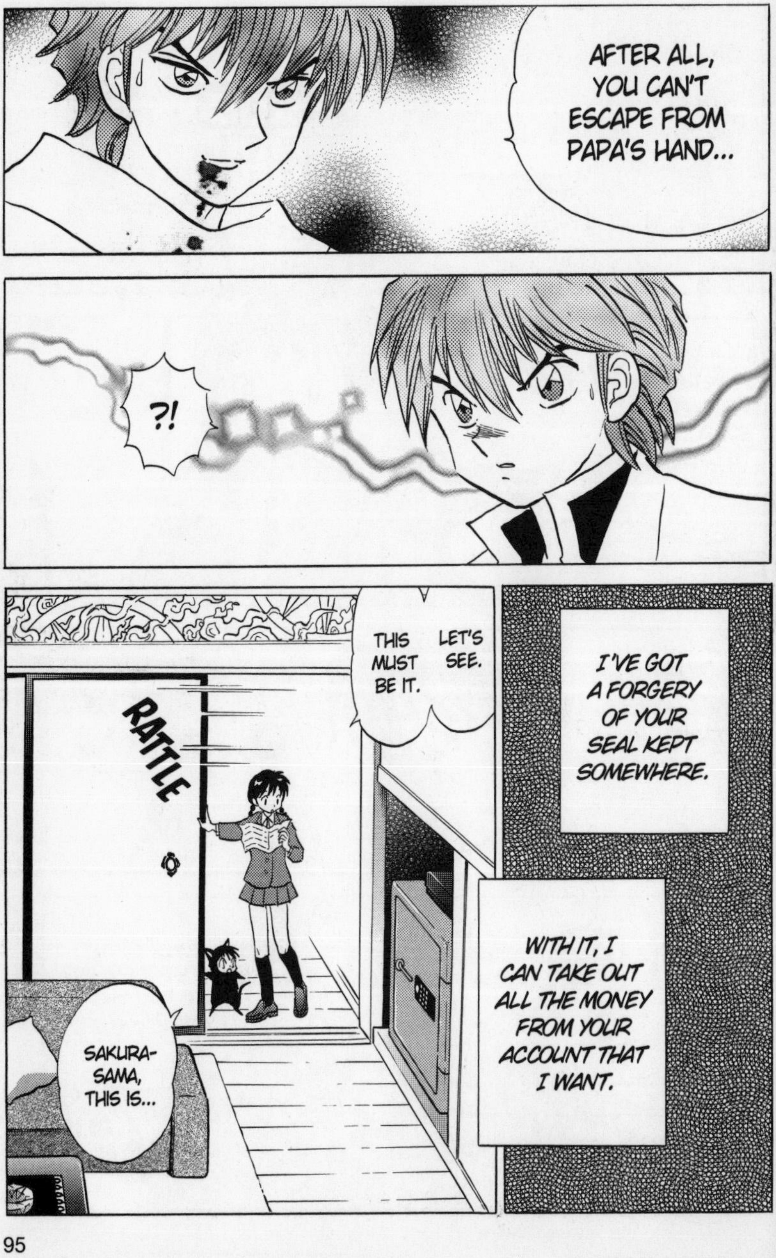
AFTER ALL, YOU CAN'T ESCAPE FROM PAPA'S HAND...
?!
I'VE GOT A FORGERY OF YOUR SEAL KEPT SOMEWHERE.
WITH IT, I CAN TAKE OUT ALL THE MONEY FROM YOUR ACCOUNT THAT I WANT.
LET'S SEE.
THIS MUST BE IT.
RATTLE
SAKURA-SAMA, THIS IS...

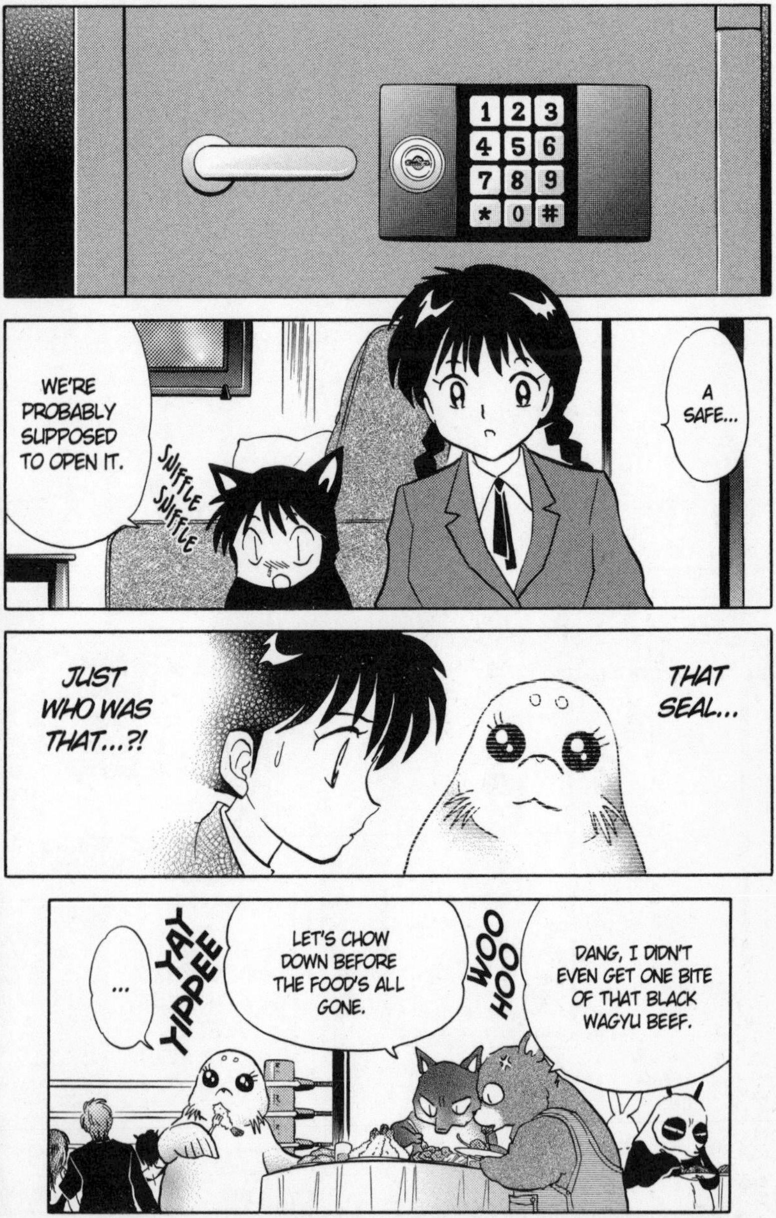
A SAFE...
SNIFFLE SNIFFLE
WE'RE PROBABLY SUPPOSED TO OPEN IT.
THAT SEAL...
JUST WHO WAS THAT...?!
DANG, I DIDN'T EVEN GET ONE BITE OF THAT BLACK WAGYU BEEF.
WOO HOO
LET'S CHOW DOWN BEFORE THE FOOD'S ALL GONE.
YAY YIPPEE
...

CHAPTER 34: HANDPRINT

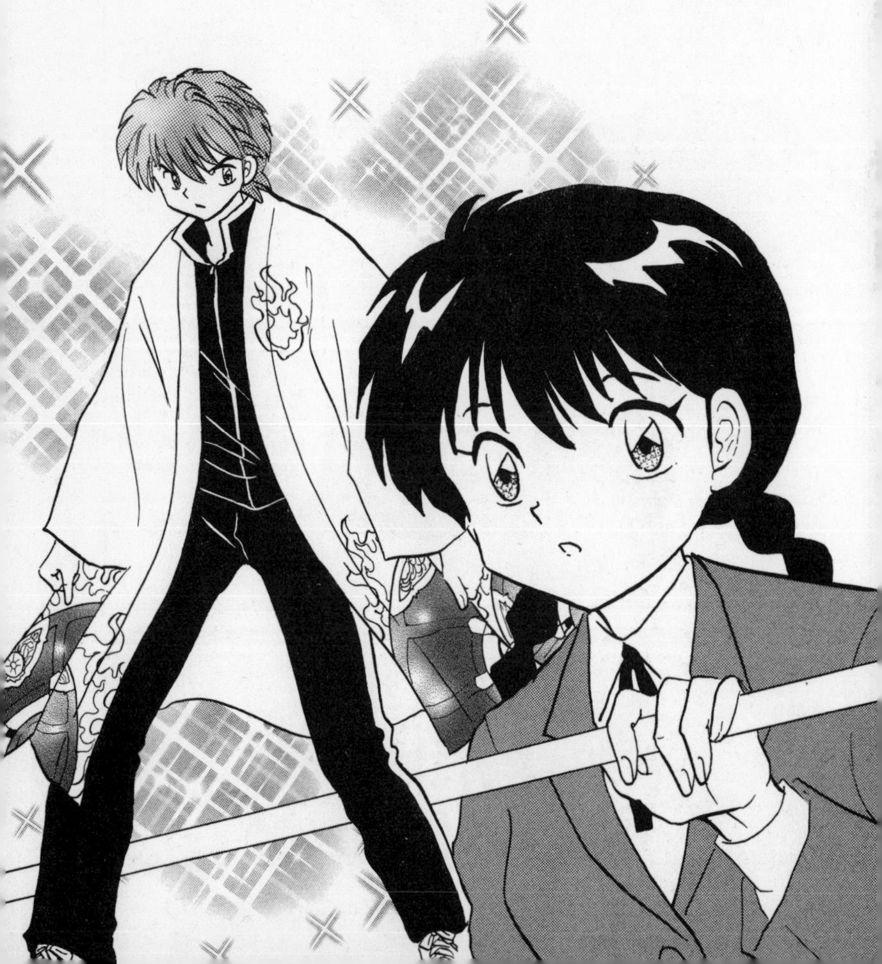

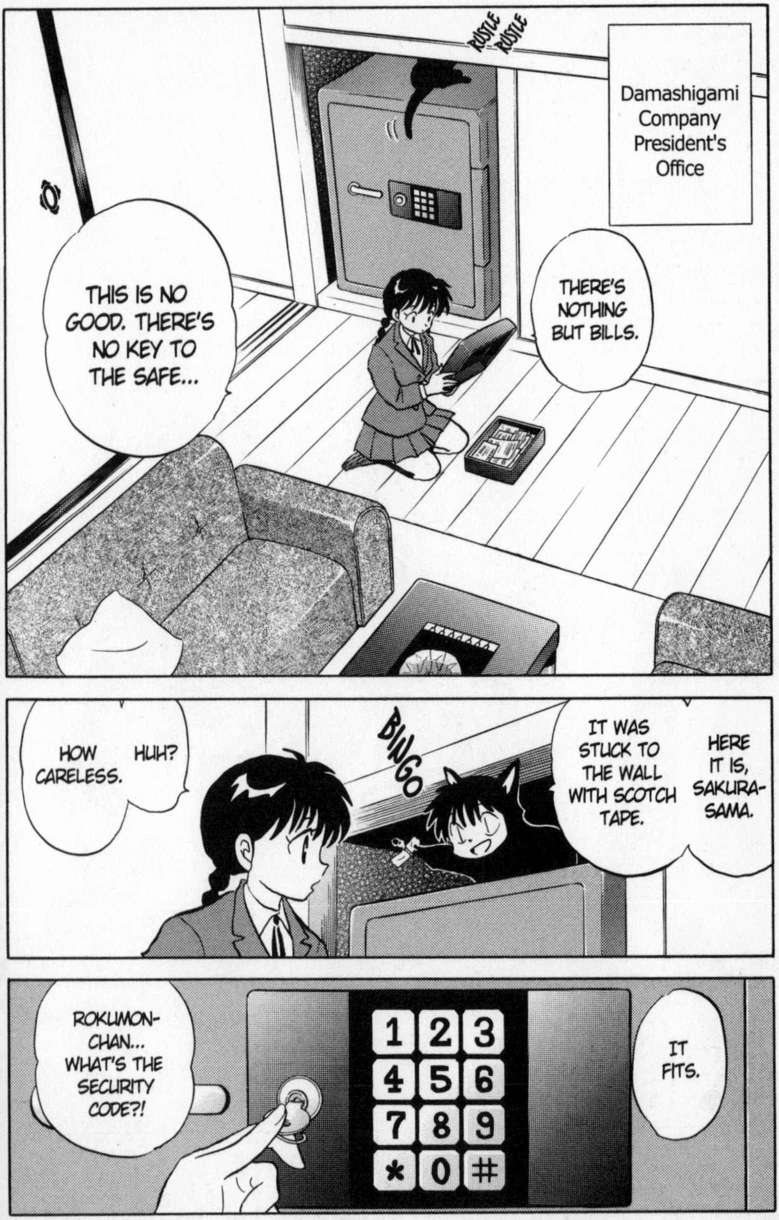
Damashigami Company President's Office
RUSTLE RUSTLE
THERE'S NOTHING BUT BILLS.
THIS IS NO GOOD. THERE'S NO KEY TO THE SAFE...
HERE IT IS, SAKURA-SAMA.
IT WAS STUCK TO THE WALL WITH SCOTCH TAPE.
BINGO
HUH?
HOW CARELESS.
IT FITS.
1 2 3
4 5 6
7 8 9
* 0 #
ROKUMON-CHAN... WHAT'S THE SECURITY CODE?!

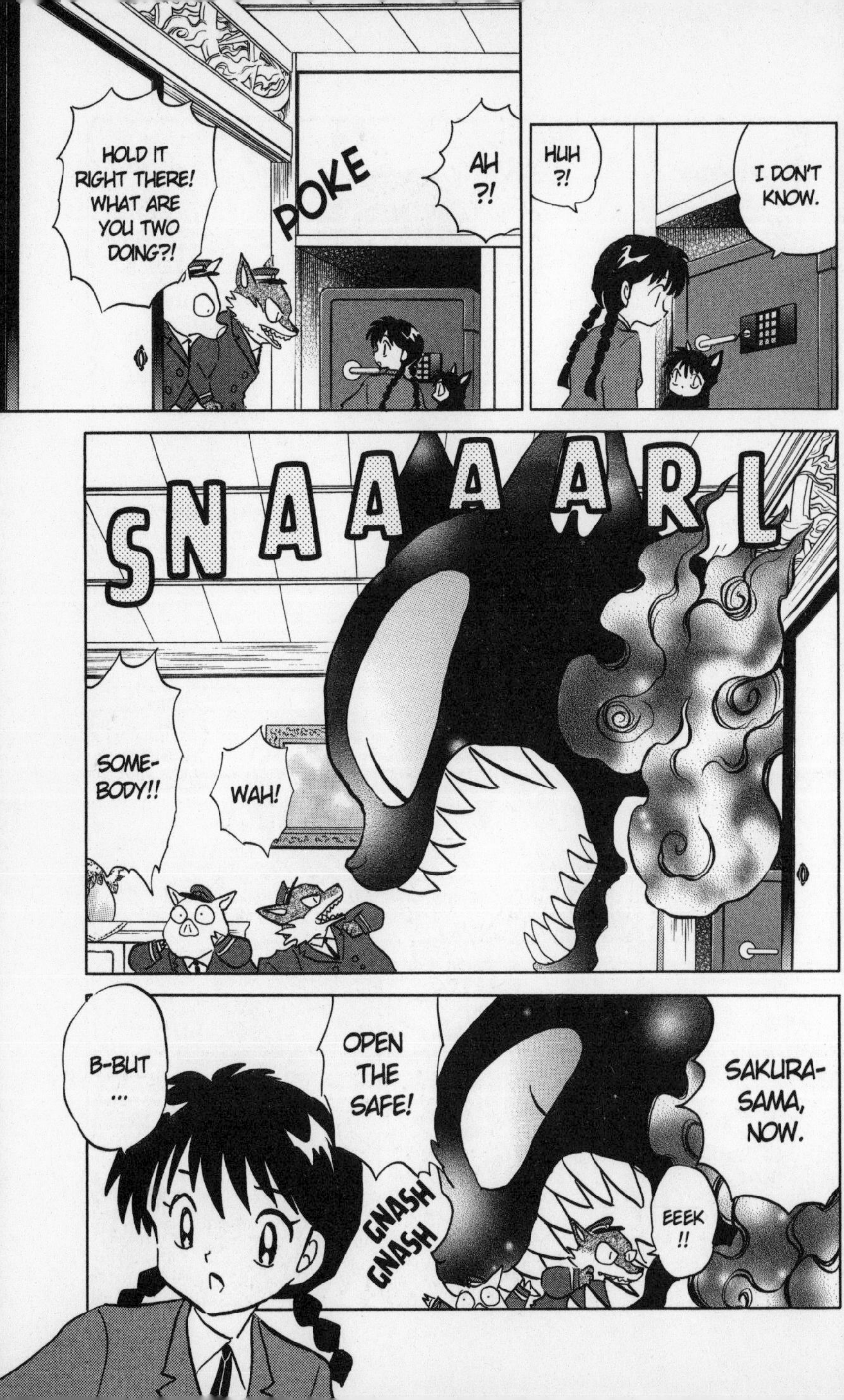
I DON'T KNOW.
HUH ?!
AH ?!
POKE
HOLD IT RIGHT THERE! WHAT ARE YOU TWO DOING?!
SNAAAARL
WAH!
SOME-BODY!!
SAKURA-SAMA, NOW.
EEEK !!
OPEN THE SAFE!
GNASH GNASH
B-BUT ...

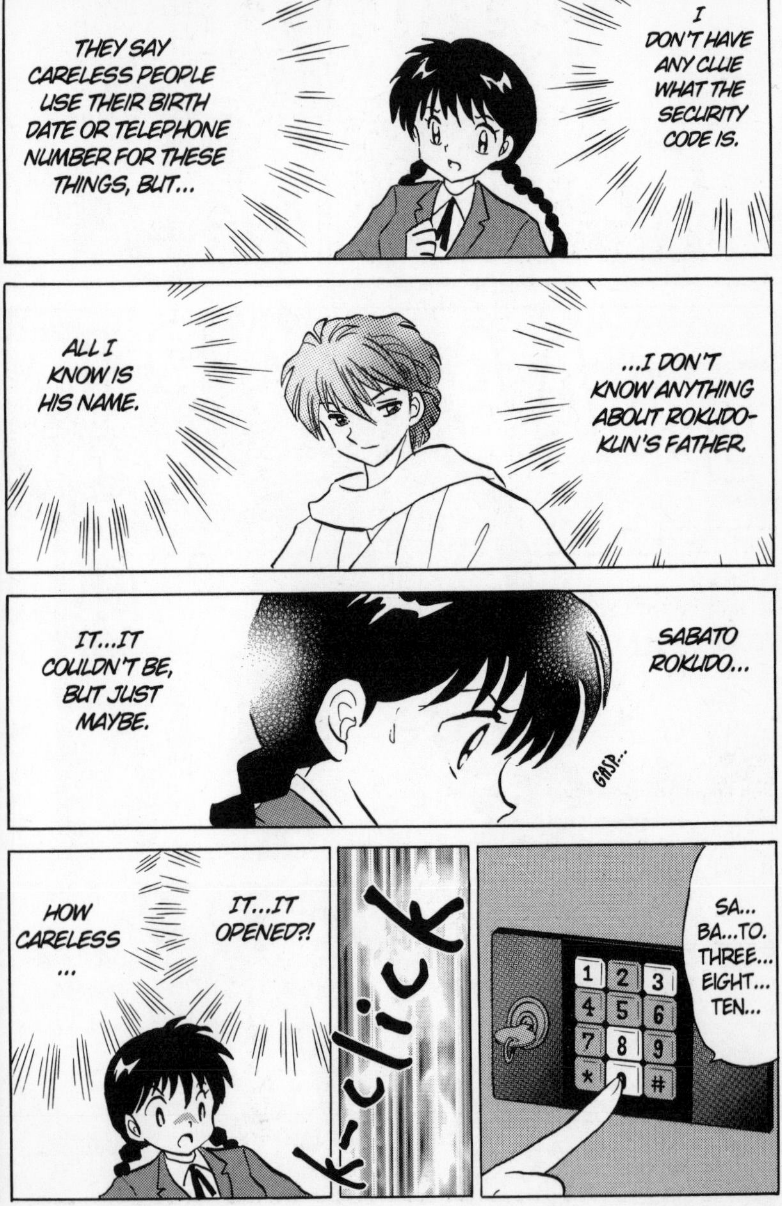
I DON'T HAVE ANY CLUE WHAT THE SECURITY CODE IS.
THEY SAY CARELESS PEOPLE USE THEIR BIRTH DATE OR TELEPHONE NUMBER FOR THESE THINGS, BUT...
...I DON'T KNOW ANYTHING ABOUT ROKUDO-KUN'S FATHER.
ALL I KNOW IS HIS NAME.
SABATO ROKUDO...
GASP...
IT...IT COULDN'T BE, BUT JUST MAYBE.
SA... BA...TO. THREE... EIGHT... TEN...
K-CLICK
IT...IT OPENED?!
HOW CARELESS...

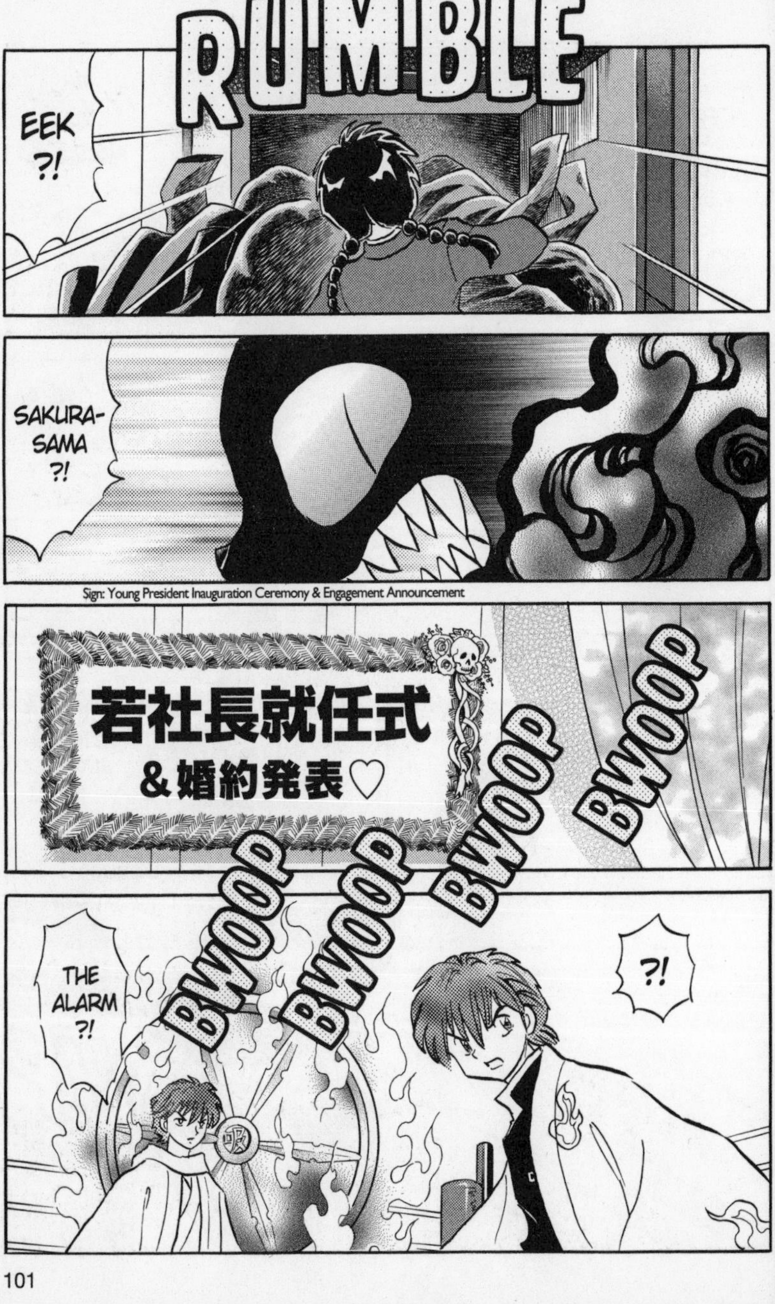

RUMBLE
EEK ?!
SAKURA-SAMA ?!
Sign: Young President Inauguration Ceremony & Engagement Announcement
若社長就任式
&婚約発表♡
BWOOP
BWOOP
BWOOP
BWOOP
?!
THE ALARM ?!

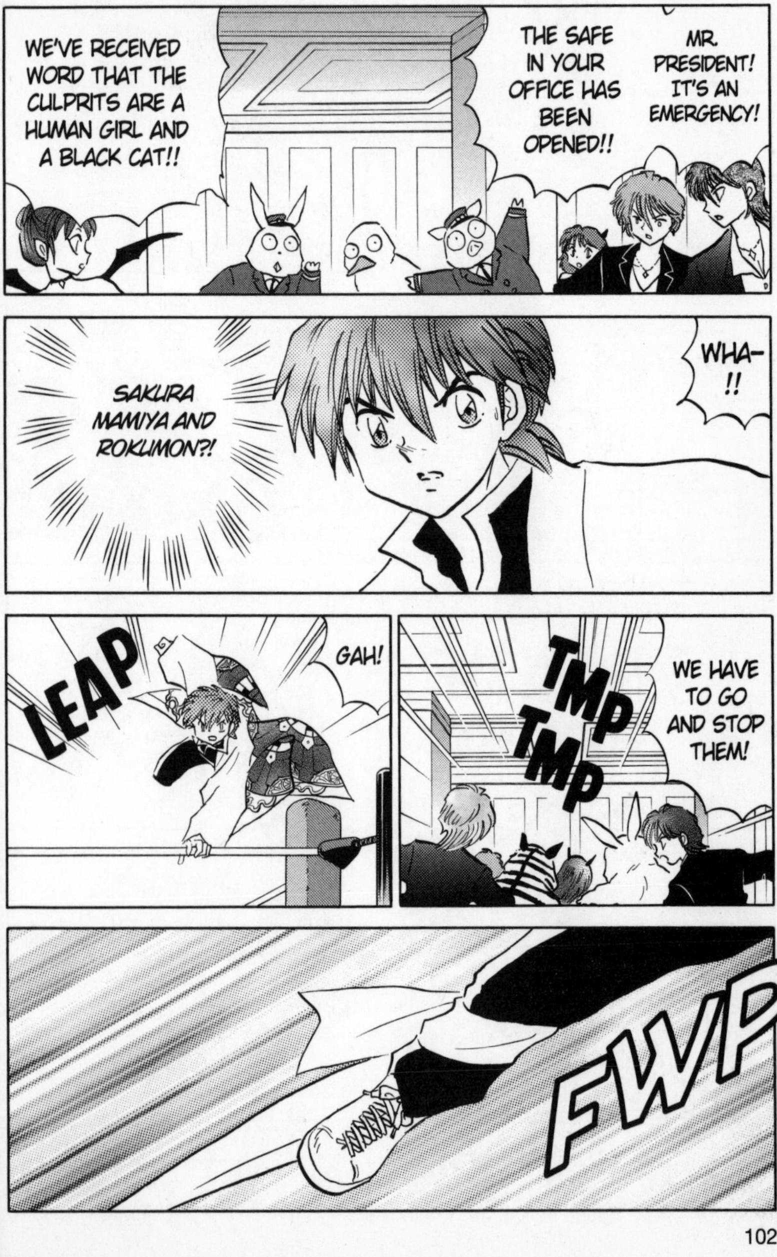
MR. PRESIDENT! IT'S AN EMERGENCY!
THE SAFE IN YOUR OFFICE HAS BEEN OPENED!!
WE'VE RECEIVED WORD THAT THE CULPRITS ARE A HUMAN GIRL AND A BLACK CAT!!
WHA- !!
SAKURA MAMIYA AND ROKUMON?!
WE HAVE TO GO AND STOP THEM!
TMP TMP
GAH!
LEAP
FWP

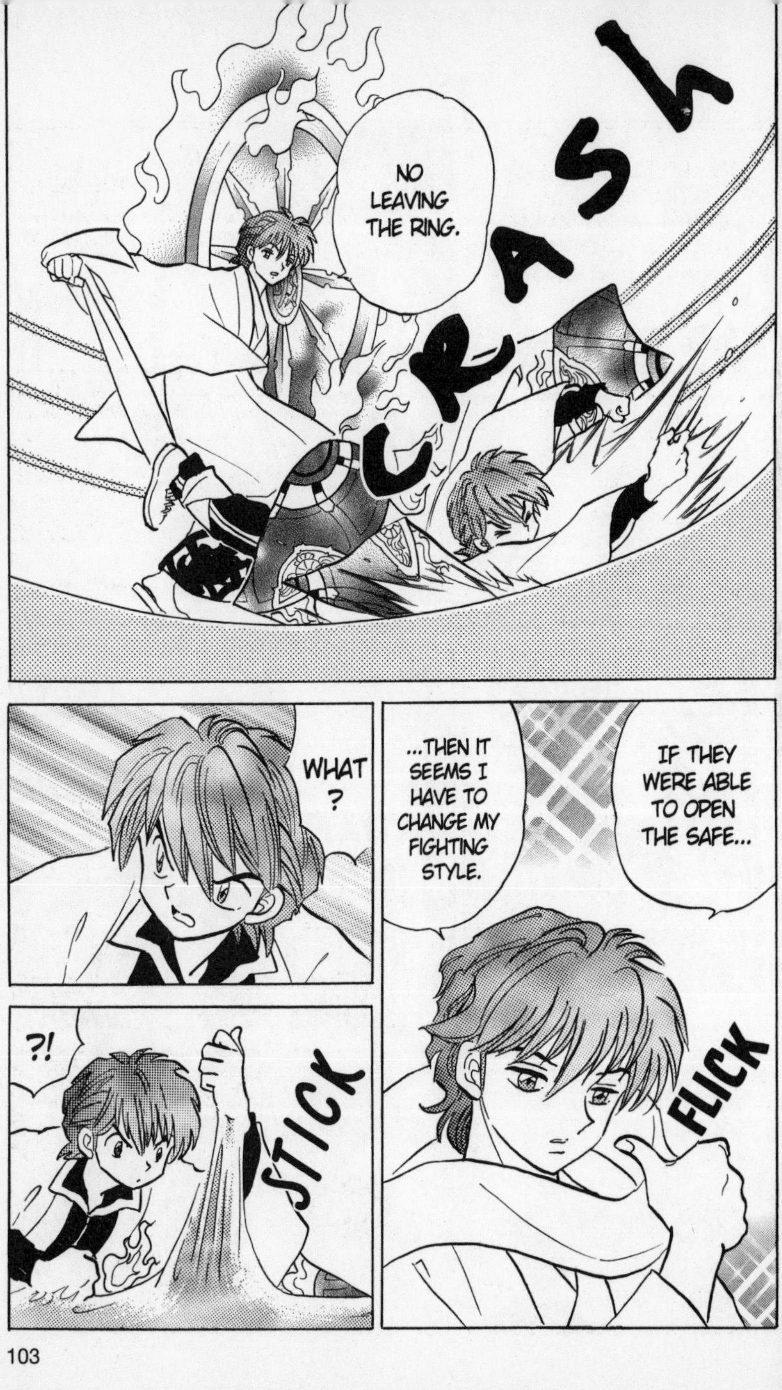
NO LEAVING THE RING.
CRASH
IF THEY WERE ABLE TO OPEN THE SAFE...
...THEN IT SEEMS I HAVE TO CHANGE MY FIGHTING STYLE.
FLICK
WHAT?
?!
STICK

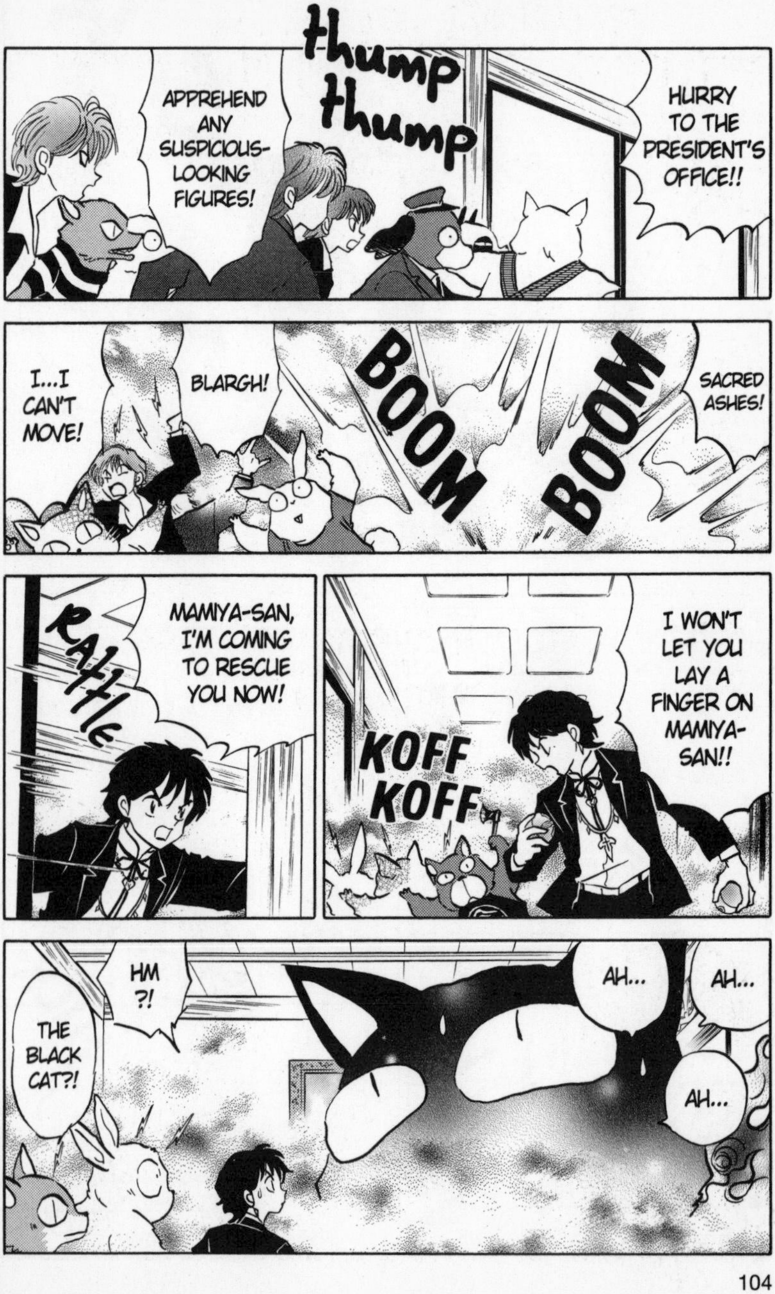
HURRY TO THE PRESIDENT'S OFFICE!!
thump thump
APPREHEND ANY SUSPICIOUS-LOOKING FIGURES!
SACRED ASHES!
BOOM
BOOM
BLARGH!
I...I CAN'T MOVE!
I WON'T LET YOU LAY A FINGER ON MAMIYA-SAN!!
KOFF KOFF
MAMIYA-SAN, I'M COMING TO RESCUE YOU NOW!
RATTLE
AH...
AH...
AH...
HM ?!
THE BLACK CAT?!

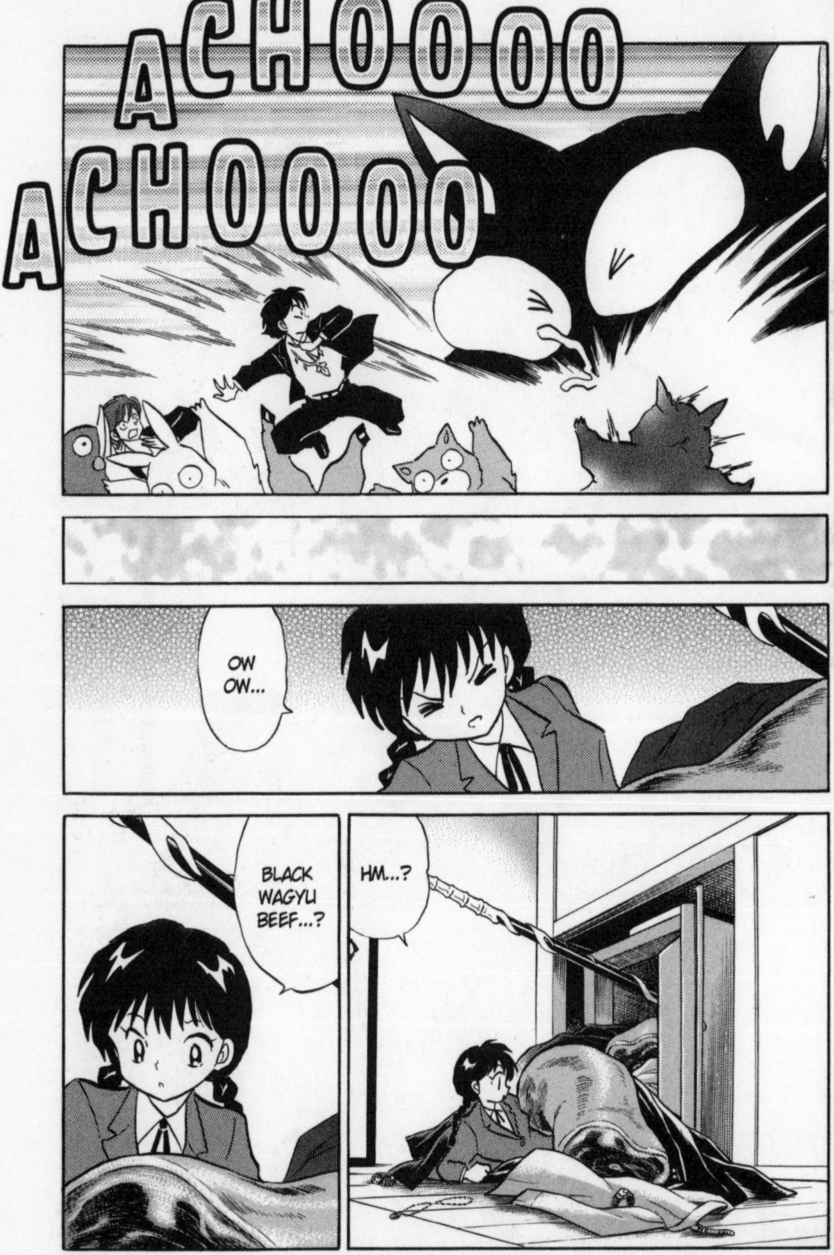
ACHOOOO
ACHOOOO
OW OW...
HM...?
BLACK WAGYU BEEF...?

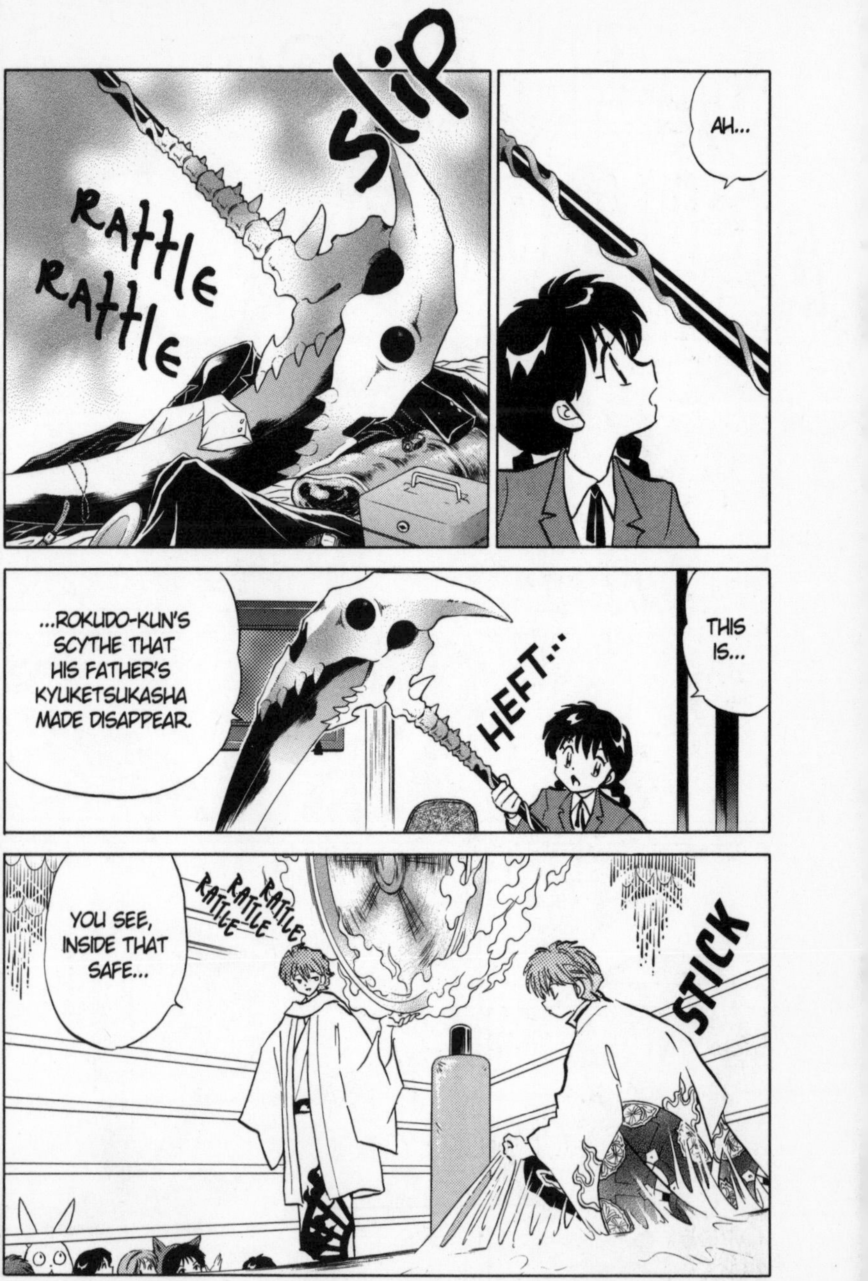
AH...
SLIP
RATTLE RATTLE
THIS IS...
HEFT...
...ROKUDO-KUN'S SCYTHE THAT HIS FATHER'S KYUKETSUKASHA MADE DISAPPEAR.
STICK
RATTLE RATTLE
YOU SEE, INSIDE THAT SAFE...

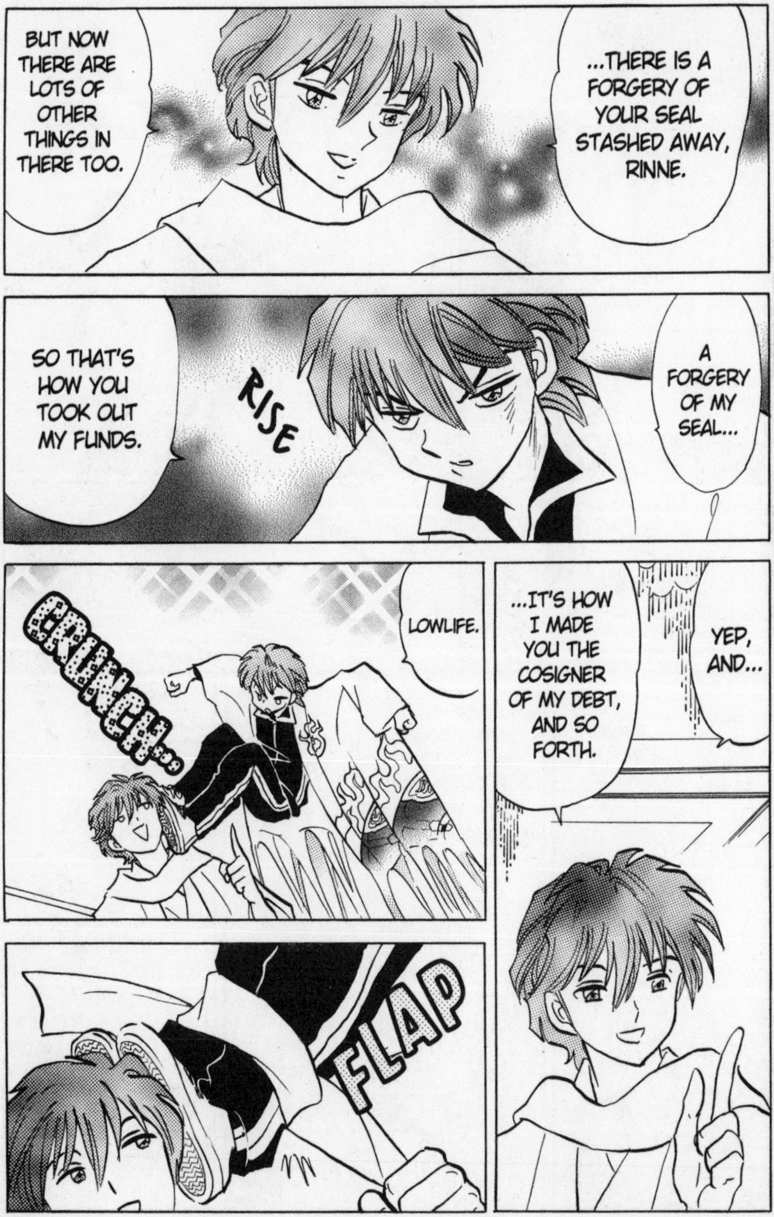
...THERE IS A FORGERY OF YOUR SEAL STASHED AWAY, RINNE.
BUT NOW THERE ARE LOTS OF OTHER THINGS IN THERE TOO.
A FORGERY OF MY SEAL...
RISE
SO THAT'S HOW YOU TOOK OUT MY FUNDS.
YEP, AND...
...IT'S HOW I MADE YOU THE COSIGNER OF MY DEBT, AND SO FORTH.
LOWLIFE.
CRUNCH...
FLAP

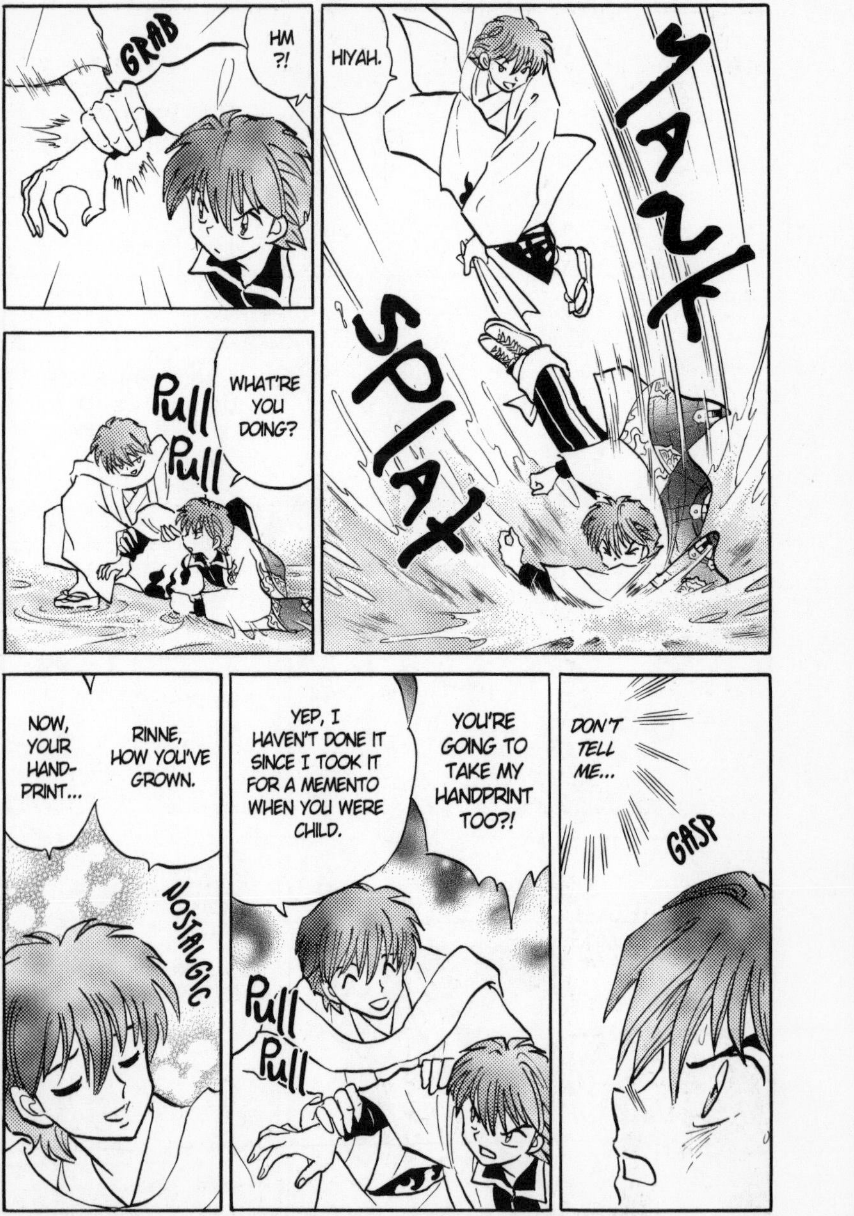
HIYAH.
SPLAT
HM ?!
GRAB
WHAT'RE YOU DOING?
Pull
Pull
DON'T TELL ME...
GASP
YOU'RE GOING TO TAKE MY HANDPRINT TOO?!
YEP, I HAVEN'T DONE IT SINCE I TOOK IT FOR A MEMENTO WHEN YOU WERE CHILD.
Pull
Pull
RINNE, HOW YOU'VE GROWN.
NOW, YOUR HAND-PRINT...
NOSTALGIC

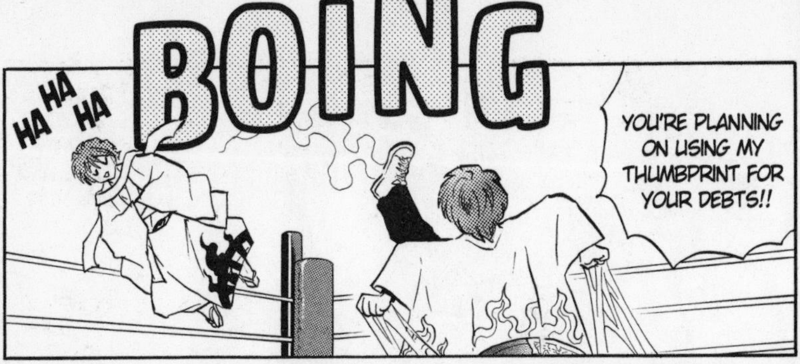
YOU'RE PLANNING ON USING MY THUMBPRINT FOR YOUR DEBTS!!
BOING
HA HA HA

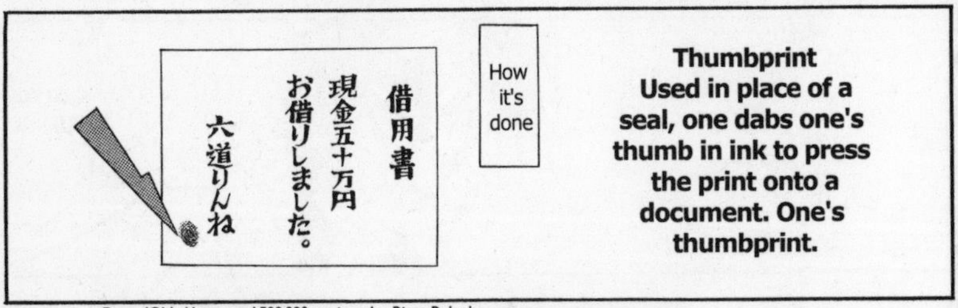
Thumbprint
Used in place of a seal, one dabs one's thumb in ink to press the print onto a document. One's thumbprint.
How it's done
借用書
現金五十万円お借りしました。
六道りんね

Paper: IOU I borrowed 500,000 yen in cash. Rinne Rokudo

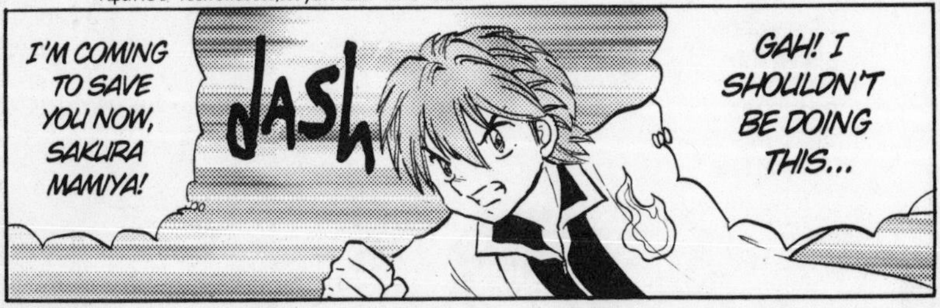
GAH! I SHOULDN'T BE DOING THIS...
DASH
I'M COMING TO SAVE YOU NOW, SAKURA MAMIYA!

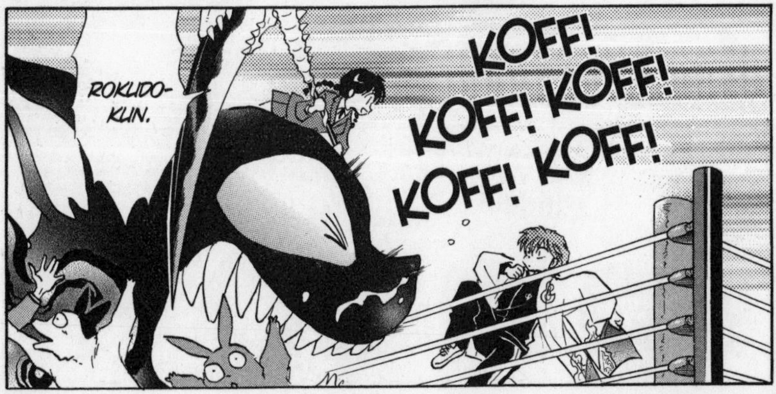
KOFF! KOFF! KOFF! KOFF! KOFF!
ROKUDO-KUN.

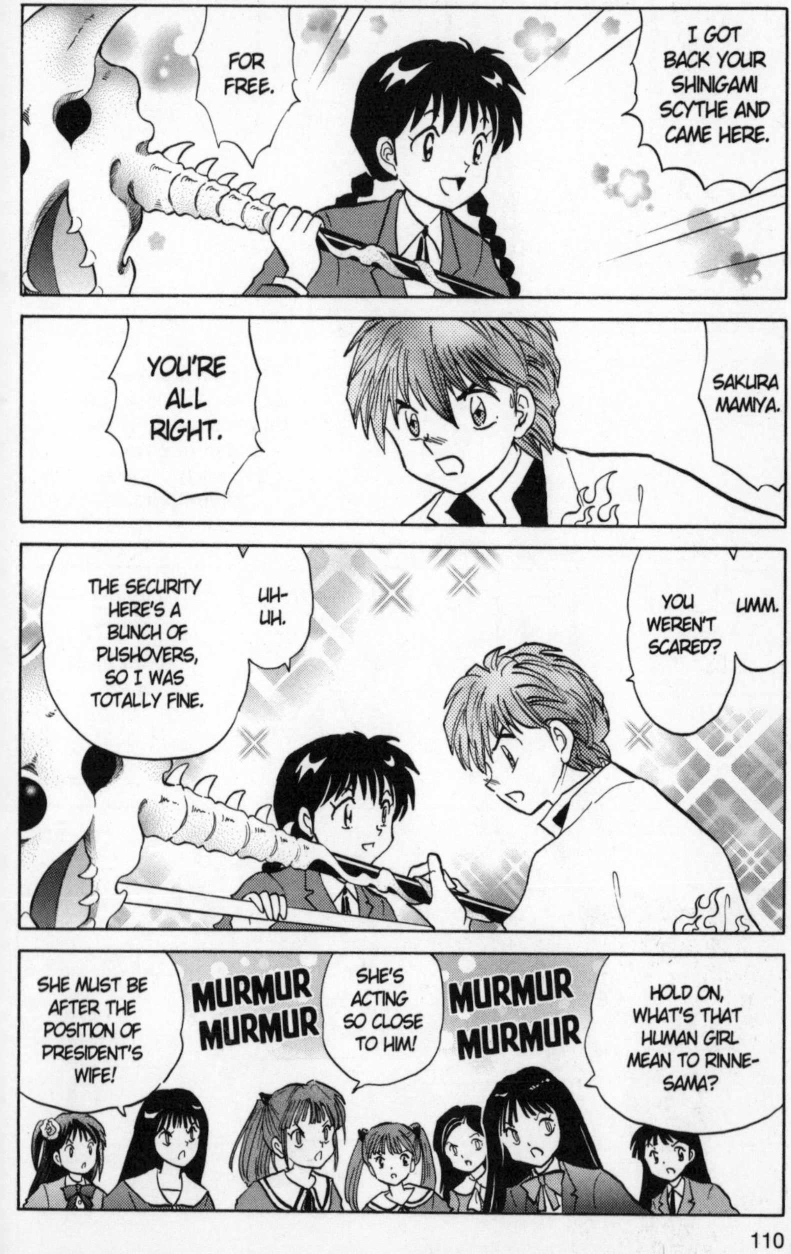
I GOT BACK YOUR SHINIGAMI SCYTHE AND CAME HERE.
FOR FREE.
SAKURA MAMIYA.
YOU'RE ALL RIGHT.
UMM.
YOU WEREN'T SCARED?
UH-UH.
THE SECURITY HERE'S A BUNCH OF PUSHOVERS, SO I WAS TOTALLY FINE.
HOLD ON, WHAT'S THAT HUMAN GIRL MEAN TO RINNE-SAMA?
MURMUR MURMUR
SHE'S ACTING SO CLOSE TO HIM!
MURMUR MURMUR
SHE MUST BE AFTER THE POSITION OF PRESIDENT'S WIFE!

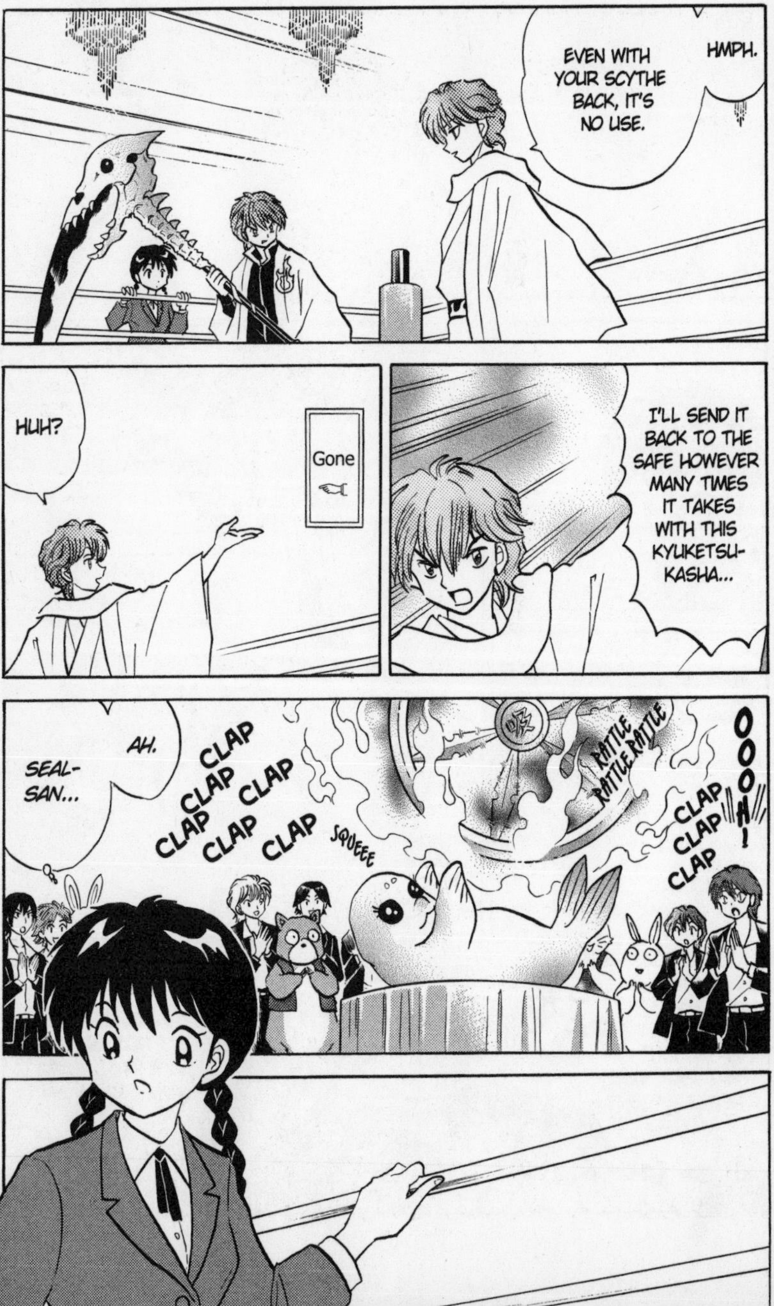
HMPH.
EVEN WITH YOUR SCYTHE BACK, IT'S NO USE.
I'LL SEND IT BACK TO THE SAFE HOWEVER MANY TIMES IT TAKES WITH THIS KYUKETSU-KASHA...
HUH?
Gone
OOOOH!
CLAP CLAP CLAP
RATTLE RATTLE RATTLE
SQUEEE
CLAP CLAP CLAP CLAP CLAP CLAP CLAP
AH.
SEAL-SAN...

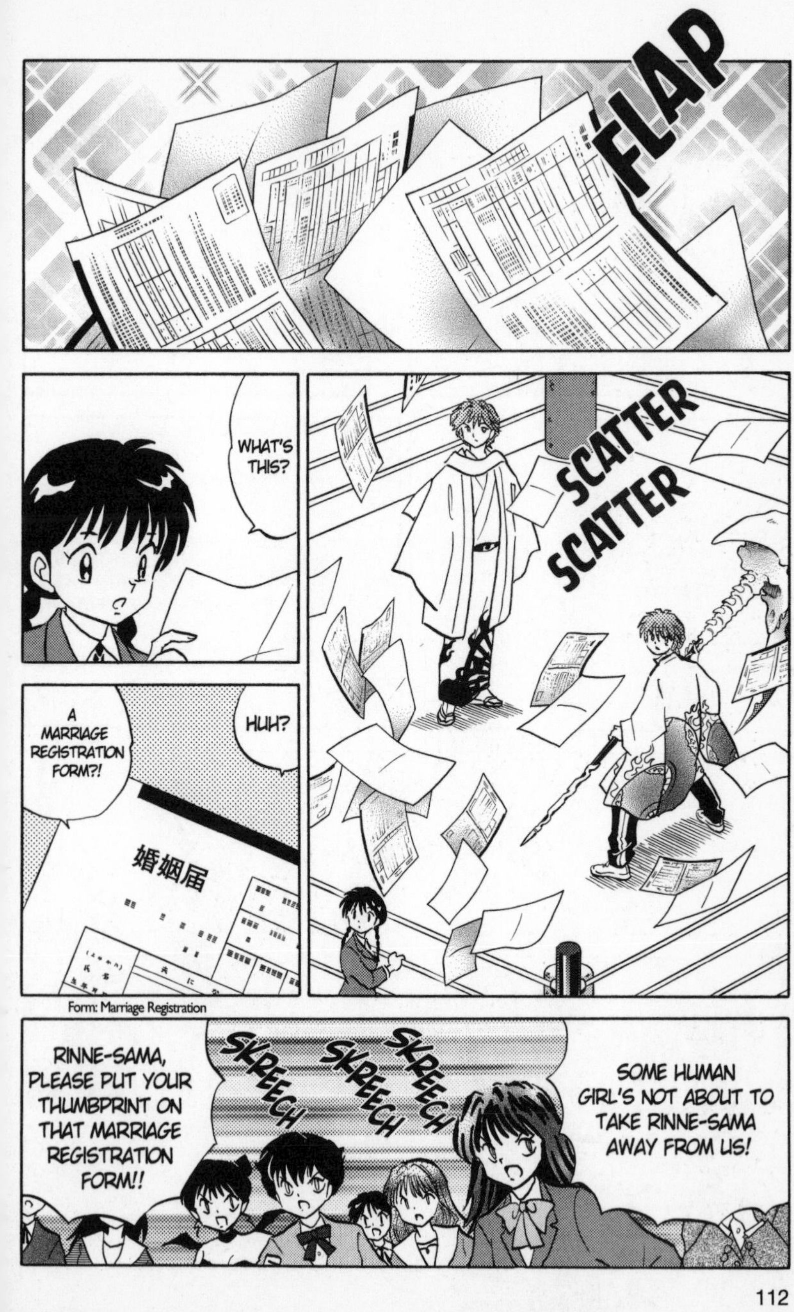
FLAP
SCATTER SCATTER
WHAT'S THIS?
HUH?
A MARRIAGE REGISTRATION FORM?!
婚姻届
SOME HUMAN GIRL'S NOT ABOUT TO TAKE RINNE-SAMA AWAY FROM US!
SKREECH SKREECH SKREECH
RINNE-SAMA, PLEASE PUT YOUR THUMBPRINT ON THAT MARRIAGE REGISTRATION FORM!!
Form: Marriage Registration

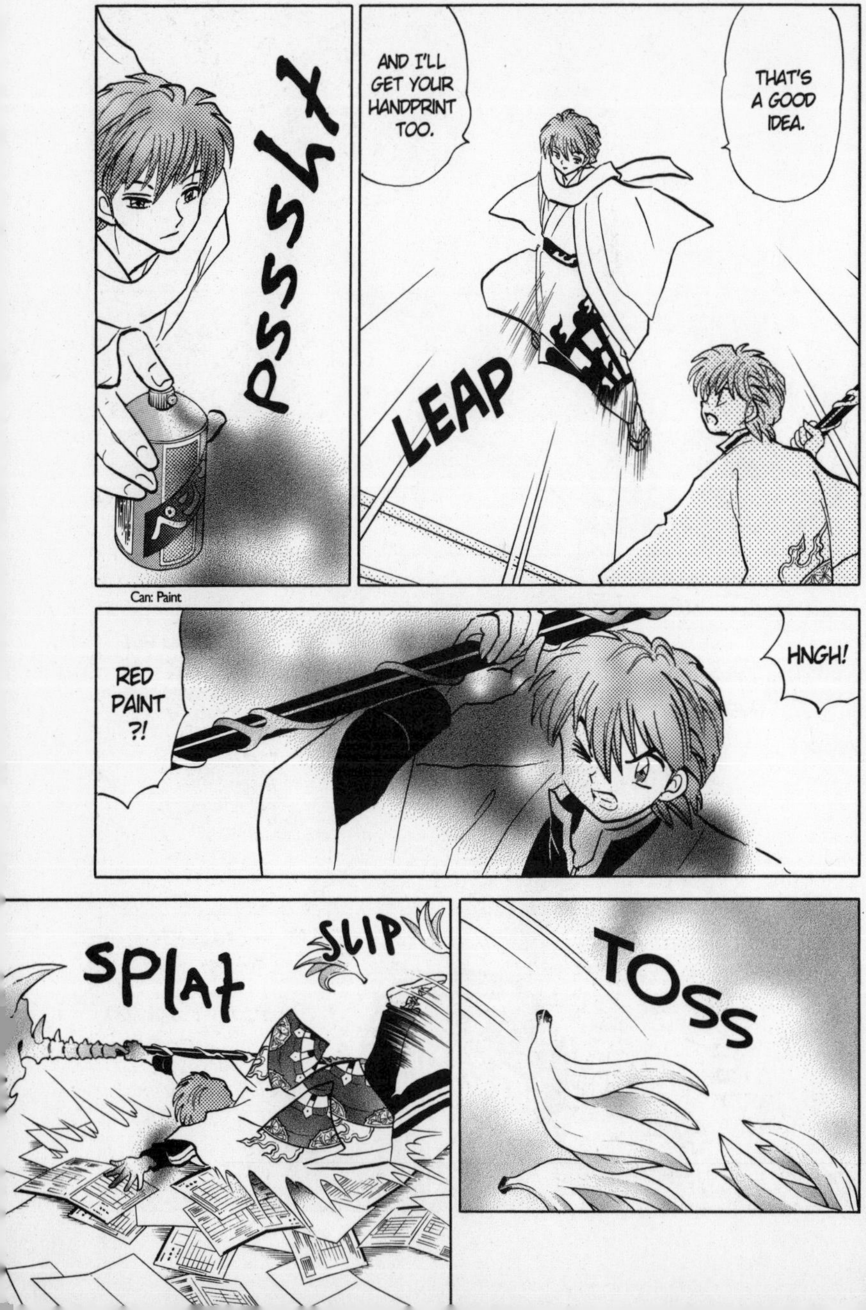
THAT'S A GOOD IDEA.
AND I'LL GET YOUR HANDPRINT TOO.
LEAP
PSSSHT
Can: Paint
HNGH!
RED PAINT ?!
TOSS
SLIP
SPLAT

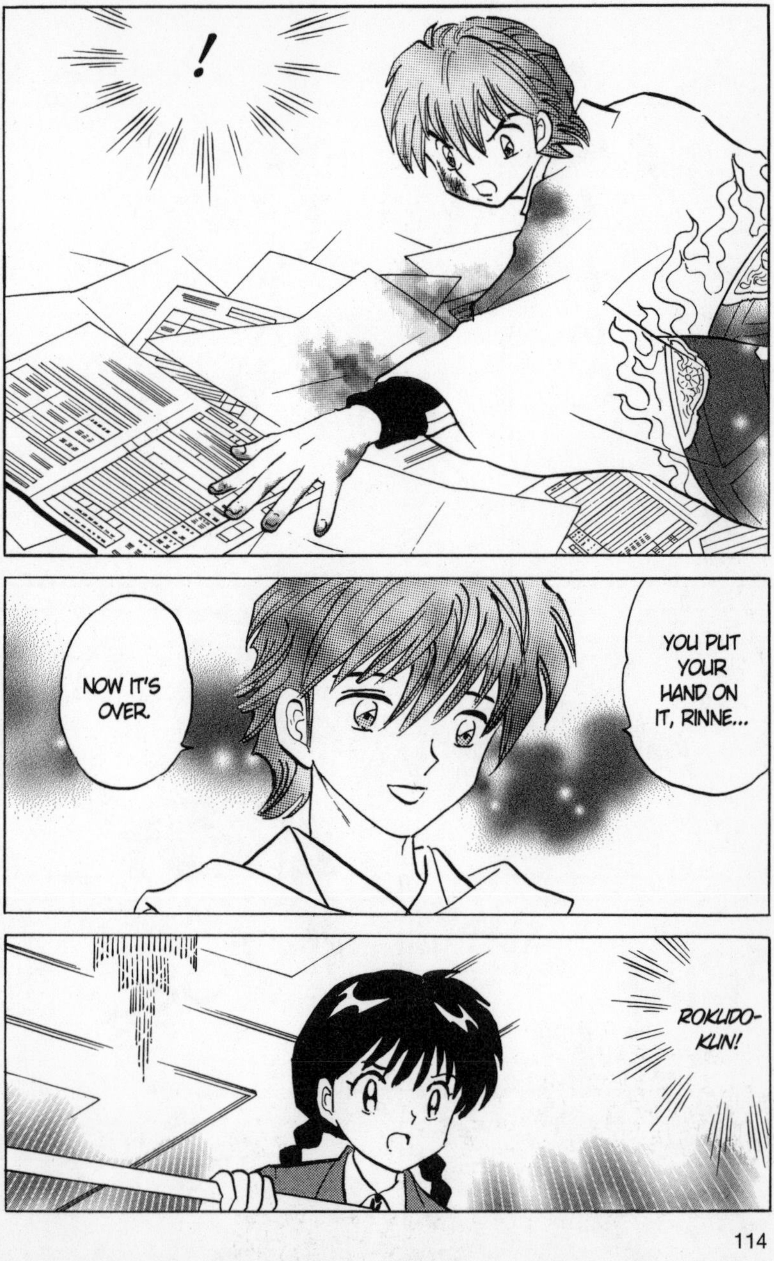
!
YOU PUT YOUR HAND ON IT, RINNE...
NOW IT'S OVER.
ROKUDO-KUN!

CHAPTER 35: YOU DON'T DISAPPROVE OF THAT?

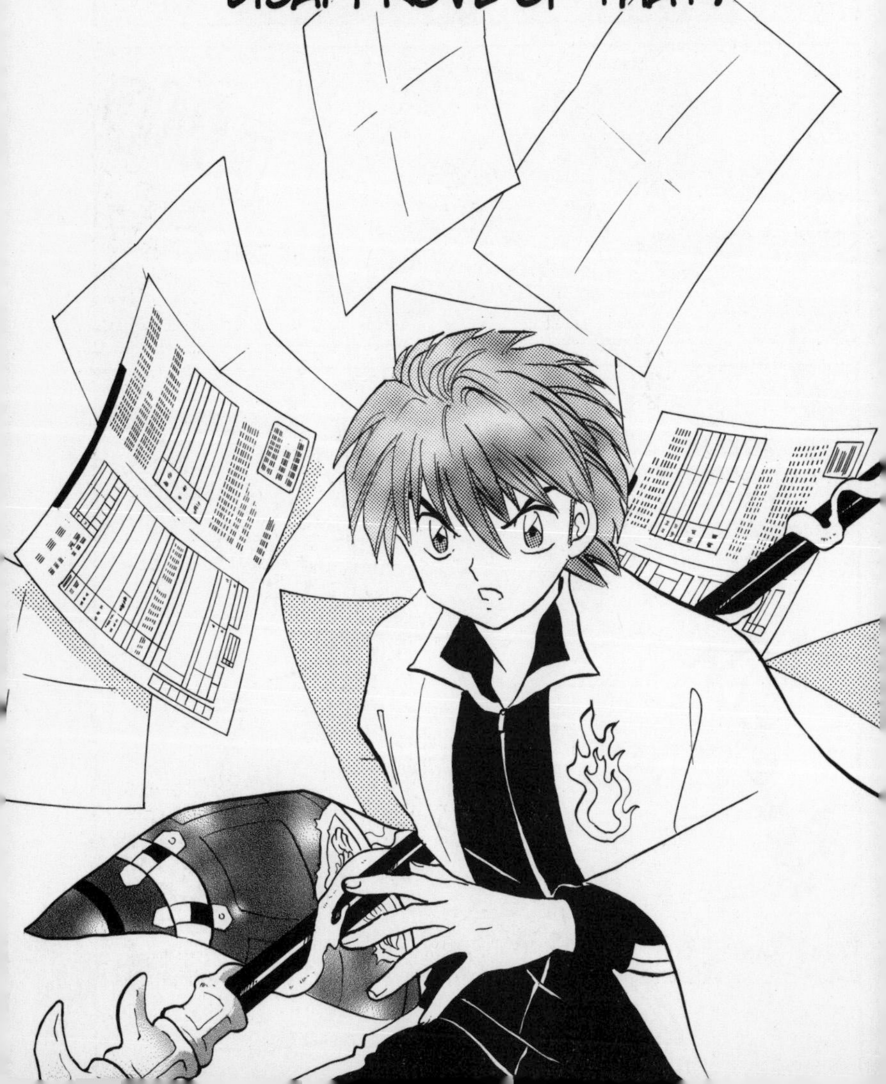

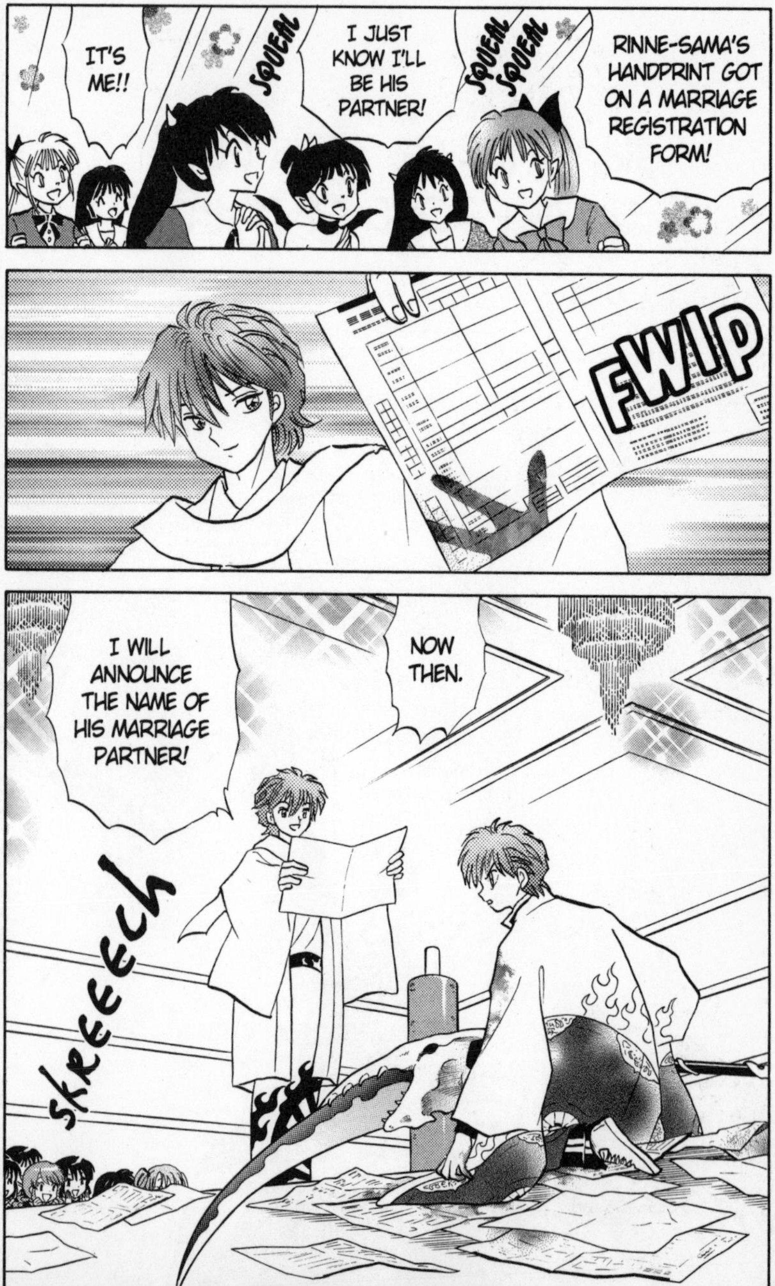
RINNE-SAMA'S HANDPRINT GOT ON A MARRIAGE REGISTRATION FORM!
SQUEAL SQUEAL
I JUST KNOW I'LL BE HIS PARTNER!
SQUEAL
IT'S ME!!
FWIP
NOW THEN.
I WILL ANNOUNCE THE NAME OF HIS MARRIAGE PARTNER!
SKREEECH

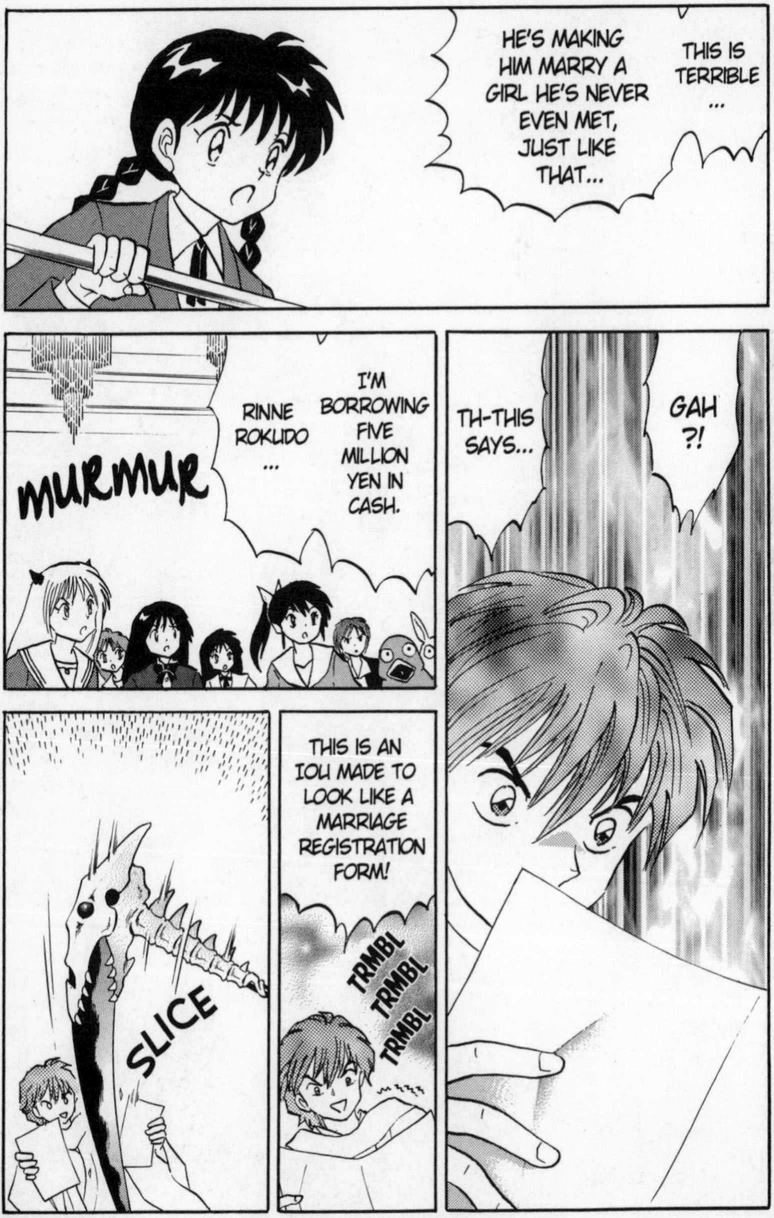
THIS IS TERRIBLE ...
HE'S MAKING HIM MARRY A GIRL HE'S NEVER EVEN MET, JUST LIKE THAT...
GAH ?!
TH-THIS SAYS...
RINNE ROKUDO ... I'M BORROWING FIVE MILLION YEN IN CASH.
MURMUR
THIS IS AN IOU MADE TO LOOK LIKE A MARRIAGE REGISTRATION FORM!
TRMBL TRMBL TRMBL
SLICE

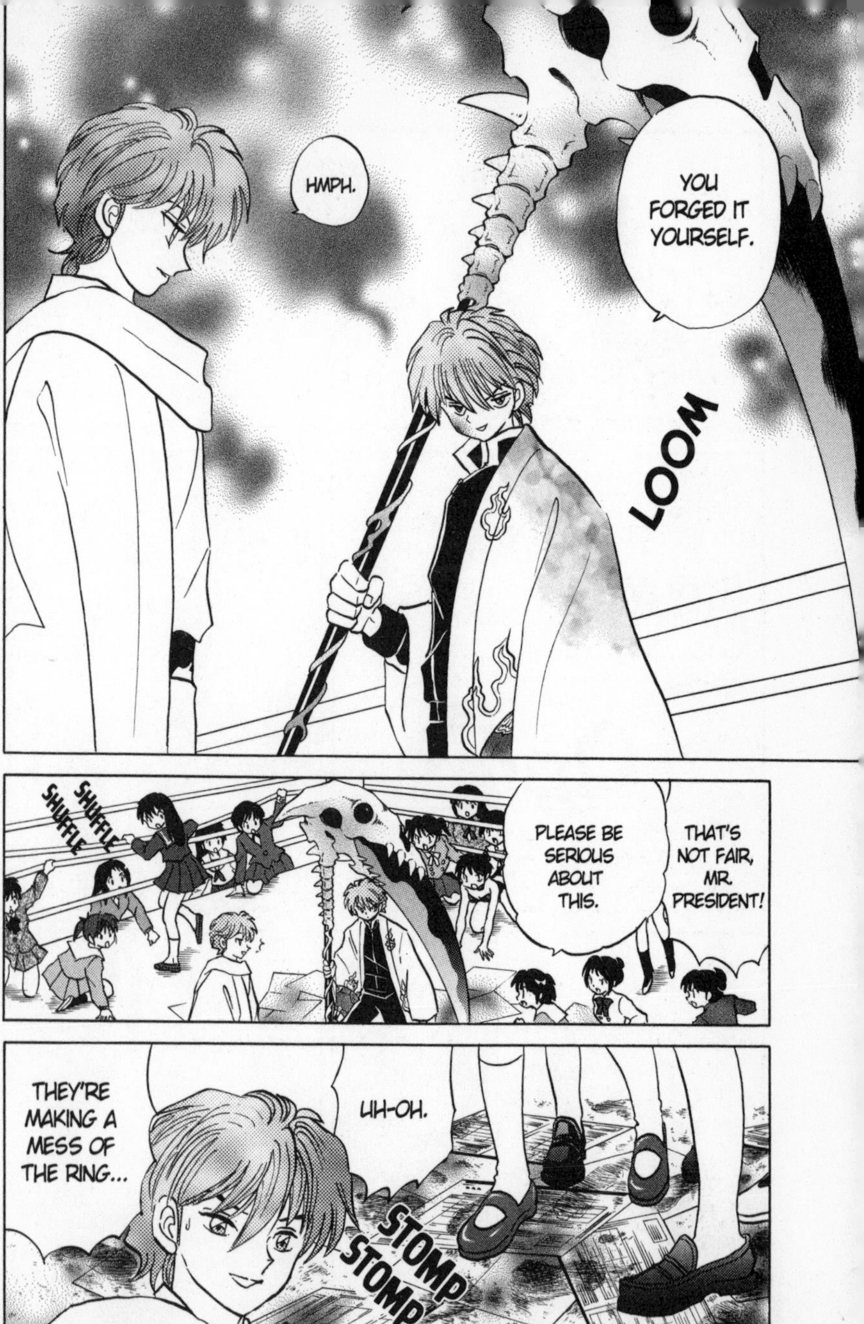
YOU FORGED IT YOURSELF.
LOOM
HMPH.
THAT'S NOT FAIR, MR. PRESIDENT!
PLEASE BE SERIOUS ABOUT THIS.
SHUFFLE SHUFFLE
UH-OH.
STOMP STOMP
THEY'RE MAKING A MESS OF THE RING...

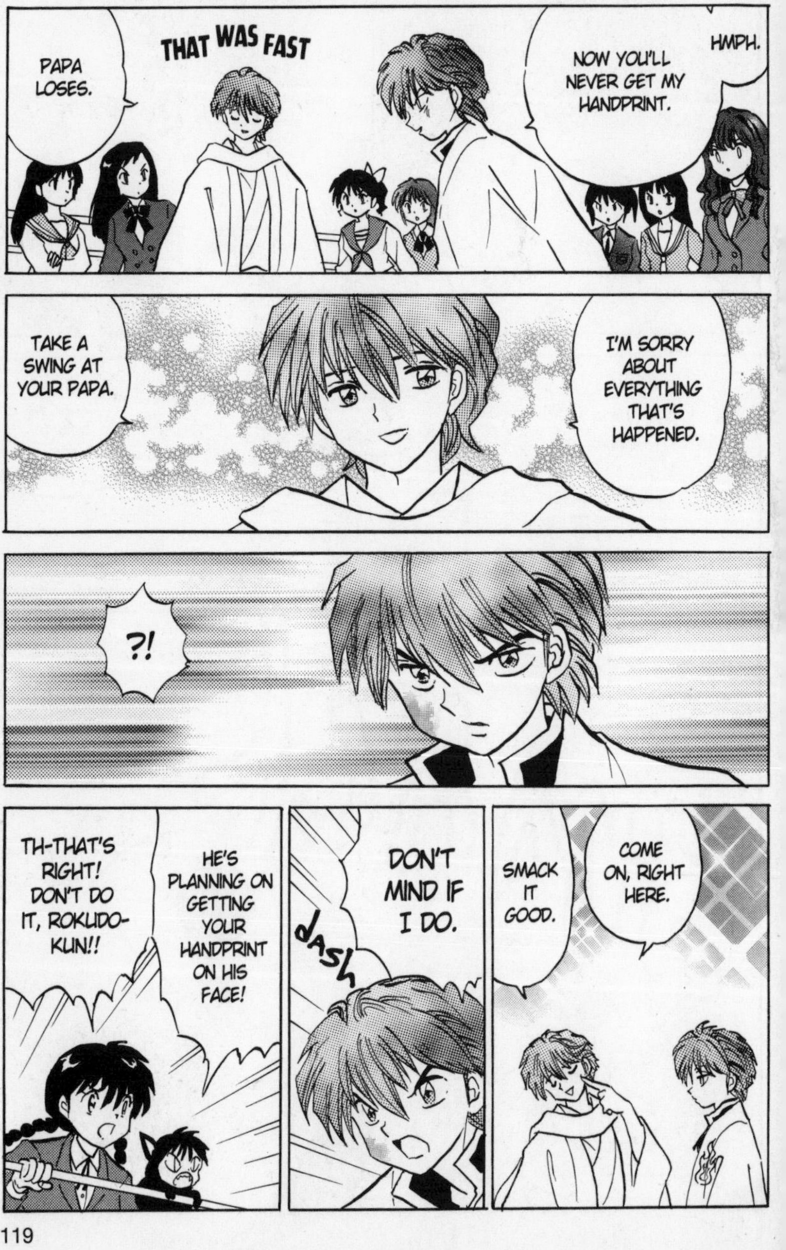
HMPH.
NOW YOU'LL NEVER GET MY HANDPRINT.
THAT WAS FAST
PAPA LOSES.
I'M SORRY ABOUT EVERYTHING THAT'S HAPPENED.
TAKE A SWING AT YOUR PAPA.
?!
COME ON, RIGHT HERE.
SMACK IT GOOD.
DON'T MIND IF I DO.
dash
HE'S PLANNING ON GETTING YOUR HANDPRINT ON HIS FACE!
TH-THAT'S RIGHT! DON'T DO IT, ROKUDO-KUN!!

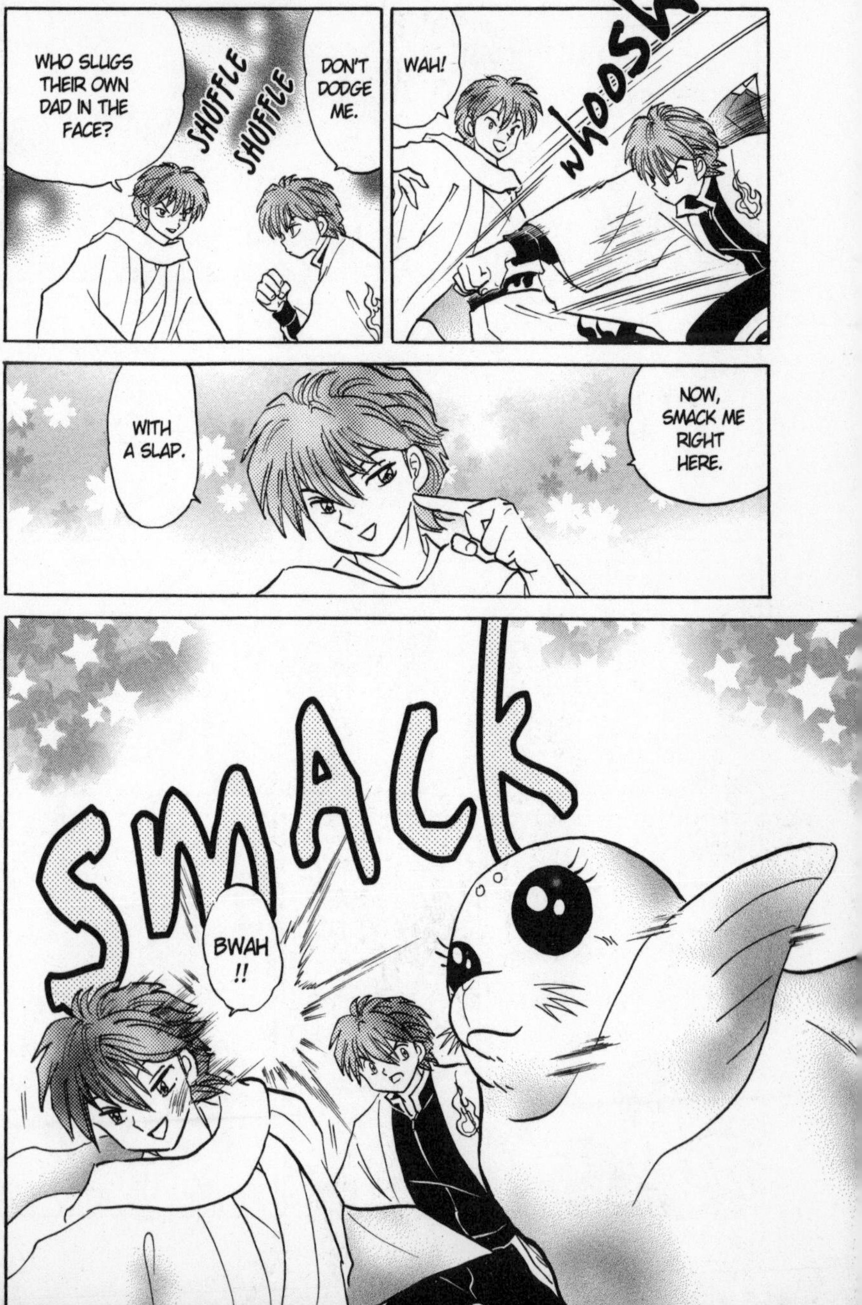
WAH!
whoosh
DON'T DODGE ME.
SHUFFLE SHUFFLE
WHO SLUGS THEIR OWN DAD IN THE FACE?
NOW, SMACK ME RIGHT HERE.
WITH A SLAP.
SMACK
BWAH !!

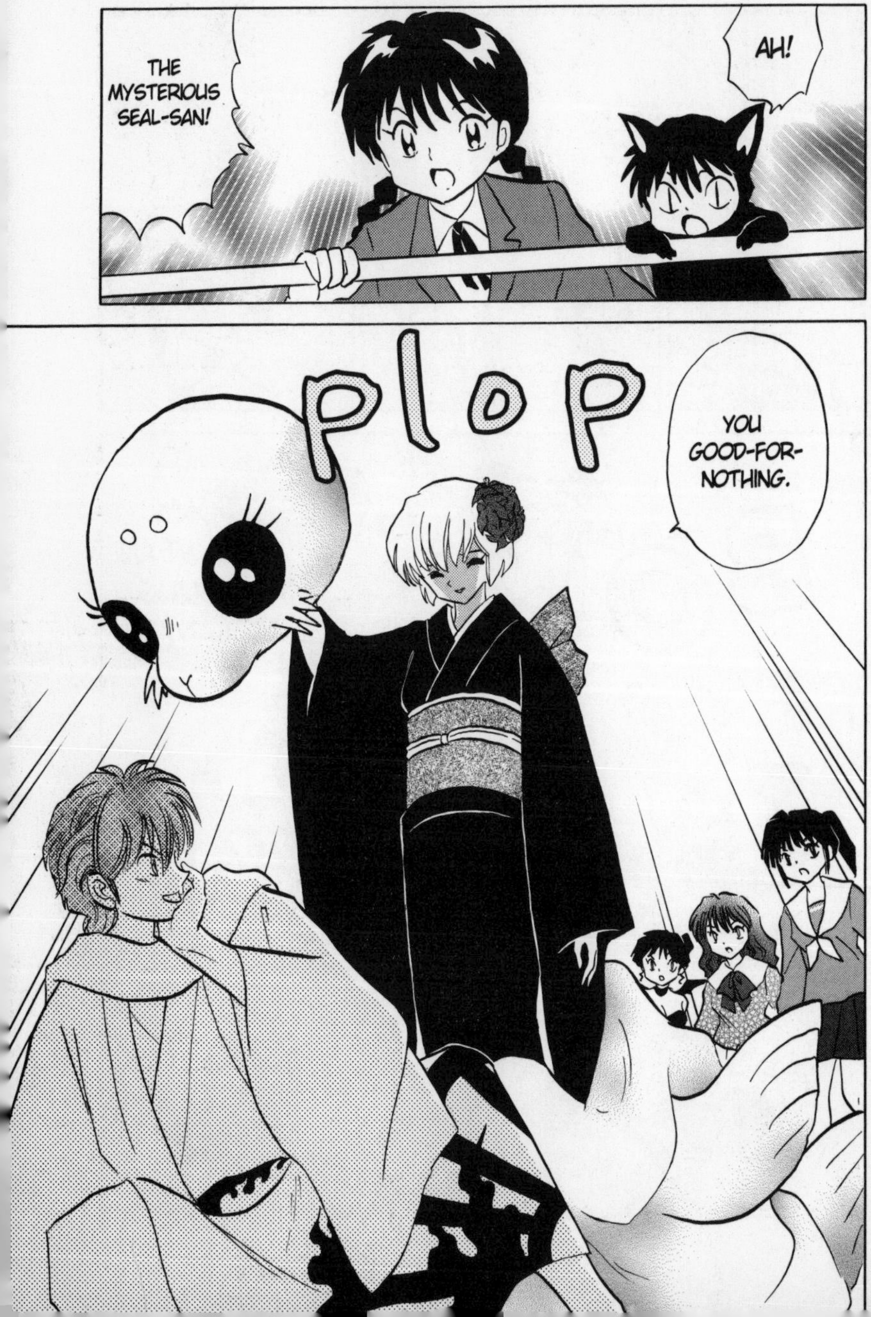
AH!
THE MYSTERIOUS SEAL-SAN!
YOU GOOD-FOR-NOTHING.
plop

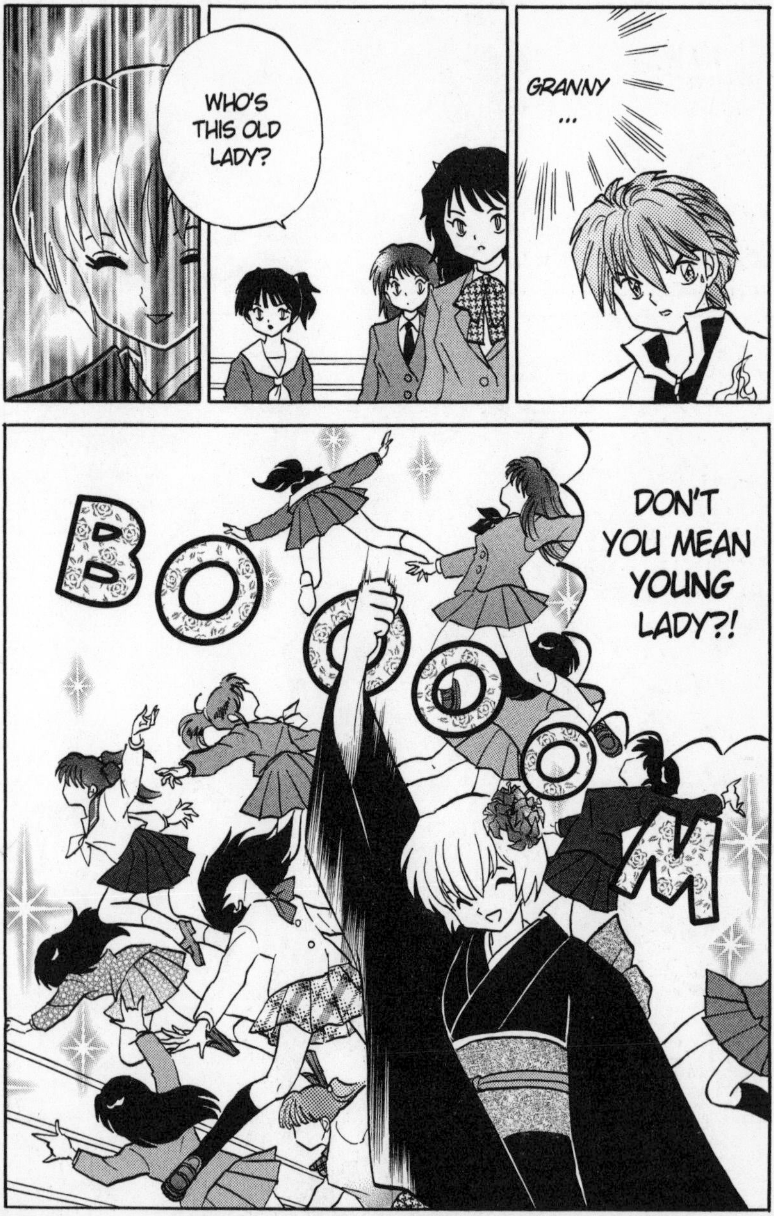
GRANNY ...
WHO'S THIS OLD LADY?
DON'T YOU MEAN YOUNG LADY?!
BOOOOOM

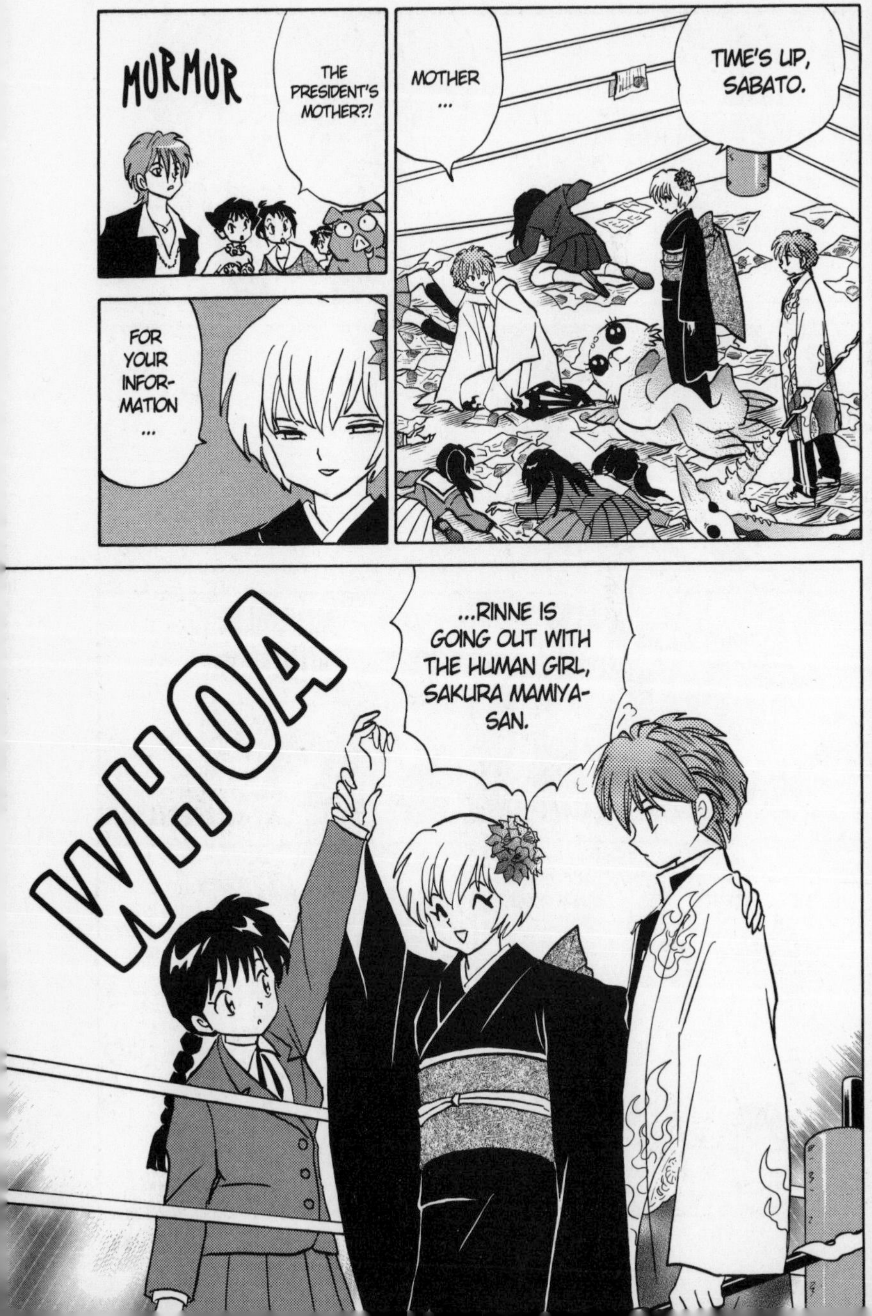
TIME'S UP, SABATO.
MOTHER ...
THE PRESIDENT'S MOTHER?!
MURMUR
FOR YOUR INFOR-MATION ...
...RINNE IS GOING OUT WITH THE HUMAN GIRL, SAKURA MAMIYA-SAN.
WHOA

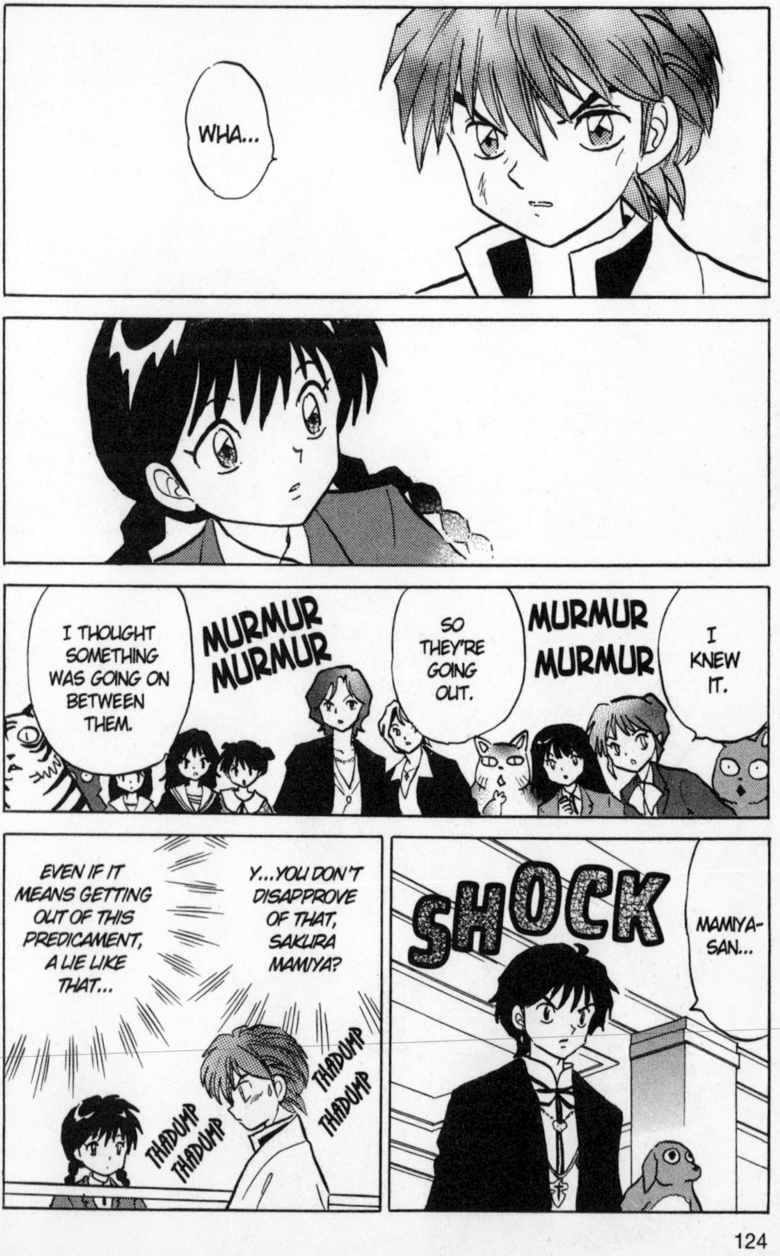
WHA...
I KNEW IT.
MURMUR MURMUR
SO THEY'RE GOING OUT.
MURMUR MURMUR
I THOUGHT SOMETHING WAS GOING ON BETWEEN THEM.
MAMIYA-SAN...
SHOCK
Y...YOU DON'T DISAPPROVE OF THAT, SAKURA MAMIYA?
EVEN IF IT MEANS GETTING OUT OF THIS PREDICAMENT, A LIE LIKE THAT...
THADUMP THADUMP
THADUMP THADUMP

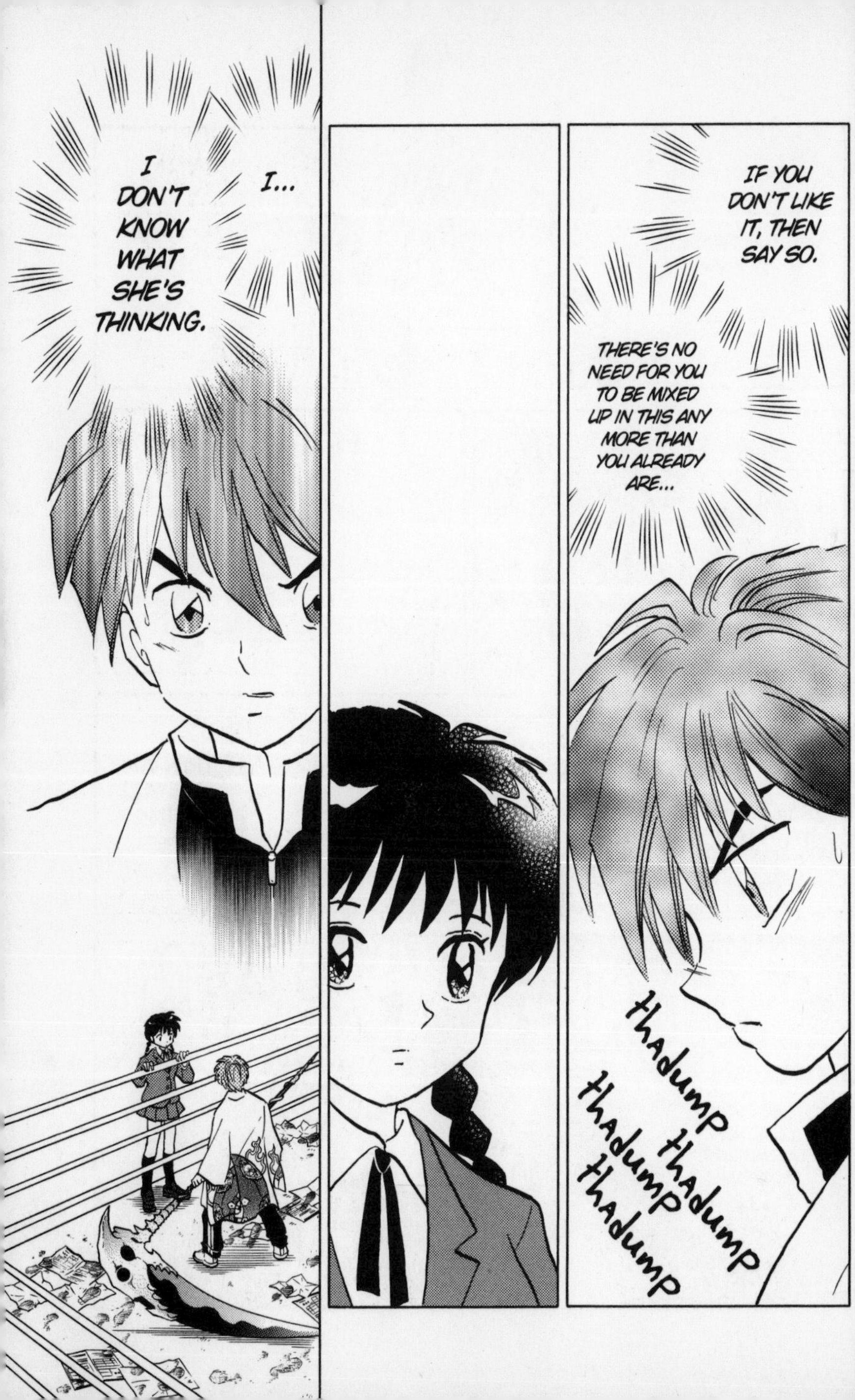
IF YOU DON'T LIKE IT, THEN SAY SO.
THERE'S NO NEED FOR YOU TO BE MIXED UP IN THIS ANY MORE THAN YOU ALREADY ARE...
thadump thadump thadump thadump
I...
I DON'T KNOW WHAT SHE'S THINKING.

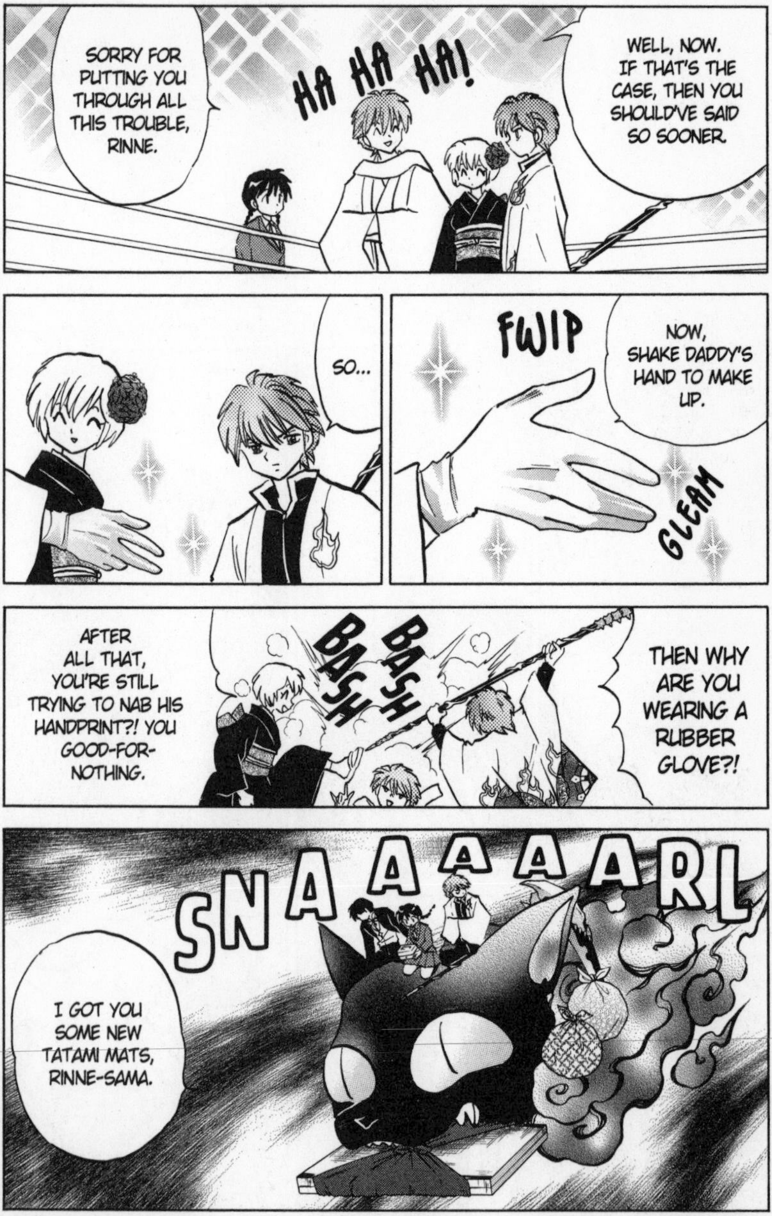
WELL, NOW. IF THAT'S THE CASE, THEN YOU SHOULD'VE SAID SO SOONER.
HA HA HA!
SORRY FOR PUTTING YOU THROUGH ALL THIS TROUBLE, RINNE.
FWIP
NOW, SHAKE DADDY'S HAND TO MAKE UP.
GLEAM
SO...
THEN WHY ARE YOU WEARING A RUBBER GLOVE?!
BASH
BASH
AFTER ALL THAT, YOU'RE STILL TRYING TO NAB HIS HANDPRINT?! YOU GOOD-FOR-NOTHING.
SNAAAAARL
I GOT YOU SOME NEW TATAMI MATS, RINNE-SAMA.

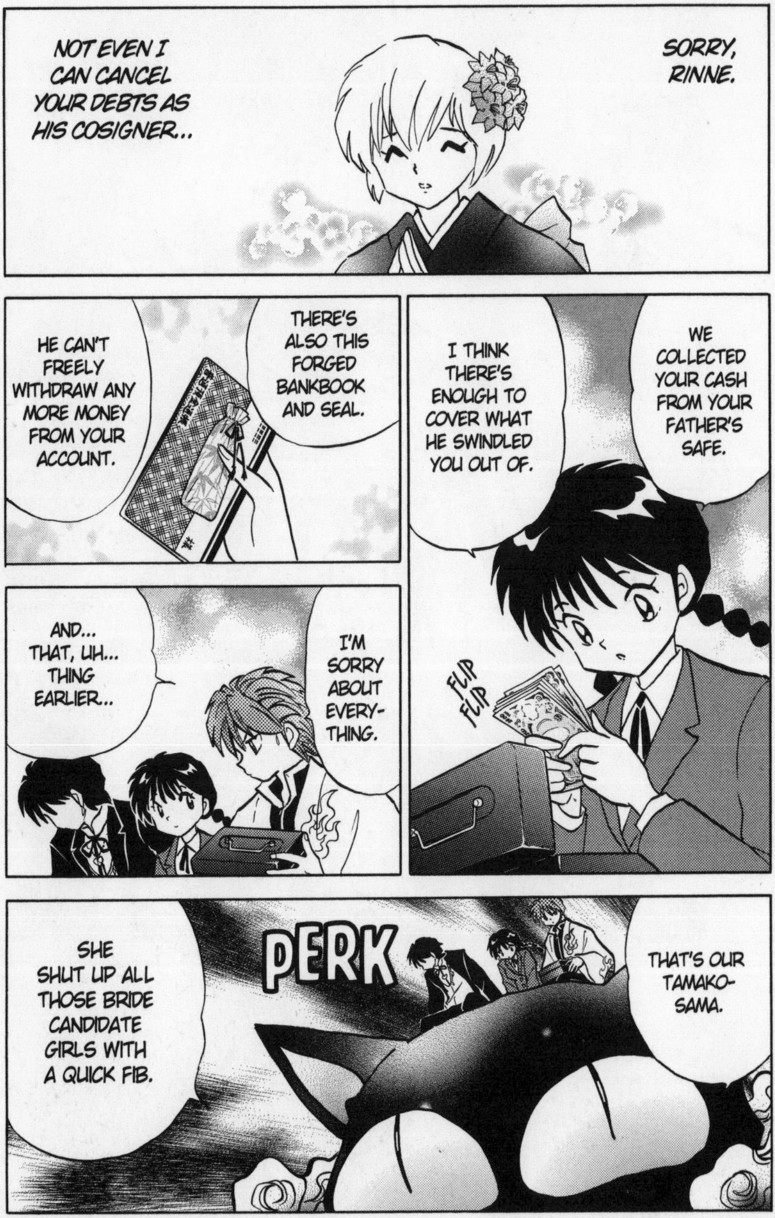
SORRY, RINNE.
NOT EVEN I CAN CANCEL YOUR DEBTS AS HIS COSIGNER...
WE COLLECTED YOUR CASH FROM YOUR FATHER'S SAFE.
I THINK THERE'S ENOUGH TO COVER WHAT HE SWINDLED YOU OUT OF.
FLIP FLIP
THERE'S ALSO THIS FORGED BANKBOOK AND SEAL.
HE CAN'T FREELY WITHDRAW ANY MORE MONEY FROM YOUR ACCOUNT.
I'M SORRY ABOUT EVERY-THING.
AND... THAT, UH... THING EARLIER...
THAT'S OUR TAMAKO-SAMA.
PERK
SHE SHUT UP ALL THOSE BRIDE CANDIDATE GIRLS WITH A QUICK FIB.

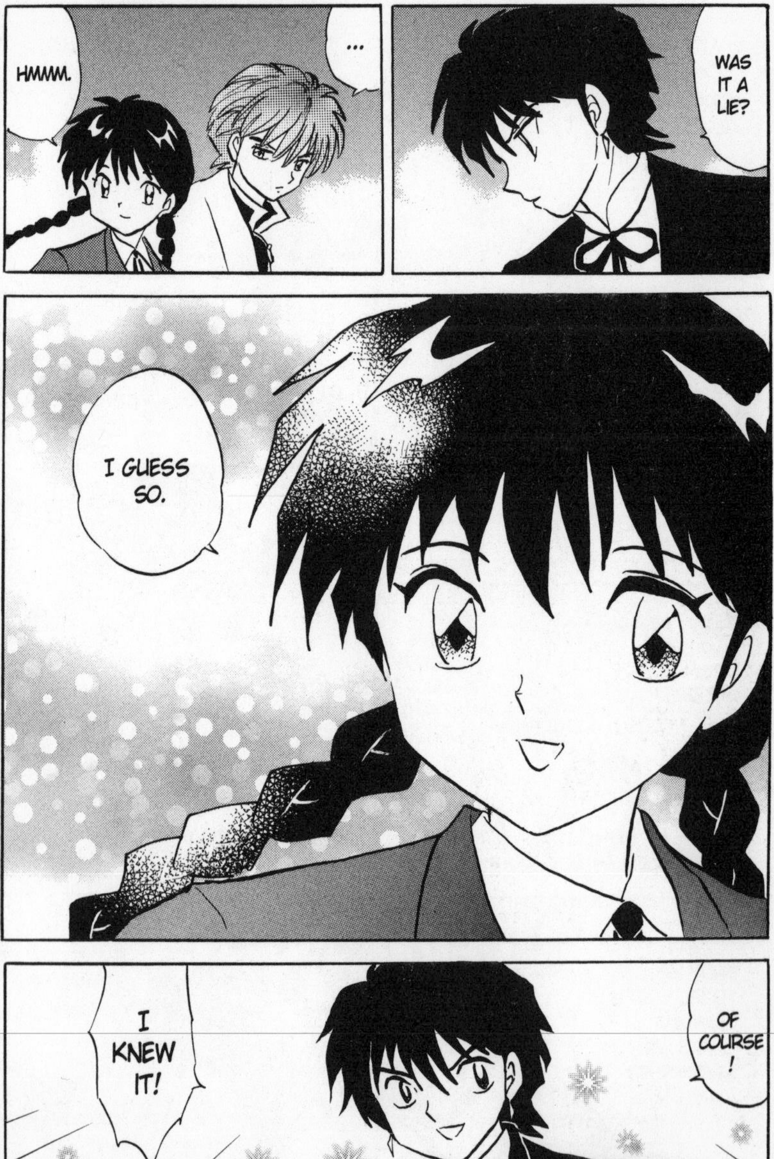
WAS IT A LIE?
...
HMMM.
I GUESS SO.
OF COURSE!
I KNEW IT!

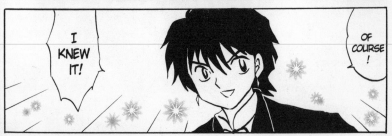

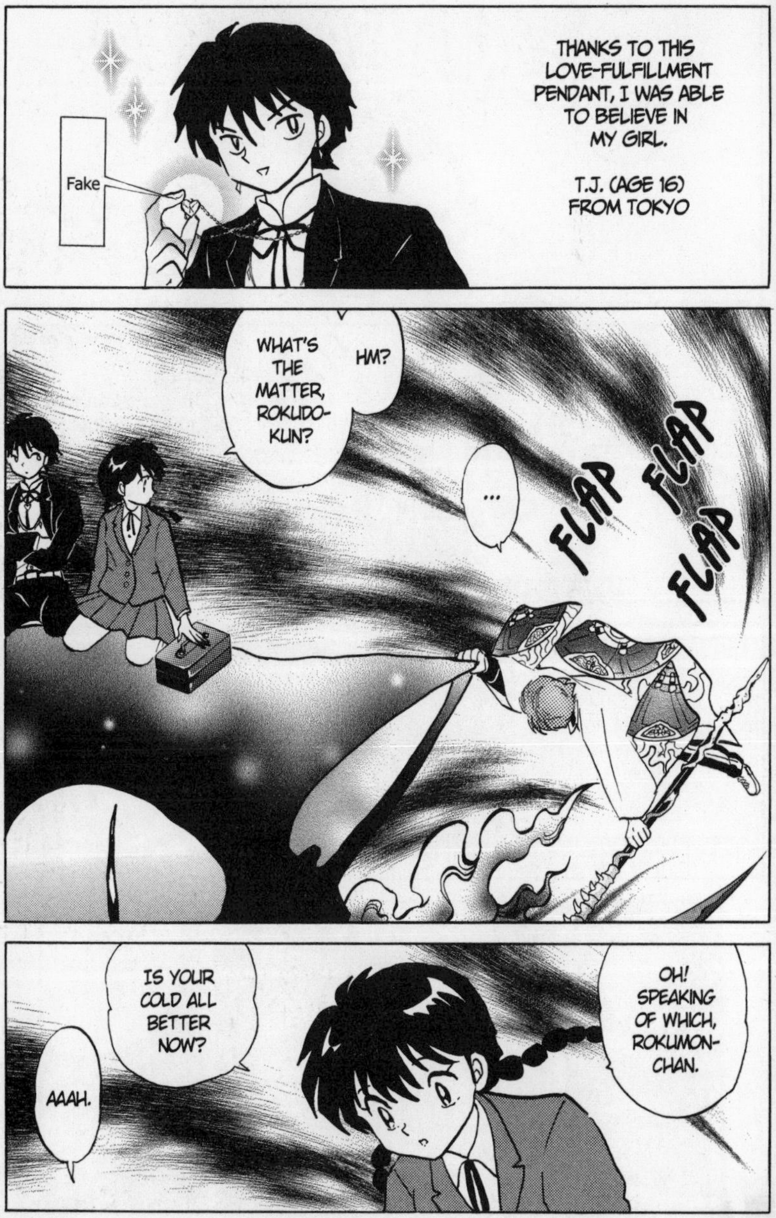
THANKS TO THIS LOVE-FULFILLMENT PENDANT, I WAS ABLE TO BELIEVE IN MY GIRL.
T.J. (AGE 16) FROM TOKYO
Fake
HM?
WHAT'S THE MATTER, ROKUDO-KUN?
...
FLAP FLAP FLAP
OH! SPEAKING OF WHICH, ROKUMON-CHAN.
IS YOUR COLD ALL BETTER NOW?
AAAH.

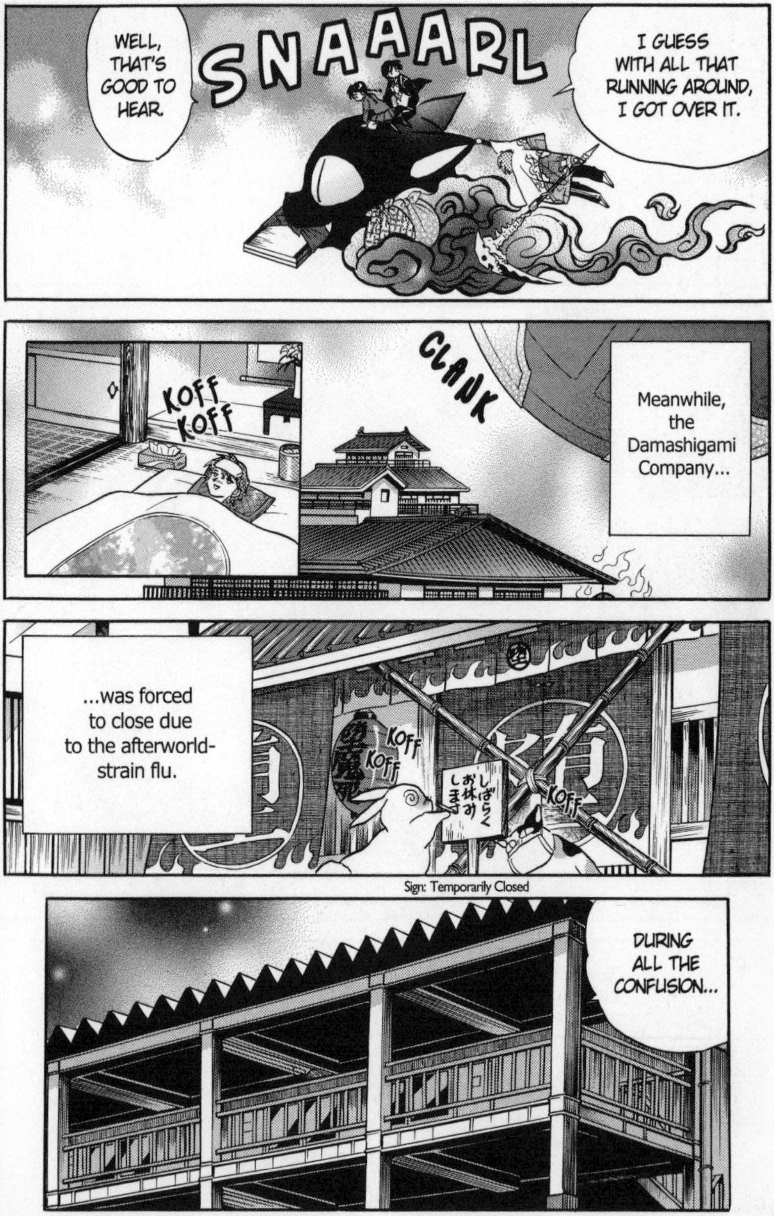
I GUESS WITH ALL THAT RUNNING AROUND, I GOT OVER IT.
SNAAARL
WELL, THAT'S GOOD TO HEAR.
Meanwhile, the Damashigami Company...
CLANK
KOFF KOFF
KOFF
しばらくお休みします
KOFF KOFF
...was forced to close due to the afterworld-strain flu.
DURING ALL THE CONFUSION...
Sign: Temporarily Closed

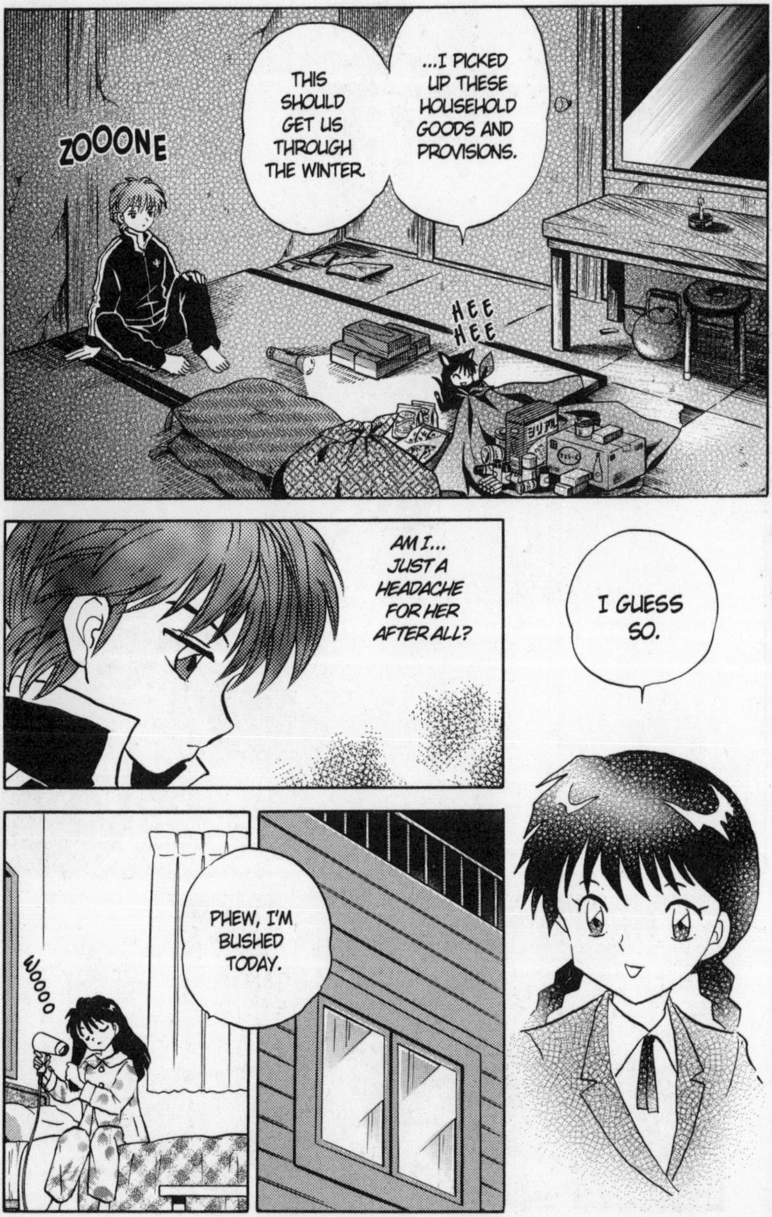
...I PICKED UP THESE HOUSEHOLD GOODS AND PROVISIONS.
THIS SHOULD GET US THROUGH THE WINTER.
ZOOONE
HEE HEE
I GUESS SO.
AM I... JUST A HEADACHE FOR HER AFTER ALL?
PHEW, I'M BUSHED TODAY.
Woooo

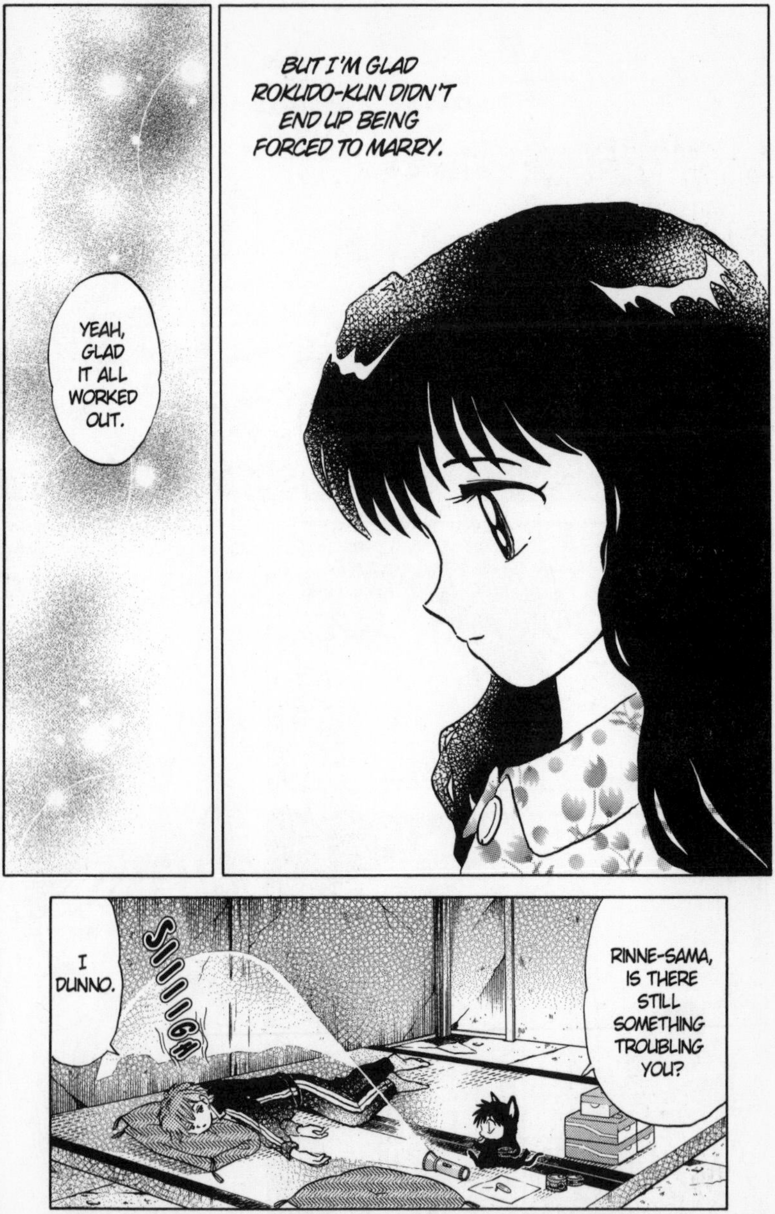
BUT I'M GLAD ROKUDO-KUN DIDN'T END UP BEING FORCED TO MARRY.
YEAH, GLAD IT ALL WORKED OUT.
RINNE-SAMA, IS THERE STILL SOMETHING TROUBLING YOU?
SIIIIIGH
I DUNNO.

CHAPTER 36: AGEHA, THE SHINIGAMI

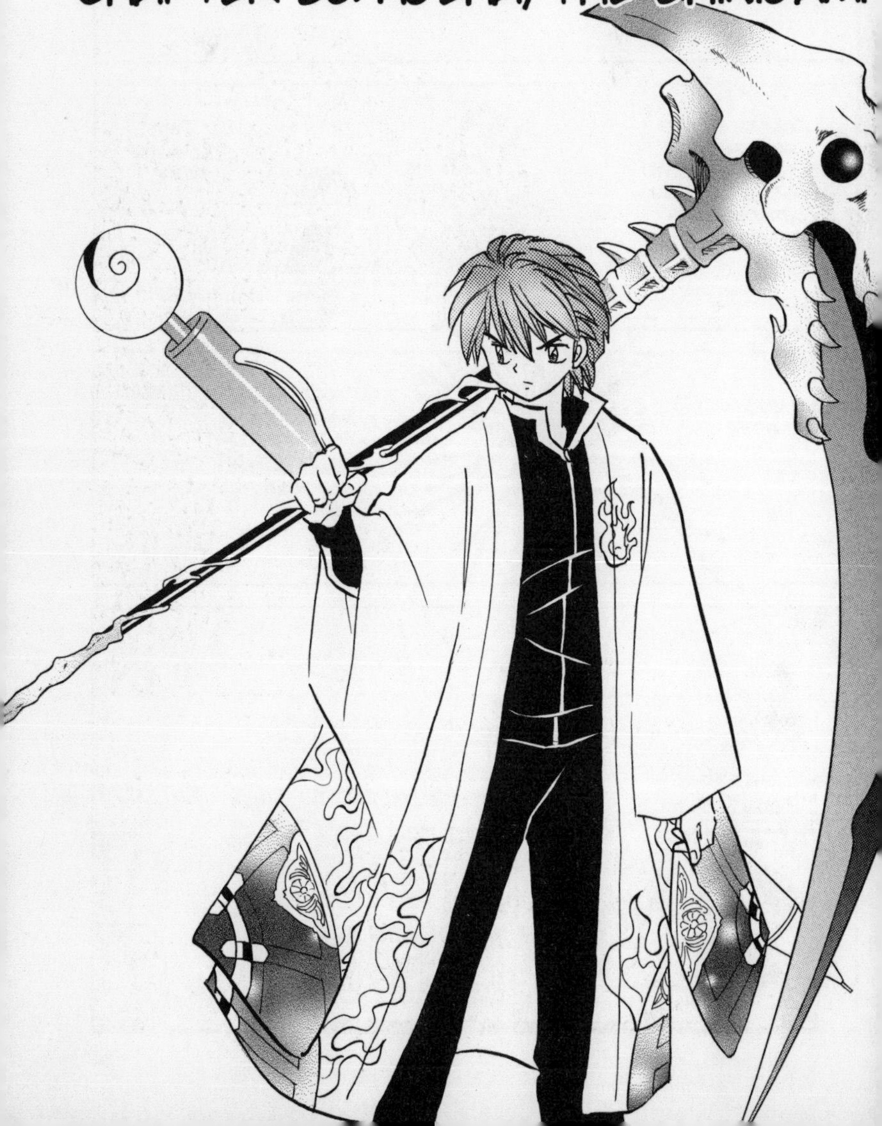

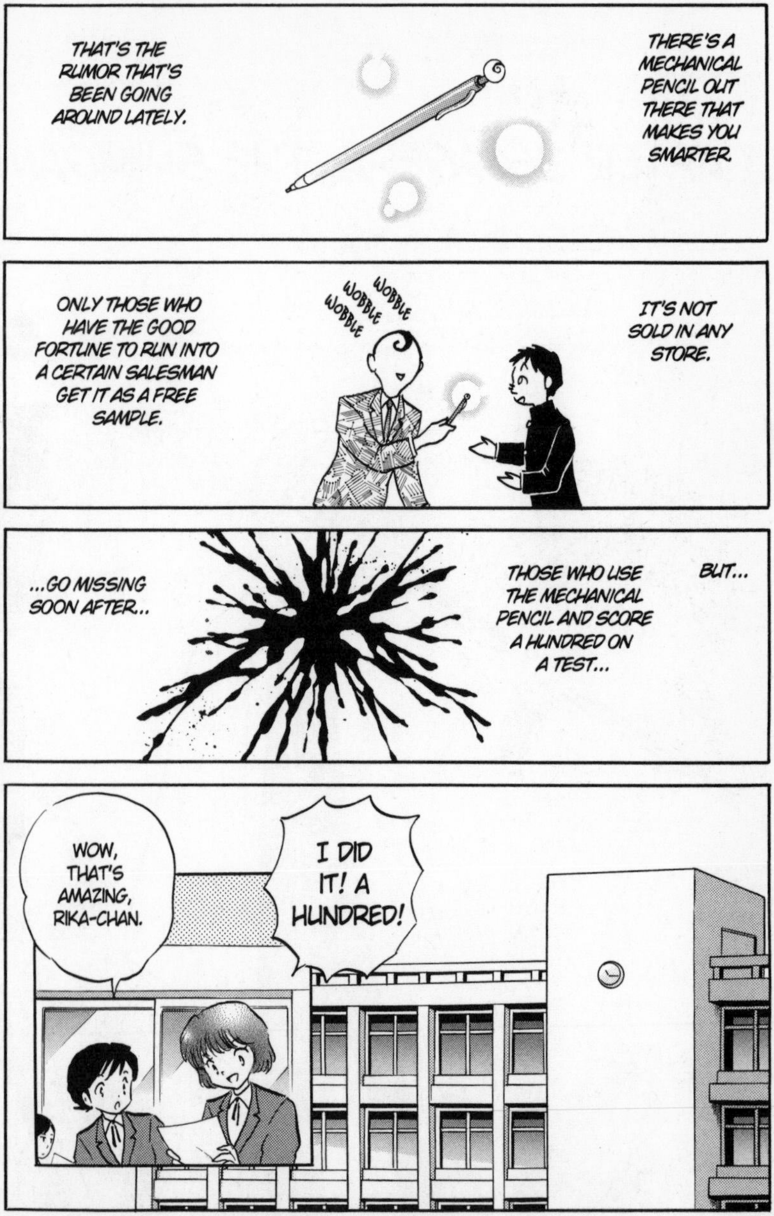
THERE'S A MECHANICAL PENCIL OUT THERE THAT MAKES YOU SMARTER.
THAT'S THE RUMOR THAT'S BEEN GOING AROUND LATELY.
IT'S NOT SOLD IN ANY STORE.
WOBBLE WOBBLE WOBBLE
ONLY THOSE WHO HAVE THE GOOD FORTUNE TO RUN INTO A CERTAIN SALESMAN GET IT AS A FREE SAMPLE.
BUT...
THOSE WHO USE THE MECHANICAL PENCIL AND SCORE A HUNDRED ON A TEST...
...GO MISSING SOON AFTER...
I DID IT! A HUNDRED!
WOW, THAT'S AMAZING, RIKA-CHAN.

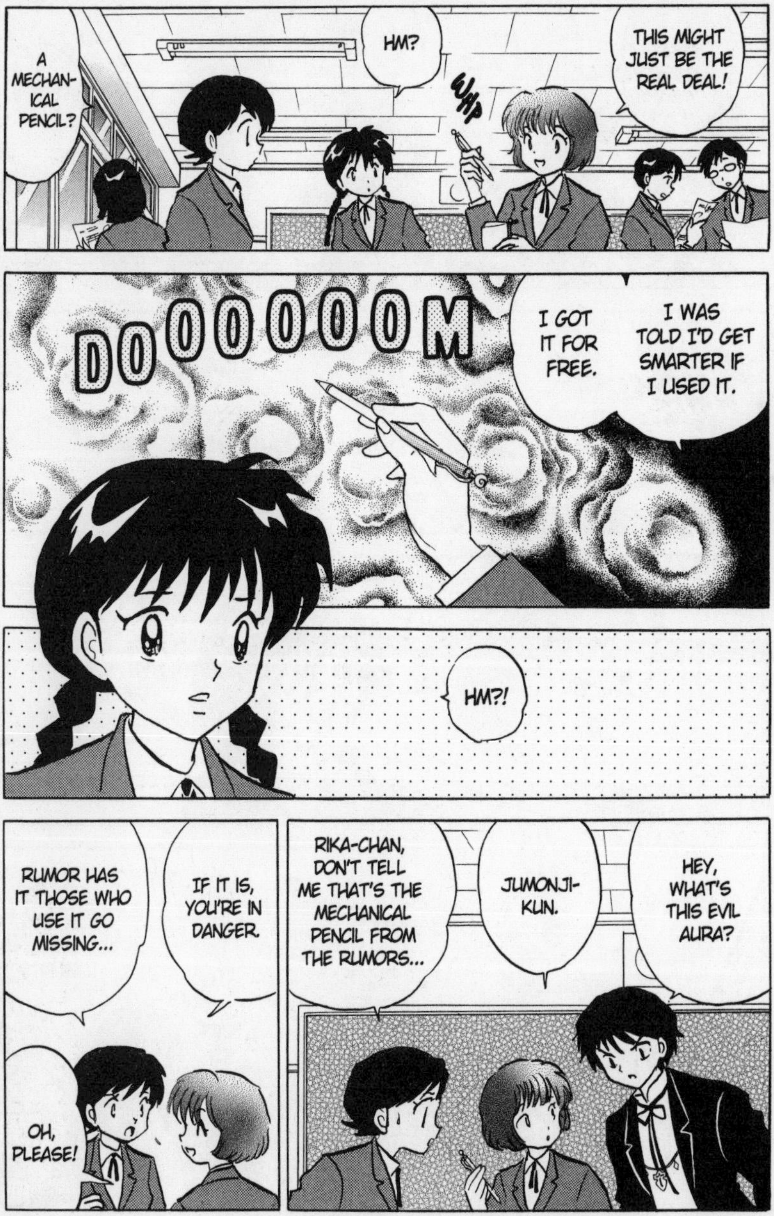
THIS MIGHT JUST BE THE REAL DEAL!
WHP
HM?
A MECHANICAL PENCIL?
I WAS TOLD I'D GET SMARTER IF I USED IT.
I GOT IT FOR FREE.
DOOOOOOM
HM?!
HEY, WHAT'S THIS EVIL AURA?
JUMONJI-KUN.
RIKA-CHAN, DON'T TELL ME THAT'S THE MECHANICAL PENCIL FROM THE RUMORS...
IF IT IS, YOU'RE IN DANGER.
RUMOR HAS IT THOSE WHO USE IT GO MISSING...
OH, PLEASE!

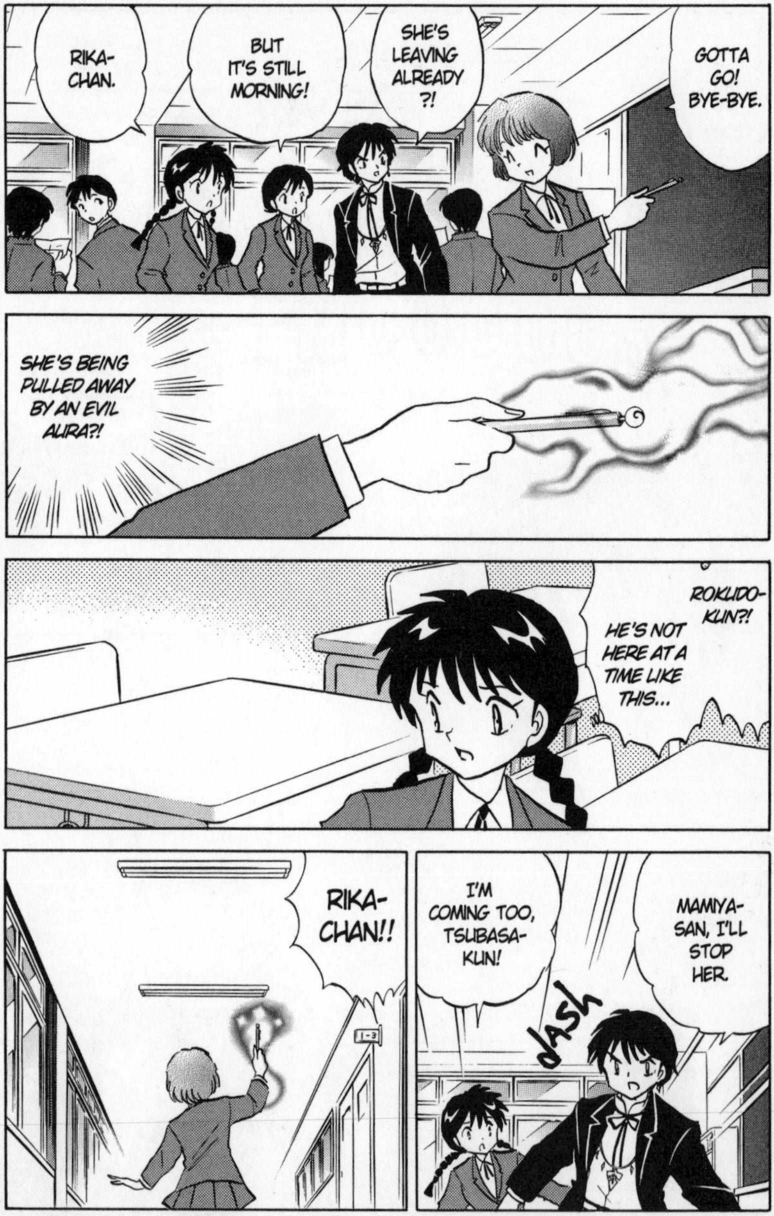
GOTTA GO! BYE-BYE.
SHE'S LEAVING ALREADY?!
BUT IT'S STILL MORNING!
RIKA-CHAN.
SHE'S BEING PULLED AWAY BY AN EVIL AURA?!
ROKUDO-KUN?!
HE'S NOT HERE AT A TIME LIKE THIS...
MAMIYA-SAN, I'LL STOP HER.
dash
I'M COMING TOO, TSUBASA-KUN!
RIKA-CHAN!!
1-3

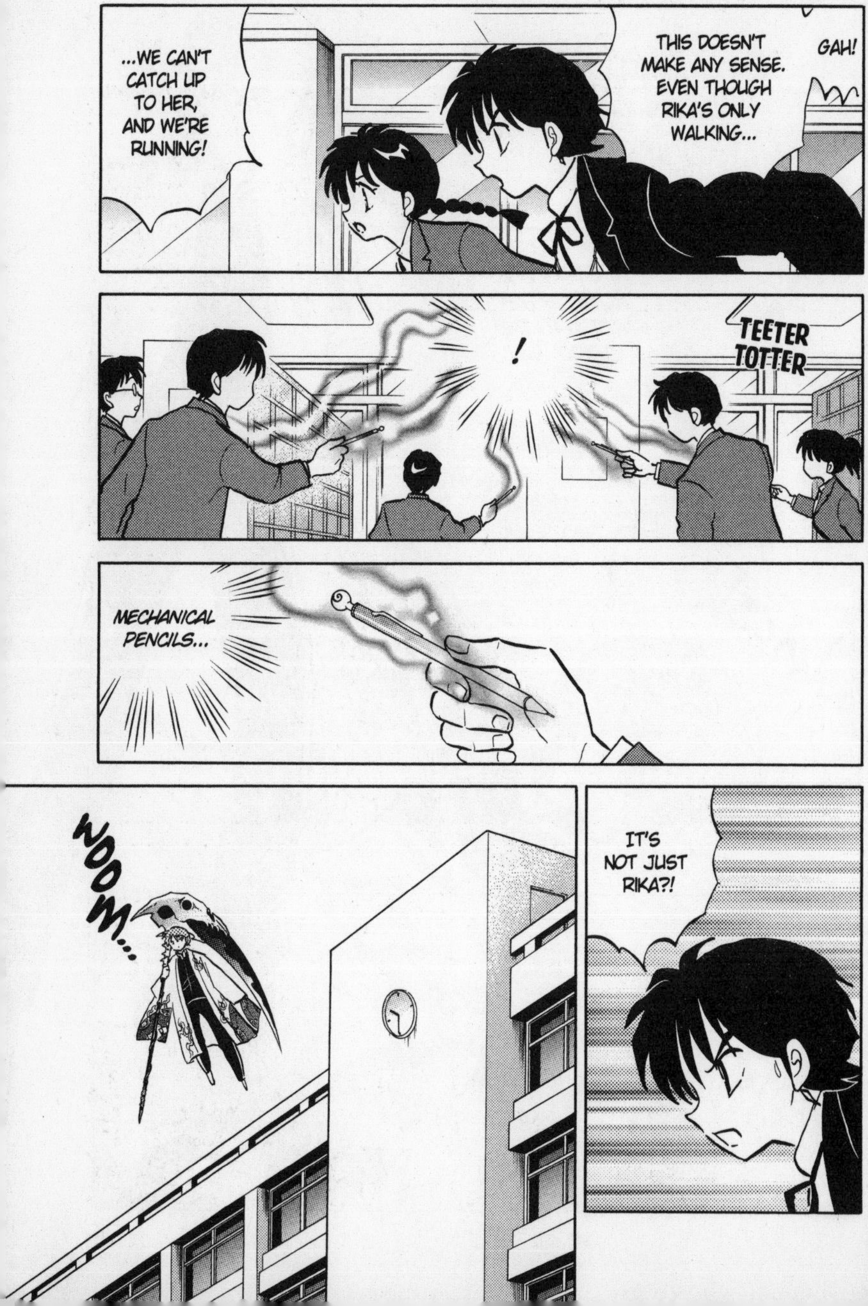
GAH!
THIS DOESN'T MAKE ANY SENSE. EVEN THOUGH RIKA'S ONLY WALKING...
...WE CAN'T CATCH UP TO HER, AND WE'RE RUNNING!
TEETER TOTTER
!
MECHANICAL PENCILS...
IT'S NOT JUST RIKA?!
WOOM...

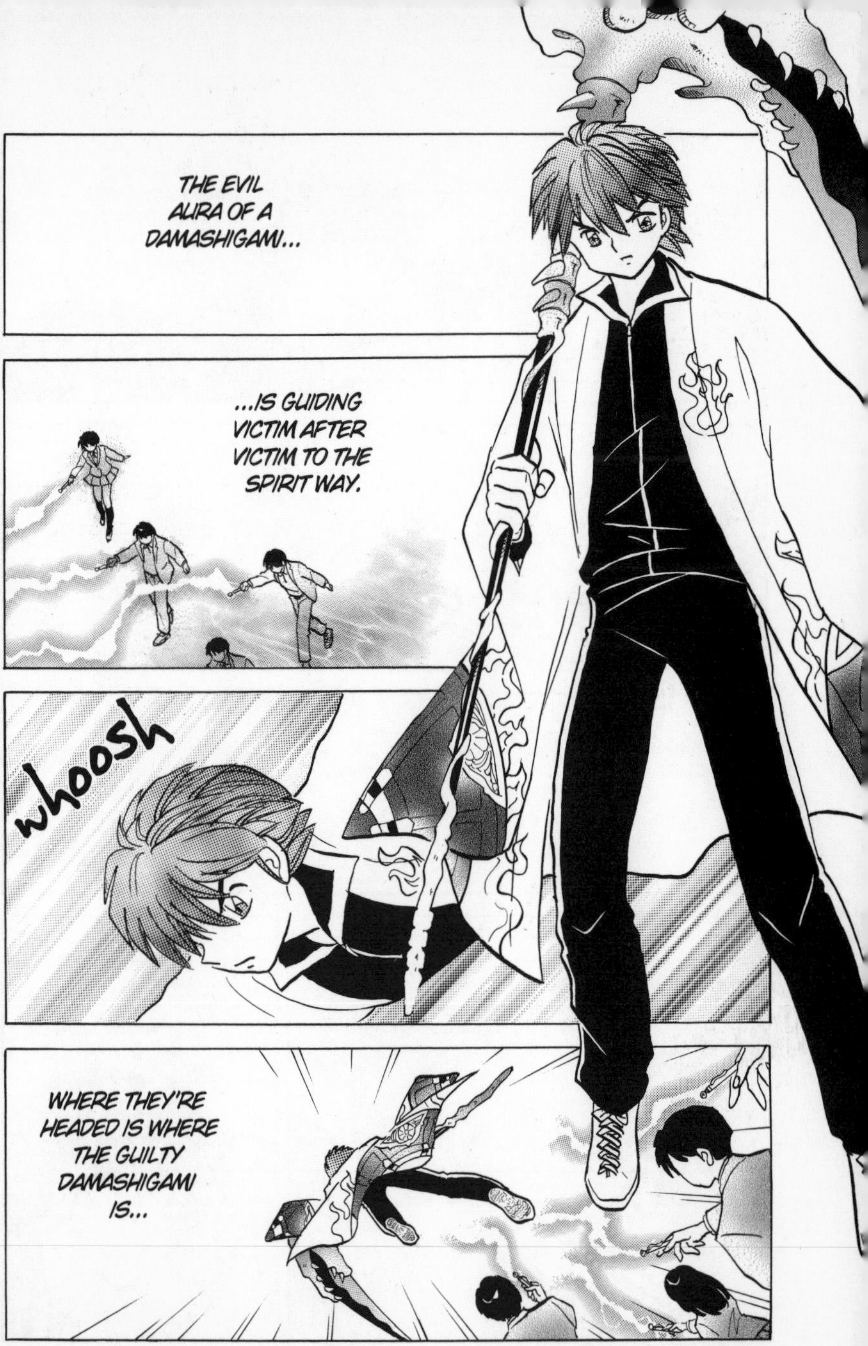
THE EVIL AURA OF A DAMASHIGAMI...
...IS GUIDING VICTIM AFTER VICTIM TO THE SPIRIT WAY.
whoosh
WHERE THEY'RE HEADED IS WHERE THE GUILTY DAMASHIGAMI IS...

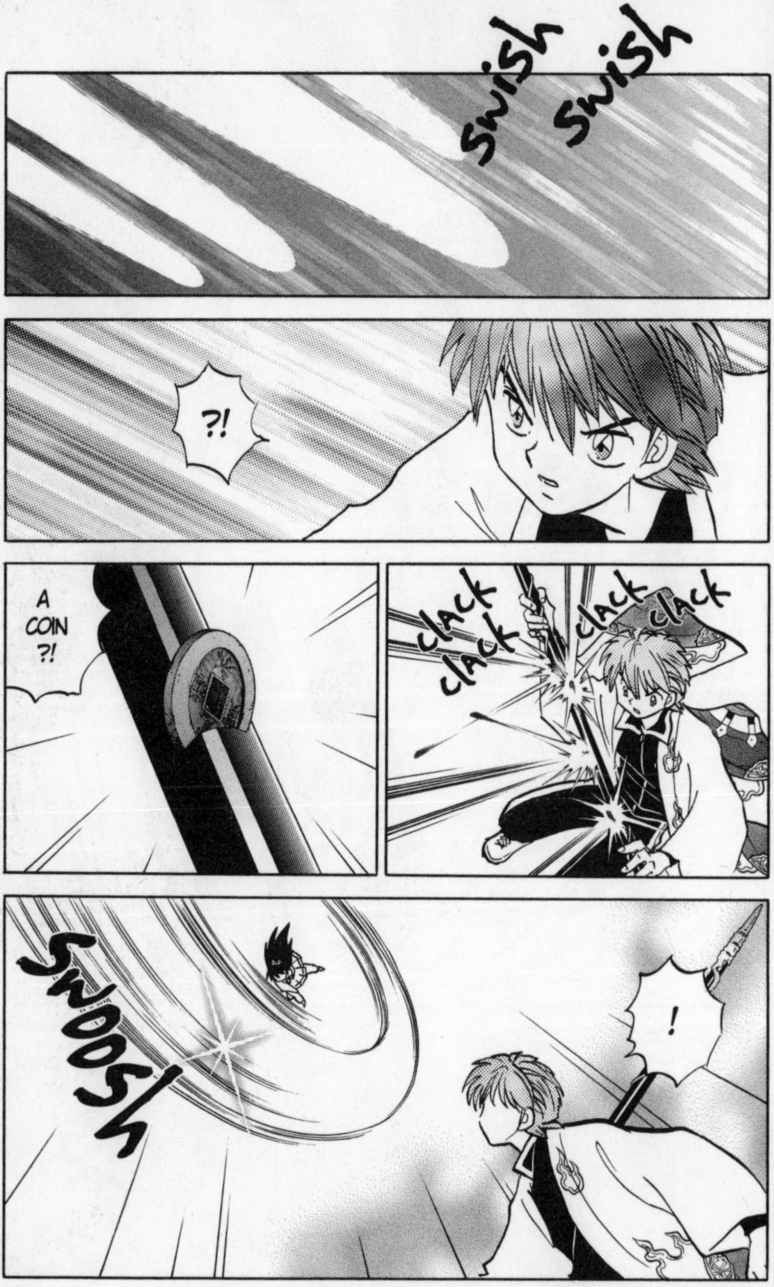
swish swish
?!
clack clack
clack clack
A COIN ?!
!
SWOOSH

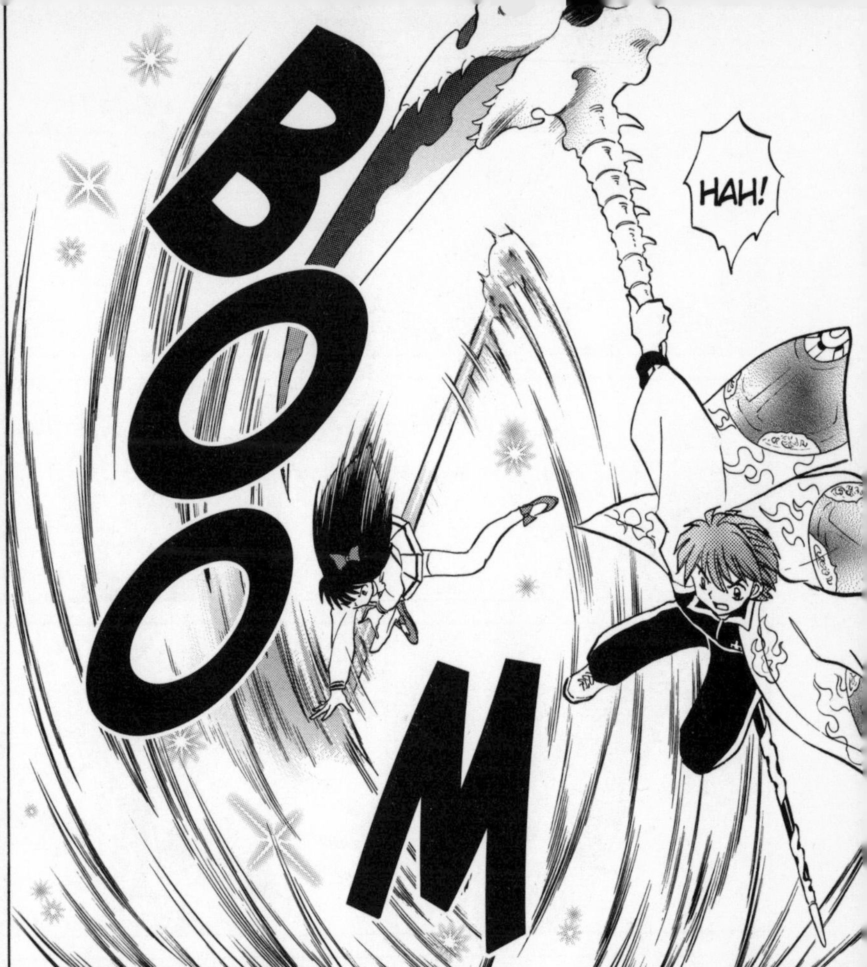
HAH!
BOOM

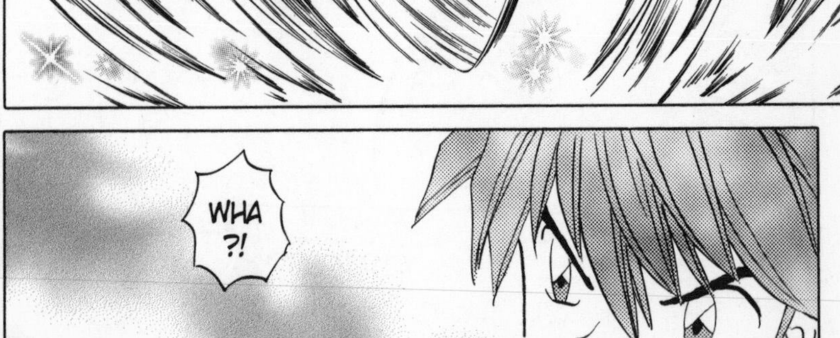
WHA ?!

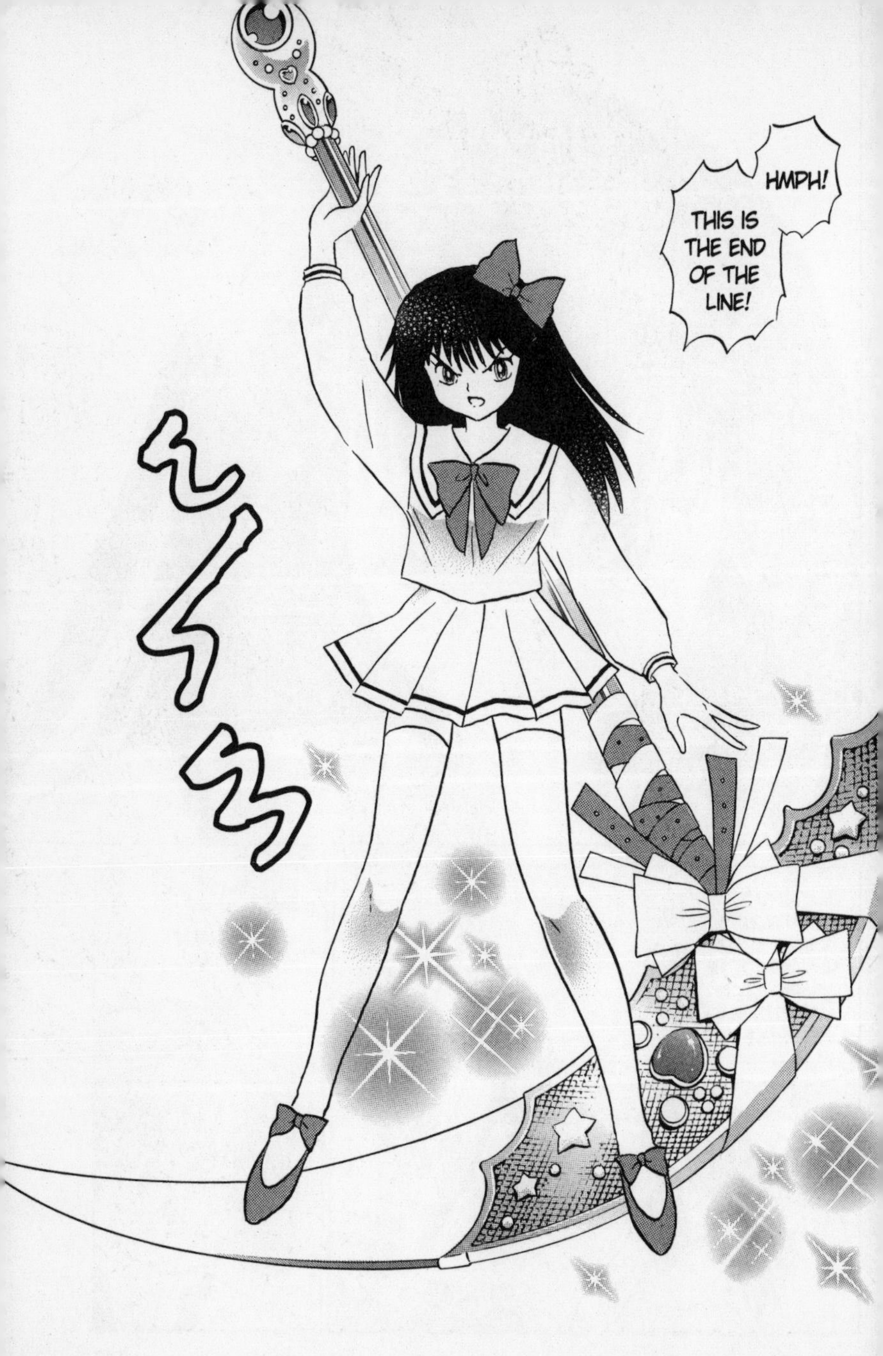
HMPH!
THIS IS THE END OF THE LINE!

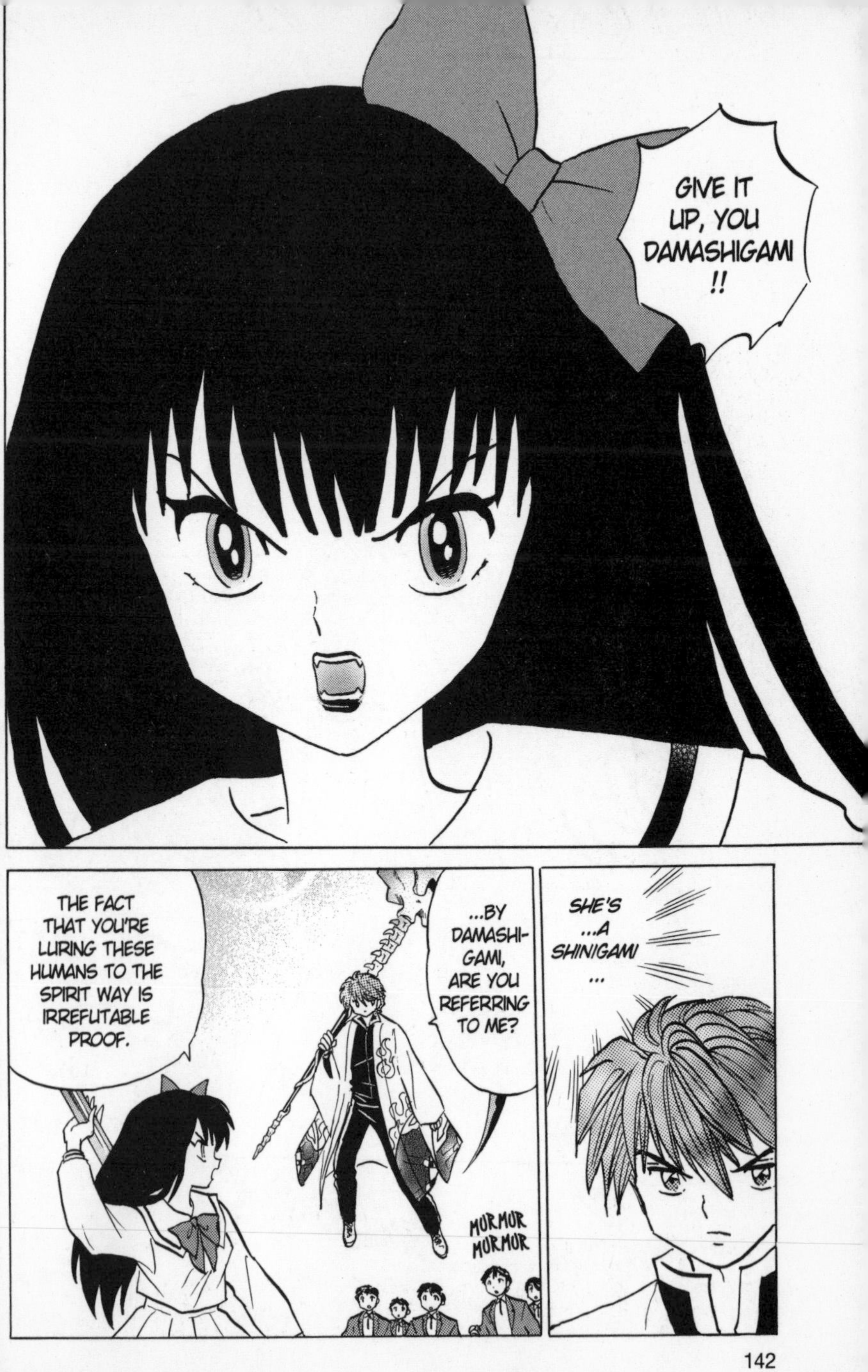
GIVE IT UP, YOU DAMASHIGAMI !!
SHE'S ...A SHINIGAMI ...
...BY DAMASHI-GAMI, ARE YOU REFERRING TO ME?
THE FACT THAT YOU'RE LURING THESE HUMANS TO THE SPIRIT WAY IS IRREFUTABLE PROOF.
MURMUR MURMUR

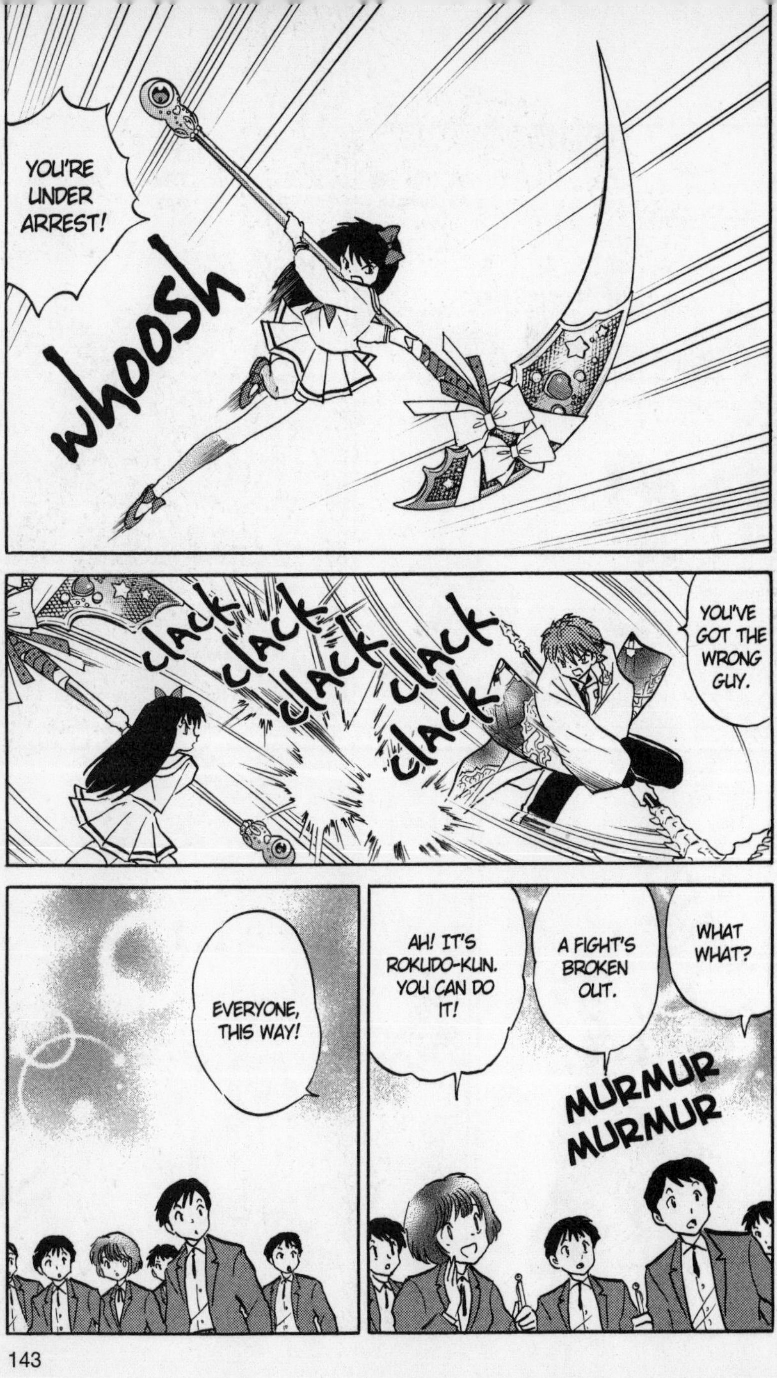
YOU'RE UNDER ARREST!
whoosh
YOU'VE GOT THE WRONG GUY.
clack clack clack clack clack
WHAT WHAT?
A FIGHT'S BROKEN OUT.
AH! IT'S ROKUDO-KUN. YOU CAN DO IT!
MURMUR MURMUR
EVERYONE, THIS WAY!

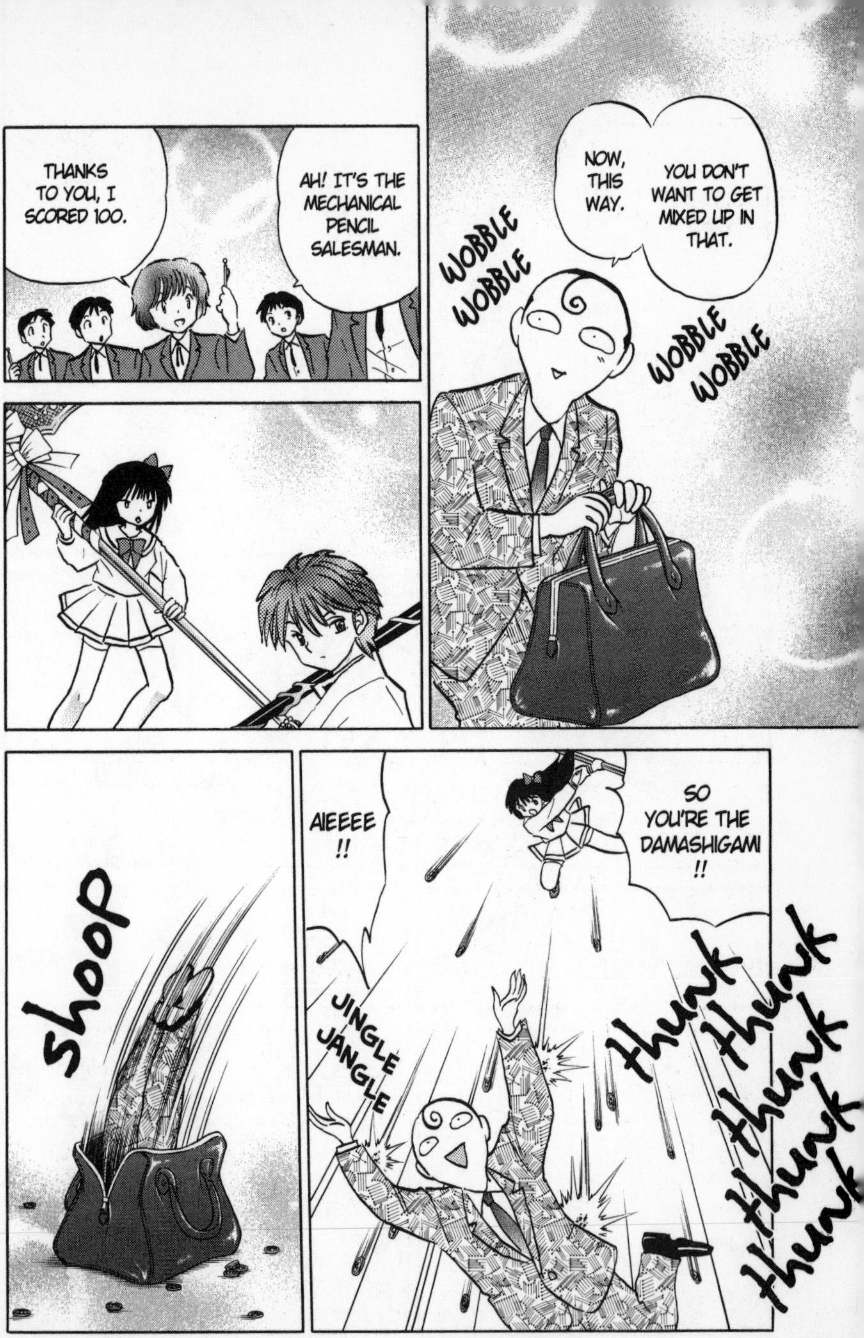
YOU DON'T WANT TO GET MIXED UP IN THAT.
NOW, THIS WAY.
WOBBLE WOBBLE
WOBBLE WOBBLE
AH! IT'S THE MECHANICAL PENCIL SALESMAN.
THANKS TO YOU, I SCORED 100.
SO YOU'RE THE DAMASHIGAMI !!
AIEEEE !!
thunk thunk thunk thunk thunk
JINGLE JANGLE
shoop

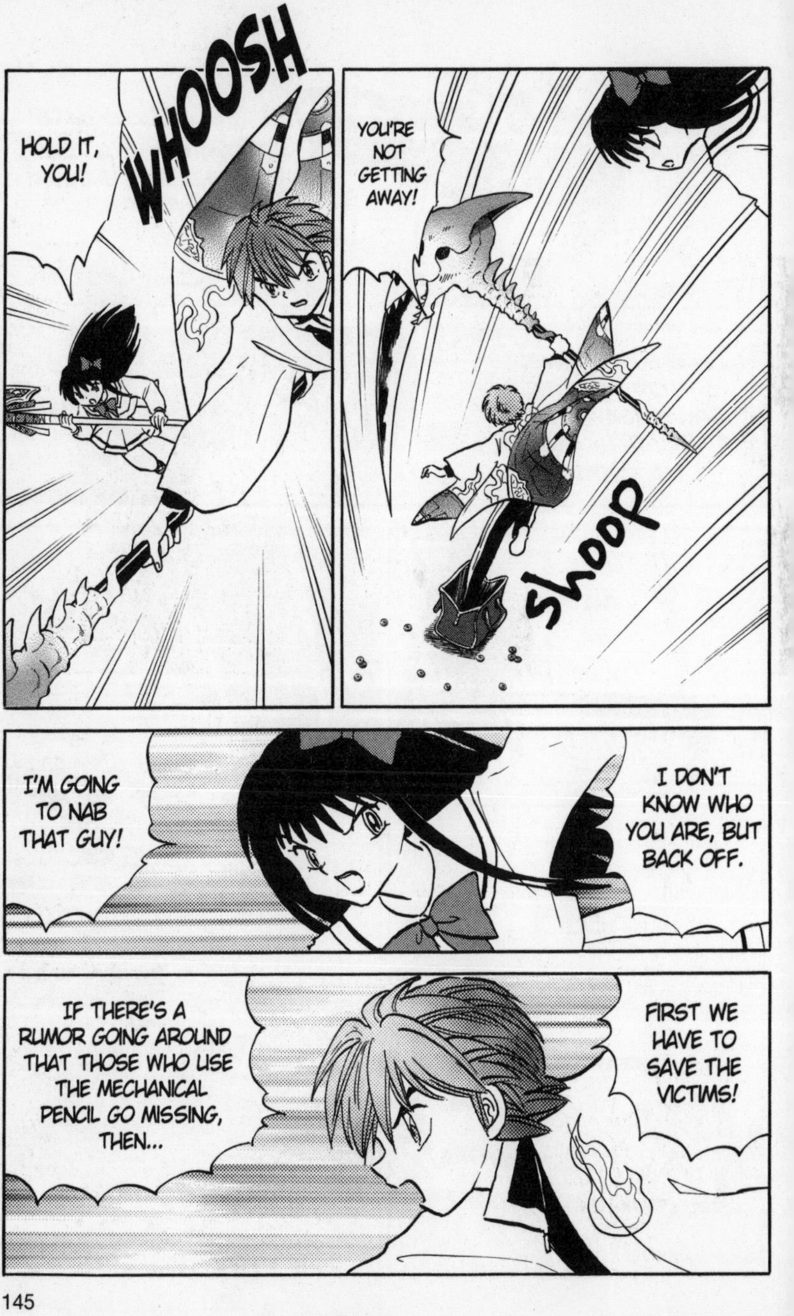
YOU'RE NOT GETTING AWAY!
SHOOP
HOLD IT, YOU!
WHOOSH
I DON'T KNOW WHO YOU ARE, BUT BACK OFF.
I'M GOING TO NAB THAT GUY!
FIRST WE HAVE TO SAVE THE VICTIMS!
IF THERE'S A RUMOR GOING AROUND THAT THOSE WHO USE THE MECHANICAL PENCIL GO MISSING, THEN...

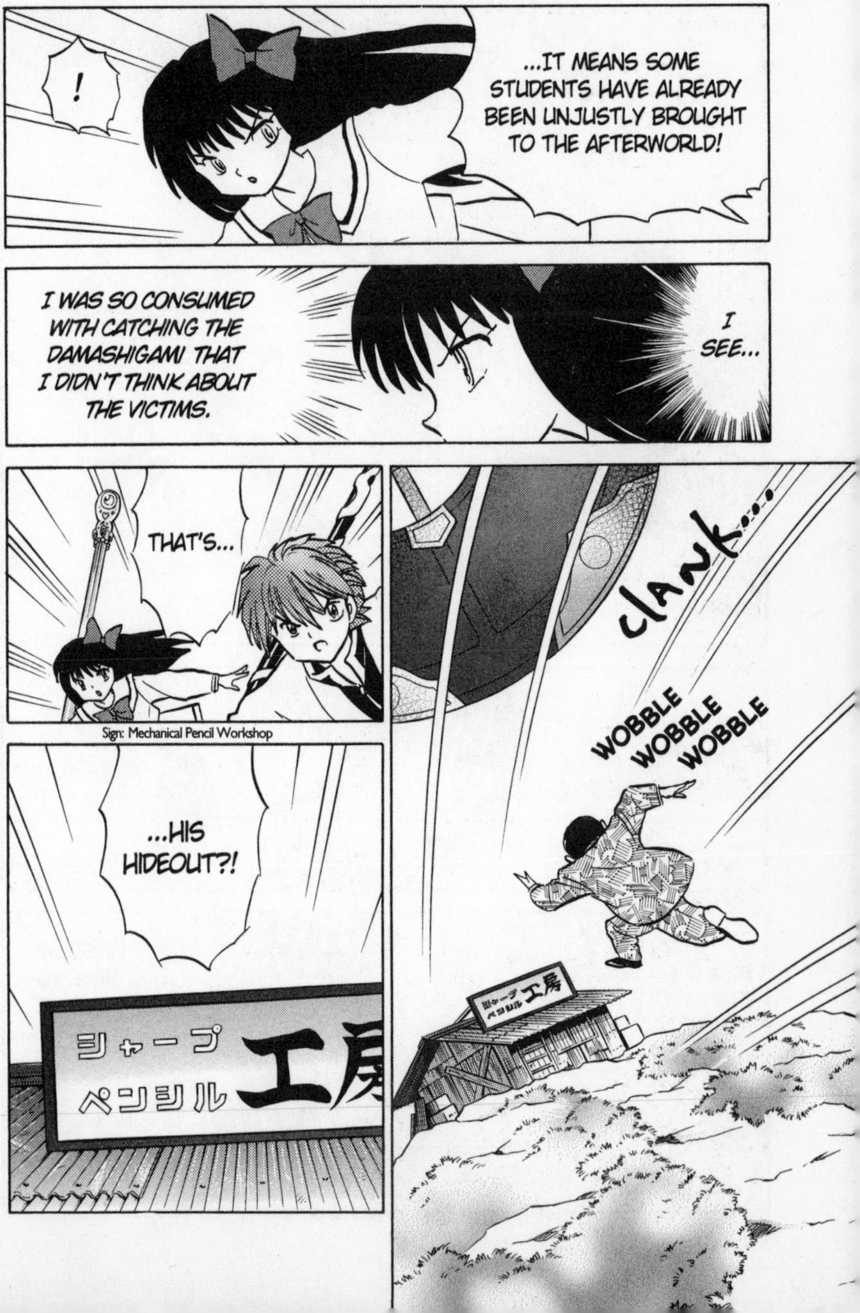
...IT MEANS SOME STUDENTS HAVE ALREADY BEEN UNJUSTLY BROUGHT TO THE AFTERWORLD!
!
I SEE...
I WAS SO CONSUMED WITH CATCHING THE DAMASHIGAMI THAT I DIDN'T THINK ABOUT THE VICTIMS.
clank...
WOBBLE WOBBLE WOBBLE
シャープペンシル工房
THAT'S...
Sign: Mechanical Pencil Workshop
...HIS HIDEOUT?!
シャープペンシル工房

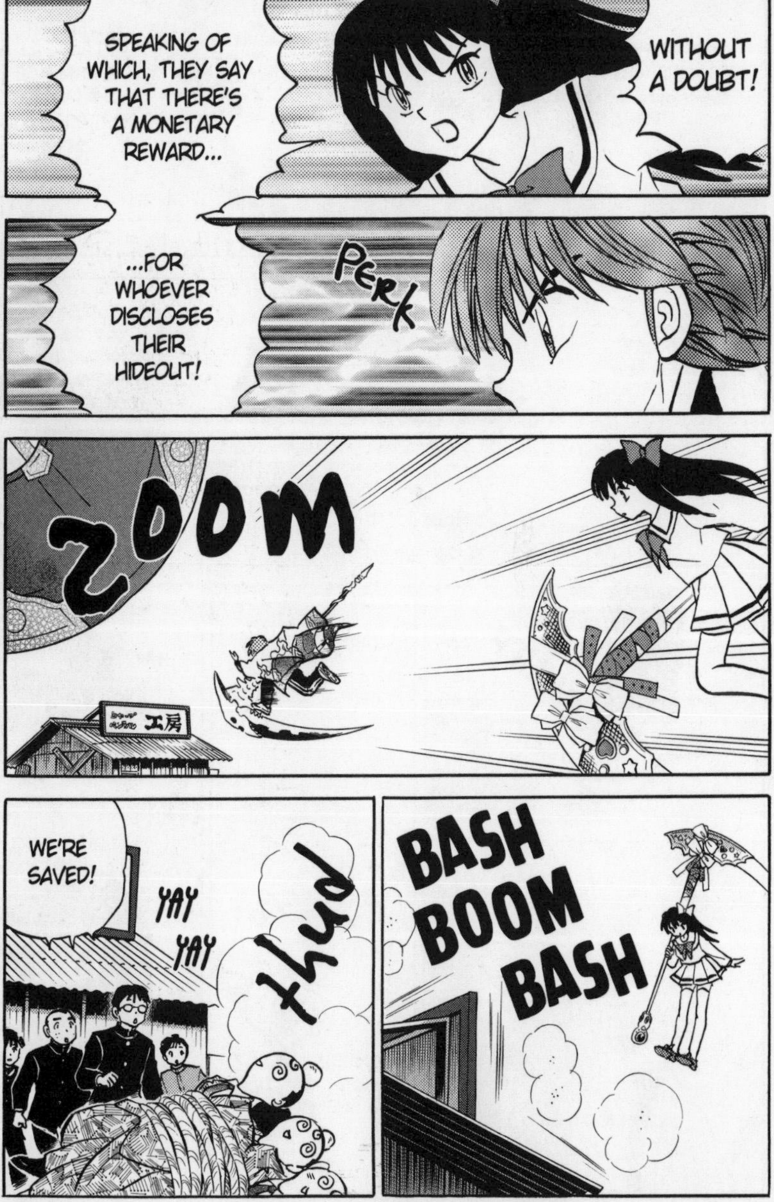
WITHOUT A DOUBT!
SPEAKING OF WHICH, THEY SAY THAT THERE'S A MONETARY REWARD...
PERK
...FOR WHOEVER DISCLOSES THEIR HIDEOUT!
ZOOM
BASH
BOOM
BASH
thud
YAY
YAY
WE'RE SAVED!

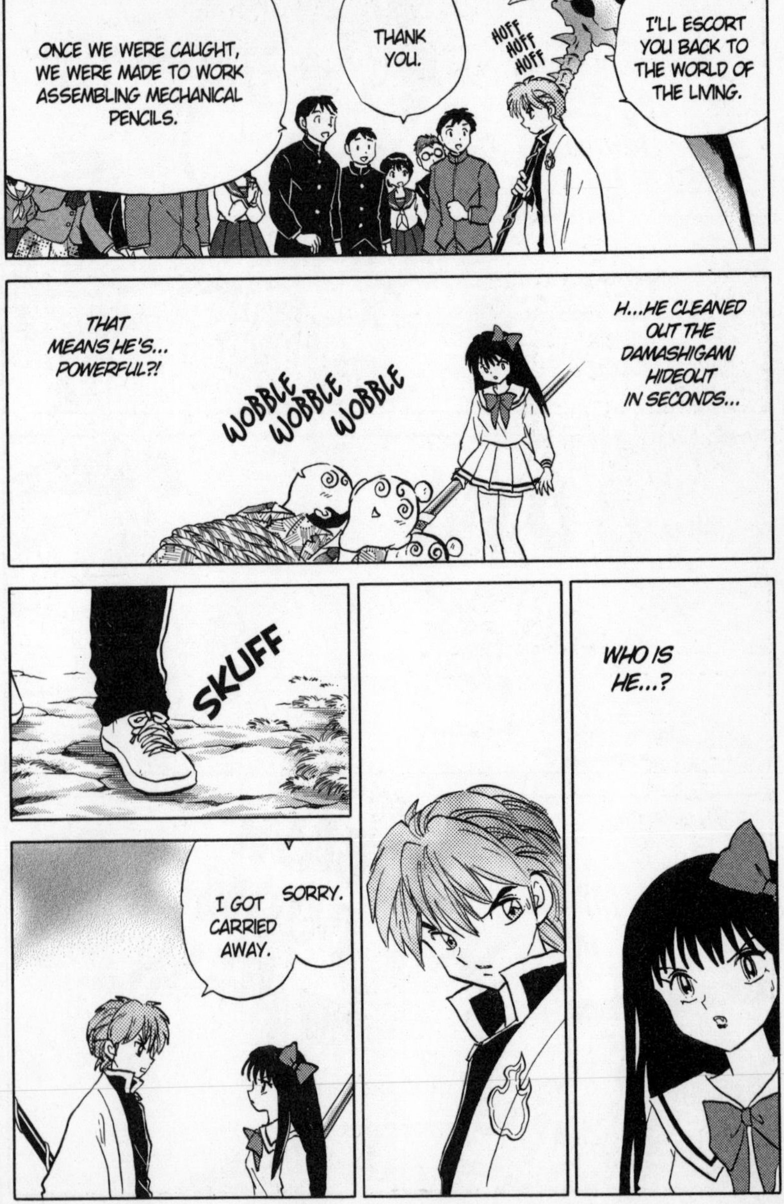
I'LL ESCORT YOU BACK TO THE WORLD OF THE LIVING.
HUFF HUFF HUFF
THANK YOU.
ONCE WE WERE CAUGHT, WE WERE MADE TO WORK ASSEMBLING MECHANICAL PENCILS.
H...HE CLEANED OUT THE DAMASHIGAMI HIDEOUT IN SECONDS...
WOBBLE WOBBLE WOBBLE
THAT MEANS HE'S... POWERFUL?!
WHO IS HE...?
SKUFF
SORRY.
I GOT CARRIED AWAY.

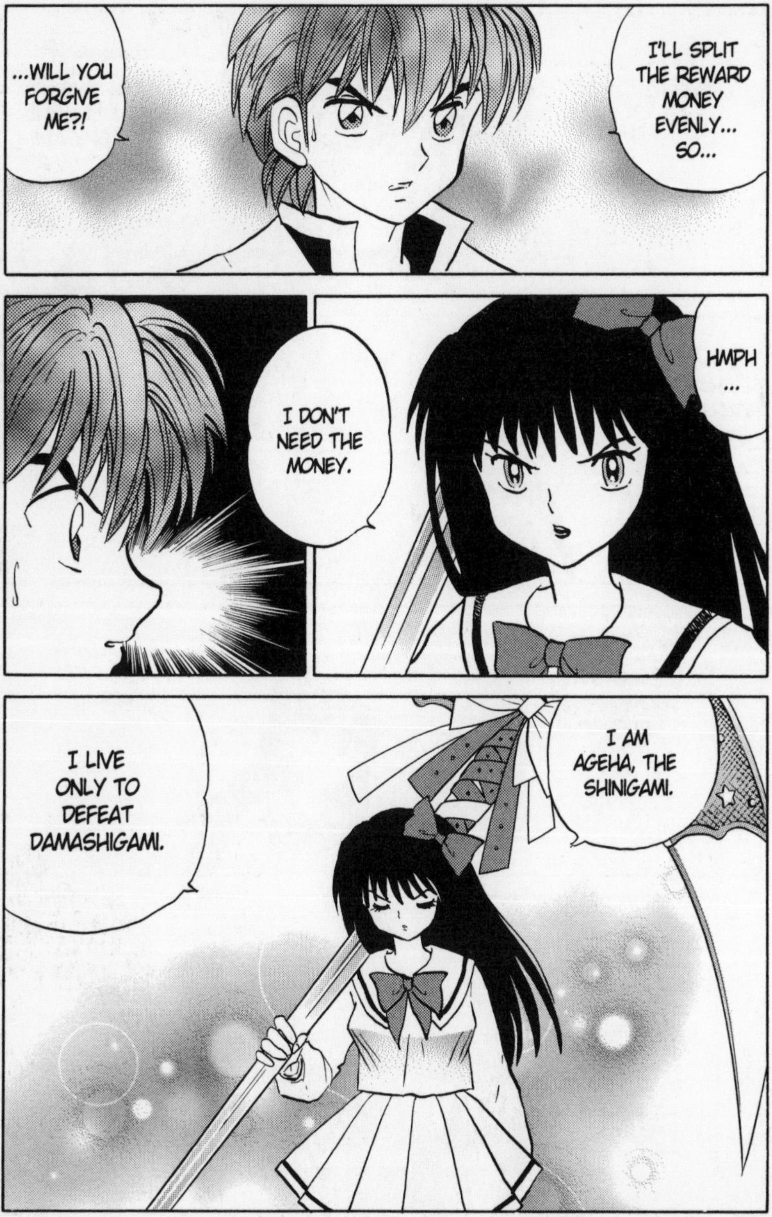
I'LL SPLIT THE REWARD MONEY EVENLY... SO...
...WILL YOU FORGIVE ME?!
HMPH ...
I DON'T NEED THE MONEY.
I AM AGEHA, THE SHINIGAMI.
I LIVE ONLY TO DEFEAT DAMASHIGAMI.

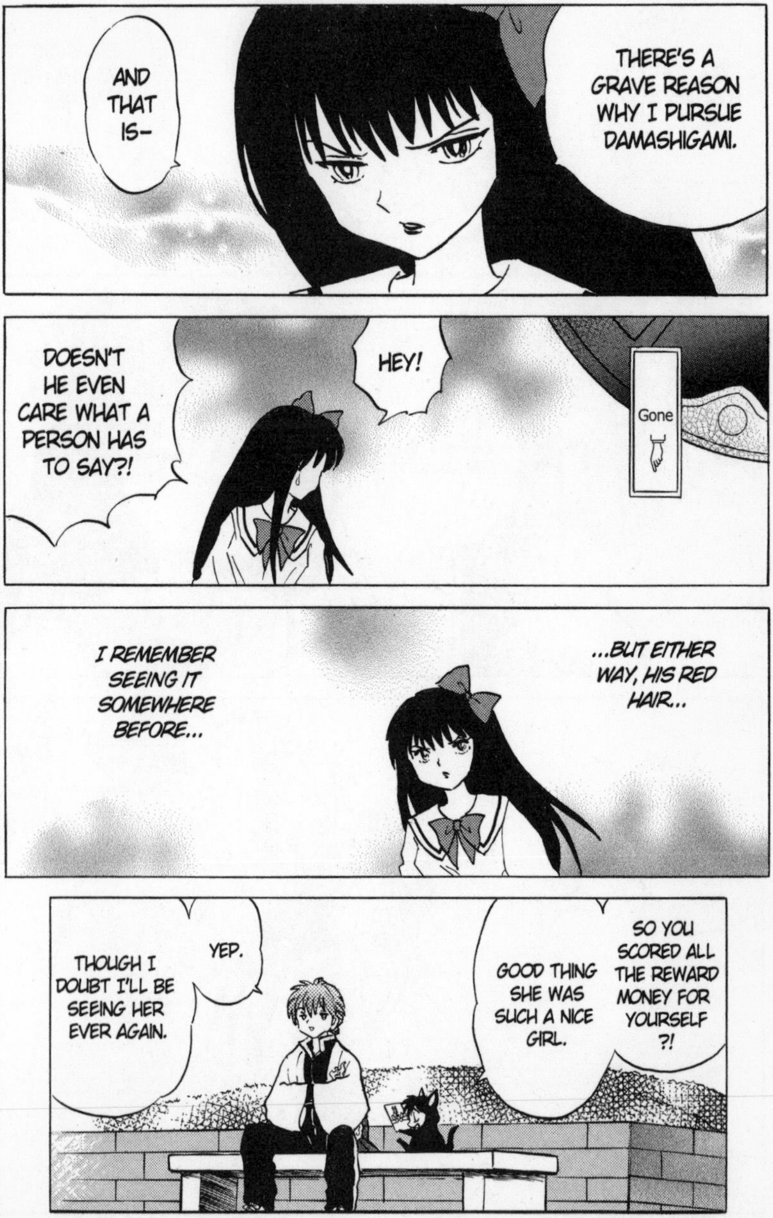
THERE'S A GRAVE REASON WHY I PURSUE DAMASHIGAMI.
AND THAT IS-
Gone
HEY!
DOESN'T HE EVEN CARE WHAT A PERSON HAS TO SAY?!
...BUT EITHER WAY, HIS RED HAIR...
I REMEMBER SEEING IT SOMEWHERE BEFORE...
SO YOU SCORED ALL THE REWARD MONEY FOR YOURSELF ?!
GOOD THING SHE WAS SUCH A NICE GIRL.
YEP.
THOUGH I DOUBT I'LL BE SEEING HER EVER AGAIN.

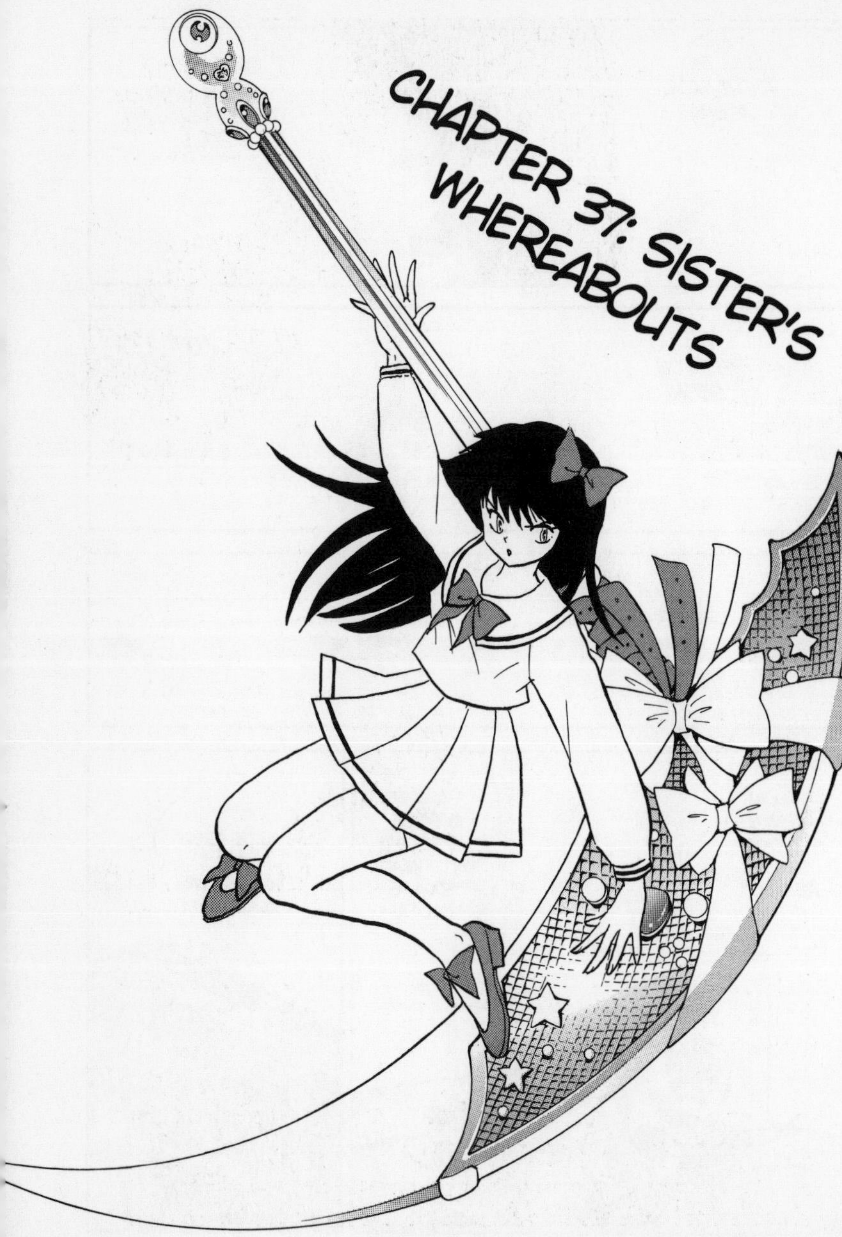
CHAPTER 37: SISTER'S WHEREABOUTS

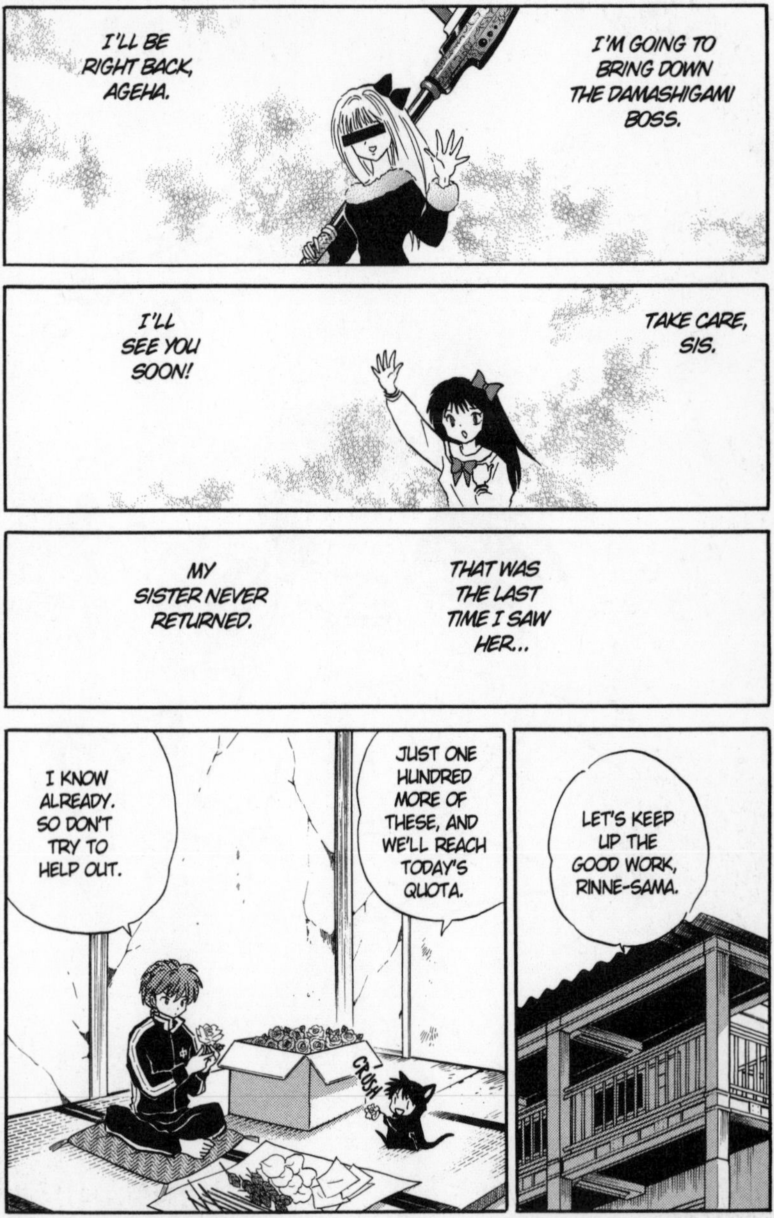
I'M GOING TO BRING DOWN THE DAMASHIGAMI BOSS.
I'LL BE RIGHT BACK, AGEHA.
TAKE CARE, SIS.
I'LL SEE YOU SOON!
THAT WAS THE LAST TIME I SAW HER...
MY SISTER NEVER RETURNED.
LET'S KEEP UP THE GOOD WORK, RINNE-SAMA.
JUST ONE HUNDRED MORE OF THESE, AND WE'LL REACH TODAY'S QUOTA.
CRUSH
I KNOW ALREADY. SO DON'T TRY TO HELP OUT.

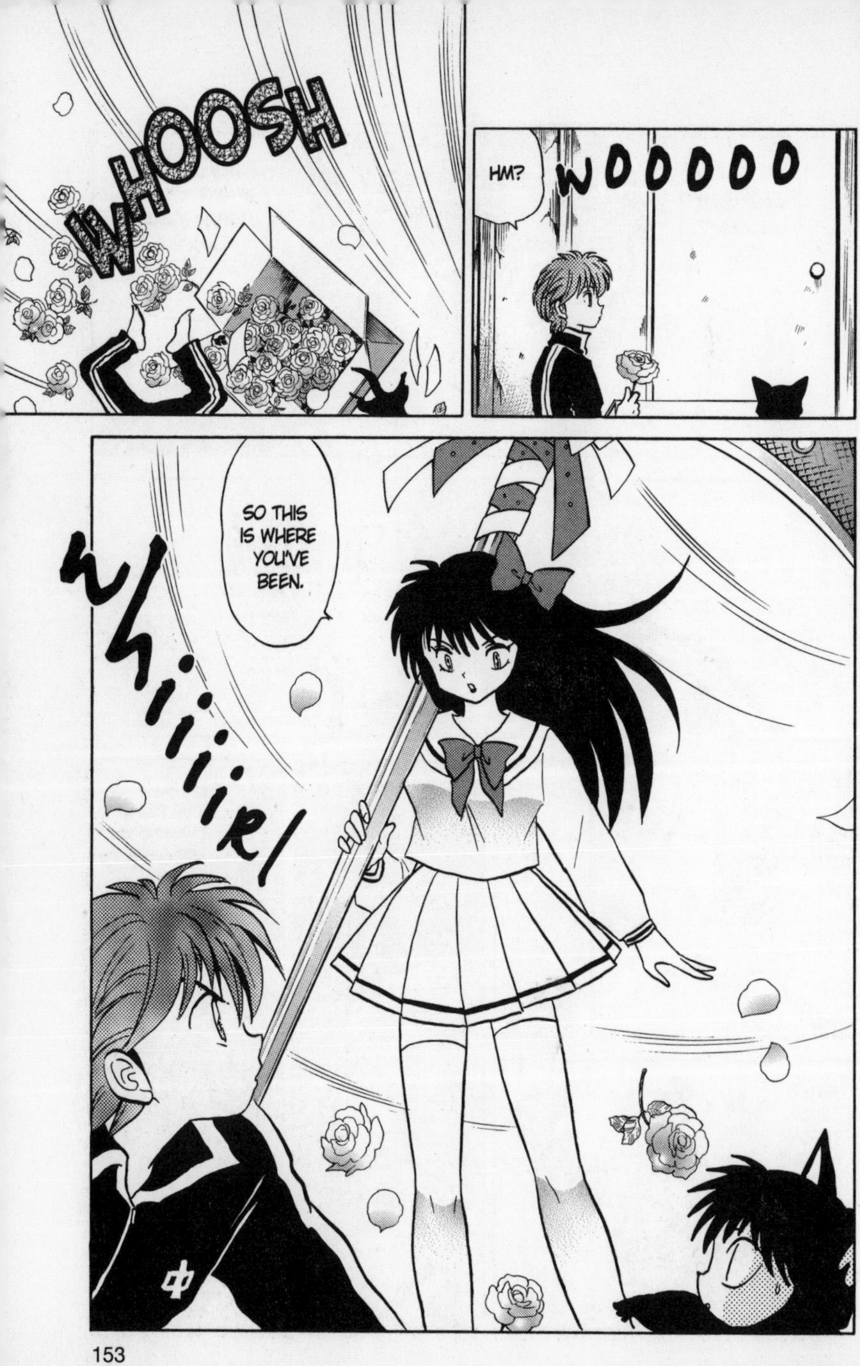

HM?
WOOOOO
WHOOSH
SO THIS IS WHERE YOU'VE BEEN.
Whiiiir!

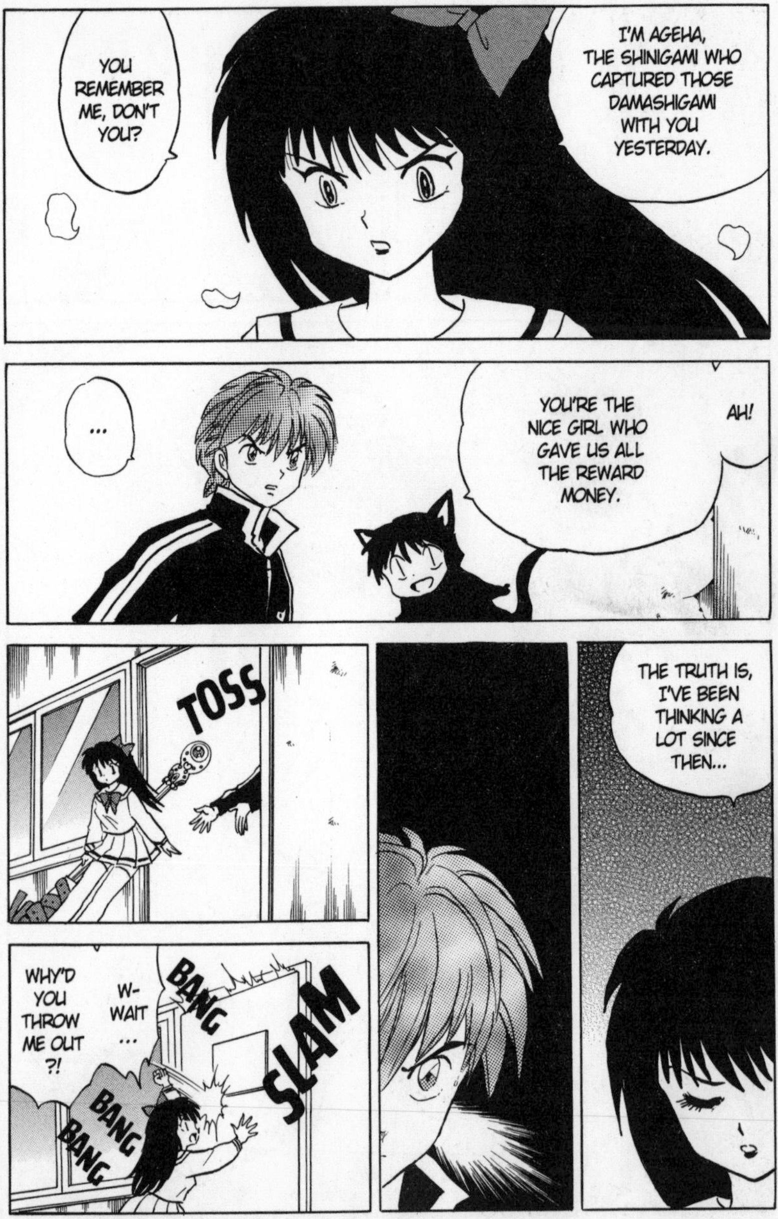
I'M AGEHA, THE SHINIGAMI WHO CAPTURED THOSE DAMASHIGAMI WITH YOU YESTERDAY.
YOU REMEMBER ME, DON'T YOU?
AH!
YOU'RE THE NICE GIRL WHO GAVE US ALL THE REWARD MONEY.
...
THE TRUTH IS, I'VE BEEN THINKING A LOT SINCE THEN...
TOSS
BANG
SLAM
W-WAIT...
WHY'D YOU THROW ME OUT?!
BANG BANG

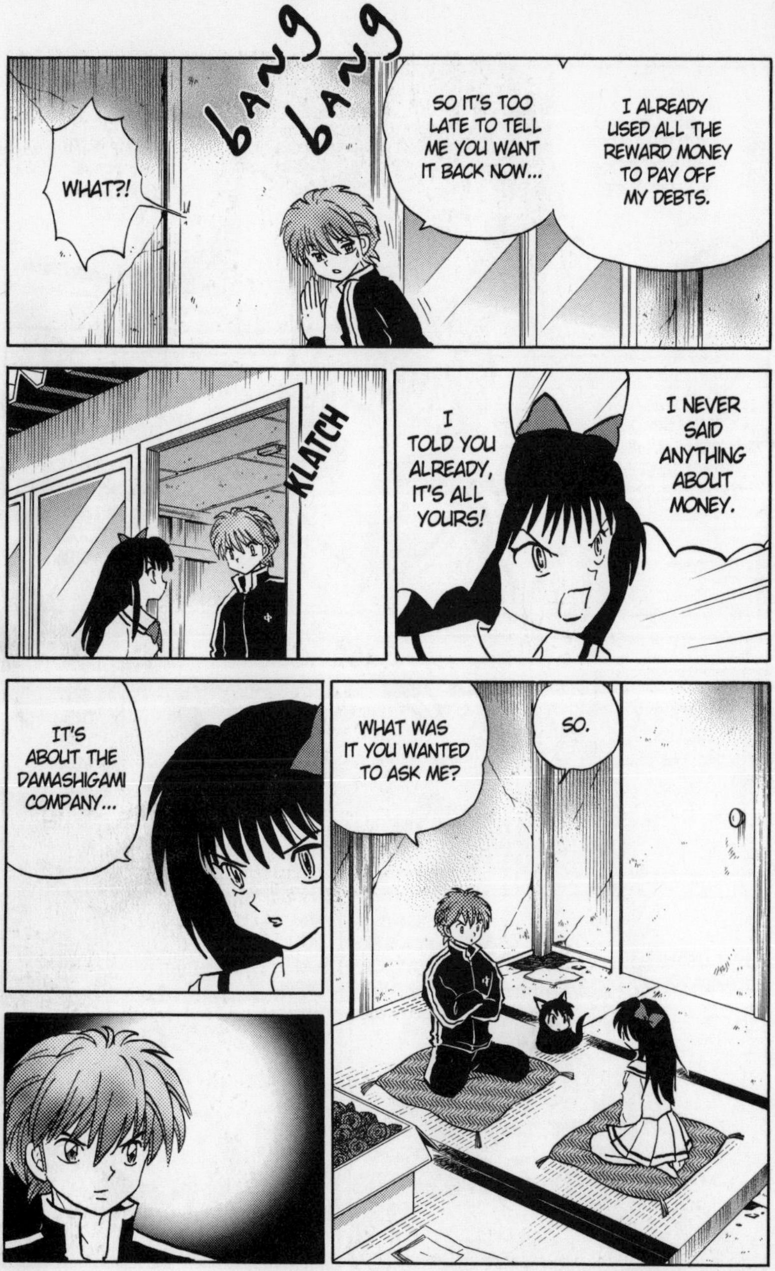
I ALREADY USED ALL THE REWARD MONEY TO PAY OFF MY DEBTS.
SO IT'S TOO LATE TO TELL ME YOU WANT IT BACK NOW...
BANG BANG
WHAT?!
I NEVER SAID ANYTHING ABOUT MONEY.
I TOLD YOU ALREADY, IT'S ALL YOURS!
KLATCH
SO.
WHAT WAS IT YOU WANTED TO ASK ME?
IT'S ABOUT THE DAMASHIGAMI COMPANY...

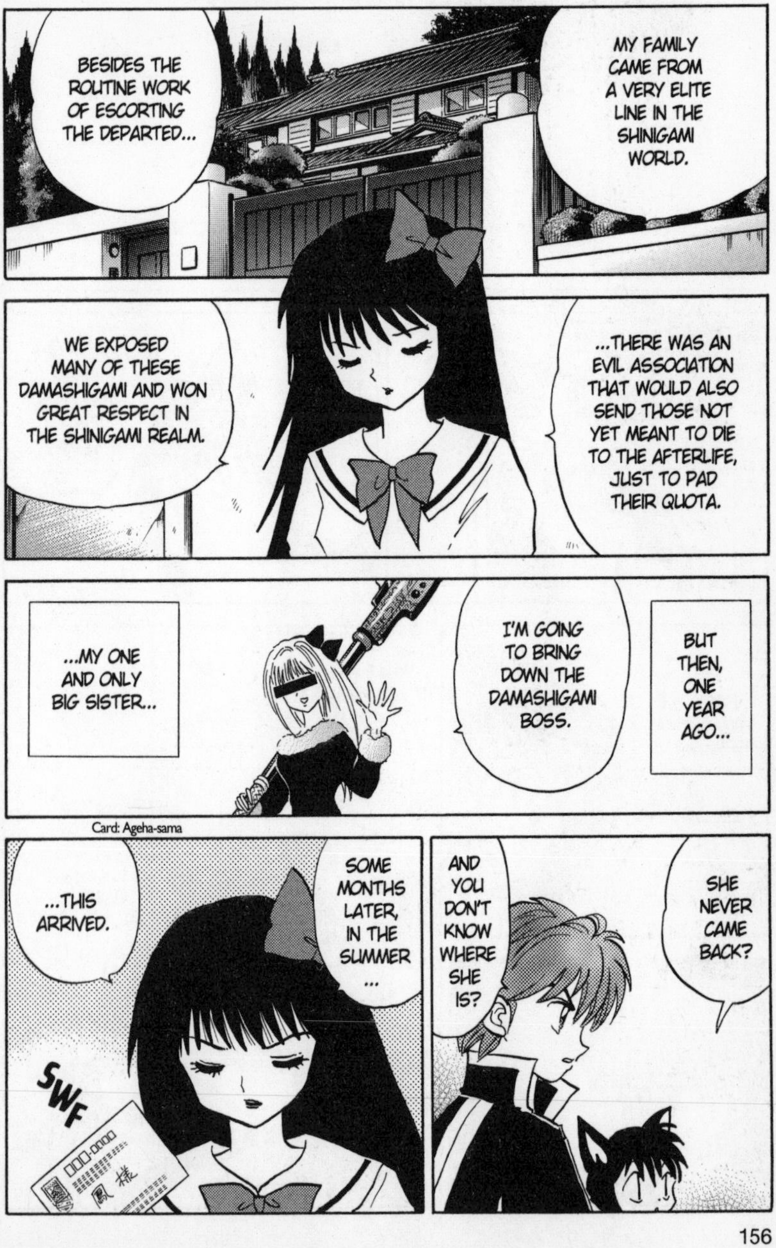
MY FAMILY CAME FROM A VERY ELITE LINE IN THE SHINIGAMI WORLD.
BESIDES THE ROUTINE WORK OF ESCORTING THE DEPARTED...
...THERE WAS AN EVIL ASSOCIATION THAT WOULD ALSO SEND THOSE NOT YET MEANT TO DIE TO THE AFTERLIFE, JUST TO PAD THEIR QUOTA.
WE EXPOSED MANY OF THESE DAMASHIGAMI AND WON GREAT RESPECT IN THE SHINIGAMI REALM.
BUT THEN, ONE YEAR AGO...
I'M GOING TO BRING DOWN THE DAMASHIGAMI BOSS.
...MY ONE AND ONLY BIG SISTER...
Card: Ageha-sama
SHE NEVER CAME BACK?
AND YOU DON'T KNOW WHERE SHE IS?
SOME MONTHS LATER, IN THE SUMMER ...
...THIS ARRIVED.
SWF

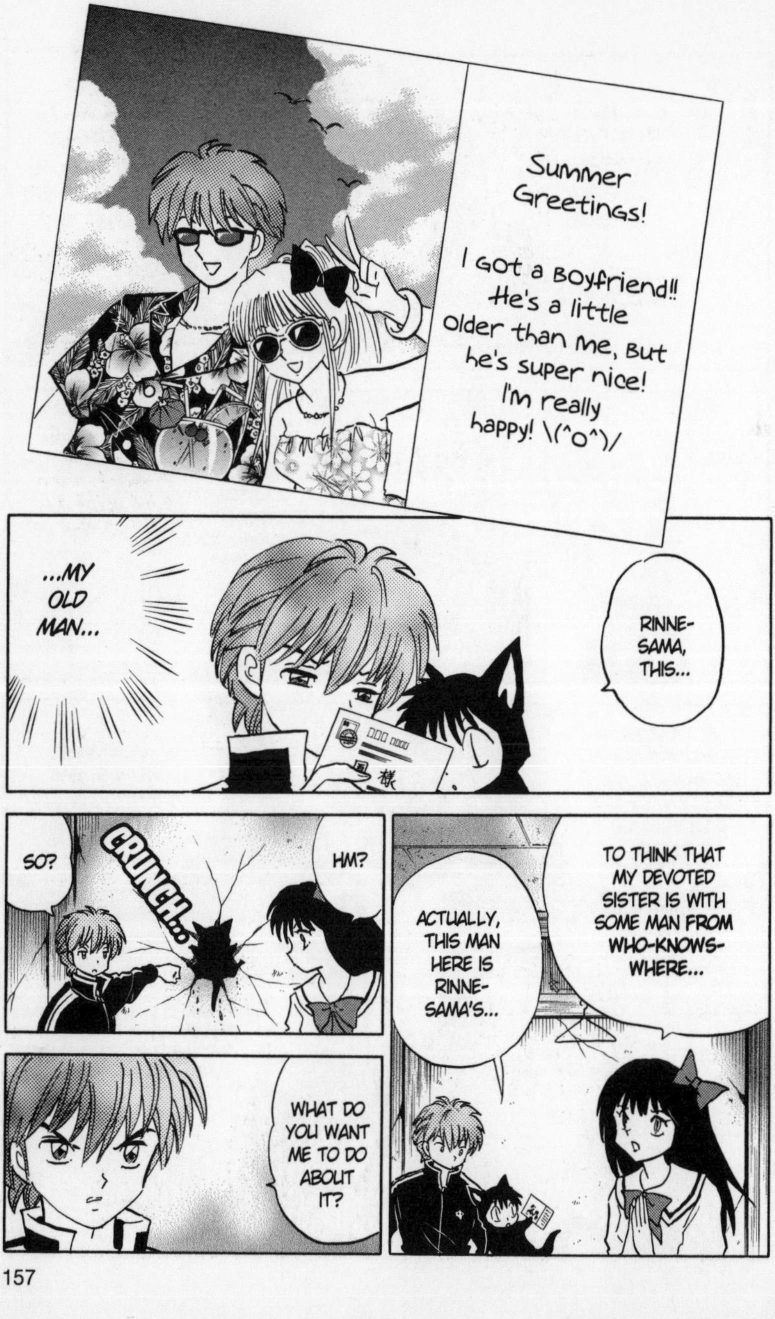
Summer Greetings!
I got a boyfriend!! He's a little older than me, but he's super nice! I'm really happy! \(^o^)/
RINNE-SAMA, THIS...
...MY OLD MAN...
TO THINK THAT MY DEVOTED SISTER IS WITH SOME MAN FROM WHO-KNOWS-WHERE...
ACTUALLY, THIS MAN HERE IS RINNE-SAMA'S...
HM?
CRUNCH...
SO?
WHAT DO YOU WANT ME TO DO ABOUT IT?

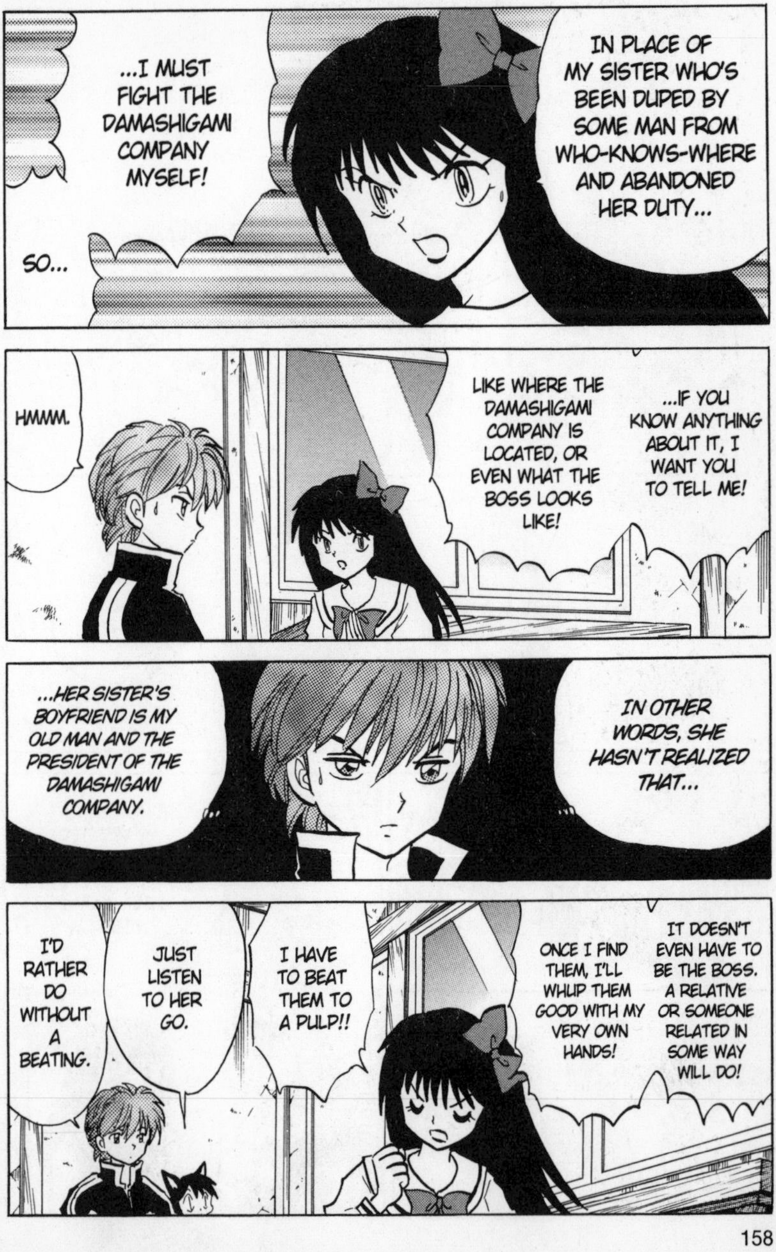
IN PLACE OF MY SISTER WHO'S BEEN DUPED BY SOME MAN FROM WHO-KNOWS-WHERE AND ABANDONED HER DUTY...
SO...
...I MUST FIGHT THE DAMASHIGAMI COMPANY MYSELF!
...IF YOU KNOW ANYTHING ABOUT IT, I WANT YOU TO TELL ME!
LIKE WHERE THE DAMASHIGAMI COMPANY IS LOCATED, OR EVEN WHAT THE BOSS LOOKS LIKE!
HMMM.
IN OTHER WORDS, SHE HASN'T REALIZED THAT...
...HER SISTER'S BOYFRIEND IS MY OLD MAN AND THE PRESIDENT OF THE DAMASHIGAMI COMPANY.
IT DOESN'T EVEN HAVE TO BE THE BOSS. A RELATIVE OR SOMEONE RELATED IN SOME WAY WILL DO!
ONCE I FIND THEM, I'LL WHUP THEM GOOD WITH MY VERY OWN HANDS!
I HAVE TO BEAT THEM TO A PULP!!
JUST LISTEN TO HER GO.
I'D RATHER DO WITHOUT A BEATING.

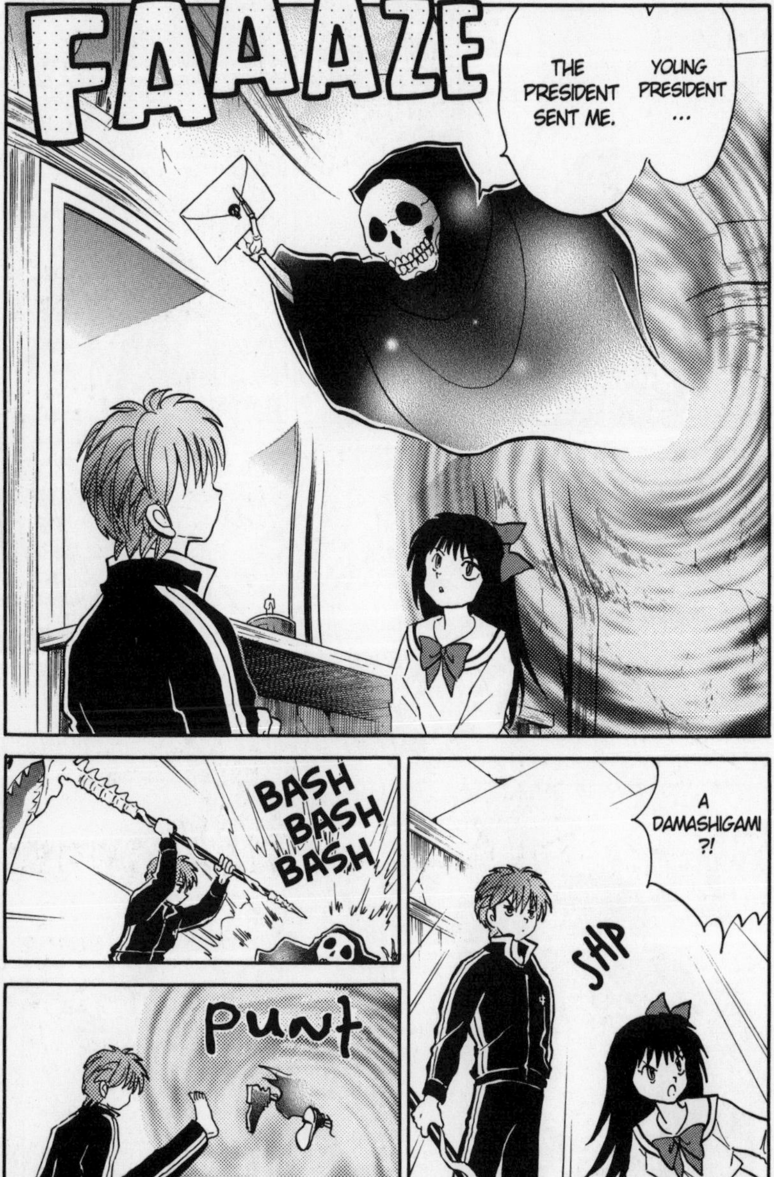
FAAAZE
YOUNG PRESIDENT ...
THE PRESIDENT SENT ME.
A DAMASHIGAMI ?!
SHP
BASH BASH BASH
punt

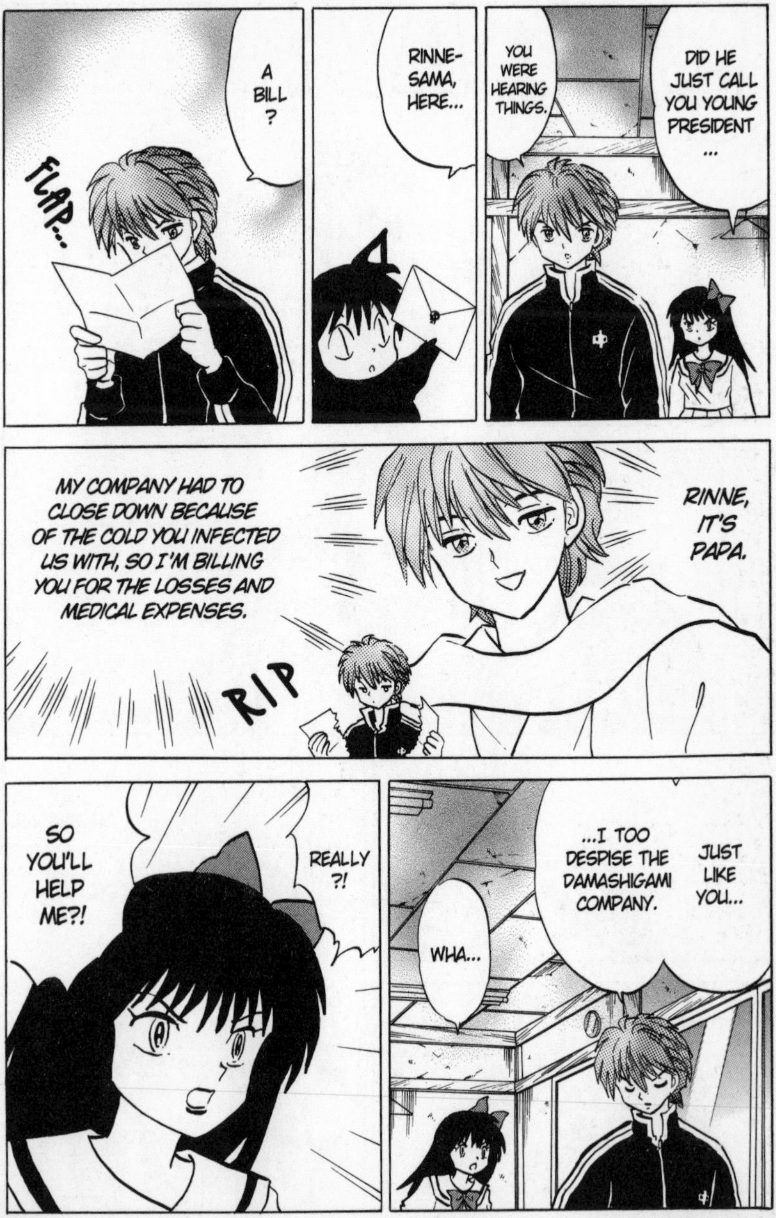
DID HE JUST CALL YOU YOUNG PRESIDENT ...
YOU WERE HEARING THINGS.
RINNE-SAMA, HERE...
A BILL ?
FLAP...
RINNE, IT'S PAPA.
MY COMPANY HAD TO CLOSE DOWN BECAUSE OF THE COLD YOU INFECTED US WITH, SO I'M BILLING YOU FOR THE LOSSES AND MEDICAL EXPENSES.
RIP
JUST LIKE YOU...
...I TOO DESPISE THE DAMASHIGAMI COMPANY.
WHA...
REALLY ?!
SO YOU'LL HELP ME?!

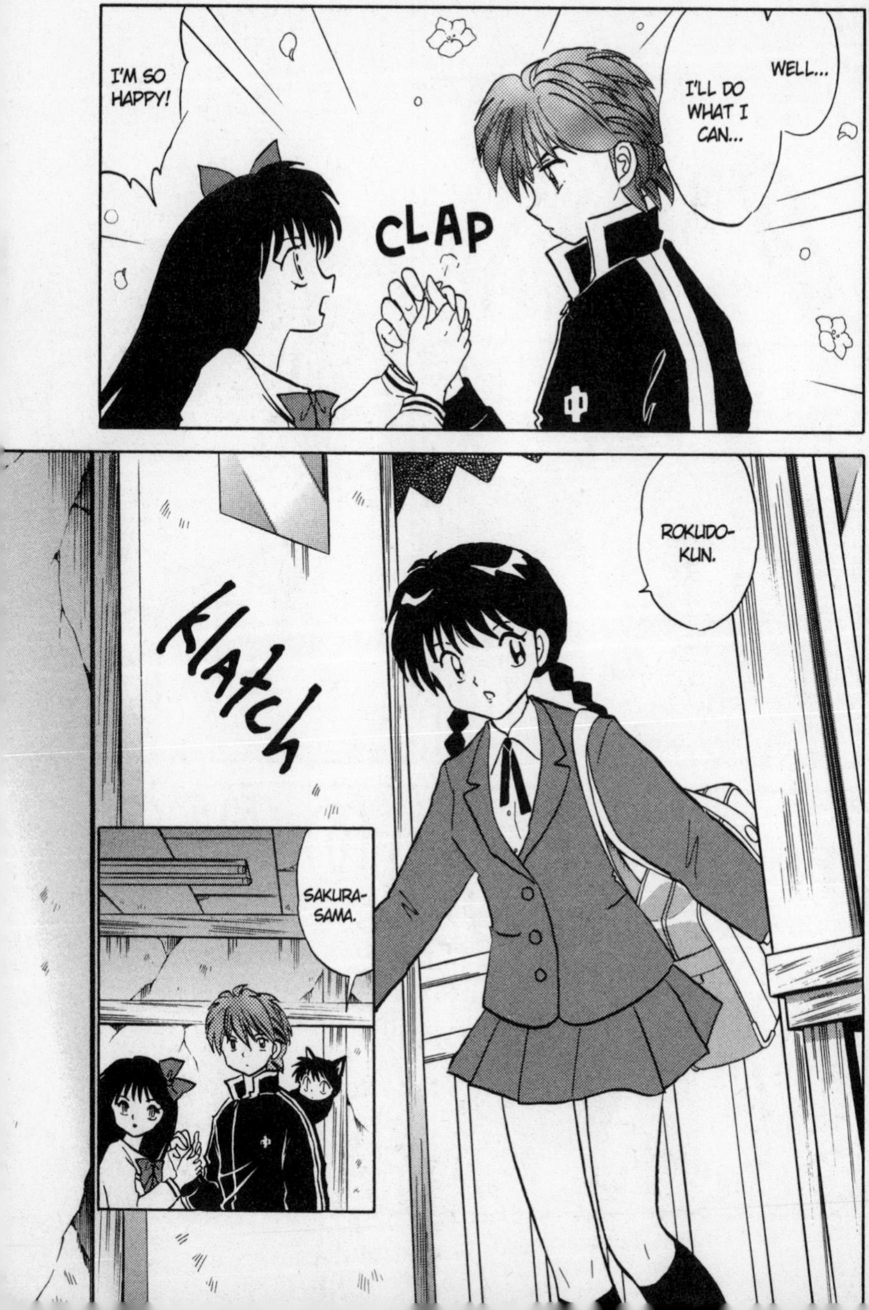
WELL... I'LL DO WHAT I CAN...
CLAP
I'M SO HAPPY!
klatch
ROKUDO-KUN.
SAKURA-SAMA.

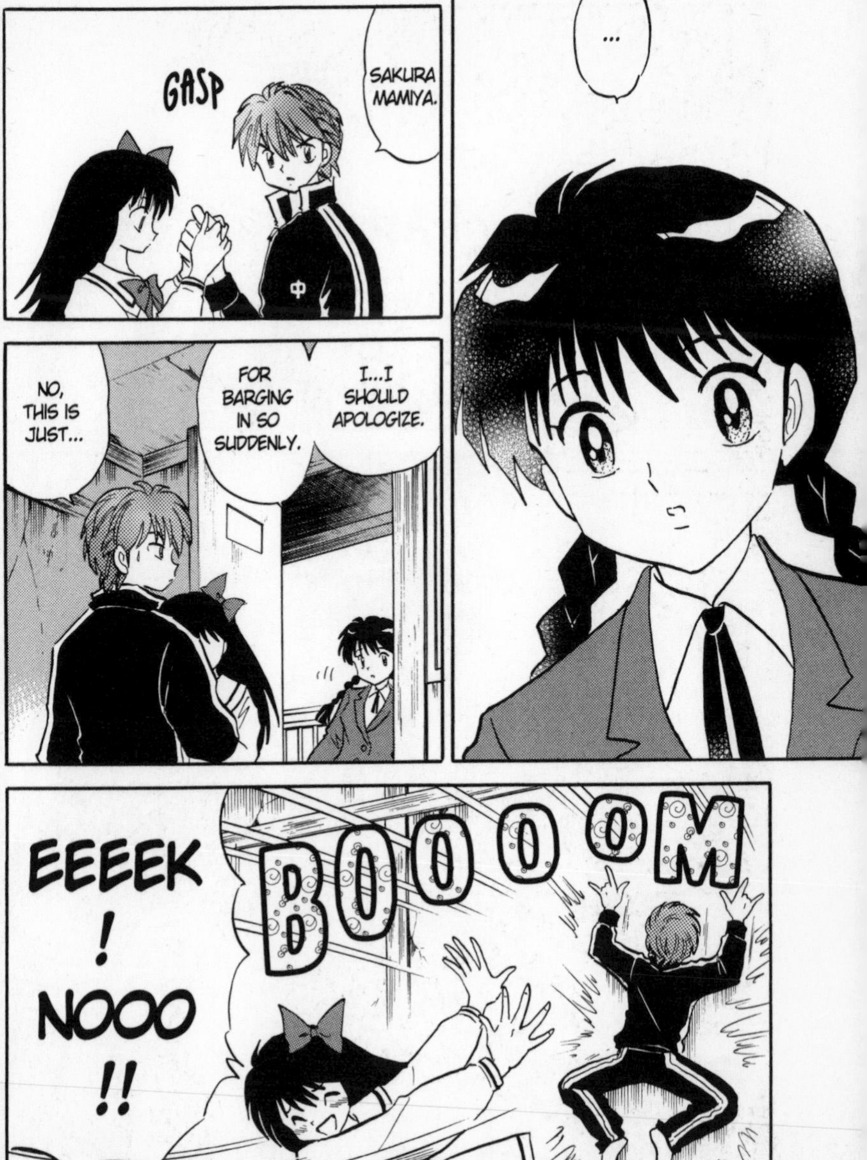
...
SAKURA MAMIYA.
GASP
I...I SHOULD APOLOGIZE.
FOR BARGING IN SO SUDDENLY.
NO, THIS IS JUST...
BOOOOM
EEEEK! NOOO!!

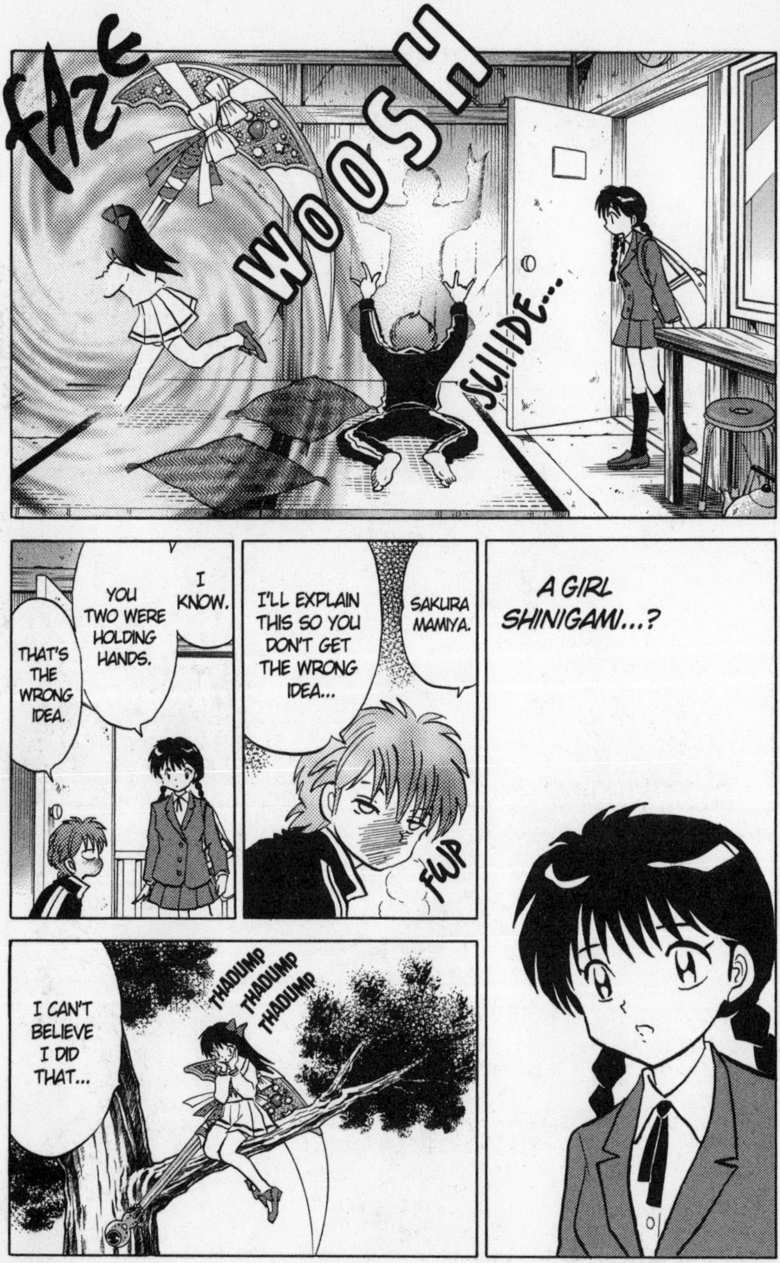
WOOSH
SLIIIDE...
FAZE
A GIRL SHINIGAMI...?
SAKURA MAMIYA.
I'LL EXPLAIN THIS SO YOU DON'T GET THE WRONG IDEA...
FWP
I KNOW.
YOU TWO WERE HOLDING HANDS.
THAT'S THE WRONG IDEA.
THADUMP
THADUMP
THADUMP
I CAN'T BELIEVE I DID THAT...

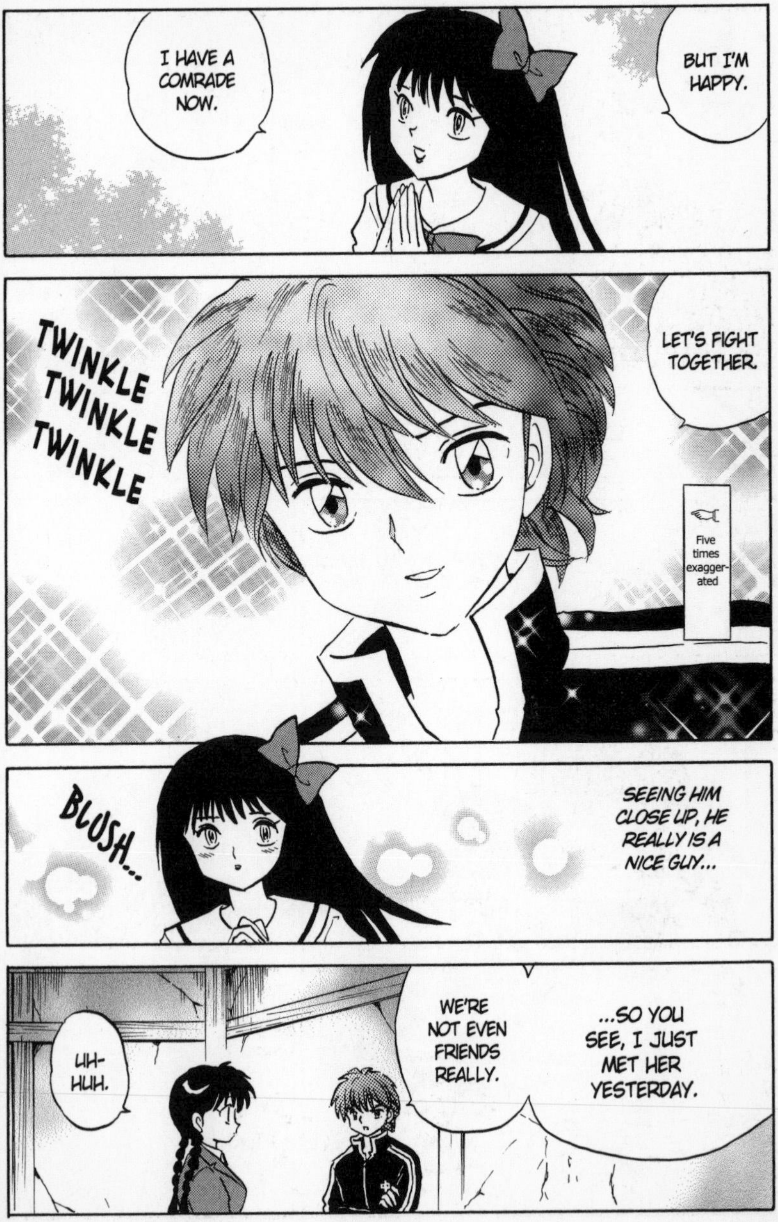

BUT I'M HAPPY.
I HAVE A COMRADE NOW.
LET'S FIGHT TOGETHER.
Five times exaggerated
TWINKLE TWINKLE TWINKLE
SEEING HIM CLOSE UP, HE REALLY IS A NICE GUY...
BLUSH...
...SO YOU SEE, I JUST MET HER YESTERDAY.
WE'RE NOT EVEN FRIENDS REALLY.
UH-HUH.

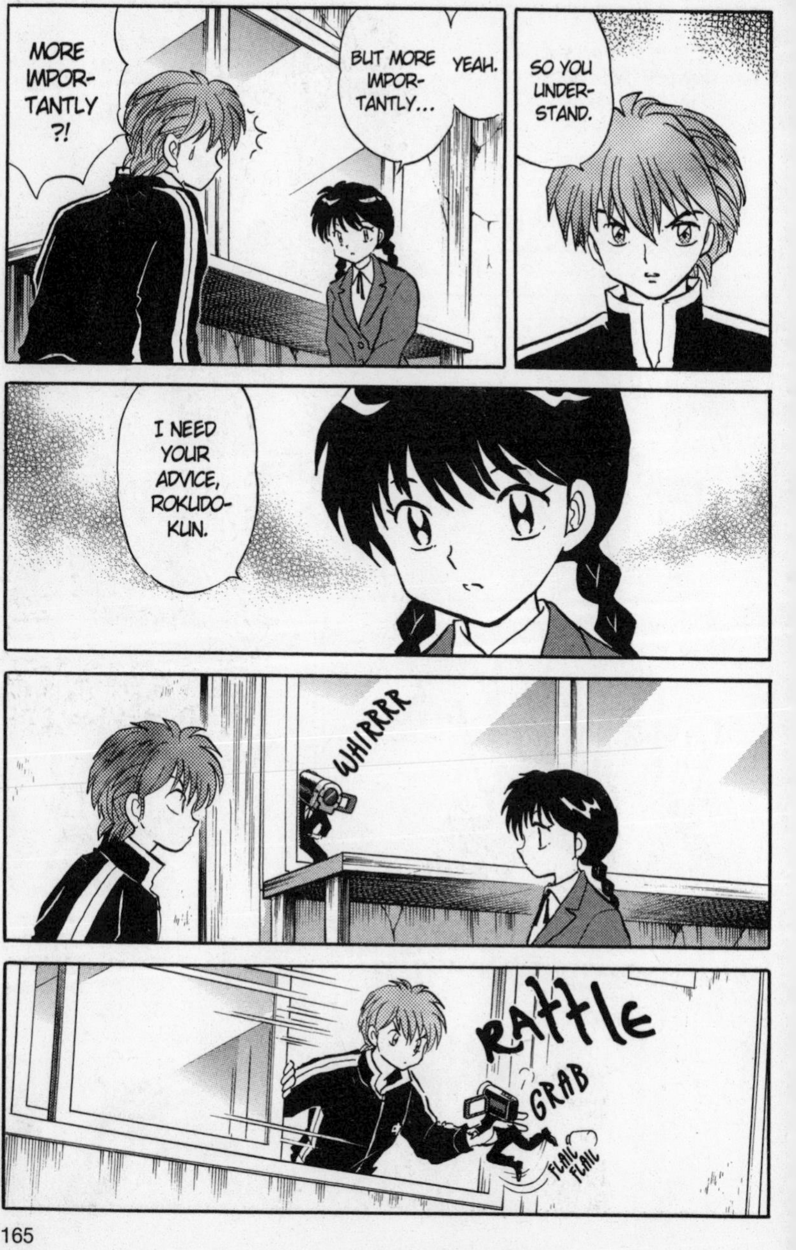

SO YOU UNDERSTAND.
YEAH.
BUT MORE IMPORTANTLY...
MORE IMPORTANTLY ?!
I NEED YOUR ADVICE, ROKUDO-KUN.
WHIRRRR
RATTLE
GRAB
FLAIL FLAIL

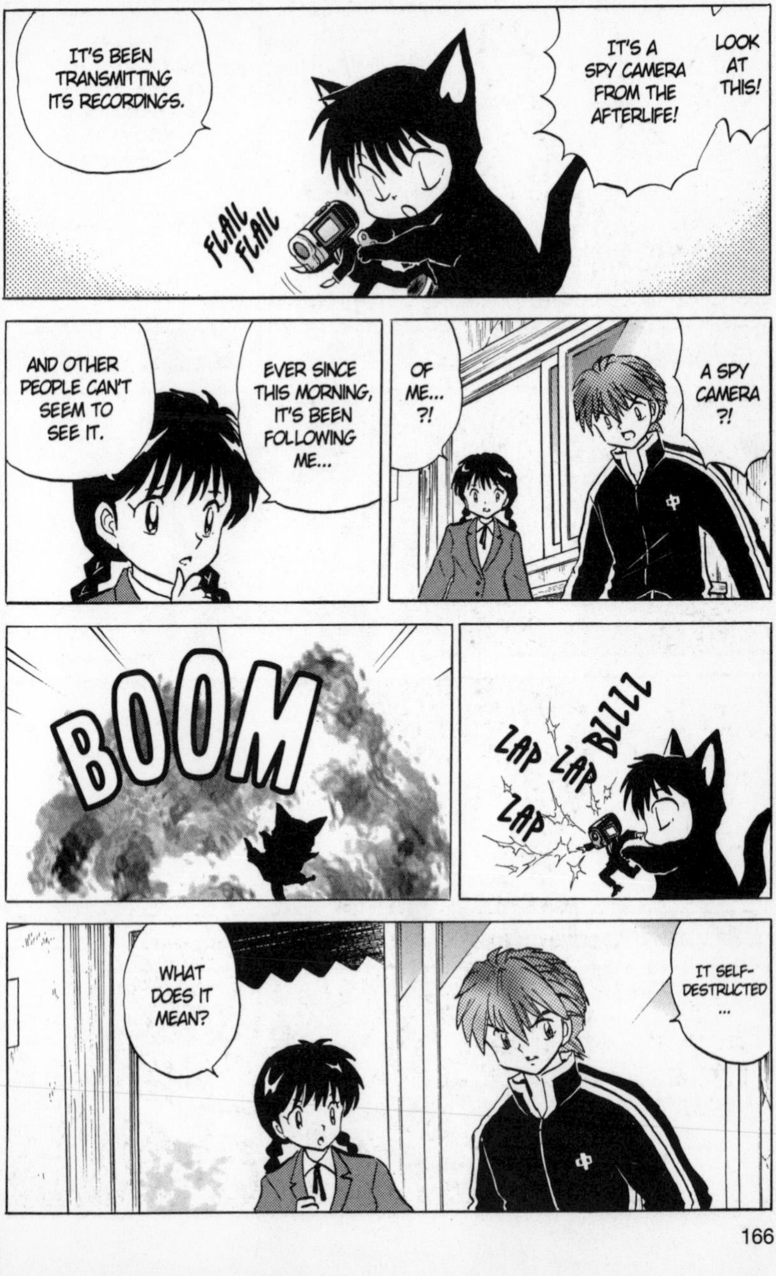
LOOK AT THIS!
IT'S A SPY CAMERA FROM THE AFTERLIFE!
IT'S BEEN TRANSMITTING ITS RECORDINGS.
FLAIL FLAIL
A SPY CAMERA ?!
OF ME... ?!
EVER SINCE THIS MORNING, IT'S BEEN FOLLOWING ME...
AND OTHER PEOPLE CAN'T SEEM TO SEE IT.
BZZZZ
ZAP ZAP
ZAP
BOOM
IT SELF-DESTRUCTED ...
WHAT DOES IT MEAN?

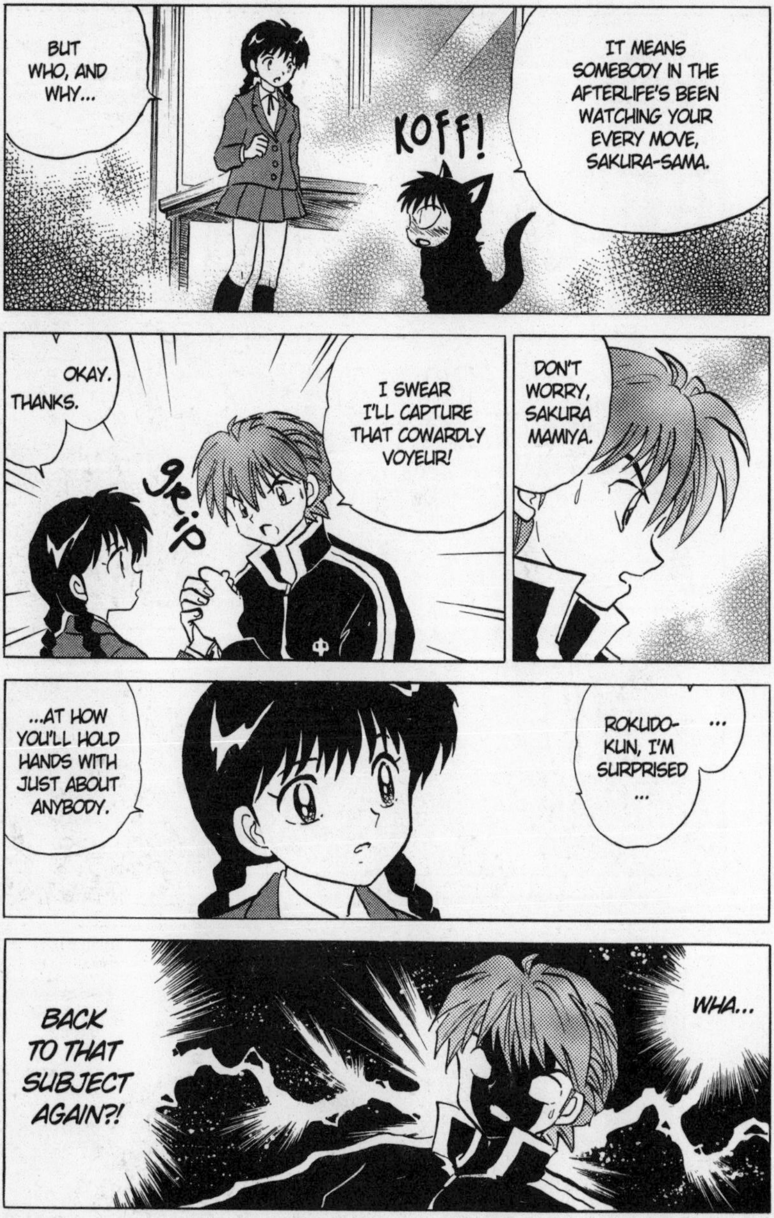
IT MEANS SOMEBODY IN THE AFTERLIFE'S BEEN WATCHING YOUR EVERY MOVE, SAKURA-SAMA.
KOFF!
BUT WHO, AND WHY...
DON'T WORRY, SAKURA MAMIYA.
I SWEAR I'LL CAPTURE THAT COWARDLY VOYEUR!
grip
OKAY. THANKS.
ROKUDO-KUN, I'M SURPRISED ... ...
...AT HOW YOU'LL HOLD HANDS WITH JUST ABOUT ANYBODY.
WHA...
BACK TO THAT SUBJECT AGAIN?!

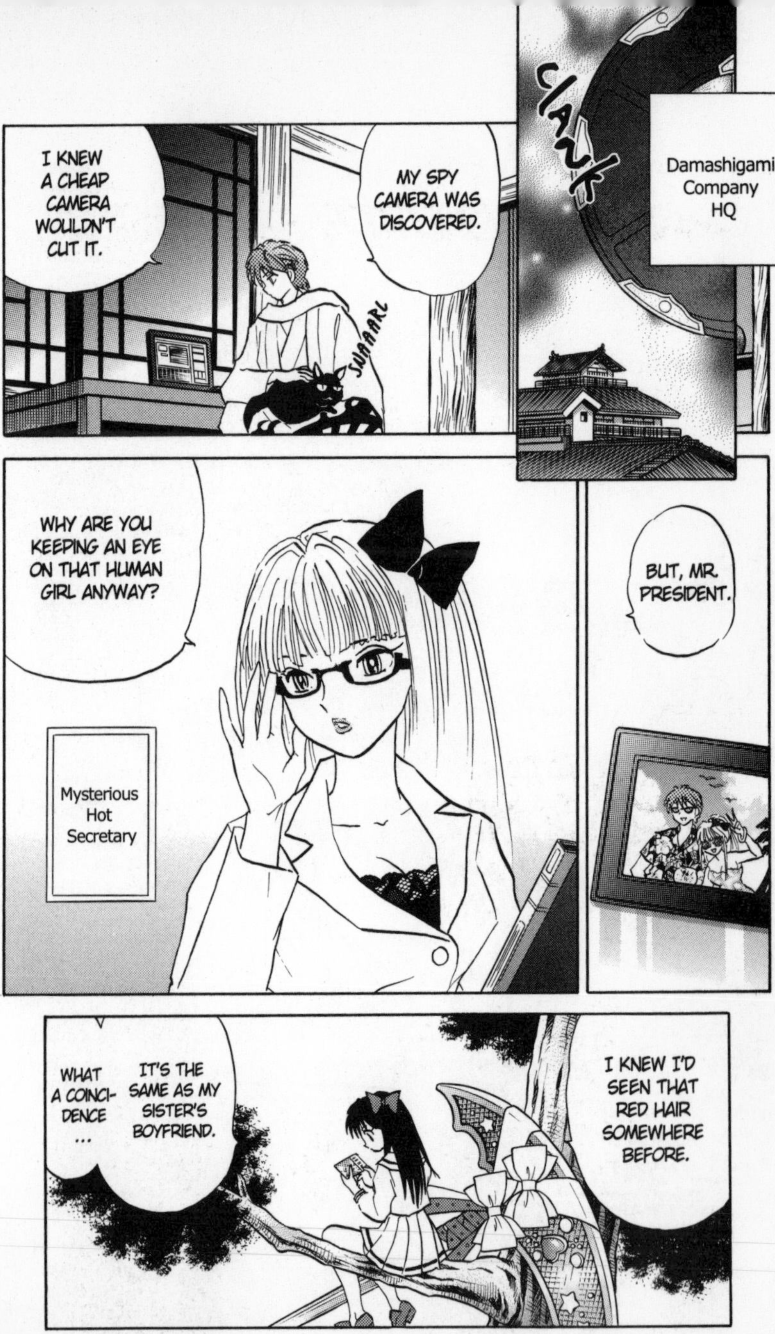
CLANK
Damashigami Company HQ
MY SPY CAMERA WAS DISCOVERED.
I KNEW A CHEAP CAMERA WOULDN'T CUT IT.
SNAAARL
BUT, MR. PRESIDENT.
WHY ARE YOU KEEPING AN EYE ON THAT HUMAN GIRL ANYWAY?
Mysterious Hot Secretary
I KNEW I'D SEEN THAT RED HAIR SOMEWHERE BEFORE.
IT'S THE SAME AS MY SISTER'S BOYFRIEND.
WHAT A COINCIDENCE...

CHAPTER 38: BRIDE SCREENING

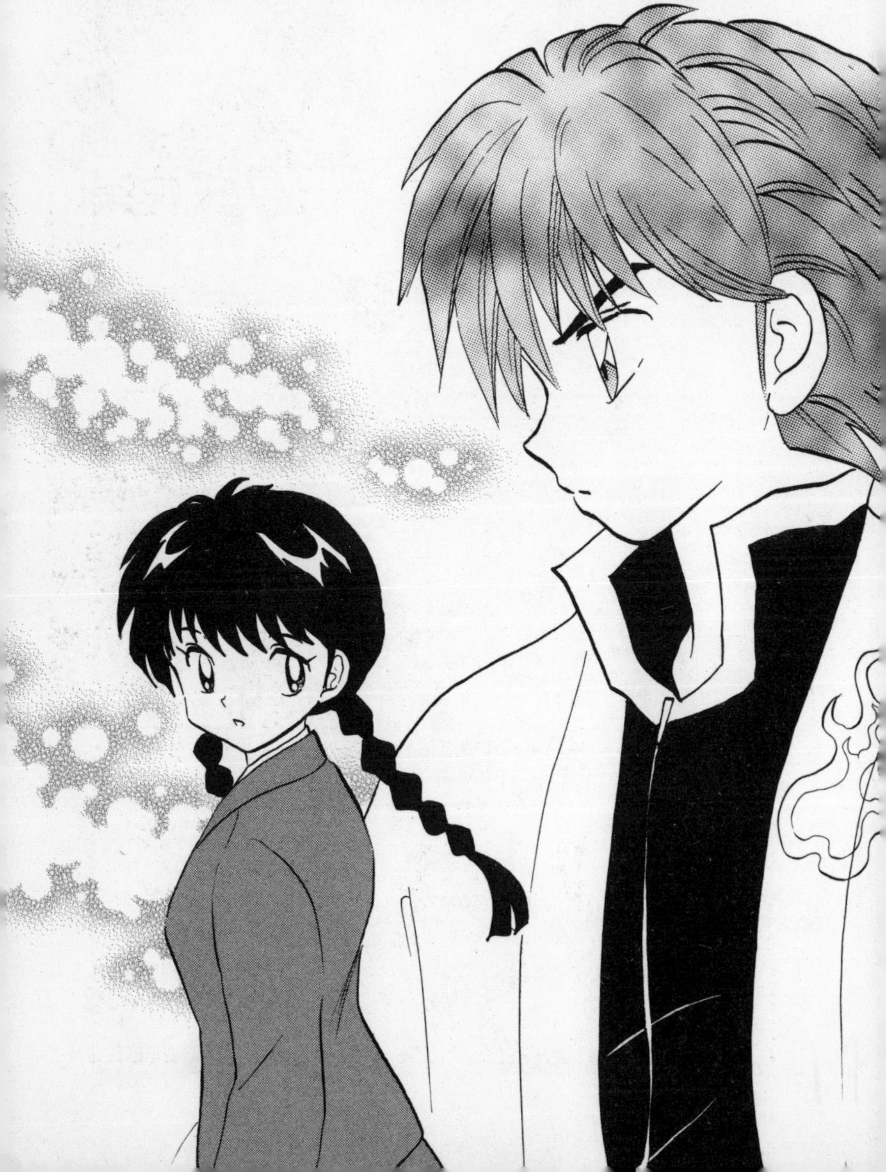

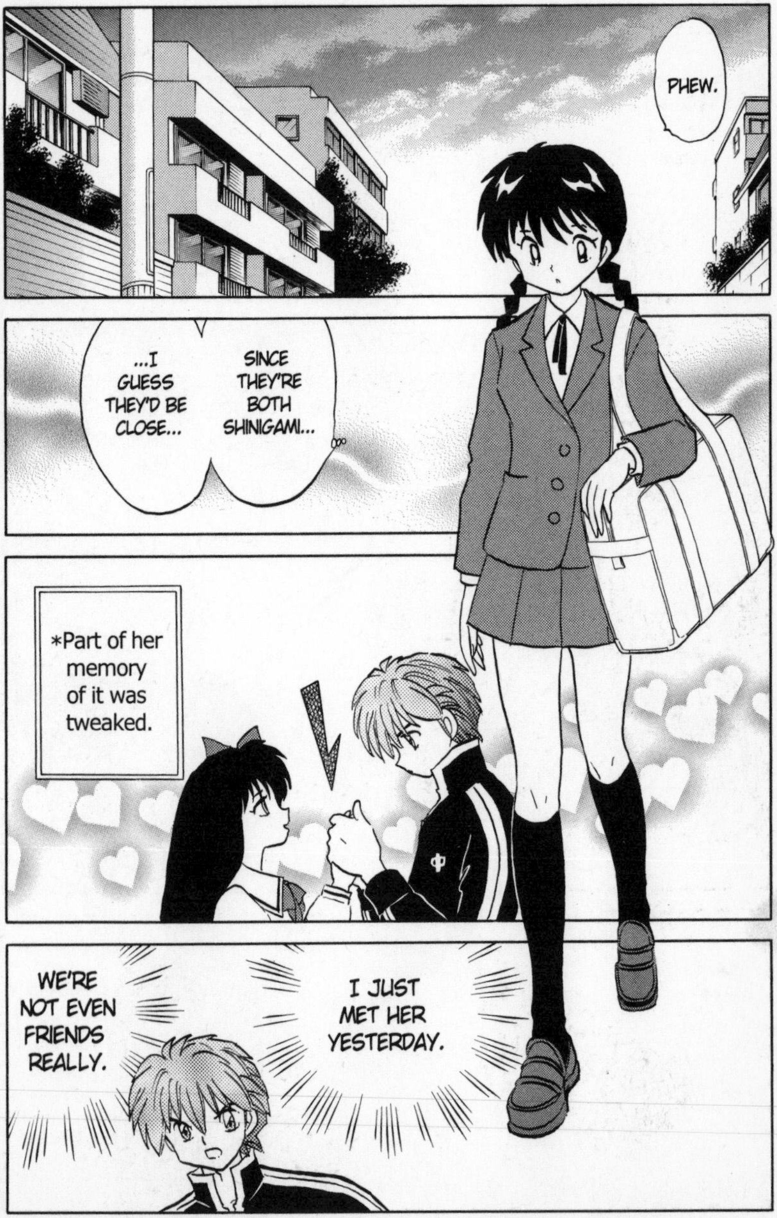
PHEW.
SINCE THEY'RE BOTH SHINIGAMI...
...I GUESS THEY'D BE CLOSE...
*Part of her memory of it was tweaked.
I JUST MET HER YESTERDAY.
WE'RE NOT EVEN FRIENDS REALLY.

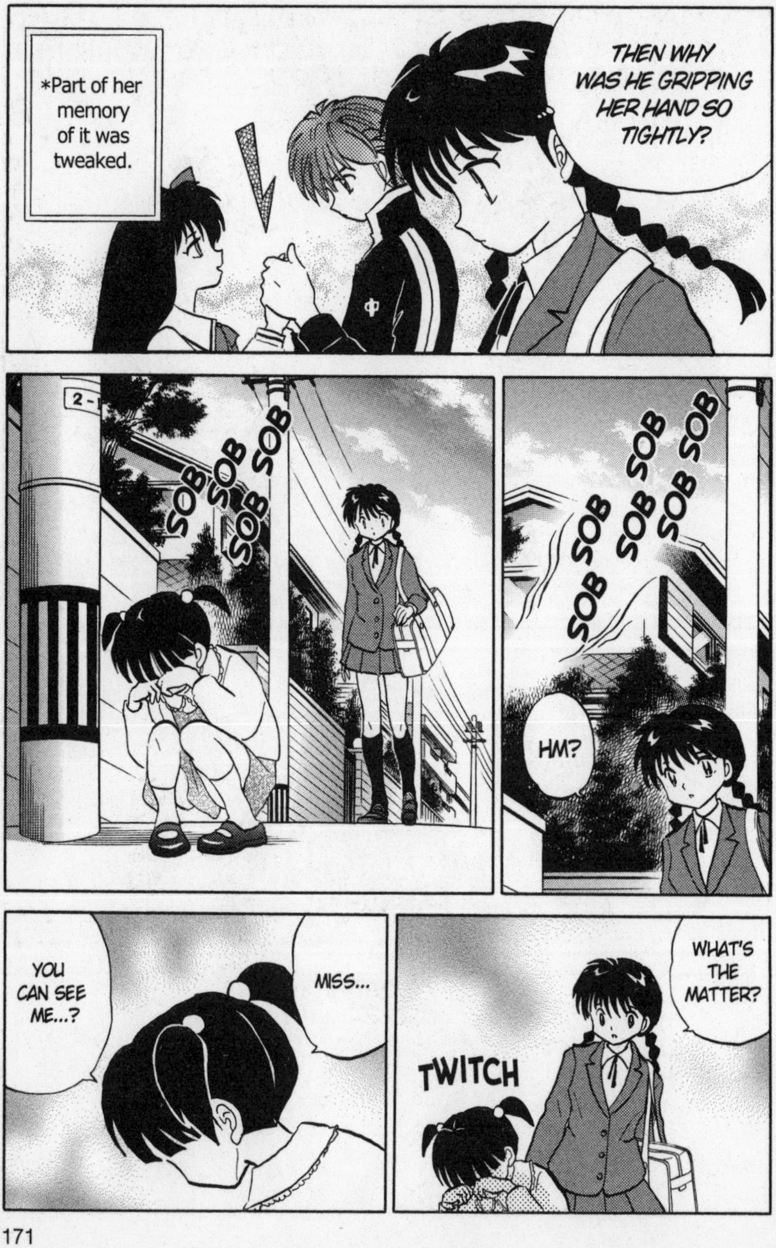
THEN WHY WAS HE GRIPPING HER HAND SO TIGHTLY?
*Part of her memory of it was tweaked.
SOB SOB
SOB SOB
SOB SOB
HM?
SOB
SOB SOB
SOB
WHAT'S THE MATTER?
TWITCH
MISS...
YOU CAN SEE ME...?

EH HEH HEH HEH HEH HEH HEH HEH.
GLOOOM
CAN I FOLLOW YOU HOME?
AAW, SHOOT.
SHE'S A GHOST!
OH, YOU CAN SEE US?
YAY YAY
LOOK AT ME.
MURMUR MURMUR
ME TOO. ME TOO.
HUH ?!
THERE'S THIRTY TIMES MORE THAN USUAL!

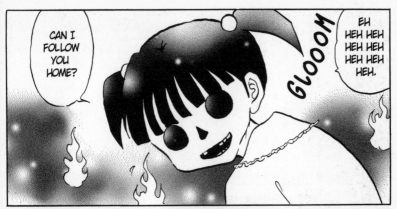

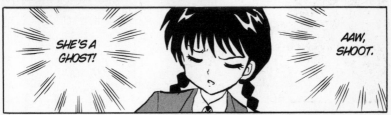

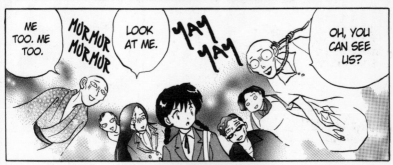

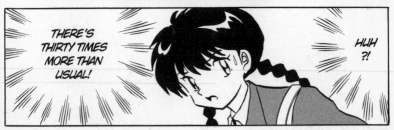

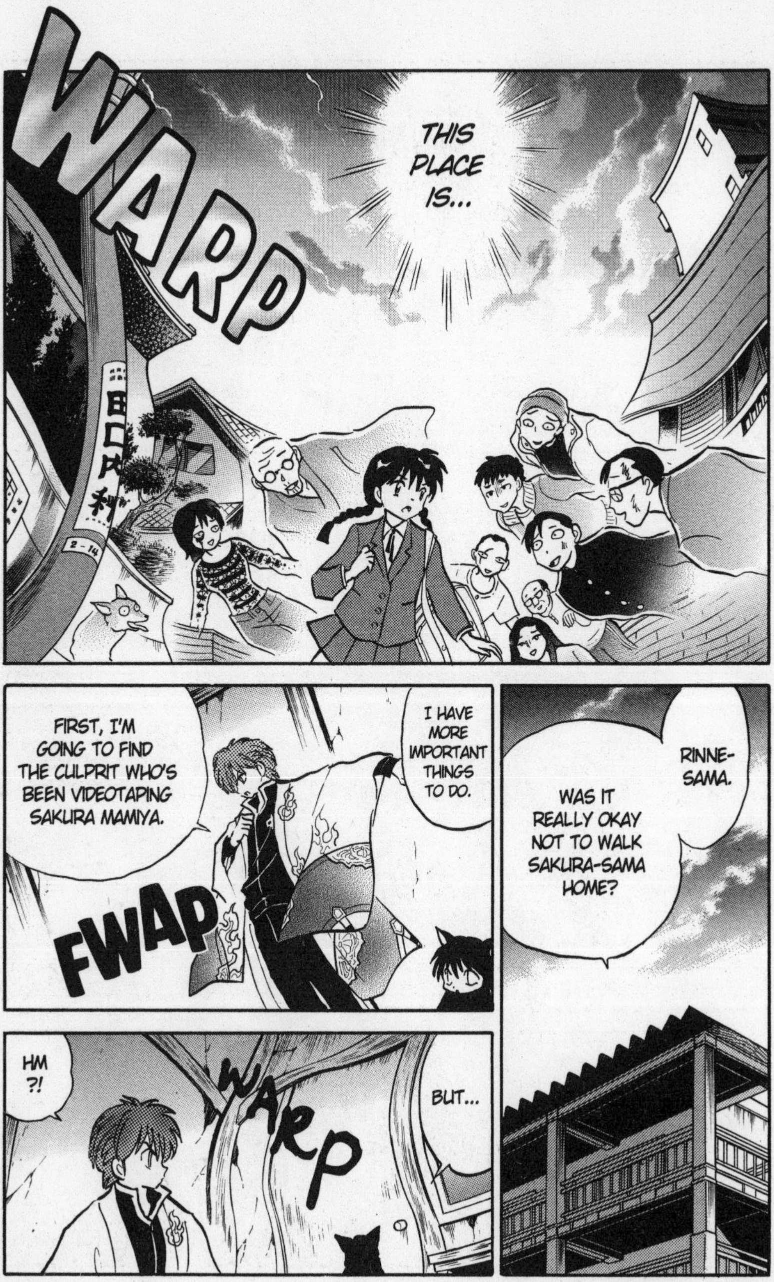
WARP
THIS PLACE IS...
RINNE-SAMA.
WAS IT REALLY OKAY NOT TO WALK SAKURA-SAMA HOME?
I HAVE MORE IMPORTANT THINGS TO DO.
FIRST, I'M GOING TO FIND THE CULPRIT WHO'S BEEN VIDEOTAPING SAKURA MAMIYA.
FWAP
BUT...
WARP
HM ?!

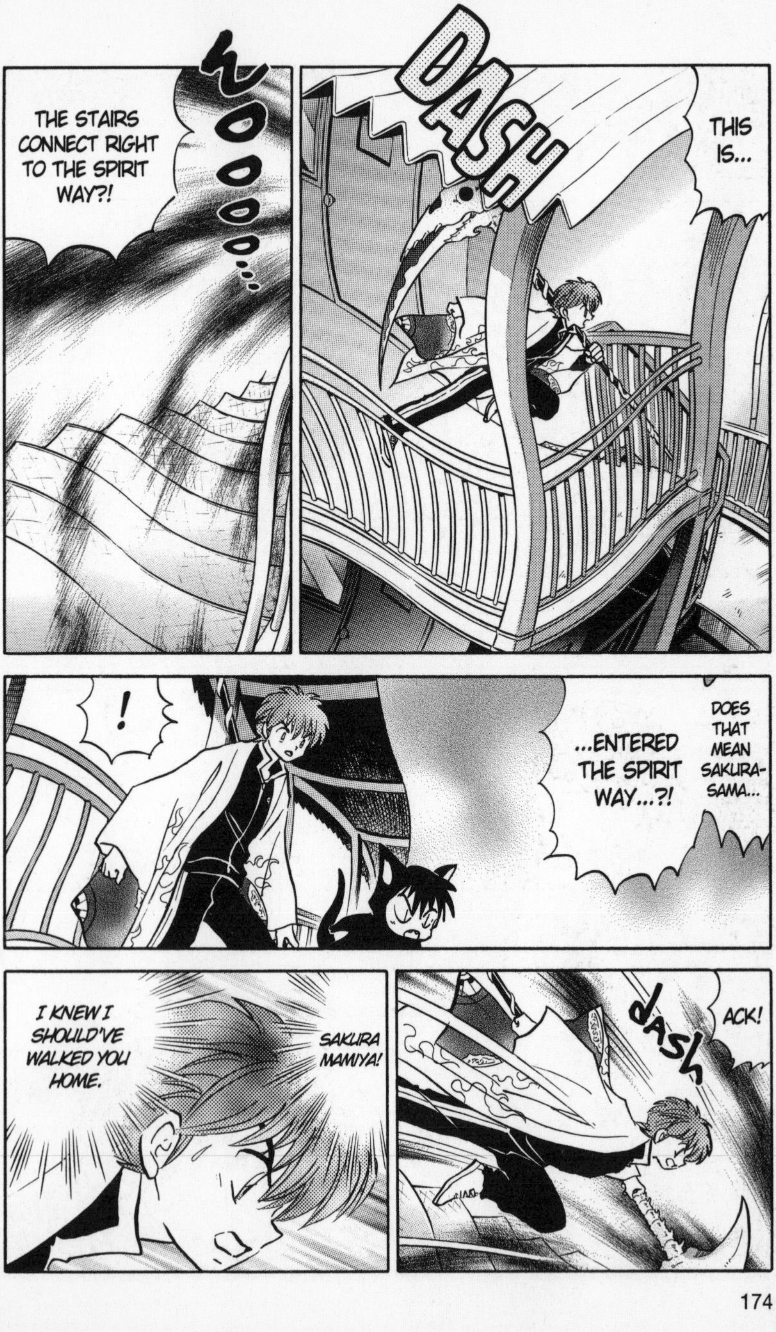
DASH
THIS IS...
WOOOOOO...
THE STAIRS CONNECT RIGHT TO THE SPIRIT WAY?!
DOES THAT MEAN SAKURA-SAMA...
...ENTERED THE SPIRIT WAY...?!
!
ACK!
dash
SAKURA MAMIYA!
I KNEW I SHOULD'VE WALKED YOU HOME.

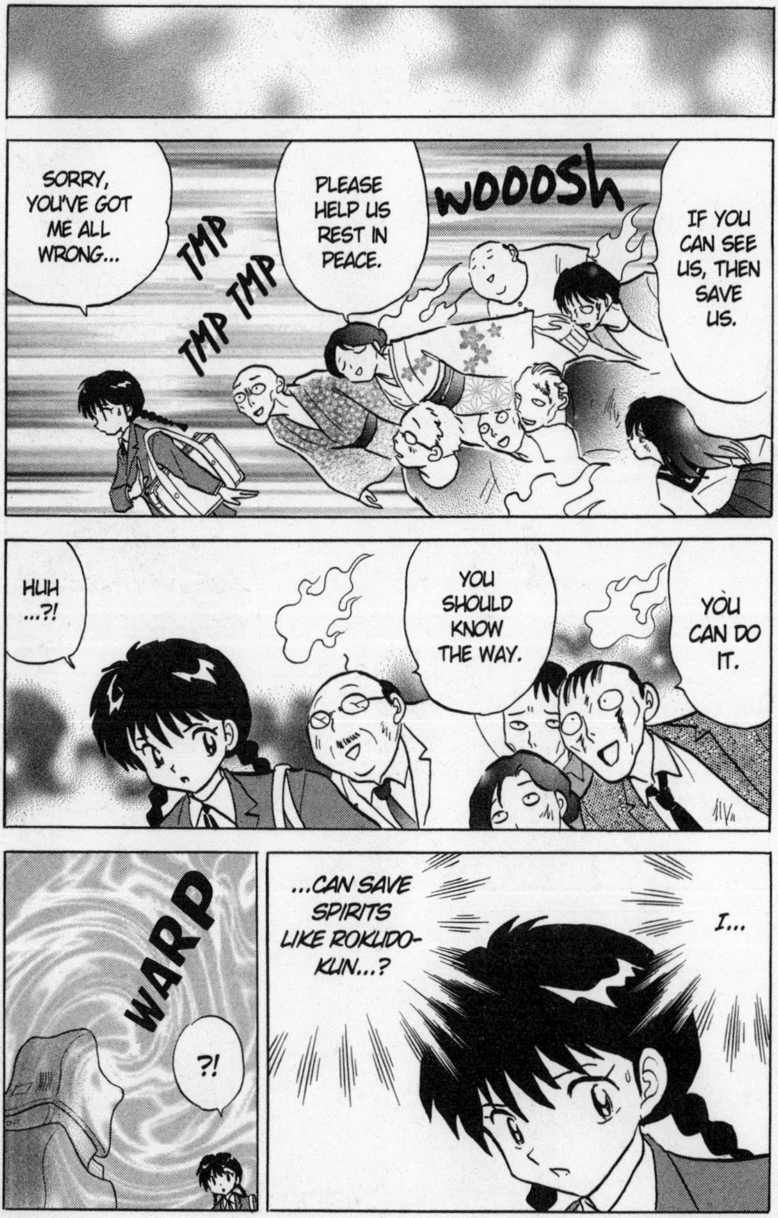
IF YOU CAN SEE US, THEN SAVE US.
WOOOSH
PLEASE HELP US REST IN PEACE.
TMP TMP TMP
SORRY, YOU'VE GOT ME ALL WRONG...
YOU CAN DO IT.
YOU SHOULD KNOW THE WAY.
HUH ...?!
I...
...CAN SAVE SPIRITS LIKE ROKUDO-KUN...?
WARP
?!

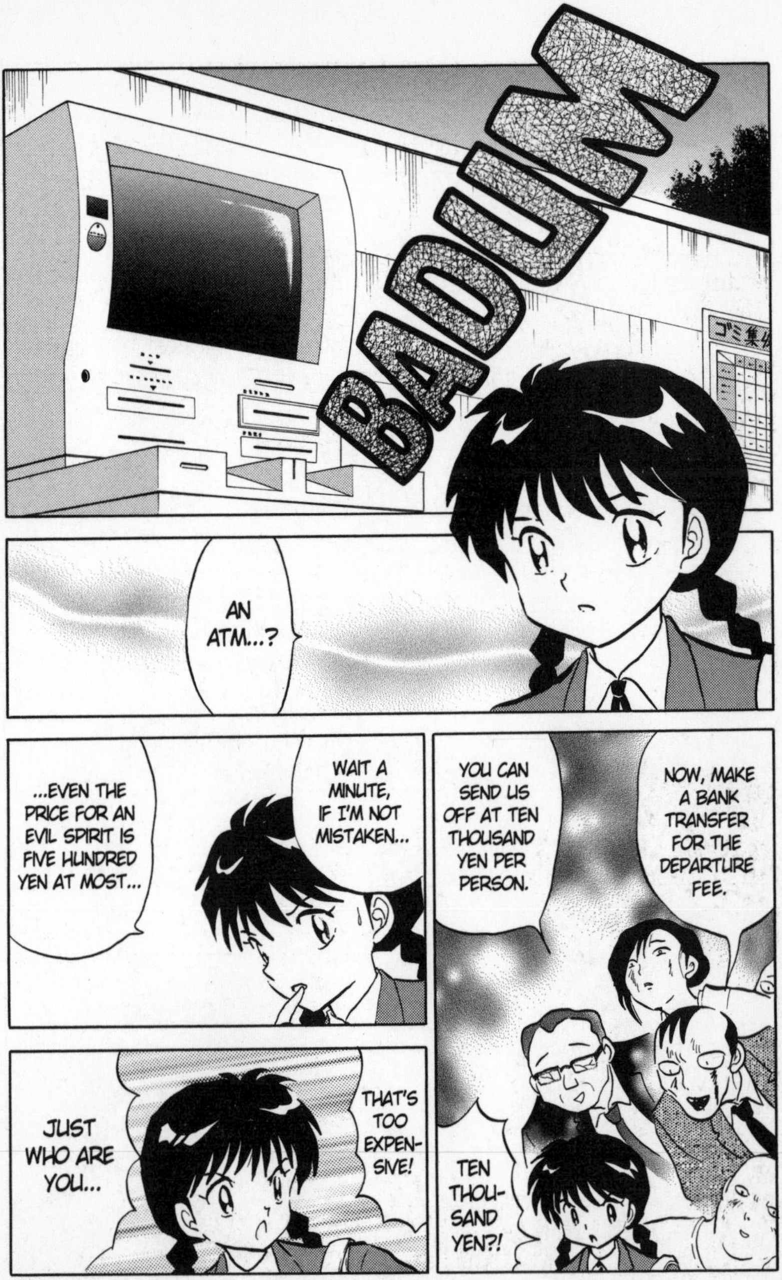
BADUM
AN ATM...?
NOW, MAKE A BANK TRANSFER FOR THE DEPARTURE FEE.
YOU CAN SEND US OFF AT TEN THOUSAND YEN PER PERSON.
TEN THOUSAND YEN?!
WAIT A MINUTE, IF I'M NOT MISTAKEN...
...EVEN THE PRICE FOR AN EVIL SPIRIT IS FIVE HUNDRED YEN AT MOST...
THAT'S TOO EXPENSIVE!
JUST WHO ARE YOU...

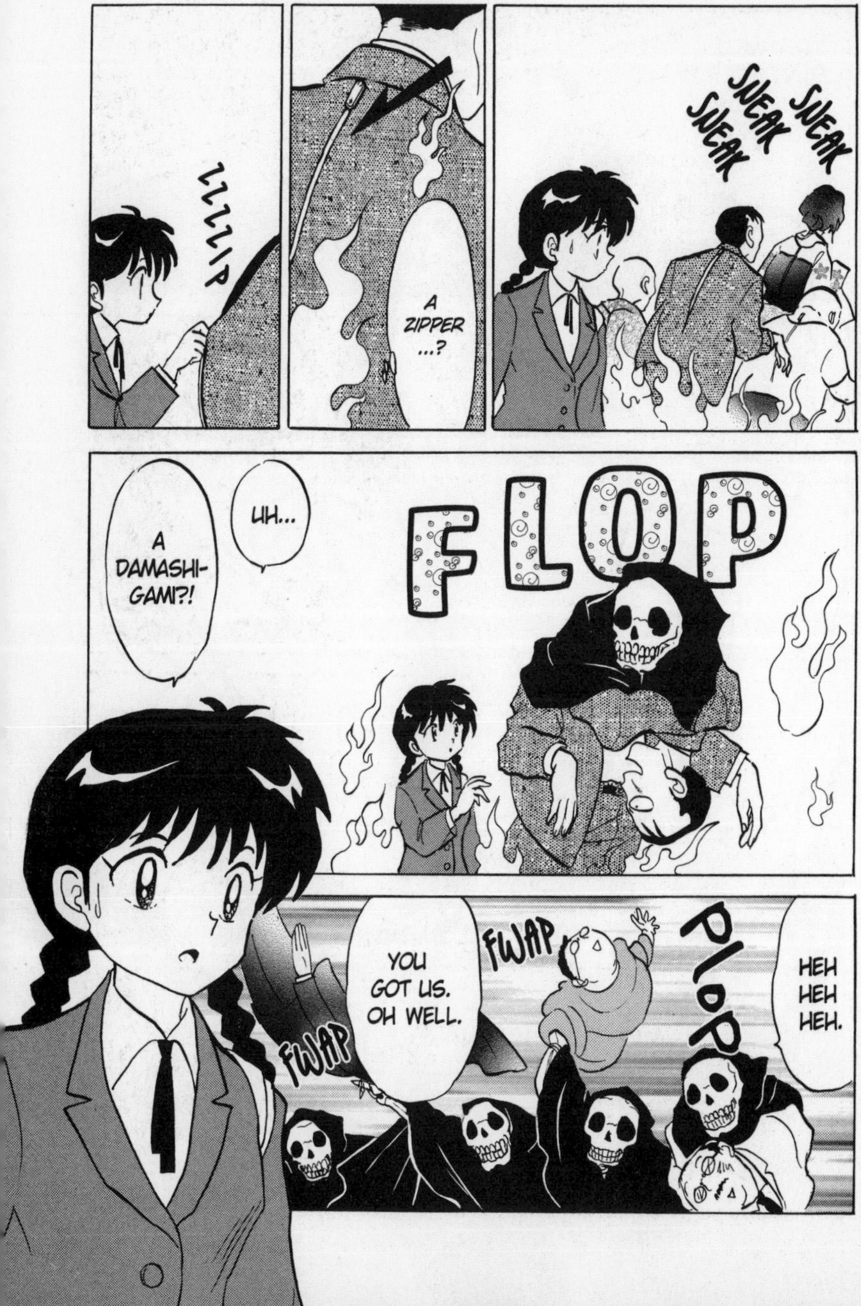
SNEAK
SNEAK
SNEAK
A ZIPPER ...?
ZZZZIP
FLOP
UH...
A DAMASHI-GAMI?!
HEH HEH HEH.
PIOP
FWAP
YOU GOT US. OH WELL.
FWAP

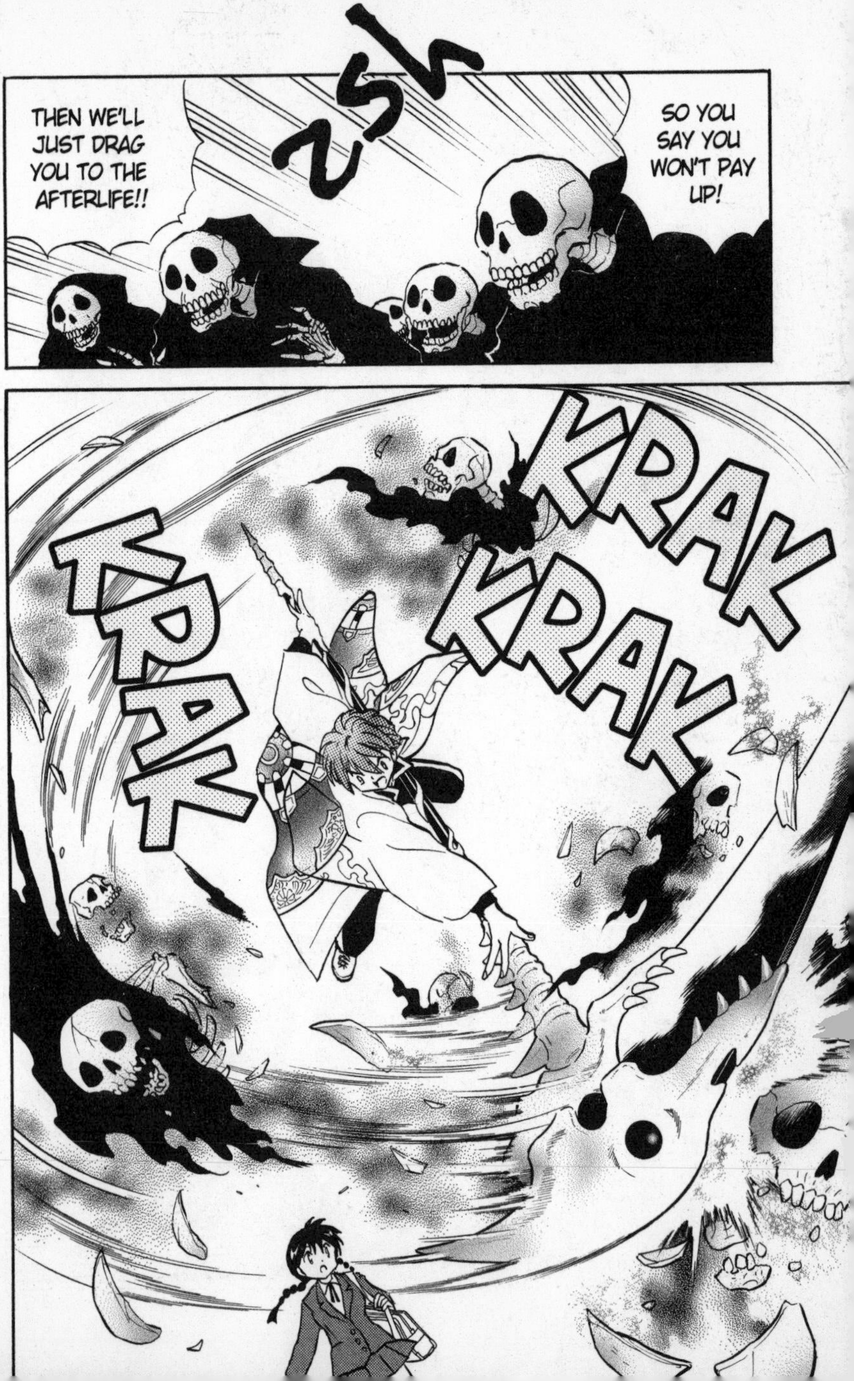
SO YOU SAY YOU WON'T PAY UP!
ZSH
THEN WE'LL JUST DRAG YOU TO THE AFTERLIFE!!
KRAK
KRAK
KRAK

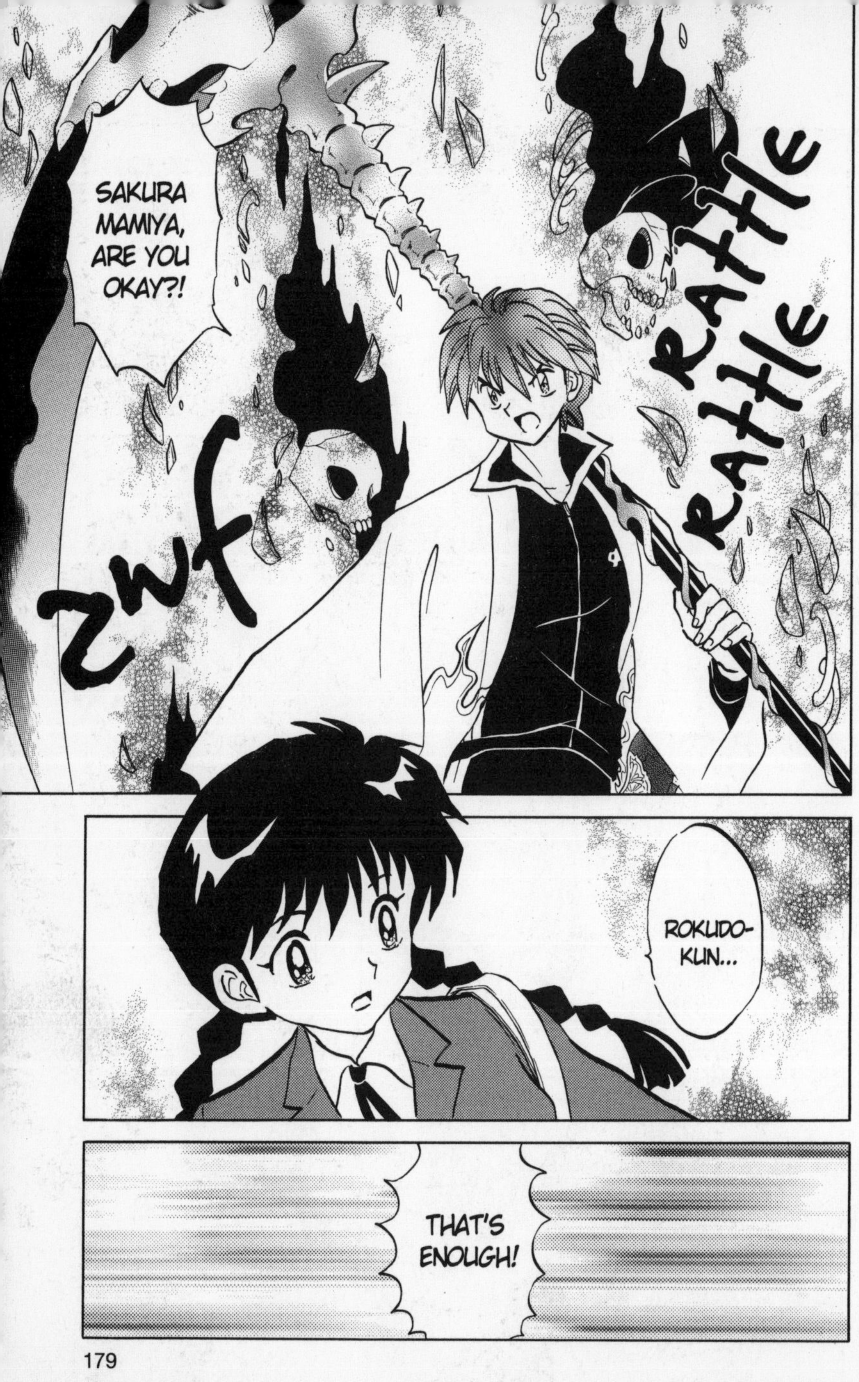
RATTLE RATTLE
SAKURA MAMIYA, ARE YOU OKAY?!
ZWF
ROKUDO-KUN...
THAT'S ENOUGH!

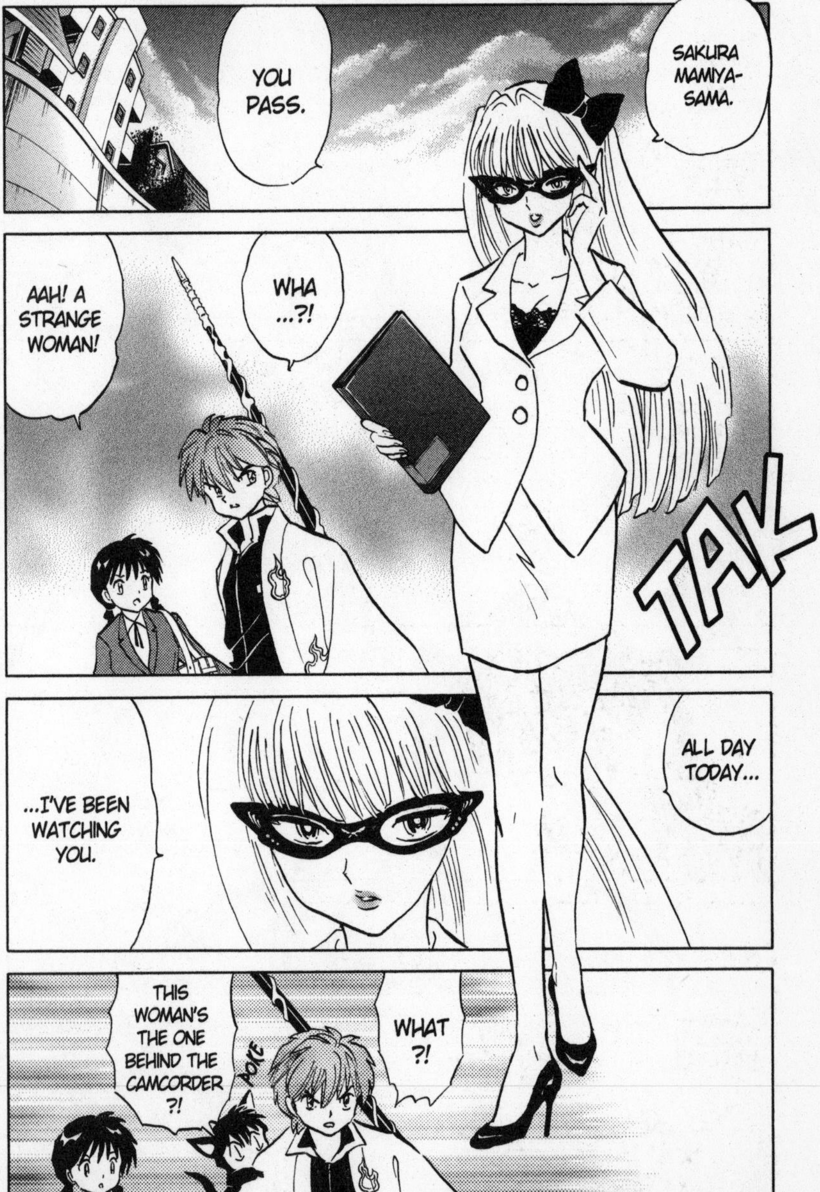
SAKURA MAMIYA-SAMA.
YOU PASS.
TAK
WHA ...?!
AAH! A STRANGE WOMAN!
ALL DAY TODAY...
...I'VE BEEN WATCHING YOU.
WHAT ?!
POKE
THIS WOMAN'S THE ONE BEHIND THE CAMCORDER ?!

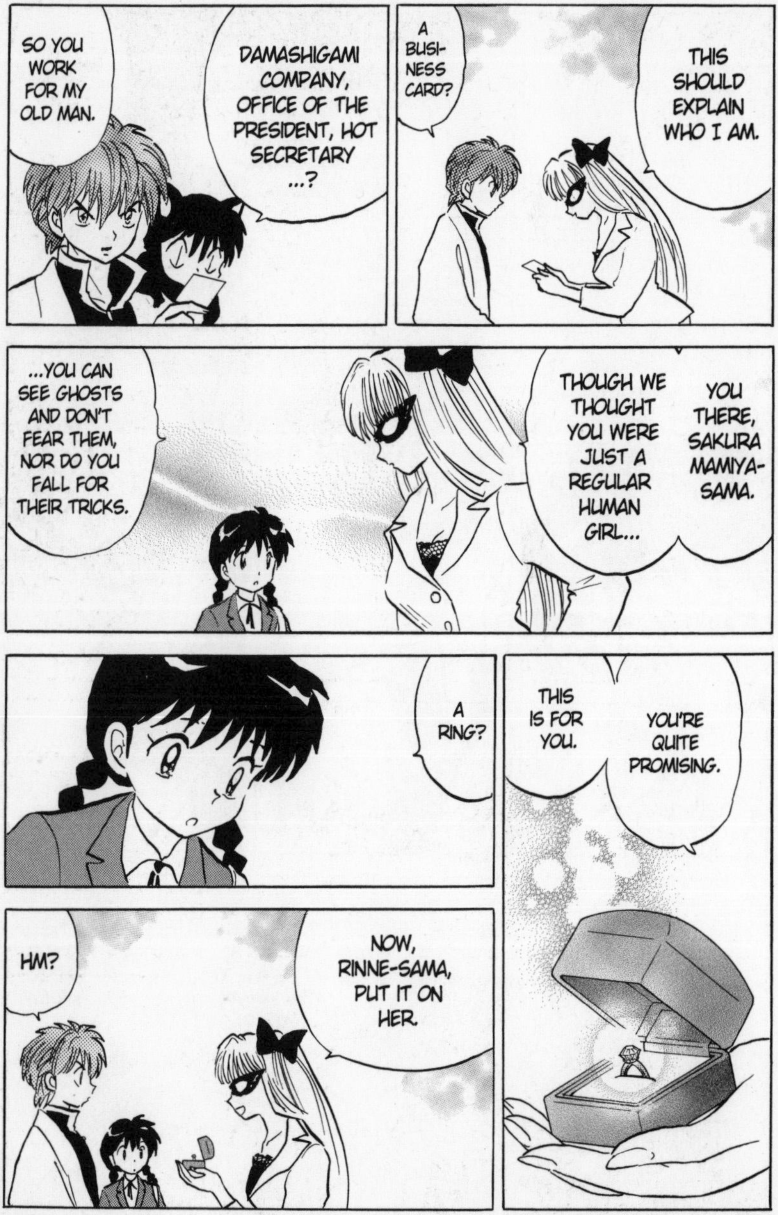
THIS SHOULD EXPLAIN WHO I AM.
A BUSI-NESS CARD?
DAMASHIGAMI COMPANY, OFFICE OF THE PRESIDENT, HOT SECRETARY ...?
SO YOU WORK FOR MY OLD MAN.
YOU THERE, SAKURA MAMIYA-SAMA.
THOUGH WE THOUGHT YOU WERE JUST A REGULAR HUMAN GIRL...
...YOU CAN SEE GHOSTS AND DON'T FEAR THEM, NOR DO YOU FALL FOR THEIR TRICKS.
YOU'RE QUITE PROMISING.
THIS IS FOR YOU.
A RING?
NOW, RINNE-SAMA, PUT IT ON HER.
HM?

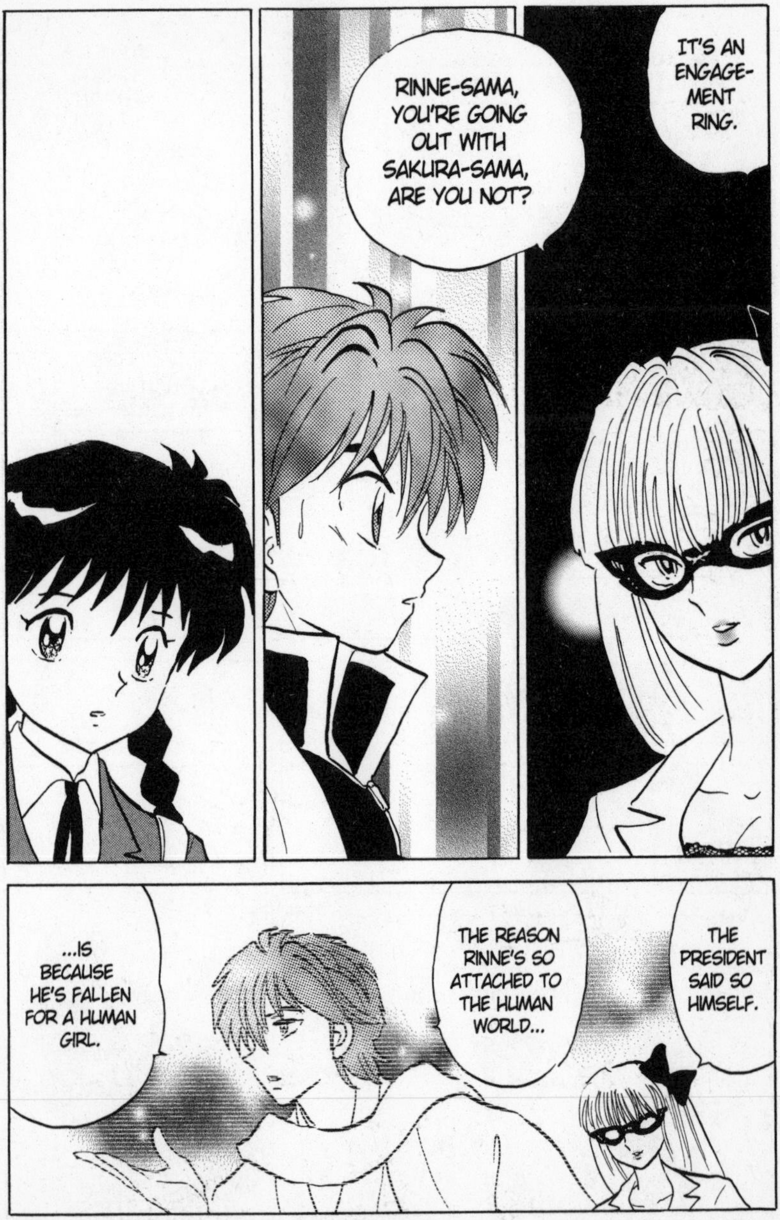
IT'S AN ENGAGE-MENT RING.
RINNE-SAMA, YOU'RE GOING OUT WITH SAKURA-SAMA, ARE YOU NOT?
THE PRESIDENT SAID SO HIMSELF.
THE REASON RINNE'S SO ATTACHED TO THE HUMAN WORLD...
...IS BECAUSE HE'S FALLEN FOR A HUMAN GIRL.

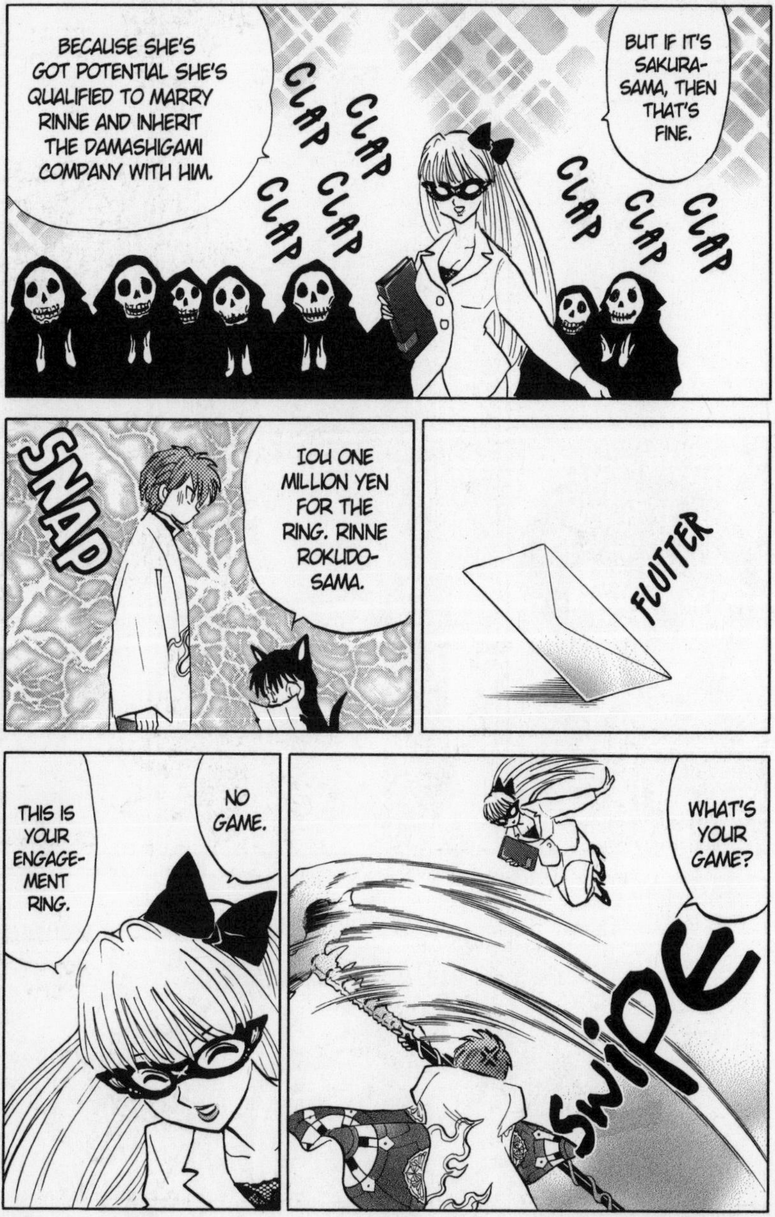
BUT IF IT'S SAKURA-SAMA, THEN THAT'S FINE.
CLAP CLAP CLAP
BECAUSE SHE'S GOT POTENTIAL SHE'S QUALIFIED TO MARRY RINNE AND INHERIT THE DAMASHIGAMI COMPANY WITH HIM.
CLAP CLAP CLAP
FLUTTER
IOU ONE MILLION YEN FOR THE RING. RINNE ROKUDO-SAMA.
SNAP
WHAT'S YOUR GAME?
SWIPE
NO GAME.
THIS IS YOUR ENGAGE-MENT RING.

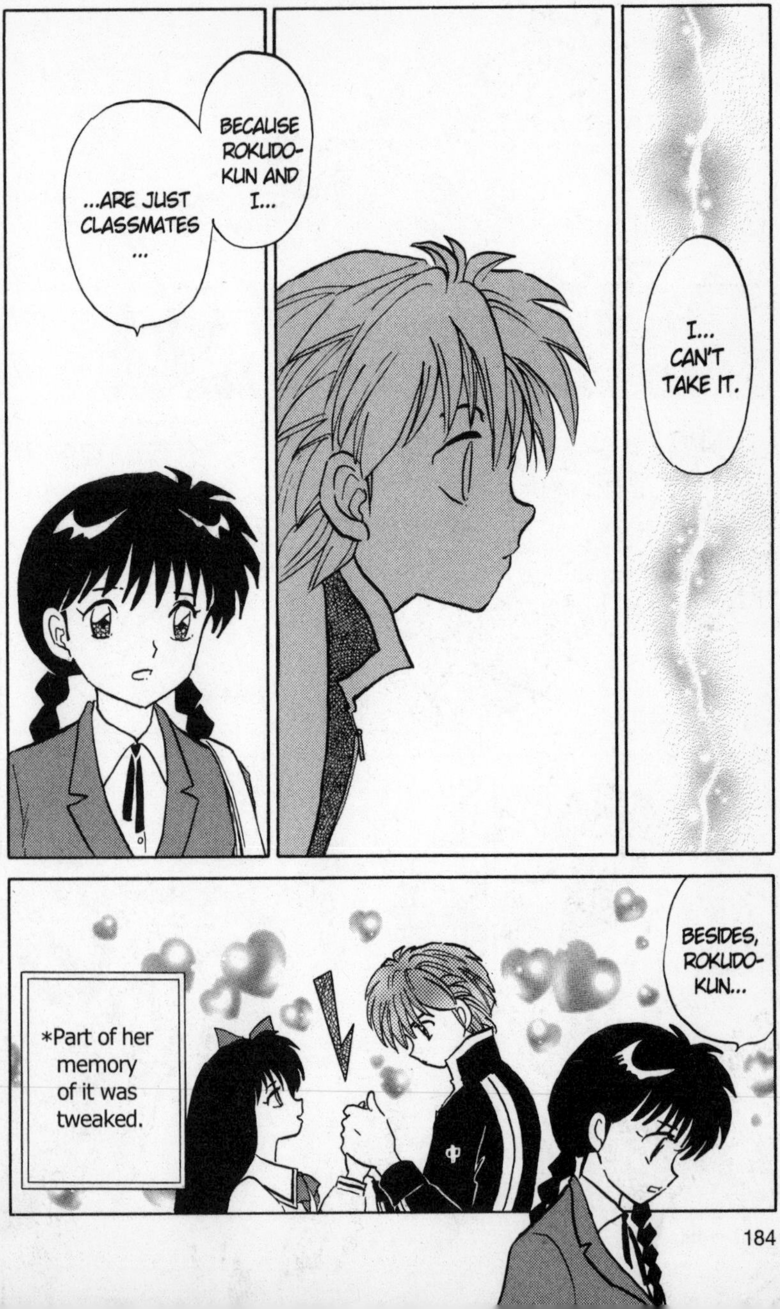
I... CAN'T TAKE IT.
BECAUSE ROKUDO-KUN AND I...
...ARE JUST CLASSMATES ...
BESIDES, ROKUDO-KUN...
*Part of her memory of it was tweaked.

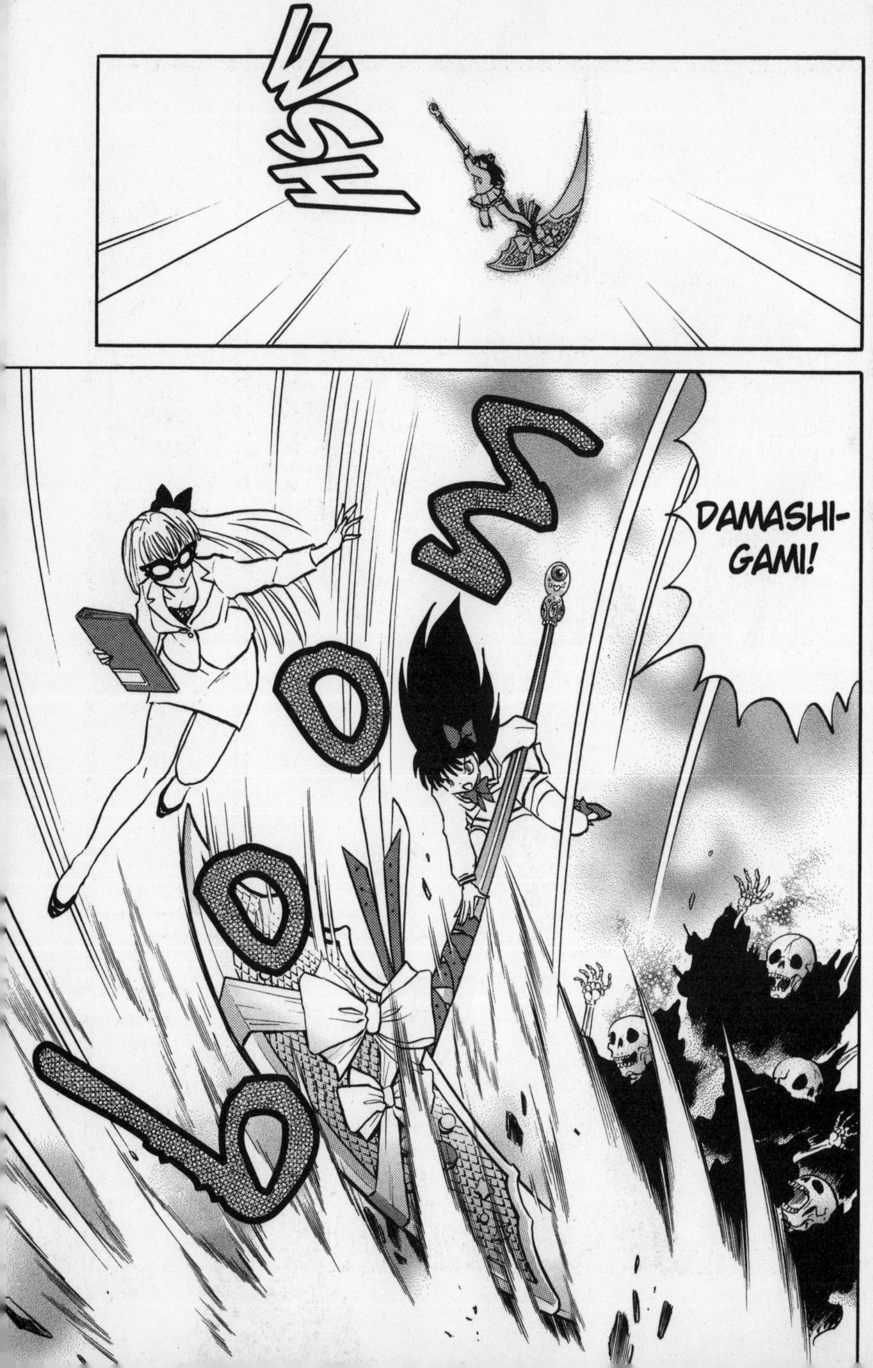
WSH
DAMASHI-
GAMI!
BOOM

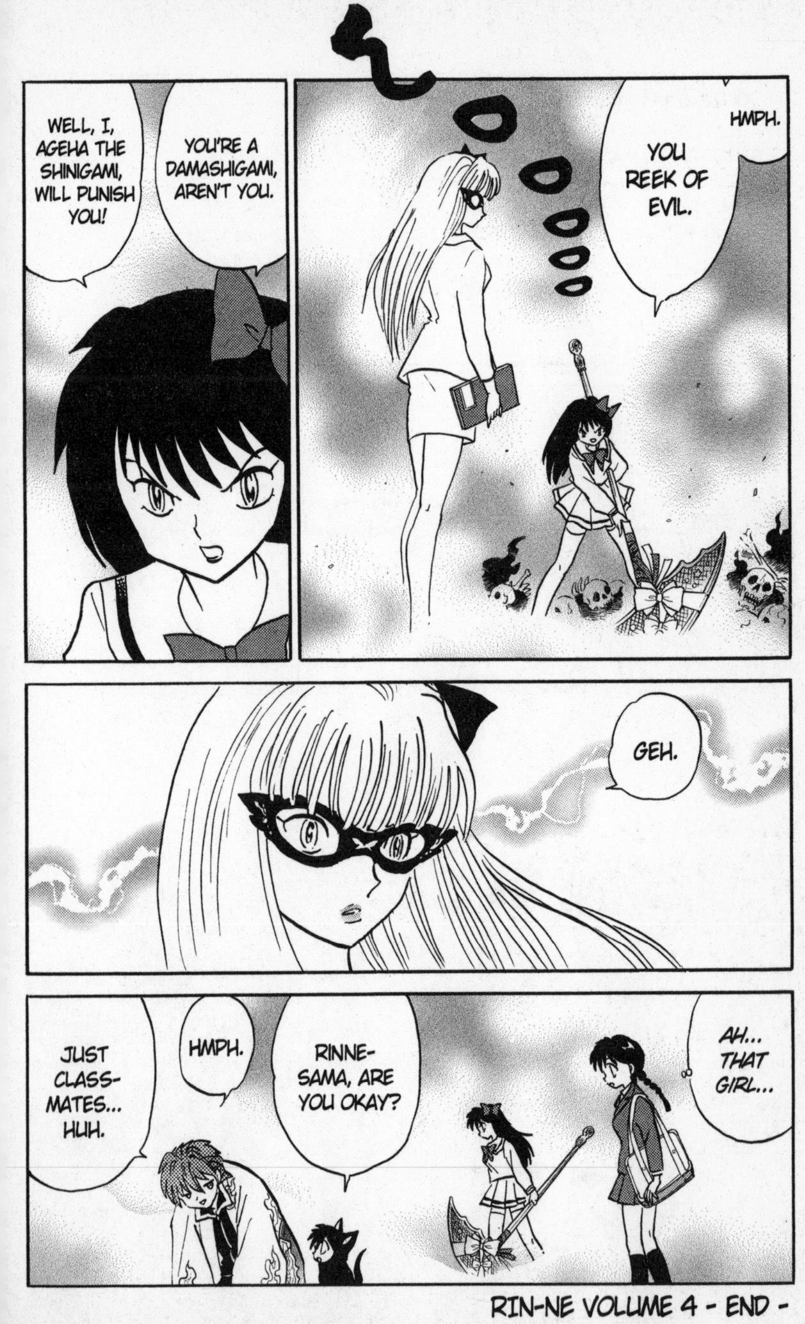
HMPH.
YOU REEK OF EVIL.
YOU'RE A DAMASHIGAMI, AREN'T YOU.
WELL, I, AGEHA THE SHINIGAMI, WILL PUNISH YOU!
GEH.
AH... THAT GIRL...
RINNE-SAMA, ARE YOU OKAY?
HMPH.
JUST CLASSMATES... HUH.

RIN-NE VOLUME 4 - END -

Translation and Cultural Notes

Chapter 30, page 34
When Rinne's father introduces himself, he says his name is "Sabato Rokudo." In kanji, it's written like this: 「六道鯖人」. *Saba* (鯖) means "mackerel" and *to* (人) in this case means "person." To put it another way, "Mackerel Man." You may also recall that Rinne's grandfather was reborn as a mackerel (see volume 1, chapter 6).

Chapter 31, page 45
Rinne catches Sabato up to no good. Sabato is wearing a *hokkamuri*, which is a visual cue that someone is a thief or burglar in Japan. Modern thieves don't really wear this anymore.

Chapter 33, page 95
People in Japan often use personal seals (stamps, chops, etc.) to "sign" official documents such as bank loans or contracts. The Japanese word for it is 「印鑑」 (*inkan*). Signatures are used too, of course, but the personal seal is very common.

Chapter 34, page 100
Here, Sakura says, "Sa...Ba...To...three...eight...ten." In Japanese, you can use the words for numbers to form parts of words, in this case *sa* (from *san* = 3), *ba* (from *hachi* = 8) and *to* (from *to-o* = 10). So we get "3, 8, 10" (or 1 and 0).

InuYasha

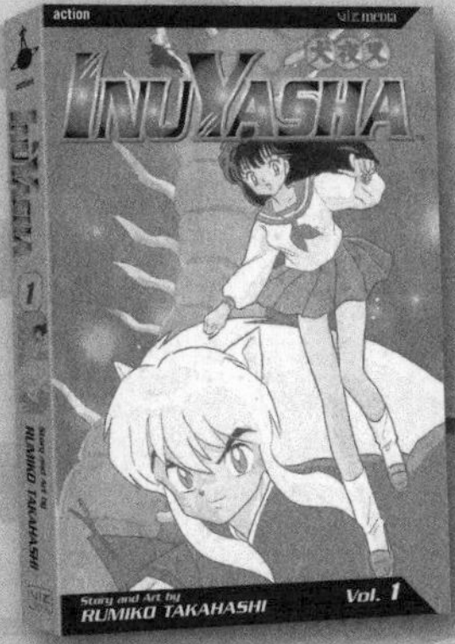
action
viz media
InuYasha
犬夜叉
Story and Art by
RUMIKO TAKAHASHI
Vol. 1

Read the action from the start with the original manga series

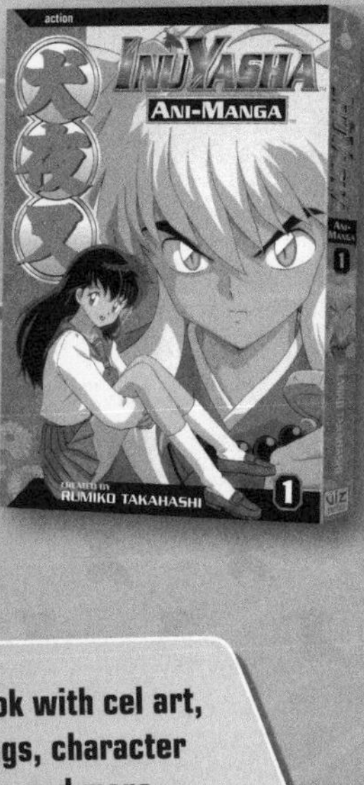
action
InuYasha
Ani-Manga
犬夜叉
CREATED BY
RUMIKO TAKAHASHI
1

Full color adaptation of the popular TV series

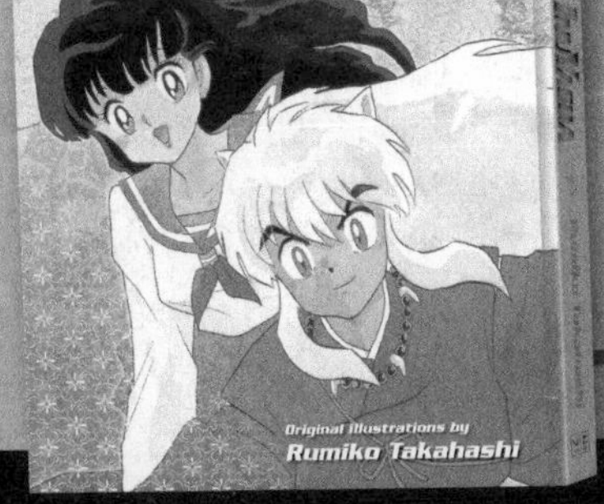
The Art of
InuYasha
犬夜叉
Original Illustrations by
Rumiko Takahashi

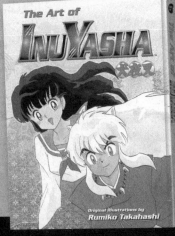

Art book with cel art, paintings, character profiles and more

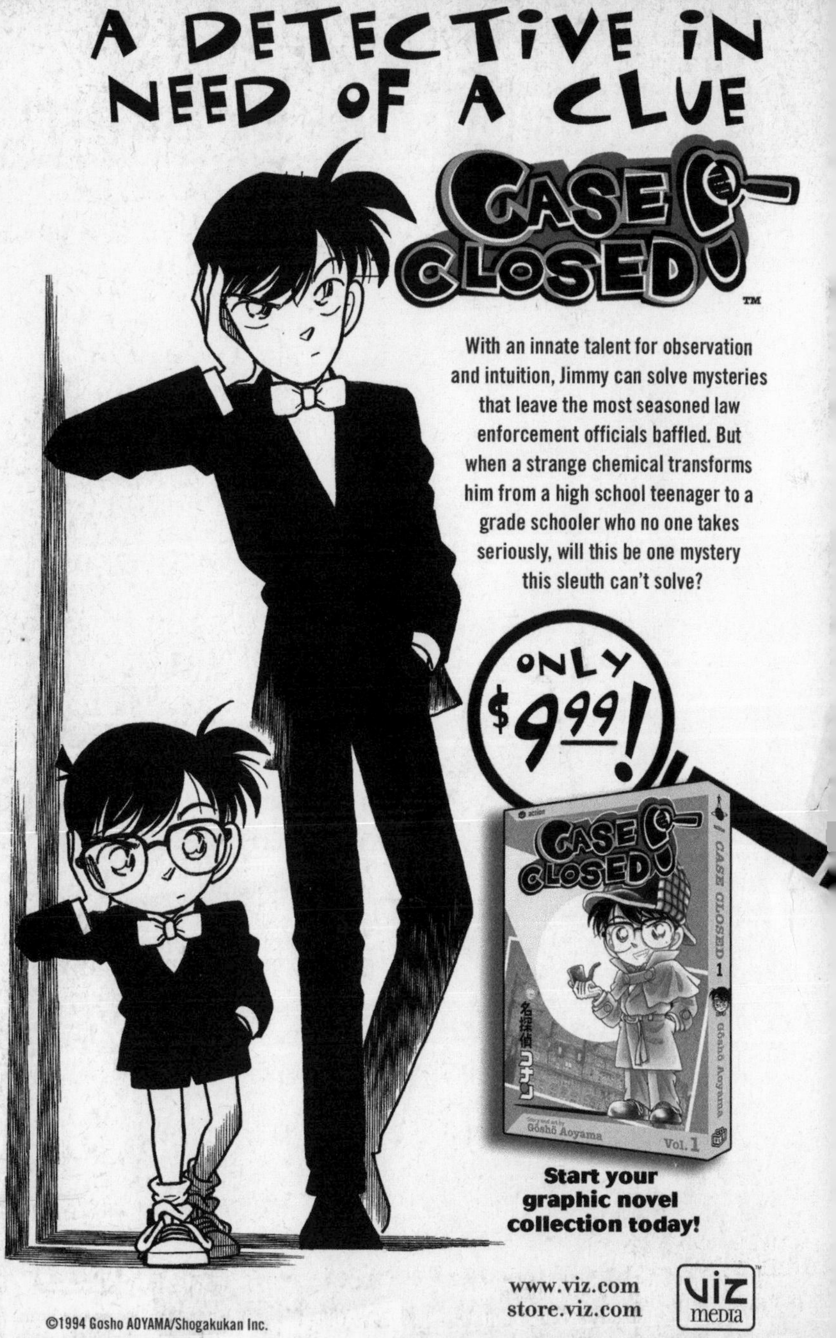
A DETECTIVE IN
NEED OF A CLUE
CASE CLOSED™
With an innate talent for observation and intuition, Jimmy can solve mysteries that leave the most seasoned law enforcement officials baffled. But when a strange chemical transforms him from a high school teenager to a grade schooler who no one takes seriously, will this be one mystery this sleuth can't solve?
ONLY $9.99!
CASE CLOSED
名探偵コナン
Gosho Aoyama
Vol. 1
Start your graphic novel collection today!
www.viz.com
store.viz.com
VIZ media
©1994 Gosho AOYAMA/Shogakukan Inc.

STUDENTS BY DAY, DEMON-FIGHTERS BY NIGHT!

KEKKAISHI
【けっかいし】

Teenagers Yoshimori and Tokine are "kekkaishi"—demon-fighters that battle bad beings side-by-side almost every night. They also quarrel with each other, but their biggest fight is the one between their families. Can Yoshimori and Tokine fight together long enough to end their families' ancient rivalry and save the world?

Join this modern-day Romeo and Juliet adventure in graphic novels, now available at store.

ONLY $9.99!